HOW TO AVOID
FORECLOSURE
ON YOUR HOME, FARM, OR BUSINESS

HOW TO AVOID
FORECLOSURE
ON YOUR HOME, FARM, OR BUSINESS

LAURENCE ADAMS MALONE, LL.B., Ph.D.

Betterway Publications, Inc.
White Hall, Virginia

Published by Betterway Publications, Inc.
Box 58
White Hall, VA 22987

This book is designed to provide useful information to persons facing possible foreclosure on their homes, farms, or businesses. It is sold with the understanding that neither the author nor the publisher is engaged in rendering legal, financial, or other professional services. If such expert assistance is required, the services of a competent professional person should be sought.

Library of Congress Cataloging-in-Publication Data

Malone, Laurence Adams.
　　How to avoid foreclosure of your home, farm, or business.

　　Includes index.
　　1. Foreclosure—United States—Popular works.
I. Title.
KF697.F6M33　1985　　346.7304′364　　85−30724
　　　　　　　　　　　　　347.3064364
　　ISBN 0−932620−58−2 (pbk.)

Printed in the United States of America
0　9　8　7　6　5　4　3　2　1

Dedicated to the American Family Farmer.

Acknowledgments

The author is indebted to the following distinguished colleagues and friends who have so generously given the author access to their superb material and experience and furnished much of the information culminating in the writing of this book. They include the Citizens Bar Association, Conrad Le Beau, Lowell Becraft, Jerome Daly, Roger Elvick, Randy Reineking, The Federal Reserve Bankers Research Institute, R. E. McMaster, Jr., Eustace Mullins, Theodore R. Thoren, F. R. Warner, P. J. Honigsber, John Welsh, E.W Kemmerer, Cornelius Maloney, and many others who so kindly gave me their time in discussing court room procedures with expertise and who made many helpful suggestions during the creation of this book.

Author's Note

Print and broadcast media are full of stories of people distraught over the prospect of losing home, farm or business. Often, we hear of a man who has held off the Sheriff or Magistrate at gunpoint. There was one story of a simple lawsuit that rescued a family from bank foreclosure in Dallas, Texas. In the same city a family named Verhoff sued the First Dallas Bank for 1.7 million dollars, charging fraud, breach of contract and usury. A jury trial was demanded; the court room was filled with high human drama. Verhoff won.

But what does one do who does not have the help of blazing headlines and knows nothing about how to take steps to help himself following a visit from the Sheriff, with a Notice of Default and letter threatening Foreclosure by sale? The magnitude of the foreclosure problem is not exaggerated in the media.

This book deals with the problems and how to resolve them for the person facing foreclosure, who has had little or no help and does not know that first step to take. The purpose of the book is to save property from being lost to the lender.

I wrote this book with specific guidelines to help the person facing foreclosure to forestall, defer, or stop foreclosure. The book is full of alternatives on what to save from foreclosure and how to do it; various areas of negotiation with a lender are explored.

The person facing foreclosure should find many good alternatives in this book; he is helped from the moment he is aware of Default in his mortgage payments. He is guided as to his steps to take. The importance of repayment and refinance is stressed, based on the borrower's equity in the property. The person

facing foreclosure in court is given step by step guidance as to how to Defend himself.

What can a person do to stop Foreclosure? This book shows you how to begin, and how to cope with the various kinds of Foreclosure in various states. The author does not attempt to give actual legal advice or other professional service. However, guidance as to when to seek legal counsel is included. Examples of actual cases of Foreclosure, as well as a Memorandum of Law applicable for use in Foreclosure cases, are in the appendices.

If you are seeking to undo something eminently unfair that has been done to you, you may lawfully get help of an attorney and of the court. If you seek to be unfair to your creditor, no one will help you as all the circumstances will become fully explored and known. You will not prevail.

The entire emphasis of this book has been to promote fair play, negotiation between you and your lender and communication on any problem you may have in paying him what you honestly owe him. Do not seek to subvert the law to shield you in some scheme to defraud your lender of what you fairly owe him.

Familiarize yourself with all the provisions of the Soldiers' and Sailors' Civil Relief Act. It may be used to protect you in situations affecting the home you own or rent. It can protect you on matters of insurance, storage liens, taxes, veteran claims, tax exemptions, divorce and a host of other financial problems. Take a good long look at the Act with an attorney who can best tell you how the Act applies to your particular situation. Laws are designed to deal fairly with you and your creditor. Any judge or officer of the court (lawyer, marshall, sheriff) will expect you to use them honestly.

Negotiations are heavily emphasized, even while court proceedings take place. A Summary of Procedures is set forth in the Appendices. Credit, loan extensions and refinancing out of foreclosure is strongly urged, and guidelines given. Avenues to sources of cash that may have been overlooked are explored.

There are many ways to win out over the finality of foreclosure. This book explores various ways to win. However, as a special cautionary note to the reader, this book was written and published with the understanding that the author is not engaged in law practice, nor in giving legal or other professional advice or service. If you have legal questions or problems, consult with an attorney familiar with the laws of your community and state.

The Publisher and Author specifically disclaim any personal liability for any loss or risk incurred, as a result of your use, direct or indirect, of any advice, guidance, suggestions, lawsuit models, or any information contained in this book.

The Author

Contents

Preface

There are at least three large farm foreclosures daily. In addition, of the sixty million homes in America, more than five percent—about three million of them—are facing foreclosure. The threat of foreclosure occurs because farmers and homeowners are late or seriously in arrears on mortgage payments. Statistics reveal an additional nine and a half million homeowners approaching thirty day delinquency. Business investors are going into bankruptcy at an alarming rate. The foreclosure rate has reached epidemic proportions.

How to Avoid Foreclosure tells you what you need to know about foreclosures, and especially the kind that you might have to face. Among other topics this book discusses:

- How the various kinds of foreclosures are processed
- How to avoid the specific foreclosure you face
- What help is available if you are facing foreclosure on your home, farm or business
- How to re-negotiate or refinance your debt with a lender
- How to reschedule payments with creditors
- How to determine whether your equity in your property is worth the cost to save it.
- Legal Karate is a name given to a series of legal moves designed to avoid or stop mortgage or non-judicial foreclosures, where Sheriff or Trustee sales are held or about to be held.

Today, our courts are often little more than collection agencies for the nation's banks and mortgage companies. While the right to a trial by jury (constitutional right) is always granted in a criminal proceeding, it is frequently denied in a civil proceeding, where the only issue is whether a certain amount of money (legal tender) is owed.

TRIAL BY MOTIONS Vs. TRIAL BY JURY has been given the nickname Legal Karate, because most court cases today are very quickly decided with MOTION HEARINGS. The most frequently used Motions are "Motion to Dismiss," and a "Motion for Summary Judgment." If the Judge grants you either Motion, your foreclosure case will never come to trial.

COMPLAINT AT LAW or SUIT at COMMON LAW. Your complaint at law or suit at common law is merely your assertion of right to have your case tried before a jury, under the 7th amendment to the Bill of Rights, U.S. Constitution, which says: "In suits at common law, where the value in controversy shall exceed twenty dollars, the right of trial by jury shall be preserved."

If you have property or an investment to save, it is important that you understand what to do immediately when you face foreclosure. You must understand the main difference between a "suit in equity," which is tried before a judge, and a "suit at law," which is tried before a jury. [When you present Motions before a judge, you are in chancery or equity jurisdiction. When you present Motions before the Court, it is practical and possible to file a "Complaint at Law," and demand a trial by jury.] Your Motion for a Continuance or a Motion for Certification of the Question are all proper Motions to present to the court. In a "Complaint at Law or Suit at Common Law," a Motion to Dismiss for any reason, such as lack of jurisdiction, or failure to state a claim upon which relief can be granted, must be tried before a jury. Further, if you hire an attorney, make sure he is zealous about upholding constitutional law both in letter and spirit. When an attorney files any of these Motions or if you do so personally, it is the right of either party to the suit to have these Motions tried before a jury. In effect, you obtain two jury trials. The first is to determine if the Court has jurisdiction, or if there is a bonafide claim upon which relief can be granted. If so, then you proceed beyond these issues to the second jury trial on the Merits of your case. The same jury could preside over both trials. While the right to a trial by jury is a constitutional right under the seventh amendment, practical experience has shown that courts don't grant jury trials in civil proceedings, unless there are material facts in dispute.

How to Avoid Foreclosure is indeed your biggest challenge. The best way to face that challenge when it occurs is to file a "Complaint" or a "Counterclaim." Go on the offensive immediately. Become the Plaintiff rather than the Defendant. In a lawsuit, the "Complaint" is when the plaintiff sues the defendant; in a "Counterclaim," the defendant who is being sued counter-sues the Plaintiff or "Counterclaims." As a Plaintiff filing Complaint, you can force the court to make decisions regarding basic issues before your case is ever tried. Such issues may deal with:

1. **Jurisdiction**—by what authority under the Constitution or laws invoked does the court have the authority to act.

2. **Parties**—the names and addresses of each party to the lawsuit, both sides. Also you may list Cross Complaints in which you may sue any of the defendants, individually, such as an Officer of the lender bank pressing for a foreclosure.

3. **The Facts**—You will need a lawyer to help you draft pleadings to show that the intent of the person(s) you are suing was to defraud, or breach the contract, or to injure you in some way. You must give dates, places and names of persons involved. You will need exhibits, such as a letter promising renewal of your loan, or offers to lend you money, shortly before they call in your note. In such an instance, you can show bad faith, or breach of contract. If you have nothing in writing from your lender that shows bad faith on his part, then affidavits from witnesses, showing that you have made good-faith offers to cor-

rect default, which he has ignored. You can use additional exhibits such as:

4. **The laws violated.** Your counsel will assist you.

5. **The Relief you are requesting of the court in—Money Damages.**

In this book, you will find model lawsuits such as the kind of lawsuit you will want to use in defending yourself against a foreclosure by a bank; and the kind of lawsuit you want to use for anyone else. Your basic lawsuits will involve the "CREDIT ISSUE." The more issues of facts in dispute that you can present to the court, the better your chances of getting a trial by jury, even in today's "equity" courts. Do not hesitate to add such issues to your lawsuit as: 1. Breach of Contract or Agreement, when the bank or other lender promises verbally to renew your loan and then turns you down at the last minute. Have a witness with you or a pocket tape recorder. The tape can be used to discredit the lender's testimony denying his promise to renew the loan, thereby winning the judge's sympathy. The Affidavit of a witness is admissible as evidence. The tape recorder is not.

YOUR LEGAL KARATE WEAPONS.

1. A well written Complaint (this is better than a Counterclaim).

2. A Motion requesting substitution of the Judge or a Motion for Disqualification of the Judge supported by an **Affidavit of Prejudice.**

3. Affidavits in opposition to Motions to Dismiss, and Affidavits in opposition to the lender's Motions for Summary or Default Judgment, raising issues of facts and law.

4. Constructive Notice—use this Motion often and attach one to your lawsuit. (See example given in this book.)

5. Affidavits in support of all your Motions.

6. Third Party Complaints and Cross Complaints.

7. Motions for a New Trial or a Motion for leave of Court to file a Counter claim, used after a judgment has been entered against you.

8. Chapter 13 proceeding (reorganization) to block entry of judgment or to stop the Sheriff from conducting a sale.

9. Adversary Proceedings in Bankruptcy Court, or Complaint before a Grand jury against any who allegedly conspired to violate your constitutional rights in violation of Title 18, Sec. 241, which could subject them to a $10,000 fine and up to ten years in prison.

10. Use Depositions to win your case throughout all of these Motions. This is the essence of Legal Karate given with step-by-step procedures in this book.

FRAUD, USURY AND CREDIT LOANS EXTENDED AS LAWFUL MONEY

Today, there are thousands of people who are losing their homes, farms, and businesses needlessly because of lender created credit money. There is a difference between legal tender (lawful money) and lender created credit money, which the lender pretends is money. Credit is Not money. Credit is the opposite of Money.

For a long time, the MONEY ISSUE debate has centered around two distinct issues: 1) that Constitutional money is gold and silver coin; 2) that the dollar is defined by the Mint Act of 1792, and is legal tender which the law requires a creditor to accept in payment of a debt. This last definition is, as yet, not well understood. It is the last and most important issue of all as it pertains to the lender–credit issue. And it is the most important issue of all because 97% of our money supply today consists of bank credit, whereas Federal Reserve Notes and United States Minted Coins comprise less than 3%. If the Constitutional guidelines as to money and credit were followed closely today, almost every institutional lender type credit loan could be legally voided because it is based on the mere bookkeeping entry of credit issuance instead of money (lawful money, legal tender).

What is Credit? Credit is the opposite of money. Money, which is legal tender for the payment of debts, is defined by Congress in 31 U.S.C.A. Section 392. This section basically describes all coins and currency issued by the United States Government as legal tender for all debts, public and private. For purposes of this article, money is either coins or currency.

Bank or institutional lender loans. When you apply for a loan at a bank or some institutional lender company, you sign a loan agreement pledging to pay back dollars with interest. When the bank accepts your promise to pay in exchange for its loan, it means your credit is good. This applies to any institutional lender. However, the next question is most interesting. What have you been loaned? The lender invariably gives you a check, which is a mere promise to pay, or he makes a bookkeeping entry of the trans-

action to your checking account. In effect, what you and he have done is exchange promises to pay. You have accepted each other's credit, yet no money exchanged hands. What do you do with the check or a check you write against your account? You spend it or pay bills with it. In either case, the check, when processed, goes back to the lender's bookkeeping department where the numbers are transferred from the check and taken from your account. Once the loan is made, the lender institution can say its deposits have increased. Actually, this fictional increase is all there is on his books since there is no actual increase of dollars in his vault. Of course, he will have your promissory note, secured by a mortgage lien on your property and / or a Deed of Trust as the case may be. His bookkeeping entry deposits are called demand deposits, which means literally that the borrowers can walk into the bank and demand the deposit.

Bank Assets. What to you think the bank's assets are? Well, it is a small amount of vault cash plus a large amount of IOUs, which are all those loan Agreements like the one you signed when you took out the loan. All those promises to pay the bank are its assets. Thus, both the bank's assets and liabilities are virtually all on paper.

Modern Money Mechanics, published by the Federal Reserve Bank of Chicago states that "deposits are merely book entries" which makes it easier to understand what the credit and electronic transfer of money is all about. What credit and so called money amounts to is merely a transfer of numbers or book entries from one bank account to another. The same thing happens when you write a check. It is merely your promise to pay. It is not legal tender, nor lawful money. When a credit card is used bank credit or book entries are created and transferred simultaneously. The next question is, if it is so easy for a bank to create credit, which is used like money, how then is this credit destroyed? The credit is destroyed when the principal of the loan is repaid. However, the interest collected by the bank on the credit loaned is transferred to another account for distribution to the lender or his stockholders. What happens is that because 97% of the nation's money supply consists of CREDIT, which is all created by private corporations (lender institutions) and because interest is charged on every dollar of credit used, debts are constantly created for which no money really exists with which to repay those debts.

By what authority—under what law—are such institutional lenders given the right to create money as lawful money or to demand lawful money, legal tender, in return for credit loaned? There is no such law or authority. Again, almost every loan in the United States can legally be voided because it is based on credit instead of money. However, if you have received a fair consideration of goods or services in exchange for your promise to repay the lender or creditor or merchant, you will be held liable for repayment.

But, where you have given your lender a Deed to your property in exchange for his mere bookkeeping entry of a credit to your checking account, you may have a legally voidable contract. Even if he has given you a Certified Check, a Cashier's Check, or Bank check, such "checks" are mere promises to pay. If you cannot walk out of that lender's bank with cash in your hand, it could well be that he does not have the cash in his vault to back up his check. If such is the case, the check is a bad check, and his practice can best be described as unlawful.

Actually, our money system today can best be described as a debt–usury system. For every dollar's worth of credit that comes into existence, a debt is created for which the lender charges interest. In general, it could be said that every bank loan made in the United States today is illegal, since all bank loans are based on credit instead of money.

Ultra Vires. The words "ultra vires" are very important words as they mean that a contract made by a corporation beyond the scope of its corporate powers is unlawful. The courts have consistently ruled that banks CANNOT LEND THEIR CREDIT, but can only lend their money, and that ALL LOANS OF CREDIT ARE ULTRA VIRES.*

(*See *1st National Bank of Tallapoosa* v. *Monre,* 69 S.E. 1123; also *Norton Grocery Co.* v. *Peoples National Bank* 144 S.E. 501; and *Federal Intermediate Credit Bank* v. *L'Herisson,* 33 F.2nd 841; and *American Express Co.* v. *Citizens State Bank 194 N.W. 427*)

Bank Charters. No bank charter gives a bank permission to lend its credit as money, and Congress never gave banks permission to create money. Therefore all such loans of credit are ultra vires and unlawful. The bank, by lending credit, has unjustly enriched itself. It pays no interest for the use of creating credit money, but charges its customers the same amount of interest as if it had loaned out lawful money. In a court of law Complaint this may be described as deception, fraud, and usury. The collection of interest on credit is in violation of all usury laws, as the lender is collecting interest on money which doesn't exist.

Believe it or not, there are more than six trillion dollars worth of illegal "credit" loans out there waiting to be challenged by Americans who are beginning to understand this issue.

Of course, you can walk off your property and let the lender have it. But you have a better chance in court to void the bank loan and keep your property. It would be much better to sue the bank or lender on fraud and usury charges and ask that all contracts which you signed on the day you took out the loan be declared "ULTRA VIRES" and therefore null and void. That includes Deeds of Trust, mortgages, notes and security Agreements. With the law on your side, why not begin?

Introduction

Lender's problems. Lender's problems arise out of default on note payments due from the borrower. Why? Today, there are thousands of people who are needlessly losing their homes, farms and businesses because of created credit, which the lender represents as "money." Credit is not money. Money is legal tender, as defined by Congress in 31 United States Code Annotated, Section 392. The mystery of how lenders, perhaps unknowingly, carry on this practice of confusing credit with money, provides you with a legal basis to fight back by suing a lender on fraud and usury charges, especially if he is bent on foreclosing on your home, farm or business.

The money issue. For a long time, the money issue debate has centered around two distinct issues: 1) that Constitutional money is gold and silver coin; and, 2) that the dollar is defined by the Mint Act of 1792 (which has never been repealed by Congress); and, 3) that a Federal Reserve Note is not a dollar, as it cannot be redeemed in gold, silver or anything of value except faith and credit.

The Bank Credit Issue. The bank credit issue is of utmost importance because 97% of our so-called money supply today consists of bank credit, whereas Federal Reserve Notes and gold and silver coins consist of less than 3% of that money supply. Why then do lenders have problems? Simply because almost every loan made in the United States can be legally voided as it is based on CREDIT and not MONEY.

What is credit? Credit is the opposite of money. Money is legal tender for payment of debt. Congress has stated in 31 U.S.C.A. Sec. 392 that all coins and currency issued by the UNITED STATES GOVERNMENT is legal tender for all debts, public and private.

The Federal Reserve Bank is a closely held private corporation (with stockholders) regulated by the Federal Government's so-called Federal Reserve Board. Banks lend you their credit in return for your promise to pay them money and interest on that money. In addition, they accept your pledge of anything from a motorcycle to your farm, home, or business as collateral for the security agreement. The lender has accepted your credit or promise to pay him a sum of money in exchange for his promise to lend you his credit. It is small wonder the lender has problems in his attempt to get money back from you for loaning you his credit. And, in this connection, the next question is the most interesting. What did the lender lend you? Well, if the lender is a bank, the bank invariably gave you a check or a deposit slip (if you have an account in that bank) showing your account has been "credited" with x number of dollars. Actually, you received no dollars. The bank lent you a credit it created as it could not and did not create any dollars as defined in 31 U.S.C.A. Sec. 392.

The Bank Credit Issue and the Money Issue. People facing foreclosure in most cases face severe loss. And indeed, they go into court to try to prevent having their property taken from them without due process of law. Some of these people become aware of a vast difference between credit and its opposite, "Money." Others are not aware that there is a difference. They are easily cheated out of their property through foreclosure proceedings and an aggressive lender's Motion in court and demand for Summary Judgment.

Another lender's problem: If the lender is a bank that claims for itself the right to create money, then it must produce in court the law that gives it such power. If it fails, then it has no claim for relief. Obviously, it will fail as no such law exists. The lender's problems go beyond mere note payments.

Borrower's Problems. The borrower has problems when his payments are too high. At the time he borrowed, he may have felt that real estate prices would continue an upward spiral. This was especially true in the last decade; prices in many areas doubled or tripled. So he bought and borrowed, often beyond his means, expecting to sell and use the profit to purchase another home without debt. Such speculation has become a major cause of foreclosures.

Loss of work in bad times has also presented the borrower with problems, leading to unusual stress, illness, arrears in payments and eventual default, a time when no payment can be made. People who have speculated and risked assuming high payments are today suffering the highest rates of foreclosure on first mortgages since the time of the Great Depression. In fact, foreclosure in times of depression or recession becomes a root cause of bank failures. Obviously, a bank that has loaned out credit is not getting back money in return when it has to foreclose on a thousand properties. Such a bank is at risk, as it faces high negative cash flow and cannot bail itself out. It is almost axiomatic that foreclosure only works for lenders when there is no "recession" or "depression." In bad times, savings and loan associations fearfully watch their real estate acquired through Foreclosure bulge dangerously. These properties become a liability as no cash flow from interest payments is realized. In bad times the properties cannot be resold.

In the major farm belts, such as Iowa, Kansas, and surrounding states, more than fifty percent of the farmers are in Foreclosure or threatened with foreclosure. High interest rates, recession-lowered prices, and imports have prevented the farmers from making enough money on produce to pay back the loans they have incurred and the interest demanded.

Many reasons surface in examining causes of Foreclosure. These include schemes for balloon payments or payments that are so high the borrower cannot meet them, real estate booms and busts, sudden blights that sweep over various areas of a city, governmental condemnation, and the farmer's problems of poor crops and prices. Both the borrower and lender are in trouble.

Negotiation. Lender's and borrower's problems are special to both. As a result, it is good to consider negotiation. This book is written with negotiation in mind. If a borrower has received money from a lender, he should make every honest effort to repay. If he cannot, the lender is in the position of having to foreclose on the borrower's collateral offered to the lender as security for the money he has received. Most lenders are willing to refinance and renegotiate an old mortgage Agreement. They are especially interested in receiving interest money. That is their cash flow.

Negotiation is preferred. The lender stands to lose money if he has to foreclose. He may lose his case in court if you can prove that you received only a created credit from your lender and no money.* Negotiation is very much the preferred road a lender would like to take with you. By early negotiation, problems can either be avoided altogether or reasonably postponed.

You are the person who creates a mortgage, the mortgagor. Foreclosure ends all rights you may have in your home, your farm or business. The rights you have in your property are among your most prized possessions.

Together, in this book let us explore how you may preserve and defend your legal rights and possessions. But first, I suggest you familiarize yourself with the following terms and definitions. Understanding these at the onset will be invaluable in helping you derive the maximum use and value from this book.

Laurence Malone

DEFINITIONS

Action — In legal practice, an action is the legal and formal demand of one's right from another person, insisted on in a court of justice.

Admissions — Voluntary acknowledgments made by a person as to the existence of certain facts, or a fact relevant to the cause of an adversary in a suit or law case.

Affiant — An affiant is one who makes an Affidavit.

Affidavit — An Affidavit is a written or printed declaration or statement of facts, made voluntarily, and confirmed by the oath of the person making

---

*See Appendices: Memorandum of Law; Case Citations.

it, taken before an officer or Notary having authority to administer the oath.

Allegation — An allegation is the assertion or declaration of a person made in relation to what the person expects to prove in an action at law.

Appellant — An appellant is one who carries his complaint from an inferior court to a superior court alleging an injustice has been done or an error has been committed by the lower court. The action is known as an Appeal.

Assumption — Pertains to the act of undertaking or adopting a debt or obligation primarily resting upon another person.

Attachment — The act of seizing another person's property by virtue of a judicial order.

Bank — Banks are of three kinds: (1) of deposit of money, (2) of discount, (3) of circulation. A bank of deposit is one that loans money upon mortgage, pawn or other security, makes loans and issues banknotes designed to circulate as money.

Bankruptcy — The term is used to indicate insolvency, an inability to pay one's debts.

Breach — The breaking or violating of a law, right, or duty, either by commission or omission.

Breach of Trust — An act done by a trustee contrary to the terms of his trust as a detriment of the trust he holds.

Case — A case is a term for an action, cause, suit or controversy at law, a question contested before a court of justice.

Caveat — A term which is an action notifying a judge or other officer to suspend a proceeding until merits of certain acts are determined. Warns a judge by formal Notice to stop procedings or to stop an officer against the performance of certain acts within his power or jurisdiction.

Certiorari — Is simply a writ of review or inquiry.

Chancery — A system of jurisprudence administered in courts of equity.

Check — A commercial device intended for payment of money, not for circulation. A promise to pay, used as a draft or order upon a bank purporting to be drawn upon a deposit of money.

Chose (in action) — A personal right, thing or article of personal property recoverable by a suit at law.

Circuit Courts — Courts whose jurisdiction extends over several counties or districts, concerned with matters and causes of action which are of Federal cognizance.

Civil (action) — An action wherein an issue is presented for trial by means of a Complaint in the protection of a right or the prevention of a wrong in a court of justice.

Claim — Is a term that represents a person's demand of a right he has.

Complaint — The first or initiatory pleading on the part of the Plaintiff in a civil action in those states having A Code of Civil Procedure. A Cross-complaint is one brought by the opposing party in a lawsuit, seeking relief against either plaintiff or co-defendant and is in the nature of an original petition.

Counterclaim — Represents the right of the defendant or plaintiff to have the claims of the parties in a lawsuit counterbalanced in whole or in part with judgment to be entered for the excess. A Counterclaim is used in a lawsuit to defeat or diminish plaintiff's demand.

Credit — Credit is the ability of a person to borrow money or obtain goods on time, in consequence of the favorable opinion held by the particular creditor or lender, as to the person's solvency and reliability.

Damages — Loss, injury or deterioration, caused by the negligence, design, or accident of one person to another, provides the basis for Damages. Damages is a pecuniary or money compensation which may be recovered in the courts by any person who has such loss, detriment or injury whether to his person, property or rights through the unlawful act or omission or negligence of another.

Deceit — A fraudulent and cheating misrepresentation, artifice or use of a device to deceive and trick another person, who is ignorant of the facts surrounding the circumstances of a transaction, personal or business, to the prejudice and damage of the person the deceit has been imposed upon.

De Facto — In fact.

Default — A failure or an omission to perform a legal duty.

Defendant — The person against whom relief or recovery is sought in an action or suit at law.

Defense — A defense which may be set up in a court of law. An equitable defense may be set up only in a court of equity.

De Jure — A term which means as a matter of right.

Demur — A term which means one takes exception to the sufficiency in point of law of a pleading or takes exception to the state of facts alleged.

Demurrable — A pleading, petition, or the like is said to be Demurrable when it does not state such facts as support the claim or defense put forward to the court.

Demurrer — See *demur.*

De Novo — A venire de novo is a writ for summoning a jury for the second trial of a case which has been sent back from a court of appeals or a higher court for a new trial.

Deponent — One who testifies or makes an oath as to the truth of certain facts, which is reduced to writing.

Deposition — Testimony of a witness taken upon interrogatories not in court. The testimony reduced to writing which is intended to be used upon the trial of an action in court.

Devise, and Devisee — The testamentary disposition of land or realty to a devisee, the person to whom lands or other real property are given.

Disclosure — The revelation of subject matter which has been held secret.

Discovery — Finding out that which was previously unknown, or hidden. The acquisition of or knowledge of acts or facts. The basis for the granting of a new trial for newly discovered facts or acts previously hidden, or which had not previously come to light.

Duces Tecum — Requires a person who is summoned to appear in court to bring with him some document, or piece of evidence to be used or inspected by the court. See Subpœna Duces Tecum.

Entry (foreclosure by) — Where the mortgagee enters upon and takes possession of mortgaged land, shuts out and bars all right existing in a mortgagor to redeem the estate, being applicable when the mortgagor has forfeited his estate by non-payment of money due on the mortgage at the time appointed.

Equity — Used here, it is a system of jurisprudence, distinct from common law courts empowered to deal with the parties of a lawsuit from the bench dealing out impartial justice as between two persons whose rights or claims are in conflict.

A court of equity is also called a court of chancery, and has the power to enforce Discovery, make decisions as to mortgages, and other fiduciary obligations, and adjust common law rights where the court of common law has no particular process for doing so. Such a court may supply a particular and preventive remedy for common law wrongs where courts of common law only give subsequent damages.

The judge acts as both judge and jury. However, if the subject matter of the lawsuit is in excess of $20, either of the parties to the suit can demand trial by jury (7th Amendment to the Bill of Rights, U.S. Constitution).

Federal District Court — Is any court of the United States to which this title may be applicable. A court of Bankruptcy is a Federal District Court. Courts of the United States: The Senate sitting as a court of impeachment, The Supreme Court, Courts of Appeals, courts of claims, courts of customs; tax courts and the like.

Findings of Fact — A determination of a fact by the court, averred by one party to a lawsuit and denied by the adversary party. Nevertheless founded on evidence in the case. Also the answer of a Jury to a specific interrogatory propounded to them as to the existence or non-existence of a fact in issue.

Foreclosure — To shut out, to bar, to destroy an equity of redemption. A termination of all rights of the mortgagor or his grantee in property covered by a mortgage. Usually a process in a court of equity, by which all further right existing in a mortgagor to redeem his property is defeated and lost to him. The estate becomes the absolute property of the mortgagee lender. If the mortgagor has made some payment, there is an equity of redemption.

Foreclosure (Statutory) — Applied to foreclosure by execution of a power of sale contained in the mortgage itself, without recourse to the courts, although it must conform to the regulations of the statutes governing such sales.

Foreclosure (Strict) — Vests the property in the mortgagee on default of payment, without any sale of the property.

Fraud — An intentional misrepresentation of truth for the purpose of inducing another in reliance upon it to part with some valuable thing or property belonging to him or to surrender his legal right to the property; a false representation of matters of fact, whether by words, conduct, writings, or by concealment of that which should have been disclosed resulting in a legal injury to the person relying on the representation.

Indictment — An accusation in writing presented by a grand jury legally convoked and sworn to the court in which it is impaneled, charging that a person therein named has done some act or been guilty of some omission which by law is a public offense, punishable on indictment.

Injunction — A prohibitive writ, restraining or forbidding a person to do some act or to permit his servants or agents to do some act which is or may be legally injurious to another.

Issue — The disputed point or question to which the parties in an action at law have narrowed their several allegations down to points of fact or law on which they are desirous of obtaining the decision of the proper tribunal.

Judgment — One which calls for the payment of a sum of money, as distinguished from one directing an act to be done or property to be restored or transferred. The judgment determines the amount due. Execution of judgment involves an order of the court requiring that the money be paid and which may therefore be satisfied out of any of the debtors property, which is within the reach of the Process.

Jurisdiction — Embraces every kind of judicial action. It gives a court the right to act in the matter brought before it.

Law (Questions of) — Questions of law are always decided by the presiding judge of the court in which the questions are raised. Questions of fact are for the jury to decide. Questions of material fact in disputes between parties should always be left to trial by Jury and for the Jury to decide. [Many judges in equity arrogate this power to themselves (wrongfully).]

Money (lawful) — As defined by the U.S. Constitution Article 1, Sec. 10, and by Black's Law Dictionary: In the usual and ordinary acceptation it means gold, silver coin, or paper money redeemable in gold or silver, which is used as circulating medium of exchange and *does not embrace notes, bonds, evidences of debt, or other personal or real estate.*

Mortgage — A mortgage creates an estate which can be conveyed by the mortgage or lien absolute in its form, but intended to secure the performance of some act such as the payment of money to a lender for his having advanced the named sum of money to the mortgagor; and which becomes void if the act is performed according to the terms prescribed at the time of the making of the mortgage conveyance. A mortgage is a conditional conveyance of land or the conditional transfer of property as security for the advancement of money from a lender (creditor), to the mortgagor. In equity, the debtor and those claiming under him remain the actual owners until barred by judicial sentence or by their own default. Today, regarded as a lien.

Mortgagee — The lender in whom the legal ownership of a property is vested.

Mortgagor — One who gives or grants a lender a conditional legal ownership in his property.

Motion — Motions for Decree, judgment, in arrest of judgment, in error, to set aside judgment and many more of almost any given name describing the motion, it simply presents a Motion addressed to the court, which must be heard and a determination made. There are Motions to Stay, to Strike, etc., etc.

Null and Void — Usually coupled in terms when used in a contract or statute and often construed by the courts as meaning voidable.

Pleadings — Allegations of fact in a cause in a lawsuit. To argue a cause in a court of justice. The Pleadings must produce a proper legal issue to the court upon which a trial is based.

Proceedings — Conduct of juridical business before a court of law: includes all possible legal steps in an action from its commencement to the execution of judgment or verdict of a jury. Calls for an act necessary to be done in order to obtain a juridical end.

Quit Claim Deed — A deed of conveyance which passes title, interest or any claim which the grantor may have in the premises. However, the deed does not profess such title is valid nor does it contain any warranty of title.

Writ of Quo Warranto — A writ which is addressed to prevent a continued exercise of authority unlawfully asserted, for instance a Writ addressed to a judge in equity who unlawfully asserts his authority to deny a petitioner his demand for trial by jury (a right protected by the 7th Amendment).

Service — Usually applied to serving papers on a party to a lawsuit.

Shin-plaster — A term used to describe a check or bank note or form of paper money which is of no value, in lawful money (gold or silver or redeemable in gold or silver).

Sine die — A final adjournment. A dismissal of a cause. A judgment for the defendant / complainant discharging him from any further appearance in court.

Summons — A writing by which a party to a lawsuit is summoned to appear in court.

Superior court — One in which actions in a lawsuit are heard that involve sums of money in excess of a specified sum.

Trustee — A person who has been appointed to sell an estate or an interest in an estate for a lender. The Trustee is a person who holds the legal title to property for the benefit of another person. He also may have the legal duty of carrying out a foreclosure sale called a Trustee sale, where a Deed of Trust has been given a lender as security for the mortgage lien on the property, of the debtor.

Ultra Vires — Acts beyond the scope and power of a corporation such as a bank. Acts which are in excess of powers granted by the authority of law or which are prohibited. Also applied when a corporation has no power to do an act but does it anyway without legal authority to perform it under any circumstances or for any purpose.

Usury — Any illegal contract for a loan or forbearance of money goods, or things in action, by which an illegal interest is reserved to the lender. An unlawful contract obtained by deceit, misrepresentation of truth, upon which a person acted in reliance on the lender's statements. An unlawful contract upon the loan of money contrived to receive the same amount of money again with exorbitant increase. Where no lawful money is given or received, fraud may be added to the charge of usury.

Venue — The county or state in which an action at law is brought for trial, or jurisdiction in which either party to a lawsuit may demand trial by jury. Venue does not arise, until an action has been started.

Waive — In modern law the term is used to denote that which is renounced, repudiated, or surrendered such as a privilege, a right or an opportunity to take advantage of some defect, irregularity or wrong. A person may waive the benefit of a tort or an injury when he abandons the remedy which the law gives him for it.

Writ — A precept in writing requiring the performance of a specific act in a suit, or a proceeding giving authority to have it done.

1
Kinds of Foreclosure

Foreclosure. To shut out, to bar, to destroy an equity of redemption, foreclosure represents a termination of all rights of the mortgagor or his grantee in any property he has covered by the mortgage he has created.

Foreclosure is a process in chancery in court, by which all right existing in a mortgagor to redeem an estate becomes the absolute property of the mortgagee. Foreclosure procedures apply when the mortgagor has forfeited his estate by non-payment of the money due on the mortgage at the time appointed. However, the mortgagor still may retain his equity of redemption.

The term Foreclosure is applied to any of various methods of enforcing payment of the debt secured by a mortgage, by taking and selling the mortgaged estate.

In addition, Foreclosure is also applied to proceedings founded upon some other liens; thus there are proceedings to foreclose a mechanic's lien. Foreclosure may be a proceeding in or out of court, when provided for by a valid contract, which subjects your property or any part thereof covered by a lien to payment of debt secured by the lien; and it has the effect of extinguishing all right, title or interest you may have in the property.

FORECLOSURES. Foreclosures occur because of default on debt secured by mortgage payments on property. The number of foreclosures is growing daily. A state of emergency exists. High interest rates and tight money wither and consume profits as well as payments. Borrowers are in deep trouble and so are lenders. Both seek a compromise that permits borrower and lender to survive, the borrower to keep his home, business and property, the lender to keep on getting his mortgage payments. There are many different kinds of Foreclosures. Let us examine them one by one, in the following order: Foreclosure on Trust Deed, Foreclosure on Mortgage, Strict Foreclosure, Entry Foreclosure. Then let us see how to stop the Foreclosure Clock from running against us.

Bear in mind that foreclosure proceedings start with a formal demand for payment, usually a letter from the lender. It may come from his attorney, his insurance company of from The Bank. This letter notice is usually a form notifying you of default. (Illus. NOTICE OF DEFAULT). Study. Realize that it is a threat to seize, sell your property, terminate all your rights in that property and evict you from the premises.

Consider. Foreclosures take time.

Foreclosures involve legal actions, required procedures, motions to be filed and heard in court, delays, a chance to re-negotiate, opportunities to defend yourself with legal motions. So don't panic. Assess your equity in your property and determine if it is worth defending.

Kinds of Foreclosures. Under a Trust Deed. Strict and by Entry.

Foreclosure proceedings are not the same in all states. If you are threatened with foreclosure, re-examine the kind of security you have given to the lender.

In most states you will have used a mortgage or a Deed of Trust as security for the sum you have borrowed. In Arizona, Kentucky and Maryland, both are required. Usage is based on legal traditions of each state. In states using only a mortgage as security, you will have to go through formal legal procedures and face proceedings in a court of law. In states using only a Deed of Trust, Foreclosure could be enforced without going to court. In either case, there is the note that you have signed, which contains the obligation to pay back the money you borrowed. This note is evidence of indebtedness. Two questions which your attorney should include in your defense in court:

Q. Did you receive any money or was it the banker's or lender's mere book entry?

Q. If a mere book entry, where is evidence you actually received legal money representing the indebtedness?

Questions like this will throw your adversary off stride, and the court may dismiss the lender's suit.

Foreclosure under a Trust Deed. This form of foreclosure may be the most terrifying because when the Notice of Default has been served on you, and that Notice has been duly recorded at the County Recorder's Office, you are in foreclosure. You must act at once to stop the Foreclosure Clock. There are only two ways you can stop that kind of Foreclosure: (1) stop it by negotiating with the lender to extend, forgive, accept payment on account. Create any delay possible if you cannot make payment on the account. (2) Challenge the Trust Deed documents, the legal description of the property, the notices, everything you can find fault with in court. Get an expert real estate (and constitutional) lawyer. (3) Examine the documents for the slightest flaw or mistake. Example: Does the document specify where to make payment? If not, you have an out for failure to make payment. This flaw may provide grounds for dismissing the lender's case and he will have to collect what he can, whenever he can. Loss of his case does not discharge your debt. You are just buying time. Further, the documents must state the full amount owed and the terms of payment such as weekly, monthly, annually, etc. The Deed note must specify the annual percentage rate of interest. Here an expert real estate attorney can examine your documents for errors and be of real help.

As a last resort you can hold off your creditor by using Bankruptcy procedures. But this is to be avoided, if at all possible.

Mortgage Deed Foreclosure. A mortgage deed can only be foreclosed through court action. Here again, have the Mortgage Deed closely examined for errors in property description, amount borrowed, terms of payment, interest rate, other terms and start the questions. Were you paid in legal money, or was it a mere book entry? Hire a Constitutional lawyer who will defend you based on your constitutional rights and definitions, who will ferret out the flaws in the lenders' case and keep on filing valid motions which have the effect of buying time. Meanwhile, negotiate and communicate with your creditor. [You may enable yourself to remain rent free, payment free in the premises indefinitely.]

If you have salvageable equity, fight for it. If you do not, and still want to remain, seek alternatives with the lender. Meanwhile, hire a lawyer. (1) Deny the lender's complaint in court, (2) Stop the Foreclosure clock with counter court actions and motions, delay court hearings, (3) challenge the documents for Usury, legal money, violations of Truth in Lending, (4) negotiate, (5) Communicate, (6) If all is about to be lost file Bankruptcy to forestall any default judgment, because if the property does not bring at sale the amount owed you could be liable for the difference; if your lender is the Government, it will reach you through chancery courts wherever you go.

Strict Foreclosure. In states such as Vermont and Connecticut, there are strict foreclosures. Strict foreclosures involve a court hearing to determine if the mortgagee has the right to foreclose. If so, the court will award the property to him. Because this type of Foreclosure moves rapidly through the court, it is imperative that you act timely in hiring a constitutional lawyer to deny the claim and take up your defense as to whether you received legal money. Legal issues such as this are important to raise in court. Find and test any and all errors in court, and in general play the "game of motions" and incur every possible delay.

Entry Foreclosure. In some of the New England states such as New Hampshire, Maine, Vermont and Connecticut, entry foreclosure is permitted under certain conditions. In such instance, the mortgagee forecloses by evicting the mortgagor and taking physical possession of the premises or property. This procedure is the swiftest of them all. Act immediately. Entry Foreclosure is essentially the same as Strict Foreclosure without benefit of court action. Every important effort on the part of the borrower must be made timely to stop the lender from proceeding.

Negotiate.

Plead for time.

Make partial payment in return for time delays.

Renegotiate payments if possible.

Hire an expert real estate lawyer.

Find flaws in the documents (there are always flaws).

File for bankruptcy if necessary. Review everything. And again:

Act timely to forestall legal actions.

Renegotiate your loan before the foreclosure clock time runs out.

Find out what to do in your state by seeking counsel.

Find errors in the documents.

Challenge the lender in court.

You have certain constitutional rights. Learn from counsel what they are. Play the game of motions to stop foreclosure.

Communicate with your lender, again and again and again. Work out a deal. Evaluate your equity. Be honest and renegotiate your loan on terms you can meet.

File Bankruptcy if desperate, as a last resort.

Finally, if you have no place to turn to and the property is your home or business or a combination of both, instead of any of the above, reassess your equity, and

1. Offer the lender a deed in lieu of fighting his foreclosure in return for occupancy for a period of time which in terms of rent would be equal to the value of your equity. He may agree as he will be thinking of time and cost in court and the possibility of losing his case as well.

2. Make sure, if you come to some agreement, that he agrees not to cast a cloud on your credit record.

In summary, here are a few guideline steps you can take immediately, when you are threatened with Foreclosure:

- Get all your data together, your notes, letters, receipts, payment books, records, whatever will help your lawyer (a ''constitutional'' lawyer) assemble pre-trial information. Assemble all evidence of debt against your property.
- Prepare your Findings of Facts.
- Familiarize yourself with applicable Court Rules and Proceedings. The Clerk of Court

will help you; also, the Librarian in the Court's Law Library can be of tremendous help.

- Investigate applicable State Statutes, particularly those Statutes that may have a bearing on your case.
- It will be necessary for you to familiarize yourself with the Trial Plan (your state), and to insist that your lawyer immediately file a Complaint on your behalf.
- Upon receipt of foreclosure letter from either an attorney, a title insurance company, or bank lender, arrange for an appointment, and take a witness. Try to negotiate. Prepare an Affidavit of your effort.
- Present testimony and Affidavits of Witnesses, of what you said to your lender, what you offered or proposed regarding refinance of your debt. Prepare testimony as to his replies.
- Have your attorney prepare Motions requesting Time for Discovery, and have him take Depositions.
- When your lender files his replies, you file Motions in Rebuttal.
- Have your attorney file Motions to take Interrogatories.
- Use Court Rules, and file Motions to Strike everything the lender brings down the pike.

Note: If the lender seeks relief in a court of equity, then it must show that it is actually paying some person interest for the funds it lends and is not merely creating the funds for the negligible cost of ink and paper. If the trial shows the latter to be the case, then the lender's only claim for relief can be the return of similar ink and paper loaned to the borrower. The ink and paper you use may take on the appearance of money, such as the ''Fractional Reserve Check'' shown. (See below example.) If the lender seeks relief in a court of both law and equity, and the above conditions apply, then the lender has no claim for relief at law and the borrower need only return in equity a check, as shown. Such a check need not possess the quality of lawful or legal tender, any more than the ink and paper used by the lender. Believe it or not but the Federal Reserve Bank of New York has published a document which says: ''MONEY DOESN'T HAVE TO BE INTRINSICALLY VALUABLE, BE ISSUED BY A GOVERNMENT, OR BE IN ANY

```
┌─────────────────────────────────────────────────────────────────────┐
│                                                                       │
│         FRACTIONAL RESERVE CHECK          No. _____         │
│                                                                       │
│   THE UNDERSIGNED                         _____ 19 _____    │
│   WILL PAY TO _____ $ _____   │
│                                                                       │
│   _____ DOLLARS      │
│   OF CREDIT TO THE BEARER ON DEMAND.                                  │
│                                           _____    │
│                                                 SIGNATURE             │
│   THIS CHECK IS REDEEMABLE IN A CERTIFICATE  _____     │
│   OF CREDIT, AT FULL FACE VALUE WHEN PRE-         NAME               │
│   SENTED TO THE ISSUER AT HIS PLACE OF      _____     │
│   RESIDENCE. VOID IF NOT PRESENTED FOR          ADDRESS              │
│   PAYMENT WITHIN SIX (6) MONTHS.           _____   │
│                                            CITY, STATE, P.O. ZIP NO.  │
│                                                                       │
└─────────────────────────────────────────────────────────────────────┘
```

SPECIAL FORM''!* So, indeed you may use just such a privately issued kind of check or promise to pay as such checkbook money constitutes payment in like kind and while not legal tender under the statutes, such money (Fractional Reserve Checks and Certificates of Credit) are legal tender at common law, and conform to the principle of natural equity by returning payment in a like kind of money received by you from the lender.

- If your attorney won't go along, find out why. If not satisfied, find one who will.
- Use every technique you can that applies to your situation. Act timely.

What are the legal weapons or security devices a lender can use against you? If he has merely lent you credit instead of money, and has taken from you significant instruments of value such as a Promissory Note, a Mortgage lien against your property, or a Deed of Trust or both or all three, such documents may not serve to provide him with the relief he seeks in a court of equity or common law.

It will pay you to know just what weapons he has in his arsenal as you are going to have to face him in a court battle if you intend to fight for your property.

We have been using the word Mortgage. When you grant a lender a mortgage, you are the mortgagor and he is the mortgagee. And you are creating an estate for him by conveyance absolute in its form, but

given to him with the intent to secure for you from him the payment of money. The conveyance is conditional upon his performing the act of giving you money in return for transfer of your property passing to him, conditionally, as security for payment of that money which you are borrowing from him and which is called a debt. In many states, a mortgage is not regarded as creating title or estate, but is merely a form of a pledge or security. If the Mortgage is a mere conveyance in effect, and is not cast as a form of conveyance of your property, cite the fact in your COMPLAINT. If the lender has merely lent you his credit, you have received nothing of value for it (no legal tender) and the mortgage you have given him is not cast as a form of conveyance of your property, your battle is almost won, especially insofar as remaining in your property is concerned.

THE TRUST DEED as a Security Device. There are two parts to a Trust Deed (see sample). The Deed itself is what is called a legal weapon because if payments are not made you can be foreclosed without the lender's having to go to court. Also, there is the note you signed that contains the amount of the debt owed, and represents your obligation to pay back the money you borrowed. (Here, again, immediately challenge whether you received money, legal tender, from the lender. The note definitely represents your indebtedness.) Where a Deed of Trust and Note are given, the lender usually uses a title, escrow or trust company specially set up to act as the Trustee. So be prepared to face both the lender and the Trustee in court if you fail to meet your loan obligations.

---

*''I Bet You Thought,'' published by the Federal Reserve Bank of New York, 1983. Also, see ''Modern Money Mechanics.'' FRB, Chicago.

Kinds of Security Devices Used in Our Fifty States. The following list embraces the kind or kinds of security you were asked to give the lender when you mortgaged your property. You gave the lender a mortgage, a mortgage note or a Deed of Trust. In some states, the lender will require both. Usage may be based upon the legal tradition of a particular county or state.

Security Forms (by state):

Alabama	Mortgage	Montana	Deed of Trust
Alaska	Deed of Trust	Nebraska	Deed of Trust
Arizona	Deed of Trust	Nevada	Deed of Trust
Arkansas	Both	New Hampshire	Mortgage
California	Deed of Trust	New Jersey	Mortgage
Colorado	Deed of Trust	New Mexico	Deed of Trust
Connecticut	Mortgage	New York	Mortgage
Delaware	Mortgage	North Carolina	Deed of Trust
Florida	Mortgage	North Dakota	Mortgage
Georgia	Mortgage	Ohio	Mortgage
Hawaii	Mortgage	Oklahoma	Mortgage
Idaho	Deed of Trust	Oregon	Deed of Trust
Illinois	Deed of Trust	Pennsylvania	Mortgage
Indiana	Mortgage	Rhode Island	Mortgage
Iowa	Mortgage	South Carolina	Mortgage
Kansas	Mortgage	South Dakota	Mortgage
Kentucky	Both	Tennessee	Deed of Trust
Louisiana	Mortgage	Texas	Deed of Trust
Maine	Mortgage	Utah	Deed of Trust
Maryland	Both	Vermont	Mortgage
Massachusetts	Mortgage	Virginia	Deed of Trust
Michigan	Mortgage	Washington	Deed of Trust
Minnesota	Mortgage	West Virginia	Deed of Trust
Mississippi	Deed of Trust	Wisconsin	Mortgage
Missouri	Deed of Trust	Wyoming	Mortgage

These Security Devices, the mortgage or the Deed of Trust that you give the lender along with your promissory note, are instruments of value. They represent value. They represent your equity in your property. And they are given as a consideration for value received. If you have received a bank loan from your banker by the mere stroke of his pen, the bank has merely lent you its credit. Your banker may have a bookkeeping entry made to your checking account for the amount you have borrowed. Still, you have received no money (legal tender). You may write checks against that account to pay creditors, and those checks will come back to your lender's bank and be cancelled. No gold or silver coins and no Federal Reserve Notes have actually changed hands. And your banker's argument in a court of law or equity asserting that you could have cashed a check at his counter and been given coin or dollars for your check will not provide him with relief. There is no law authorizing a banker or lender to create money by lending his credit. You may pay him back by lending him your credit by using a Fractional Reserve Check. You have then paid him back with the same kind of ink and paper that he used. Credit is the opposite of money. Memorize it.

Furthermore, he has taken a Deed of Trust from you or a Mortgage granting him a lien on your property. He has taken from you an instrument of significant value in return for "credit" which he has created out of thin air. This is why you must get your facts together, state them in a Complaint and file the Complaint at once with the Clerk of Court, upon receiving a letter threatening Foreclosure.

Foreclosure actions take time, and you have a chance to win. But bear in mind that when you give a Deed of Trust, this deed empowers the lender (trustee) to sell the property if we fail to meet our loan obligations. So the Money vs. Credit issue becomes very important, and if it can be used, it must be used at once to stop the lender from going ahead with sale.

RECORDING REQUESTED BY

AND WHEN RECORDED MAIL TO

NAME
STREET
ADDRESS
CITY &
STATE

Attn: _____   REFERENCE NUMBER

IMPORTANT NOTICE

IF YOUR PROPERTY IS IN FORECLOSURE BECAUSE YOU ARE BEHIND IN YOUR PAYMENTS, IT MAY BE SOLD WITHOUT ANY COURT ACTION, and you may have the legal right to bring your account in good standing by paying all of your past due payments plus permitted costs and expenses within three months from the date this Notice of Default was recorded.

This amount is $ _____ as of _____ , and will increase until your account becomes current. You may not have to pay the entire unpaid portion of your account, even though full payment was demanded, but you must pay the amount stated above. After three months from the date of recordation of this document (which date of recordation appears hereon), unless the obligation being foreclosed upon permits a longer period, you have only the legal right to stop the foreclosure by paying the entire amount demanded by your creditor. To find out the amount you must pay, or to arrange for payment to stop the foreclosure, or if your property is in foreclosure for any other reason, contact:

If you have any questions, you should contact a lawyer or the government agency which may have insured your loan.

Remember, **YOU MAY LOSE LEGAL RIGHTS IF YOU DO NOT TAKE PROMPT ACTION.**

NOTICE OF DEFAULT

THE FOLLOWING COPY OF NOTICE THE ORIGINAL OF WHICH WAS FILED FOR RECORD
ON _____ IN THE OFFICE OF _____ COUNTY
THE RECORDER OF _____ CALIFORNIA
IS SENT TO YOU INASMUCH AS AN EXAMINATION OF THE TITLE TO SAID TRUST PROPERTY
SHOWS YOU MAY HAVE AN INTEREST IN THE TRUSTEE'S SALE PROCEEDINGS

NOTICE IS HEREBY GIVEN: THAT _____

_____ is duly appointed Trustee under a Deed of Trust

and   executed by

                                                           as Trustor, to secure certain obligations

in favor of

                                                           , as beneficiary

recorded   , as instru-   , in   , page   of Official Records
                              ment no.   book   in the Office of the
Recorder of   County, California, describing land
therein as:

including   note   for the   sum of $ said obligations

that a breach of, and default in, the obligations for which such Deed of Trust is security has accurred in that payment has not been made of:

that by reason thereof, the present beneficiary under such Deed of Trust has deposited with said duly appointed Trustee, such Deed of Trust and all documents evidencing obligations secured thereby, and the undersigned does hereby declare all sums secured thereby immediately due and payable and does hereby elect to cause the trust property to be sold to satisfy the obligations secured thereby

Dated _____

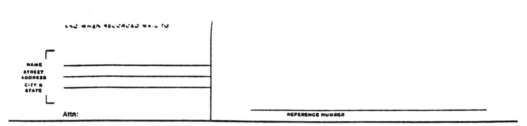

NOTICE OF RESCISSION

NOTICE WAS RECORDED ON		IN THE OFFICE OF THE RECORDER OF
		COUNTY CALIFORNIA
DOC NO.	IN BOOK	PAGE	OF OFFICIAL RECORDS.

whereas, _____

_____ is duly appointed Trustee under a Deed of Trust

executed by

dated

in favor of

recorded   as instru-   In   , as beneficiary
Recorder of   ment no.   book   page   , of Official Records
therein as: In the Office of the
                                                                                                County, California, describing land

and that:

On the day and in the book and page set forth above a Notice of Default was recorded

Notice is now given that said Notice of Default is hereby rescinded, cancelled, and withdrawn It is understood, however, that this Notice of Rescission shall not in any manner be construed as waiving or affecting any breach or default — past, present, or future, under said Deed of Trust or as impairing any right or remedy thereunder, but it is, and shall be deemed to be, only an election, without prejudice, not to cause a sale to be made pursuant to said notice, and shall in nowise jeopardize or impair any right, remedy, or privilege of the Beneficiary and/or the Trustee, under said Deed of Trust nor modify nor alter in any respect any of the terms, covenants, conditions thereof, and said Deed of Trust and all obligations secured thereby are hereby reinstated and shall be and remain in force and affect the same as if said Notice of Default had not been made and given

_____

_____

Dated _____   _____

$ _____   _____ , 19 ____

_____ after date, for value received, _____ promise

to pay to the order of _____ the sum

of _____ **Dollars,**

at _____ with interest at the rate of _____ per

centum per annum until paid; said interest payable _____

No. _____   _____

                     _____

Due _____   Address _____

This Deed, made and entered into this _____ day of _____, 19 _____, by and between

_____

_____

parties of the first part; and _____

_____

TRUSTEE, parties of the second part;

Witnesseth: that for and in consideration of the sum of TEN DOLLARS, ($10.00), the said parties of the first part do hereby grant, bargain, sell and convey unto the said parties of the second part, WITH GENERAL WARRANTY OF TITLE, certain real estate in the

_____, State of _____, more particularly described as follows:

Also including (but not excluding any fixtures which would ordinarily be construed as a part of the realty) any and all storm sashes, storm doors, vestibules, wire screens, wire doors, window shades, awnings, trees, shrubs, oil burner or other furnace equipment, domestic hot water boiler and equipment, and refrigerators, and stoves, used in the building upon said premises at the time of the execution of this deed of trust, or hereafter erected thereon, including, as well, all apparatus and fixtures of every description for watering, heating, ventilating, air conditioning, and screening said premises, together with all and singular the improvements, ways, easements, rights, privileges, and appurtenances to the same belonging, or in anywise appertaining

As further security for the debt hereby secured and the interest thereon and all of the sums authorized to be expended by the Trustees or the noteholder, the first parties hereby also sell, transfer and assign unto the noteholder, prior and superior to any and all other claims or demands thereto, the rents, issues, and income of and from the above described property accrued and hereafter to accrue, with full power and authority, at such holder's election, to collect and give receipts in full for the same and to apply all sums so collected, less a reasonable commission thereof which is hereby authorized to be paid to any agent employed by the noteholder to execute the provisions of this paragraph, and after deduction also of expenditures for repairs and upkeep of said property, to the payment of the indebtedness described in and secured by this Deed of Trust. There shall be no duty upon the said noteholder, however, to exercise such election and the noteholder may permit the first parties at any time and from time to time to collect said rents, issues, and income to their own use in which event the same shall in no way be deemed a waiver by, or to work an estoppel upon, the said noteholder thereafter to assert such holder's full rights and authority hereunder, provided, further, that no prepayment of any said rents, issues, or income for the whole or any portion of the said property, shall be procured, or permitted, or valid, without the written consent of the noteholder. If, moreover, upon default in the payment of any amount secured by this Deed of Trust, the first parties, or their successors in title to the property herein conveyed shall be or remain in possession thereof, or any part thereof, they shall be obligated to pay to the noteholder a fair and reasonable rental for the premises so occupied so long as they remain, or are allowed to remain, in such possession.

In Trust, However, to secure the prompt payment of _____ certain negotiable promissory note _____ bearing even

date herewith, for _____ Dollars,

($ _____) made by _____

_____

and payable to the order of _____

_____ after date, at the office of First American Bank of Virginia, McLean, Virginia or at such other place as the holder of the note may designate from time to time in writing, without offset, with interest at the rate of _____ per centum (_____) per annum until paid, providing for monthly installments to interest and principal, with the balance of the indebtedness, if not sooner paid, due and payable on _____ 19 _____;

_____

_____

_____

_____

_____

_____

_____

_____

_____

_____

_____

_____

_____

_____

_____

_____

said note waiving the homestead exemption as to the Makers and Endorsers thereof; and waiving notice of maturity, presentment, demand, protest and notice of protest, notice of non-payment and dishonor of the note, and having been identified by the Notary Public before whom these presents are acknowledged.

The maker of this note shall pay the Noteholder a late charge of $.05 for each $1.00 of each payment more than 15 days in arrears.

The privilege is reserved to pay the unpaid principal balance in full at any time, provided that for a period of ten years from date hereof, there shall be a prepayment fee of 1% of the unpaid principal balance.

In case the note is collected through an attorney-at-law, or under the advice thereof, the undersigned agree to pay all costs of collection, including reasonable attorneys fees.

Also In Trust, to secure the payment of any renewals or extensions of said debt as and when the same shall become due and payable, and of all costs and expenses incurred in respect thereto, and of all costs and expenses, including reasonable counsel fees incurred or paid by the Trustees or by any party hereby secured, on account of any litigation at law or in equity which may arise in respect to this trust or the said property while this trust continues, and of all moneys which may be advanced as herein provided, with interest at the rate of_____% per annum on all such costs and sums so advanced from the date of such advance; and also in trust to secure the performance of all the covenants on the part of the grantors herein covenanted to be performed.

Except as herein otherwise provided, this deed of trust shall be construed in accordance with the provisions of Section 55-59 of the 1950 Code of Virginia, as amended.

Should one of the Trustees herein named die or decline or fail to execute this trust, then the other Trustee shall have all the title, rights, powers and authority, and be charged with all the duties that are hereby conferred or charged upon both, unless and until a co-Trustee be appointed; but in any such event, or if both Trustees so die or decline or fail to execute this trust, (or for any other reason) if the holder of said note shall so desire, the said noteholder is hereby authorized and empowered to appoint by an instrument recorded where this Deed of Trust is recorded, another or two other Trustees in the place and stead of either or both of those herein originally named or in the place and stead of any other Trustee or Trustees later substituted therefor, all of whom successively shall while so acting have all the title, rights, powers and authority, and be charged with all the duties that are conferred or charged upon the Trustees herein originally named. Such power to appoint a substitute Trustee or Trustees shall not be deemed exhausted by any one or more such appointments, but rather shall continue unimpaired regardless of the number of prior appointments, and the recitals in every appointment shall be conclusive of the facts therein stated.

The said parties of the first part covenant: to pay the indebtedness hereby secured as and when the same shall become due and payable; to pay all taxes and assessments on said premises when due and immediately thereafter exhibit the official receipts to the holder of the said note; to keep the improvements now on said property or any that may hereafter be erected thereon insured, for such coverage, including Fire, Extended Coverage, Flood, and War Damage, in an approved stock insurance company for such amount and in such company or companies as may be required by or acceptable to the noteholder, and to assign the same with loss payable to the noteholder, and any amount received from said insurance shall be applied in reduction or payment of the debt hereby secured or to the repair or rebuilding of the improvements, as the noteholder may direct; to pay promptly any and all sums which have or may at any time hereafter become due for labor and materials furnished in or about the construction of any improvements on said land, and to satisfy forthwith any indebtedness for which a notice of intention to claim Mechanics' or Materialmen's Liens may at any time be filed against said land and premises; not to do nor suffer to be done anything to depreciate or impair the value of the said property; and upon default or neglect in the performance of any of said covenants the holder of said note may, at his option, declare the entire indebtedness hereby secured due and payable immediately, and may also pay such taxes and assessments, and have the said improvements insured, and pay and satisfy any debt for labor and materials furnished in, on, or about the said premises, and take steps to prevent depreciation or impairment of the value of the said property, and all expenses thereof shall be secured hereby, repayable upon demand, and shall bear interest at the rate of _____% per annum from the date of any such payment or payments.

The first parties hereby agree to make an additional payment to the noteholder monthly during the time that the indebtedness remains unpaid, of an amount equal to one-twelfth of annual taxes and assessments and/or premiums on insurance on the property on which the Note is secured or any other insurance policies, the premiums for which are collected by the noteholder.

The said parties of the first part covenant that the improvements to be erected on the real estate hereby conveyed will be completed within twelve months from the date hereof.

Any default in the payment of any lien or encumbrances senior hereto shall give the holder of the note secured hereby the option to call said note for payment in full regardless of the payment status of the note secured hereby or, in the sole discretion of the holder of the note secured hereby, it may cure the default and add the cost and expenses of curing same to the amount due under this deed of trust and note secured hereby.

Exemptions waived.
Subject to all upon default.
Renewal or extension permitted.
Reinstatement permitted.

In the event of default in the payment of said note or any installment of principal or interest as and when the same shall become due and payable, or upon default in any respect in any of the covenants herein contained, the Trustees here named, or the Trustee or Trustees acting in the execution of this trust shall, upon being requested by the holders of the note hereby secured, sell the property hereby conveyed at public auction for cash upon the premises, or at the front door of the Court House of the County or City wherein the said property is located, or at some other place in the said County or City selected by the Trustees (and a bidder's deposit of as much as 10% of the principal then due on the note may be required), after advertising the time, terms and place of sale in at least two weekly issues of some newspaper either published or having a general circulation in the said County or City, at the discretion of the Trustees, and shall convey the same to, and at the cost of, the purchaser thereof, who shall not be required to see to the application of the purchase money, and from the proceeds of said sale, shall pay, FIRST, all proper costs, charges, and expenses, including a Trustees' commission of 5% of the gross amount of sale, or the sum of $500.00, whichever is greater, which trustee's commission shall include fees to counsel for the trustees in conducting such sale, of not less than $200.00; second, all taxes, levies and assessments, with costs and interest, against the said property hereby conveyed due on date of sale; third, the total amount of principal, including any advances thereon, unpaid on said indebtedness, with interest to date, whether the same be due or not; and the balance, if any, shall be paid to the owner of the said property hereby conveyed at the time of said sale upon delivery of possession of the said property hereby conveyed, less the cost, if any, in obtaining possession thereof; provided, however, that the trustee, or trustees, as to such residue, shall not be bound by any inheritance, devise, conveyance, assignment or lien of or upon the grantor's equity, without actual notice thereof prior to distribution.

And it is further covenanted and agreed, that if the said property shall be advertised for sale as herein provided, and not sold, the Trustee or Trustees acting herein shall be entitled to one-half of the commission herein provided, to be computed on the amount of the unpaid debt hereby secured at the time of the first advertisement.

It is understood and agreed, that upon payment of all of the said principal and interest, and the fulfillment and performance of all of the covenants and agreements of the said note and of this Deed of Trust, then upon the request and at the cost of the parties of the first part a proper release and discharge of this Deed of Trust shall be executed as to so much of the property hereby conveyed as has not been sold but any right to demand a marginal release is hereby waived. Until then the first parties and their successors in title to the said property expressly waive all rights they may have to demand interim partial or protanto releases of this Deed of Trust. If a sale is had hereunder, the persons in possession of the property so sold shall be deemed to be tenants at will of the purchaser or purchasers.

In the event the above described property is sold, or title is otherwise transferred except by death, the entire indebtedness hereby secured shall become due and payable, at the option of the holder of said note. In the event the lender elects to allow this loan to be assumed, it shall not relieve the maker of the Note from any liability.

NOTICE: THE DEBT SECURED HEREBY IS SUBJECT TO CALL IN FULL OR THE TERMS THEREOF BEING MODIFIED IN THE EVENT OF SALE OR CONVEYANCE OF THE PROPERTY HEREBY CONVEYED.

<u>Witness</u> the following signatures and seals:

_____(SEAL)

_____(SEAL)

_____ of _____

_____ of _____, To-wit:

I, _____, a Notary Public in and for the said

_____, whose commission will expire on the _____day

of _____, 19 _____, do hereby certify that _____

_____

_____

_____

_____

whose name   signed to the foregoing and attached deed dated _____ ____, 19 _____,

ha   acknowledged the same before me in my   aforesaid

GIVEN under my hand   this ____day of _____, 19 _____

_____
                                            Notary Public

DEED OF TRUST

After Recordation Mail To:

[Space Above This Line For Recording Data]

DEED OF TRUST

THIS DEED OF TRUST ("Security Instrument") is made on .... ,
19 .... The grantor is ....
.... ("Borrower"). The trustee is ....
of ...., Virginia, and .... of ....,
Virginia, trustees (any one of whom may act and who are referred to as "Trustee"). The beneficiary is ....
.... , which is organized and existing
under the laws of .... , and whose address is ....
.... ("Lender").
Borrower owes Lender the principal sum of ....
.... Dollars (U.S. $ ....). This debt is evidenced by Borrower's note
dated the same date as this Security Instrument ("Note"), which provides for monthly payments, with the full
debt, if not paid earlier, due and payable on ....
This Security Instrument secures to Lender: (a) the repayment of the debt evidenced by the Note, with interest,
and all renewals, extensions and modifications; (b) the payment of all other sums, with interest, advanced under
paragraph 7 to protect the security of this Security Instrument; and (c) the performance of Borrower's convenants
and agreements under this Security Instrument and the Note. For this purpose, Borrower irrevocably grants
and conveys to Trustee, in trust, with power of sale, the following described property located in ....
...., Virginia:

which has the address of .... , ... ,
                                                    [Street]   [City]
Virginia ...., ("Property Address");
              [Zip Code]

TOGETHER WITH all the improvements now or hereafter erected on the property, and all easements,
rights, appurtenances, rents, royalties, mineral, oil and gas rights and profits, water rights and stock and all
fixtures now or hereafter a part of the property. All replacements and additions shall also be covered by this
Security Instrument. All of the foregoing is referred to in this Security Instrument as the "Property."

BORROWER COVENANTS that Borrower is lawfully seised of the estate hereby conveyed and has the right
to grant and convey the Property and that the Property is unencumbered, except for encumbrances of record.
Borrower warrants and will defend generally the title to the Property against all claims and demands, subject
to any encumbrances of record.

THIS SECURITY INSTRUMENT combines uniform convenants for national use and non-uniform covenants
with limited variations by jurisdiction to constitute a uniform security instrument covering real property.

VIRGINIA—Single Family—**FNMA/FHLMC UNIFORM INSTRUMENT**

293 (8/84)

UNIFORM COVENANTS. Borrower and Lender covenant and agree as follows:

1. Payment of Principal and Interest; Prepayment and Late Charges. Borrower shall promptly pay when due the principal of and interest on the debt evidenced by the Note and any prepayment and late charges due under the Note.

2. Funds for Taxes and Insurance. Subject to applicable law or to a written waiver by Lender, Borrower shall pay to Lender on the day monthly payments are due under the Note, until the Note is paid in full, a sum ("Funds") equal to one-twelfth of: (a) yearly taxes and assessments which may attain priority over this Security Instrument; (b) yearly leasehold payments or ground rents on the Property, if any; (c) yearly hazard insurance premiums; and (d) yearly mortgage insurance premiums, if any. These items are called "escrow items." Lender may estimate the Funds due on the basis of current data and reasonable estimates of future escrow items.

The Funds shall be held in an institution the deposits or accounts of which are insured or guaranteed by a federal or state agency (including Lender if Lender is such an institution). Lender shall apply the Funds to pay the escrow items. Lender may not charge for holding and applying the Funds, analyzing the account or verifying the escrow items, unless Lender pays Borrower interest on the Funds and applicable law permits Lender to make such a charge. Borrower and Lender may agree in writing that interest shall be paid on the Funds. Unless an agreement is made or applicable law requires interest to be paid, Lender shall not be required to pay Borrower any interest or earnings on the Funds. Lender shall give to Borrower, without charge, an annual accounting of the Funds showing credits and debits to the Funds and the purpose for which each debit to the Funds was made. The Funds are pledged as additional security for the sums secured by this Security Instrument.

If the amount of the Funds held by Lender, together with the future monthly payments of Funds payable prior to the due dates of the escrow items, shall exceed the amount required to pay the escrow items when due, the excess shall be, at Borrower's option, either promptly repaid to Borrower or credited to Borrower on monthly payments of Funds. If the amount of the Funds held by Lender is not sufficient to pay the escrow items when due, Borrower shall pay to Lender any amount necessary to make up the deficiency in one or more payments as required by Lender.

Upon payment in full of all sums secured by this Security Instrument, Lender shall promptly refund to Borrower any Funds held by Lender. If under paragraph 19 the Property is sold or acquired by Lender, Lender shall apply, no later than immediately prior to the sale of the Property or its acquistion by Lender, any Funds held by Lender at the time of application as a credit against the sums secured by this Security Instrument.

3. Application of Payments. Unless applicable law provides otherwise, all payments received by Lender under paragraphs 1 and 2 shall be applied: first, to late charges due under the Note; second, to prepayment charges due under the Note; third, to amounts payable under paragraph 2; fourth, to interest due; and last, to principal due.

4. Charges; Liens. Borrower shall pay all taxes, assessments, charges, fines and impositions attributable to the Property which may attain priority over this Security Instrument, and leasehold payments or ground rents, if any. Borrower shall pay these obligations in the manner provided in paragraph 2, or if not paid in that manner, Borrower shall pay them on time directly to the person owed payment. Borrower shall promptly furnish to Lender all notices of amounts to be paid under this paragraph. If Borrower makes these payments directly, Borrower shall promptly furnish to Lender receipts evidencing the payments.

Borrower shall promptly discharge any lien which has priority over this Security Instrument unless Borrower: (a) agrees in writing to the payment of the obligation secured by the lien in a manner acceptable to Lender; (b) contests in good faith the lien by, or defends against enforcement of the lien in, legal proceedings which in the Lender's opinion operate to prevent the enforcement of the lien or forfeiture of any part of the Property; or (c) secures from the holder of the lien an agreement satisfactory to Lender subordinating the lien to this Security Instrument. If Lender determines that any part of the Property is subject to a lien which may attain priority over this Security Instrument, Lender may give Borrower a notice identifying the lien. Borrower shall satisfy the lien or take one or more of the actions set forth above within 10 days of the giving of notice.

5. Hazard Insurance. Borrower shall keep the improvements now existing or hereafter erected on the Property insured against loss by fire, hazards included within the term "extended coverage" and any other hazards for which Lender requires insurance. This insurance shall be maintained in the amounts and for the periods that Lender requires. The insurance carrier providing the insurance shall be chosen by Borrower subject to Lender's approval which shall not be unreasonably withheld.

All insurance policies and renewals shall be acceptable to Lender and shall include a standard mortgage clause. Lender shall have the right to hold the policies and renewals. If Lender requires, Borrower shall promptly give to Lender all receipts of paid premiums and renewal notices. In the event of loss, Borrower shall give prompt notice to the insurance carrier and Lender. Lender may make proof of loss if not made promptly by Borrower.

Unless Lender and Borrower otherwise agree in writing, insurance proceeds shall be applied to restoration or repair of the Property damaged, if the restoration or repair is economically feasible and Lender's security is not lessened. If the restoration or repair is not economically feasible or Lender's security would be lessened, the insurance proceeds shall be applied to the sums secured by this Security Instrument, whether or not then due, with any excess paid to Borrower. If Borrower abandons the Property, or does not answer within 30 days a notice from Lender that the insurance carrier has offered to settle a claim, then Lender may collect the insurance proceeds. Lender may use the proceeds to repair or restore the Property or to pay sums secured by this Security Instrument, whether or not then due. The 30-day period will begin when the notice is given.

Unless Lender and Borrower otherwise agree in writing, any application of proceeds to principal shall not extend or postpone the due date of the monthly payments referred to in paragraphs 1 and 2 or change the amount of the payments. If under paragraph 19 the Property is acquired by Lender, Borrower's right to any insurance policies and proceeds resulting from damage to the Property prior to the acquisition shall pass to Lender to the extent of the sums secured by this Security Instrument immediately prior to the acquisition.

6. Preservation and Maintenance of Property; Leaseholds. Borrower shall not destroy, damage or substantially change the Property, allow the Property to deteriorate or commit waste. If this Security Instrument is on a leasehold, Borrower shall comply with the provisions of the lease, and if Borrower acquires fee title to the Property, the leasehold and fee title shall not merge unless Lender agrees to the merger in writing.

7. Protection of Lender's Rights in the Property; Mortgage Insurance. If Borrower fails to perform the convenants and agreements contained in this Security Instrument, or there is a legal proceeding that may significantly affect Lender's rights in the Property (such as a proceeding in bankruptcy, probate, for condemnation or to enforce laws or regulations), then Lender may do and pay for whatever is necessary to protect the value of the Property and Lender's rights in the Property. Lender's actions may include paying any sums secured by a lien which has priority over this Security Instrument, appearing in court, paying reasonable attorneys' fees and entering on the Property to make repairs. Although Lender may take action under this paragraph 7, Lender does not have to do so.

Any amounts disbursed by Lender under this paragraph 7 shall become additional debt of Borrower secured by this Security Instrument. Unless Borrower and Lender agree to other terms of payment, these amounts shall bear interest from the date of disbursement at the Note rate and shall be payable, with interest, upon notice from Lender to Borrower requesting payment.

If Lender required mortgage insurance as a condition of making the loan secured by this Security Instrument, Borrower shall pay the premiums required to maintain the insurance in effect until such time as the requirement for the insurance terminates in accordance with Borrower's and Lender's written agreement or applicable law.

8. Inspection. Lender or its agent may make reasonable entries upon and inspections of the Property. Lender shall give Borrower notice at the time of or prior to an inspection specifying reasonable cause for the inspection.

9. Condemnation. The proceeds of any award or claim for damages, direct or consequential, in connection with any condemnation or other taking of any part of the Property, or for conveyance in lieu of condemnation, are hereby assigned and shall be paid to Lender.

In the event of a total taking of the Property, the proceeds shall be applied to the sums secured by this Security Instrument, whether or not then due, with any excess paid to Borrower. In the event of a partial taking of the Property, unless Borrower and Lender otherwise agree in writing, the sums secured by this Security Instrument shall be reduced by the amount of the proceeds multiplied by the following fraction: (a) the total amount of the sums secured immediately before the taking, divided by (b) the fair market value of the Property immediately before the taking. Any balance shall be paid to Borrower.

If the Property is abandoned by Borrower, or if, after notice by Lender to Borrower that the condemnor offers to make an award or settle a claim for damages, Borrower fails to respond to Lender within 30 days after the date the notice is given, Lender is authorized to collect and apply the proceeds, at its option, either to restoration or repair of the Property or to the sums secured by this Security Instrument, whether or not then due.

Unless Lender and Borrower otherwise agree in writing, any application of proceeds to principal shall not extend or postpone the due date of the monthly payments referred to in paragraphs 1 and 2 or change the amount of such payments.

10. Borrower Not Released; Forbearance By Lender Not a Waiver. Extension of the time for payment or modification of amortization of the sums secured by this Security Instrument granted by Lender to any successor in interest of Borrower shall not operate to release the liability of the original Borrower or Borrower's successors in interest. Lender shall not be required to commence proceedings against any successor in interest or refuse to extend time for payment or otherwise modify amortization of the sums secured by this Security Instrument by reason of any demand made by the original Borrower or Borrower's successors in interest. Any forbearance by Lender in exercising any right or remedy shall not be a waiver of or preclude the exercise of any right or remedy.

11. Successors and Assigns Bound; Joint and Several Liability; Co-signers. The covenants and agreements of this Security Instrument shall bind and benefit the successors and assigns of Lender and Borrower, subject to the provisions of paragraph 17. Borrower's covenants and agreements shall be joint and several. Any Borrower who co-signs this Security Instrument but does not execute the Note: (a) is co-signing this Security Instrument only to mortgage, grant and convey that Borrower's interest in the Property under the terms of this Security Instrument; (b) is not personally obligated to pay the sums secured by this Security Instrument; and (c) agrees that Lender and any other Borrower may agree to extend, modify, forbear or make any accommodations with regard to the terms of this Security Instrument or the Note without that Borrower's consent.

12. Loan Charges. If the loan secured by this Security Instrument is subject to a law which sets maximum loan charges, and that law is finally interpreted so that the interest or other loan charges collected or to be collected in connection with the loan exceed the permitted limits, then: (a) any such loan charge shall be reduced by the amount necessary to reduce the charge to the permitted limit; and (b) any sums already collected from Borrower which exceeded permitted limits will be refunded to Borrower. Lender may choose to make this refund by reducing the principal owed under the Note or by making a direct payment to Borrower. If a refund reduces principal, the reduction will be treated as a partial prepayment without any prepayment charge under the Note.

13. Legislation Affecting Lender's Rights. If enactment or expiration of applicable laws has the effect of rendering any provision of the Note or this Security Instrument unenforceable according to its terms, Lender, at its option, may require immediate payment in full of all sums secured by this Security Instrument and may invoke any remedies permitted by paragraph 19. If Lender exercises this option, Lender shall take the steps specified in the second paragraph of paragraph 17.

14. Notices. Any notice to Borrower provided for in this Security Instrument shall be given by delivering it or by mailing it by first class mail unless applicable law requires use of another method. The notice shall be directed to the Property Address or any other address Borrower designates by notice to Lender. Any notice to Lender shall be given by first class mail to Lender's address stated herein or any other address Lender designates by notice to Borrower. Any notice provided for in this Security Instrument shall be deemed to have been given to Borrower or Lender when given as provided in this paragraph.

15. Governing Law; Severability. This Security Instrument shall be governed by federal law and the law of the jurisdiction in which the Property is located. In the event that any provision or clause of this Security Instrument or the Note conflicts with applicable law, such conflict shall not affect other provisions of this Security Instrument or the Note which can be given effect without the conflicting provision. To this end the provisions of this Security Instrument and the Note are declared to be severable.

16. Borrower's Copy. Borrower shall be given one conformed copy of the Note and of this Security Instrument.

17. Transfer of the Property or a Beneficial Interest in Borrower. If all or any part of the Property or any interest in it is sold or transferred (or if a beneficial interest in Borrower is sold or transferred and Borrower is not a natural person) without Lender's prior written consent, Lender may, at its option, require immediate payment in full of all sums secured by this Security Instrument. However, this option shall not be exercised by Lender if exercise is prohibited by federal law as of the date of this Security Instrument.

If Lender exercises this option, Lender shall give Borrower notice of acceleration. The notice shall provide a period of not less than 30 days from the date the notice is delivered or mailed within which Borrower must pay all sums secured by this Security Instrument. If Borrower fails to pay these sums prior to the expiration of this period, Lender may invoke any remedies permitted by this Security Instrument without further notice or demand on Borrower.

18. Borrower's Right to Reinstate. If Borrower meets certain conditions, Borrower shall have the right to have enforcement of this Security Instrument discontinued at any time prior to the earlier of: (a) 5 days (or such other period as applicable law may specify for reinstatement) before sale of the Property pursuant to any power of sale contained in this Security Instrument; or (b) entry of a judgment enforcing this Security Instrument. Those conditions are that Borrower: (a) pays Lender all sums which then would be due under this Security Instrument and the Note had no acceleration occurred; (b) cures any default of any other covenants or agreements; (c) pays all expenses incurred in enforcing this Security Instrument, including, but not limited to, reasonable attorneys' fees; and (d) takes such action as Lender may reasonably require to assure that the lien of this Security Instrument, Lender's rights in the Property and Borrower's obligation to pay the sums secured by this Security Instrument shall continue unchanged. Upon reinstatement by Borrower, this Security Instrument and the obligations secured hereby shall remain fully effective as if no acceleration had occurred. However, this right to reinstate shall not apply in the case of acceleration under paragraphs 13 or 17.

NON-UNIFORM COVENANTS. Borrower and Lender further covenant and agree as follows:

19. Acceleration; Remedies. Lender shall give notice to Borrower prior to acceleration following Borrower's breach of any covenant or agreement in this Security Instrument (but not prior to acceleration under paragraphs 13 and 17 unless applicable law provides otherwise). The notice shall specify: (a) the default; (b) the action required to cure the default; (c) a date, not less than 30 days from the date the notice is given to Borrower, by which the default must be cured; and (d) that failure to cure the default on or before the date specified in the notice may result in acceleration of the sums secured by this Security Instrument and sale of the Property. The notice shall further inform Borrower of the right to reinstate after acceleration and the right to bring a court action to assert the non-existence of a default or any other defense of Borrower to acceleration and sale. If the default is not cured on or before the date specified in the notice, Lender at its option may require immediate payment in full of all sums secured by this Security Instrument without further demand and may invoke the power of sale and any other remedies permitted by applicable law. Lender shall be entitled to collect all expenses incurred in pursuing the remedies provided in this paragraph 19, including, but not limited to, reasonable attorneys' fees and costs of title evidence.

If Lender invokes the power of sale, Lender or Trustee shall give to Borrower (and the owner of the Property, if a different person) notice of sale in the manner prescribed by applicable law. Trustee shall give public notice of sale by advertising, in accordance with applicable law, once a week for two successive weeks in a newspaper having general circulation in the county or city in which any part of the Property is located, and by such additional or any different form of advertisement the Trustee deems advisable. Trustee may sell the Property on the eighth day after the first advertisement or any day thereafter, but not later than 30 days following the last advertisement. Trustee, without demand on Borrower, shall sell the Property at public auction to the highest bidder at the time and place and under the terms designated in the notice of sale in one or more parcels and in any order Trustee determines. Trustee may postpone sale of all or any parcel of the Property by advertising in accordance with applicable law. Lender or its designee may purchase the Property at any sale.

Trustee shall deliver to the purchaser Trustee's deed conveying the Property with special warranty of title. The recitals in the Trustee's deed shall be prima facie evidence of the truth of the statements made therein. Trustee shall apply the proceeds of the sale in the following order: (a) to all expenses of the sale, including, but not limited to, Trustee's fees of ....% of the gross sale price and reasonable attorneys' fees; (b) to the discharge of all taxes, levies and assessments on the Property, if any, as provided by applicable law; (c) to all sums secured by this Security Instrument; and (d) any excess to the person or persons legally entitled to it. Trustee shall not be required to take possession of the Property prior to the sale thereof or to deliver possession of the Property to the purchaser at the sale.

20. Lender in Possession. Upon acceleration under paragraph 19 or abandonment of the Property, Lender (in person, by agent or by judicially appointed receiver) shall be entitled to enter upon, take possession of and manage the Property and to collect the rents of the Property including those past due. Any rents collected by Lender or the receiver shall be applied first to payment of the costs of management of the Property and collection of rents, including, but not limited to, receiver's fees, premiums on receiver's bonds and reasonable attorneys' fees, and then to the sums secured by this Security Instrument.

21. Release. Upon payment of all sums secured by this Security Instrument, Lender shall request Trustee to release this Security Instrument and shall surrender all notes evidencing debt secured by this Security Instrument to Trustee. Trustee shall release this Security Instrument without charge to Borrower. Borrower shall pay any recordation costs.

22. Substitute Trustee. Lender, at its option, may from time to time remove Trustee and appoint a successor trustee to any Trustee appointed hereunder. Without conveyance of the Property, the successor trustee shall succeed to all the title, power and duties conferred upon Trustee herein and by applicable law.

23. Identification of Note. The Note is identified by a certificate on the Note executed by any Notary Public who certifies an acknowledgment hereto.

24. Riders to this Security Instrument. If one or more riders are executed by Borrower and recorded together with this Security Instrument, the covenants and agreements of each such rider shall be incorporated into and shall amend and supplement the covenants and agreements of this Security Instrument as if the rider(s) were a part of this Security Instrument. [Check applicable box(es)]

☐ Adjustable Rate Rider ☐ Condominium Rider ☐ 2-4 Family Rider

☐ Graduated Payment Rider ☐ Planned Unit Development Rider

☐ Other(s) [specify]

NOTICE: THE DEBT SECURED HEREBY IS SUBJECT TO CALL IN FULL OR THE TERMS THEREOF BEING MODIFIED IN THE EVENT OF SALE OR CONVEYANCE OF THE PROPERTY CONVEYED.

BY SIGNING BELOW, Borrower accepts and agrees to the terms and covenants contained in this Security Instrument and in any rider(s) executed by Borrower and recorded with it.

.... (Seal)
                                                                                          —Borrower

.... (Seal)
                                                                                          —Borrower

.... (Seal)
                                                                                          —Borrower

.... (Seal)
                                                                                          —Borrower

[Space Below This Line For Acknowledgment]

STATE OF VIRGINIA, ... County ss:......................................

The foregoing instrument was acknowledged before me this ....
                                                                                          (date)

by ....
                              (person acknowledging)

My Commission expires: ....
                                                          Notary Public

VA Form 26-6344 (Home Loan)
APR 1978, USE OPTIONAL.
TITLE 38 U.S.C. § 1810
ACCEPTABLE TO FEDERAL NATIONAL
MORTGAGE ASSOCIATION.

VIRGINIA

DEED OF TRUST

THIS DEED, made this   **day of**   **, in the year 19   , between**

Grantors, and

Trustees:

WITNESSETH, that the said grantors do grant and assign with General Warranty to the said Trustees the following property, in the

, county or city of

in the State of Virginia, to wit:

and also all fixtures now or hereafter attached to or used in connection with the property herein described.

IN TRUST to secure to the holder thereof the payment of a certain promissory note bearing even date herewith in the principal sum of

                                        Dollars ($), with interest from date at the rate of   per centum (%) per annum on the unpaid balance until paid, and made by grantors, payable to the order of   at
                    , or at such other place as the holder may designate in writing delivered or mailed to the grantors, said principal and interest being payable in monthly installments of
            Dollars ($) commencing on the first day of   ,
19   , and continuing on the first day of each month thereafter until the note is fully paid, except that, if not sooner paid, the entire indebtedness shall be due and payable on the first day of   ,
      . Privilege is reserved to prepay at any time, without premium or fee, the entire indebtedness or any part thereof not less than the amount of one installment, or one hundred dollars ($100.00), whichever is less. Prepayment in full shall be credited on the date received. Partial prepayment, other than on an installment due date, need not be credited until the next following installment due date or thirty days after such prepayment, whichever is earlier.

This deed of trust is also given to secure the reimbursement to the holder of said note and to Trustees, and any purchaser or purchasers under any sale or sales as provided by this Trust, for any and all costs and expenses incurred in respect thereto, including reasonable counsel fees incurred or paid on account of any litigation at law or in equity which may arise in respect to this Trust, or to indebtedness on the property heretofore mentioned, or in obtaining possession of the premises after any sale which may be made as hereinafter provided for.

This deed is made under the provisions of § § 55-58 and 55-59 of the Code of Virginia and shall be construed to impose and confer upon the parties hereto and the beneficiary hereunder all of the duties, rights and obligations prescribed in said § 55-59, and, in short form provided in § 55-60, the following provisions:

Deferred purchase money.   Subject to all upon default.
Exemptions waived.   Right of anticipation reserved.
Renewal or extension permitted.   Substitution of trustee permitted and
                                             such substitution may be made at the
                                             discretion of the beneficiary or beneficiaries
                                             for any reason whatsoever.
                                             Any trustee may act.

1.   In addition to the monthly payment of principal and interest, the grantors and their assigns will also pay to the holder of the note, as trustee, on the due date of each month until it is fully paid, a sum equal to the premiums that will next become due and payable on policies of fire and other hazard insurance plus taxes and assessments next due, on the mortgaged property (all as estimated by the holder of the note, and of which the grantors are notified), less all sums already paid therefor, divided by the number of months to elapse before one month prior to the date when such premiums, taxes, and assessments will become payable, such sums to be held by the holder of the note in trust to pay said premiums, taxes, and assessments, or, if necessary, apply the same toward payment of the principal and interest.

2.   The aggregate of the amounts payable pursuant to the above paragraph and those payable on the note secured hereby, shall be paid in a single payment each month, to be applied to the following items in the order stated: (1) Taxes, assessments, fire and other hazard insurance premiums; (2) interest on the indebtedness secured hereby; and (3) amortization of the principal of said indebtedness. Any deficiency in the amount of such aggregate monthly payment shall, unless made good prior to the due date of the next such payment, constitute default under this Deed of Trust. At the option of the holder of the note, grantors will pay a "late charge" not exceeding four per centum of any installment when paid more than fifteen days after the due date thereof to cover the extra expense involved in handling delinquent

payments, but such "late charge" shall not be payable out of the proceeds of any sale made to satisfy the indebtedness secured hereby unless such proceeds are sufficient to discharge the entire indebtedness and all proper costs and expenses secured thereby.

3.   Grantors will continuously maintain hazard insurance, of such type or types and amounts as the holder of the note may from time to time require, on the improvements now or hereafter on said premises, and except when payment for all such premiums has theretofore been made under Paragraph Numbered 1 hereof, will pay promptly when due any premiums therefor. All insurance shall be carried in companies approved by the holder of the note and the policies and renewals thereof shall be held by the holder of the note and have attached thereto loss payable clauses in favor of and in form acceptable to the holder of the note. In event of loss the grantors will give immediate notice by mail to the holder of the note, who may make proof of loss if not made promptly by the grantors, and each insurance company concerned is hereby authorized and directed to make payment for such loss directly to the holder of the note instead of to the grantors and the holder of the note jointly, and the insurance proceeds, or any part thereof, may be applied by the holder of the note at its option either to the reduction of the indebtedness hereby secured or to the restoration or repair of the property damaged. In event of foreclosure of this Deed of Trust, or other transfer of title to the said premises in extinguishment of the indebtedness secured hereby, all right, title, and interest of the grantors in and to any insurance policies then in force shall pass to the purchaser or grantee.

4.   The grantors further assign to the holder of the note, as additional security, any rents which may now or hereafter be due upon the real property above described, it being understood that if, by reason of default under any of the terms hereof, the holder of the note collects said rents, such holder shall have the right of employing agents for that purpose and paying a percentage of the rents collected for such collection.

WITNESS the following signatures and seals.

_____ (SEAL)

_____ (SEAL)

_____ (SEAL)

_____ (SEAL)

STATE OF VIRGINIA,   )
CITY OF   )   **TO WIT:**
COUNTY OF   )

   I,   , a Notary Public for the city or county aforesaid in the State of Virginia, do certify that   , whose name   signed to writing above, bearing date on the   day of   , 19   , ha   acknowledged the same before me in my   and State aforesaid.

   Given under my hand and official seal this   day of   , 19   .

   My commission expires on the   day of   , 19   .

_____

Notary Public.

| This form is used in connection with deeds of trust insured under the one- to four-family provisions of the National Housing Act. |

DEED OF TRUST NOTE

| FHA CASE NUMBER: |

, Virginia.

$, 19

FOR VALUE RECEIVED, the undersigned promise(s) to pay to

,

or order, the principal sum of

Dollars ($),

with interest from date at the rate of   per centum (%),
per annum on the unpaid balance until paid. The said principal and interest shall be payable at the office of

, in

, or at such other place as the holder hereof may designate in writing, in monthly installments of

Dollars ($),
commencing on the first day of   , 19   , and on the first day of each month thereafter
until the principal and interest are fully paid, except that the entire indebtedness evidenced hereby, if not sooner paid,
shall be due and payable on the first day of

If default be made in the payment of any installment under this Note, and if such default is not made good prior to
the due date of the next such installment, the entire principal sum and accrued interest shall at once become due and
payable without notice at the option of the holder of this Note. Failure to exercise this option shall not constitute a
waiver of the right to exercise the same in the event of any subsequent default.

Presentment, protest, and notice are hereby waived. The drawers and endorsers of this Note also waive the benefit
of the homestead exemption as to this debt.

This Note and the interest are secured by the first Deed of Trust of even date herewith on property located in

County, Virginia, and this Note is to be construed according to the laws of
Virginia.

_____   _____

_____   _____

THIS IS TO CERTIFY that this is the Note described in and secured by Deed of Trust of even date herewith, and
in the same principal amount as herein stated, to

, trustee(s), on real estate

located in   County, Virginia.

Dated   , 19

_____
(Notary Public)

SHORT FORM DEED OF TRUST AND ASSIGNMENT OF RENTS (INDIVIDUAL)

A P N

This Deed of Trust, made this   day of   , between

, herein called TRUSTOR,

whose address is

    (number and street)   (city)   (state)   (zip)

, a California corporation, herein called TRUSTEE, and

, herein called BENEFICIARY,

Witnesseth: That Trustor IRREVOCABLY GRANTS, TRANSFERS AND ASSIGNS to TRUSTEE IN TRUST, WITH POWER OF SALE, that property in   County, California, described as:

TOGETHER WITH the rents, issues and profits thereof, SUBJECT, HOWEVER, to the right, power and authority given to and conferred upon Beneficiary by paragraph (10) of the provisions incorporated herein by reference to collect and apply such rents, issues and profits.

For the Purpose of Securing: 1. Performance of each agreement of Trustor incorporated by reference or contained herein. 2. Payment of the indebtedness evidenced by one promissory note of even date herewith, and any extension or renewal thereof, in the principal sum of $ executed by Trustor in favor of Beneficiary or order. 3. Payment of such further sums as the then record owner of said property hereafter may borrow from Beneficiary, when evidenced by another note (or notes) reciting it is so secured.

To Protect the Security of This Deed of Trust, Trustor Agrees: By the execution and delivery of this Deed of Trust and the note secured hereby, that provisions (1) to (14), inclusive, of the fictitious deed of trust recorded in Santa Barbara County and Sonoma County October 18, 1961, and in all other counties October 23, 1961, in the book and at the page of Official Records in the office of the county recorder of the county where said property is located, noted below opposite the name of such county, viz.:

COUNTY	BOOK	PAGE	COUNTY	BOOK	PAGE	COUNTY	BOOK	PAGE	COUNTY	BOOK	PAGE
Alameda	435	684	Kings	792	833	Placer	895	301	Sierra	29	335
Alpine	1	250	Lake	362	39	Plumas	151	5	Siskiyou	468	181
Amador	104	348	Lassen	171	471	Riverside	3005	523	Solano	1105	182
Butte	1145	1	Los Angeles	T2055	899	Sacramento	4331	62	Sonoma	1851	689
Calaveras	145	152	Madera	810	170	San Benito	271	383	Stanislaus	1715	456
Colusa	296	617	Marin	1508	339	San Bernardino	5567	61	Sutter	572	297
Contra Costa	3978	47	Mariposa	77	292	San Francisco	A332	905	Tehama	401	289
Del Norte	78	414	Mendocino	579	530	San Joaquin	2470	311	Trinity	93	366
El Dorado	568	456	Merced	1547	538	San Luis Obispo	1151	12	Tulare	2294	275
Fresno	4626	572	Modoc	184	851	San Mateo	4078	420	Tuolumne	135	47
Glenn	422	184	Mono	52	429	Santa Barbara	1878	860	Ventura	2062	386
Humboldt	657	527	Monterey	2194	538	Santa Clara	5336	341	Yolo	653	245
Imperial	1091	501	Napa	639	86	Santa Cruz	1431	494	Yuba	334	486
Inyo	147	598	Nevada	305	320	Shasta	684	528			
Kern	3427	60	Orange	5889	611	San Diego	Series 2 Book 1961, Page 183887				

(which provisions, identical in all counties, are printed on the reverse hereof) hereby are adopted and incorporated herein and made a part hereof as fully as though set forth herein at length; that he will observe and perform said provisions; and that the references to property, obligations, and parties in said provisions shall be construed to refer to the property, obligations, and part   Deed of Trust.

The undersigned Trustor requests that a copy of any Notice of Default and of any Notice of   at his address hereinbefore set forth.

STATE OF CALIFORNIA, } SS.

COUNTY OF

On   before me, the under-signed, a Notary Public in and for said State, personally appeared

     known to me to be the person__ whose name__ subscribed to the within instrument and acknowledged that   executed the same. WITNESS my hand and official seal.

Signature

Title Order No.

Escrow or Loan No.

BEWARE! BEWARE!

Short Form Deed of Trust

WITH POWER OF SALE (INDIVIDUAL)

AS TRUSTEE

Attn:_____
TS#:_____ SPACE ABOVE THIS LINE FOR RECORDER'S USE_____

NOTICE OF TRUSTEE'S SALE

NOTICE

YOU ARE IN DEFAULT UNDER A _____ DATED _____.
UNLESS YOU TAKE ACTION TO PROTECT YOUR PROPERTY, IT MAY BE SOLD AT A PUBLIC SALE. IF
YOU NEED AN EXPLANATION OF THE NATURE OF THE PROCEEDING AGAINST YOU, YOU SHOULD
CONTACT A LAWYER.

ON _____ , at _____ .M.,
as duly appointed Trustee under and pursuant to Deed of Trust executed by _____
_____ as Trustor for
the benefit and security of _____
_____ as Beneficiary, dated _____
_____, 19____ , and recorded as Instrument No. _____
on _____ , 19____ , _____
County, State of California,
WILL SELL AT PUBLIC AUCTION TO HIGHEST BIDDER FOR CASH, A CASHIER'S CHECK DRAWN ON A
STATE OR NATIONAL BANK, A STATE OR FEDERAL CREDIT UNION, OR A STATE OR FEDERAL SAVINGS
AND LOAN ASSOCIATION DOMICILED IN THE STATE OF CALIFORNIA (payable at time of sale in
lawful money of the United States) at _____
_____
all right title and interest conveyed to and now held by it under said Deed of Trust
in the property situated in said County and State described as:

The street address and other common designation, if any, of the real property described
above is purported to be:

THE UNDERSIGNED TRUSTEE DISCLAIMS ANY LIABILITY FOR INCORRECT INFORMATION FURNISHED.

THAT said sale is made without covenant or warranty regarding title, possession or
encumbrances, or as to insurability of title.

THE total amount of the unpaid balance of said obligations together with advances, and
estimated costs and expenses, is $_____.

THAT notice of breach of said obligation and election to sell said real property was
recorded as Instrument No._____ on_____ , 19____ , of
Official Records in the office of the County Recorder of _____
County, State of California.

Trustee or party conducting Sale

                                          BY:
Dated:_____   By: _____

-
-
-

         T. S. Officer _____

         T. S. No. _____

         Your Ref. _____

Gentlemen:

We have recently completed our Trustee's Sale proceedings under your above reference. We are enclosing the Return and Account of Sale, _____

_____

The Trustee's Deed has been forwarded to the office of the county recorder wherein the property was located with instructions to mail it to you after recordation. The processing of the Trustee's Deed by the county recorder normally takes one month.

Please acknowledge receipt of the enclosures and return for our file.

Dated _____

                Very truly yours,

                Foreclosure Department

T.S. Officer_____
T.S. No. _____
Your Ref._____

We are enclosing the Notice of Default and the Declaration of Default in connection with your foreclosure proceeding.

Please check carefully to see that the statement of breach on the enclosed Notice of Default and the Declaration of Default is correctly set forth. Also complete the Declaration of Default with all information called for and then sign, date, and return both documents to us in the enclosed envelope as soon as possible. Also include all receipts for advances already made under the terms of the deed of trust when returning said documents.

Please include your check in the amount shown below under "deposit required" when you return the first above mentioned papers. This amount will cover all fees and expenses until the end of the three month reinstatement period. If there is no reinstatement of your loan, we will ask for the balance of the estimated amount approximately ten days before the end of the three month reinstatement period when we ask for your instructions to proceed with the advertising of the Notice of Trustee's Sale.

Deposit required . . . . $

Balance of estimated total amount required
    before advertising   . . . . $

Total estimated amount of fee and expenses
    at the time of sale   . . . . $_____

Sincerely,

Foreclosure Department

Enclosures

F-3

MAIL TAX STATEMENTS TO:

——————SPACE ABOVE THIS LINE FOR RECORDER'S USE——————

Name
Street Address

City
State
Zip

Trustee's Deed Upon Sale

Trustee Sale No._____

The undersigned grantor declares:

(1) The Grantee herein was—was not the foreclosing beneficiary.

(2) The amount of the unpaid debt together with costs was..$_____

(3) The amount paid by the grantee at the trustee sale was.............................$_____

(4) The documentary transfer tax is..$_____

(5) The survey monument fee is...$_____

(6) Said property is in ( ) unincorporated area: ( ) City of _____, and

(herein called Trustee), as the

duly appointed Trustee under the Deed of Trust hereinafter described, does hereby grant and convey, but without warranty, express or implied, to

(herein called Grantee), all of its right, title and interest in and to that certain property situated in the City of
, County of   , State of California, described as follows:

TRUSTEE STATES THAT:

This conveyance is made pursuant to the powers conferred upon Trust by that certain Deed of Trust dated
and executed by
as trustor, and recorded
in Book   , Instrument No.   , Page   . of Official Records of
County, California, and after fulfillment of the conditions specified in said Deed of Trust authorizing this conveyance.

Default occurred as set forth in a Notice of Default and Election to Sell which was recorded in the office of the Recorder of said County.

All requirements of law regarding the mailing and recording of copies of notices and the posting and publication and recording of copies of the Notice of Sale have been complied with.

Said property as sold by said Trustee at public auction on   at the place named in the Notice of Sale,
in the County of   , California, in which the property is situated. Grantee being the highest bidder at such sale, became the purchaser of said property and paid therefor to said Trustee the amount bid, being $, in lawful money of the United States,
or by the satisfaction, pro tanto, of the obligations then secured by said Deed of Trust.

IN WITNESS WHEREOF, said   , as Trustee, has
this day, caused its corporate name and seal to be hereunto affixed by its Vice-President and Assistant Secretary, thereunto duly authorized by resolution of its Board of Directors.

Dated: _____

as Trustee aforesaid.

STATE OF CALIFORNIA
COUNTY OF   } ss

On this_____ _ _____ day of_____, 19_____.
before me, the undersigned, a Notary Public in and for said County and State,

personally appeared ____ _____ _____ _____

known to me to be the_____ President,

and _____

known to me to be the_____ Secretary
of the corporation that executed the within instrument, and known to me to be the persons who executed the within instrument on behalf of the corporation therein named and, acknowledged to me that such corporation executed the same, pursuant to its laws, or a resolution of its Board of Directors.

WITNESS my hand and official seal.

Signature_____

By _____

By _____

Name (Typed or Printed)

(This area for official seal)

DO NOT RECORD
REQUEST FOR FULL RECONVEYANCE
To be used only when note has been paid.

To _____ Dated _____

The undersigned is the legal owner and holder of all indebtedness secured by the within Deed of Trust. All sums secured by said Deed of Trust have been fully paid and satisfied; and you are hereby requested and directed, on payment to you of any sums owing to you under the terms of said Deed of Trust, to cancel all evidences of indebtedness, secured by said Deed of Trust, delivered to you herewith together with said Deed of Trust, and to reconvey, without warranty, to the parties designated by the terms of said Deed of Trust, the estate now held by you under the same.

MAIL RECONVEYANCE TO   _____

_____   _____

_____

_____   *By* _____

_____   *By* _____

Do not lose or destroy this Deed of Trust OR THE NOTE which it secures. Both must
be delivered to the Trustee for cancellation before a reconveyance will be made.

2
When Foreclosure Threatens

WHEN FORECLOSURE THREATENS. If you are seriously behind in your mortgage payments to your lender you may be sure he is aware of it. And he will let you know he is aware by sending you a letter threatening Foreclosure. Such a letter will contain a legal notice telling you that you are in Default. The notice itself will be labeled "NOTICE OF DEFAULT" (see example).

The accompanying letter may obligingly remind you of the fact that you have failed to make your monthly payments of $1,000 per month, which was due and payable on the 10th of each and every month, commencing in June of 1983; and, that you are in arrears three payments totaling $3,000 plus interest and penalties. The letter will go on to point out that in view of your Default, the mortgagee (lender) by this Notice of Default declares the entire mortgage indebtedness due and payable. The letter will further advise you that formal demand is being made upon you for the principal balance owing of $170,000, together with interest due of $6,300, bringing the total amount you now owe to the total sum opf $176,300. The letter will also go on to make demand for immediate payment in full.

Warning Notice Letters. Warning notice letters such as the example just given you are going to put you to test for some quick action and some very clear thinking if you want to save your property and your home, farm or business. You may be dealing with a very hard-nosed lender. Your lender may be an institutional lender (a bank, either commercial or a savings and loan, a finance company) or a private lender. In either case, you are going to have to know what weapons the lender can use against you in foreclosure proceedings.

Time and Money are of the essence. Try to reinstate your loan with your lender before he has an attorney start foreclosure action in court. Find out quickly what kind of foreclosure you would be up against, that is whether foreclosure would occur under a Trust Deed, whether by Entry or by Strict foreclosure. You will need to know what can happen and how quickly it can happen. You will also need to know the procedure that is applicable in your situation in your state. The law library in your county court house will give you this information. Among the data you will want to gather will be information on how to file a COMPLAINT. You will also want to look over your mortgage documents very carefully for significant misspellings, typographical errors, statements that include full disclosure of items such as interest rate charges, the full amount of the loan and interest, look for the annual percentage rate and the method your lender used in calculating the annual percentage rate of your loan. Under the Truth in Lending Law, which was enacted by Congress and became law on 1 July 1969, specific methods of calculating the annual percentage rate must be used. The law is known as Regulation Z. Take a copy of your documents to an expert real estate broker or lawyer and have him examine them for errors. Have them determine the fully disclosed interest on the mortgage.

These documents should show and fully disclose:
- Interest on the mortgage
- Transaction Charges
- Loan fees
- Appraisal fee
- Amount of insurance
- Premiums for property insurance
- Premiums for health or accidental death
  insurance (if any)
- Any other service charges.

All these costs are required by law to be set forth and fully disclosed as finance costs.

If any charge or fee has not been calculated into the annual percentage rate, a discrepancy has occurred and you have a basis for claim that the lender violated the law by not including a cost he was supposed to include in the Annual Percentage Rate.

APPRAISING YOUR PROPERTY. You will find Appraisers of Real Estate among the Real Estate brokers listed in the yellow pages of your telephone directory. If times have gotten bad, and real estate has slumped, the value of your property may have tumbled. Your equity may have vanished. Your lender may be very worried about whether he is going to get back the amount of money he loaned you on your property. If such is the situation, you may want to stop his foreclosure by legal means in order to gain time and to continue to have a place in which to live. Once you know whether your property is worth saving, there will be many questions you can decide in order of importance and come up with the answers for yourself.

Marshal your facts. You may be in a foreclosure procedure sooner than you think. Certainly one of the facts you will want to find out in a hurry is whether you have a greater net worth than the amount owed. Determine your assets by appraisal of them. Calculate your liabilities. Add both up in separate columns and subtract your liabilities from your assets to determine your net worth. If your net worth is comfortably greater than your liabilities you probably can bail yourself out of a bad situation by negotiation with your lender. You may have to make some sacrifices. To begin with, you should have asked the seller or the real estate agent for an Appraisal. If you don't have one, get one. When you mortgaged your property, your lender had your property appraised. No ques-

tion about it. And you should have obtained a copy of that appraisal. If not, you are going to have to get an appraiser quickly to get the job done. You need to know what your equity is in your property, and whether that equity is worth saving. Over and above these facts, you must determine in your own heart and mind whether your property is worth saving. In the meantime, communicate with your lender. Your lender may only be threatening you with foreclosure. He may not want to go through the time consuming and costly process of foreclosure. If you give him a good reason for delay, he may give you an opportunity to bring your account back into good standing.

If you lost your job or have been ill, or if you have had to shoulder other problems of a financial nature which would provide you with a legitimate excuse for default, to not hesitate to discuss the matter with him. Ask for time to rearrange your affairs and catch up on your payments. Give your lender a good reason not to foreclose and he will probably accept it.

What to do when you are in Default or Arrears. Once you have talked to the law librarian and read the procedure for foreclosure in your state, you will become aware of the rights your state gives you to stop or avoid foreclosure, and in addition to knowing what your rights are, you will want to know what steps your lender can take against you in foreclosure.

It is of utmost importance that you read and become thoroughly familiar with all the documents pertaining to your indebtedness. Communicate with your lender. Be sure to answer his letters. Better still, go see him and talk to him, even if it is only to discuss the entire matter. Try to avoid discussing any legal aspects of the situation with him. The truth of the matter is that an institutional lender has tremendous liability in seeing to it that he has fulfilled all the requirements of regulation Z, the Truth in Lending Law when he makes a mortgage loan (either first or second mortgage) and the chances of some member of his staff making an error is so great, that few institutions escape being found out for their errors except through the carelessness of the borrower. So talk to your lender and try to arrange to pay him under some acceptable plan. Be truthful about your financial position and give him plenty of alternatives and options to choose from...and keep cool.

3
How to Refinance Your Debts

HOW TO REFINANCE. Once you have received a letter threatening Foreclosure along with the NOTICE OF DEFAULT, you will have to employ every delaying tactic suggested here to avoid foreclosure. Getting your property appraised, making up a financial statement to see where you stand as to your net worth; finding out what your rights are in your state by a visit to the law library at the county court house are all steps you must take while you are in negotiations with your lender, whether he is a private lender or an institutional lender. Most people who have a farm or home who have had to put a mortgage or give a Deed of Trust as a security device for money borrowed will want to know where they stand creditwise, as soon as trouble threatens. So will your lender. Most people will have their mortgage with a bank.

Negotiation with the Lender Bank. Banks and bank officers at all costs seek to avoid loss and maintain a steady cash flow from the loans they have made, especially on real estate. The loan officer who originally made the loan for you is the man you want to see (if the bank has gone no further than to send you a threatening letter). First, that loan officer is going to listen to you carefully to make sure that you have an acceptable offer or proposal. He is not going to go along with you if he thinks what you propose is going to result in a bad situation's becoming worse. He will be thinking of his job and whether he will be blamed for costing the bank money. You will not only want to make a refinancing proposal that is acceptable to him, but one you feel will be acceptable to his senior officer. Find out. Indeed, he will be the first to let you know.

On the other hand, banks are usually loath to foreclose. Foreclosure costs the bank legal fees, interrupts the cash flow, snarls the bookkeeping (and you know what computers are, today). If you have been out of work, see to it that you have a promise of work and can tell the bank so. Or if no job is in prospect, ask for time delay on the basis that you are taking training, lasting six weeks or so, so that you will be qualified for a better position and can not only catch up on your payments but accelerate them or perhaps pay off your debt at a faster rate. If that doesn't work, reveal your equity and ask for a larger mortgage, for a longer term; one that will absorb your default even if it costs you a higher interest rate. Almost any of these alternatives may be acceptable to your bank. You will be talking to your lender from a position of mutual benefit. It is the only thing he will listen to, as a solution.

Negotiations with a Third Party Bank (commercial or a Savings and Loan). If your lender will not reach an acceptable Agreement with you, ask him for time to deal with another bank. He may allow your request, especially if his bank is a small bank overloaded with defaulting loans, and the bank from which you propose seeking a new loan is a large bank, well able to refinance your mortgage.

You must realize, in negotiating with any lender, that he is looking for an out from a bad situation, that of Default on your part. You will not find him sympathetic to tales of woe. He is not going to risk his job by granting any requests unless they are sound. No one will help you without a current picture of your financial situation. That picture ust be realistic, based on facts, and it must reveal clearly why things are going to get better for you.

You must realize from the start of your discussions with your lender that both of you are in trouble because of your Default. Foreclosure means big trouble. It can mean the loss of your home or business and all that you have put into it. It can mean loss to the lender bank and cast a shadow on the loan officer who granted you the loan. So when you go to a third party bank, let them know that your lender bank recommended it, and why. Do not hesitate to indicate that your lender bank is not granting loans of any kind. Your third party bank will be aware of that fact and may readily accept your proposal to refinance your property, especially if you have salvageable equity in it. Finding a proper solution will not only please a third party bank, it will relieve you as well as your lender bank. But it must be to the bank's advantage to do so. No bank exists just to help you out of a bad situation. Lenders want to make money. Lender banks that have to foreclose and go to sale have to take property they don't want. It is illiquid, it does not represent cash flow, and while it is an asset, it can turn into a severe loss to the bank. The Sale may not bring the price the property is worth. The bank will have to pay legal fees, court costs, escrow service charges, and a host of other expenses before it has disposed of the property. Sometimes it gets saddled with a piece of property no one wants. In this case the bank or lender institution is indeed highly motivated to listen to whatever you propose so long as it is reasonable and of mutual benefit. If you have to go to a third party bank maintain a good attitude and make a fair and reasonable offer.

- Have you covered all bases with institutional lenders?
- Have you tried to negotiate an acceptable proposal with your lender bank?
- Have you talked with the person in charge of your loan?
- Have you had a friendly attitude?
- Have you responded to your lender's letter notice of Default?
- Have you kept your appointments promptly with your loan officer?
- Have you kept in touch with him by telephone, assuring him that you are making every effort to resolve the default problem?
- Have you shown him you are eager to reach an acceptable solution to the problem, one of mutual benefit?
- Have you asked what he thinks you should do?
- Have you made it clear to him that you believe the problem is temporary and that you want to work closely with the bank in cooperation with his ideas in resolving the problem of Default?
- Have you asked your lender for his ideas, alternatives, options?
- Have you taken a pencil and paper along with you in meeting with him so you could write down all his suggestions?
- Have you asked him the bank's attitude toward taking the property by Foreclosure?
- Have you asked him what steps the bank would take first?

If your lender bank is in no position or refuses to extend your loan, and a third party bank also refuses, you may wish to return to your loan officer at your lender bank and start to ask questions which will alert him to the fact that he has a real fighter on his hands. Take along a small tape recorder and have a list of well prepared questions written out. Upon seeing him, immediately ask if he minds your asking some questions. Take out your tape recorder and ask his permission to record his answers to your questions, on the basis that you do not want to miss any important points he may make in his replies. No one likes to be recorded unless he is well prepared. You may expect him to be intimidated, or at least concerned.

Begin by asking him about The Truth in Lending Law, Regulation Z.

- Ask him to explain Regulation Z to you.
- Ask him if he can spare you a copy of the Regulation.
- Ask him if he realizes you may have to file for bankruptcy prior to foreclosure sale, if his bank persists in Foreclosure proceedings against you.
- Ask him, if he is still talking Foreclosure, if he would consider a final offer. Be prepared with a good one.
- If he still will not cooperate, you can do two things.
- You can get a copy of Regulation Z. Hire an expert to search your documents for errors of any kind. Hire an attorney to file a COMPLAINT and become the Plaintiff. And, you can still try to find a private lender.

Negotiating with a Private Lender. A private lender is not going to be impersonal. As you will have discovered, institutional lenders can and most do remain on a rather formal basis with you. They deal with many borrowers on a regular day to day basis. Private lenders have an altogether different attitude. First, a private lender is dealing with his own money and wants all the interest he can get for lending it out. Many private lenders are just as well off financially as a small bank, and can afford to make large real estate loans. If so, such a lender will be just as sophisticated, and deal with you at the same arm's length, as a lender bank. But being a private lender, he will also use his status as leverage for every advantage he can find. You will need to have your proposal well defined and supportable, and be able to present your goals very clearly to a private lender. It will be necessary for you to tell him honestly that foreclosure is a possibility and that you would like to avoid it. Avoidance of foreclosure is a goal. You can explain about high costs of legal actions, loss of time and money, difficulty in getting to court when you are working and many other reasons for avoidance of Foreclosure. You need not go so far as to tell him you have already filed a COMPLAINT, as that can be dropped if he pays off your lender bank and accepts your proposal.

If your loan is already in the hands of a private lender who has threatened to foreclose, you can reverse all these procedures, go to the institutional lender or to the FHA. Write to the Department of Housing and Urban Development in Washington, D.C., and ask for assistance in applying for a mortgage loan. You will receive guidance about whom to see locally and you can go from there.

Failing in all these tactics, you actually have an ally in a court of equity or common law, as you can fight a foreclosure by all the methods given elsewhere in this book. Meanwhile, if you feel you must deal with your private lender and negotiate new terms with him to gain time, try to find out from him what he would do with the money you owe him, if he had it put in his hand within 24 hours. As an opener, he will probably begin to tell you a bit about his business and how he keeps money working for him by investing.

A sensible investor will always consider a sensible proposal. You may have to have a small auction sale to liquidate some of your more valued personal belongings and to raise the money to cover your Default. Offer him an advantage in a new mortgage that contains better terms for both of you. Work out your alternatives. If you fail to move your lender, get back to discussing foreclosure and all its unpleasantness with him. Let him know that you intend to pay off the loan one way or another, even if it is not entirely satisfactory to him and that if he forces you into foreclosure you will use every delaying tactic given you in your rights by the state to defend your home and your property.

Hopefully, he will see the handwriting on the wall and begin to offer you some options and try to steer the discussion away from legal action. He too may be playing for time. On the other hand, he may allow you to make smaller payments over a period of time, payments that you can manage, and defer the big payoff by setting up a balloon payment payable at a much later date, with higher interest, of course. Still, it will give you time to remain in your home and in your job, and to work things out to a better advantage. If yout payments of $250 per month were three months in arrears, he might offer to reduce them to what you could pay, say $100 per month and create a balloon payment for you to meet at the end of a shorter mortgage term. Private lenders have many different goals from institutional lenders. If you can provably show a private lender why you got into Default and that you are sincere in wanting to pay him what you owed him, he probably will find a solution acceptable to you as well as to himself. It may be a compromise, but it will be better than protracted legal action.

4
How to Change Your Loan

How to change your loan and the nature of your loan. A loan is usually defined as an advance of money with an absolute promise to repay, a sum of money given to another person, lender or borrower, to be used by the borrower and returned either in specie or in kind.

There are, of course, various kinds of loans such as loan certificates, and a loan for consumption, in which case the article is not to be returned in specie but in kind. There are loans for exchange in which one delivers personal property to another and the latter person agrees to return to the lender a similar thing at a future time without any reward for its use; and there are gratuitous loans which is the gratuitous lending of an article to the borrower for his personal use. But the loan we are concerned with involves an advancement of money. As pointed out earlier in this book, **CREDIT IS NOT MONEY.**

You cannot change the nature of your loan unless it is recorded at the Town Hall, with the Town Clerk. Your lender may be very reluctant to change the nature of your original loan. However, there are instances when it can be done. Let us say, you have made a careful analysis of your situation and managed to borrow $10,000 from a friend. You may feel your lender bank has dealt harshly with you in its firm refusal to work out some solution to your financial crisis and is bent on forcing a Foreclosure. You want to save your home and you also want to make it possible to reduce your mortgage and your mortgage payments to the point where you can also handle repayment of the $10,000 to your friend.

Go to your lender bank and tell them you are **prepared to enter into an entirely new mortgage by paying off $10,000 on the principal of the old mort-**gage and that you want a new mortgage with much lower terms and a greater number of years in which to pay off the principal sum. By paying off the $10,000 principal, you will have increased your equity in your property and your lender should be more than happy to oblige you with the relaxed terms you seek.

You will undoubtedly be asked to fill out a new credit application by your lender in any state which requires a Deed of Trust (See example, CREDIT LINE DEED OF TRUST pg. 62–64). You will or may be asked to fill out a MORTGAGE LOAN RATING SHEET. In addition, there is a CREDIT LINE COLLATERAL LOAN AGREEMENT, which you will be called upon to fill out and sign in a loan secured by a Deed of Trust (See example, CREDIT LINE COLLATERAL LOAN AGREEMENT pg. 61).

Read and familiarize yourself with all the terms and conditions of these documents. Any kind of Modification Agreement that you enter into with a lender on your property must always be recorded in the land records, in accordance with state laws applicable to your property. (See example entitled MODIFICATION AGREEMENT pg. 65–66.)

If you are making a mortgage loan application for a Fixed Rate / Fixed Term Mortgage, you will be asked to fill out a MORTGAGE LOAN APPLICATION DISCLOSURE. (See example, MORTGAGE LOAN APPLICATION DISCLOSURE, FIXED RATE / FIXED TERM pg. 67). In this example, the loan amount is $50,000 with a term of 30 years and an initial interest rate of 13%. The payment on this example would be $553.10, the amount required to reduce the principal balance to zero by the end of the term of your loan amortization. Given the example above, the interest portion of the payment would be a monthly interest figure of $541.67. Subtracting the interest $541.67 from the payment of $553.67 leaves $11.43, or the amount the principal balance is reduced in the first month of the loan. Continuous repetition of these steps in reduction of the loan will complete amortization by the end of 30 years.

Your lender may also be willing to change your mortgage to one with a balloon payment. Once he clearly understands your financial situation, he may be able to change the terms of your mortgage agreement by lending you the money (by bookkeeping entry of a credit) in the amount you are in arrears, by relaxing the size of the payments due monthly and by pushing the "front-end" load of your mortgage to the end of its term into what is called a BALLOON payment. (See example of a BALLOON MORTGAGE LOAN APPLICATION DISCLOSURE pg. 80.) This kind of transaction will involve three primary documents: The Note or loan contract itself, the Balloon Payment Note Rider, that will explain the special characteristics of a balloon loan, and the MORTGAGE / DEED OF TRUST that places a lien on your property. You will want to examine carefully the NOTICE TO CUSTOMERS FEDERAL TRUTH-IN-LENDING DISCLOSURE STATEMENT. Such a statement is required by law and is applicable to any kind of mortgage you obtain. It may be well at this point to remind you that there are several kinds of mortgage loans. They are:

- Fixed Rate / Fixed Term (Conventional)
- Fixed Term / Variable Rate (Adjustable)
- FHA / HUD
- VA
- BALLOON MORTGAGE

If you have been to all the institutional lenders and have been unable to refinance your loan, you may call or write to the Department of Housing and Urban Development for an FHA application. Usually, federal savings and loan banks have such application forms on hand, and may be interested in clearing off your old mortgage with an FHA Mortgage. (See example of FHA / VA Applicants Statements Form pg. 71.)

If you go the VA route you will have to fill out a REQUEST FOR DETERMINATION OF ELIGIBILITY AND AVAILABLE LOAN GUARANTY ENTITLEMENT. (See example pg. 73.) There is also an additional form entitled "VERIFICATION OF VA BENEFIT-RELATED INDEBTEDNESS." (See example pg. 74.) These forms will have to be accompanied by your RESIDENTIAL LOAN APPLICATION (see example, pg. 76–79). We have discussed BALLOON payment at the mortgage's term end. And, it is reasonable to ask, just what is a balloon payment. When a person buys a piece of property and places a first and second mortgage on it, he may wish to keep his payments and the terms of the two mortgages well within his means. To do so, he may create what is called a balloon payment which will come due in a lump sum at the end of the period of time agreed on. A Balloon payment is a real threat to the loss of your property. You are dealing with a living nightmare. Hopefully, you figured under the terms of your second mortgage you would be able to pay, for example, $150 per month interest (no principal) for a term of three years. At the end of that time you would still owe the principal sum under that second mortgage of $10,000 or $20,000. And it comes due. It is called a Balloon. And it will have to be paid off in full, in a matter of weeks, or perhaps days. If you do not pay it off, the lender bank will get out a letter immediately threatening foreclosure and declare you in default. Nonpayment of your second mortgage BALLOON PAYMENT will force foreclosure on the first mortgage as well. You are in a situation which calls for innovation. You can either negotiate with your lender and combine interest with principal payment over an additional three years, or if he is a private lender, suggest that he take the Balloon note to his bank, discount it and get money for it and that you will make the payments due on it for him.

Remind your lender that if you pay off the lump sum, a large portion of it is going to go to Uncle Sam for taxes. He may be willing to go on collecting interest and payment of the principal at a reduced rate to ease his own tax burden.

Refinancing with a bank may be difficult, but it is not impossible. Most banks would rather work out a schedule of payments with you during which period of time they will continue to realize a cash flow. Banks are not happy with foreclosures, nor are they with court room Karate.

WHEREAS, _____

_____ hereinafter
called "BORROWER", has requested FIRST AMERICAN BANK OF VIRGINIA, McLEAN, VIRGINIA hereinafter called
"LENDER", to lend to Borrrower certain sums of money from time to time, the security for which loan, or loans, is to be a
_____Deed of Trust on the property hereinafter described and

WHEREAS, the parties hereto desire to set forth an agreement to provide for the manner in which such loans may be
made.

NOW, THEREFORE, in consideration of any financial accommodation given, or to be given, to the Borrower by the
Lender and the mutual covenants herein contained, the parties agree as follows:

1. Borrower agrees to execute a Deed of Trust, on the following described property, in the amount of $ _____
_____ for the benefit
of Lender for the purpose of securing existing loans, future loans or advances made by Lender to Borrower:

All of that certain property, together with the improvement thereon, located in _____,
Virginia, more particularly described as:

2. Said Deed of Trust shall be a lien on the said property, subject only to the following liens:

(1)   Current Real Estate Taxes
(2)

3. Lender shall be furnished, at Borrower's expense, a title insurance policy, or Certificate of Title, at Lender's option,
containing no exceptions unsatisfactory to Lender, showing the Deed of Trust to be recorded as a lien on the aforesaid real
estate, subject only to the aforesaid liens. All expenses for attorney's fees, title examination, title insurance premiums,
recordation taxes, etcetera, shall be at the cost of the Borrower.

4. Subject to paragraph 5 hereof, Borrower may thereafter borrow from the Lender funds to be secured by the aforesaid
Deed of Trust in an aggregate amount not to exceed $ _____
_____ . (The amount of the Deed of Trust).

5. As Advances are requested by Borrower, then Borrower shall execute a Request For Advance form and such other
loan documents as requested by Lender, in the amount of the Advance approved; which Advance is to be secured by the
aforesaid Deed of Trust. Borrower shall cause, at his expense, an endorsement to be issued to the Title Insurance Policy, or
Certificate of Title, as the case may be, hereinbefore referred to in Paragraph 3, showing the promissary note to be secured
by the Deed of Trust subject only to any other liens previously approved by Lender.

6. Lender agrees that at any time there is no indebtedness secured by the aforesaid Deed of Trust, it will upon written
request of Borrower, at his expense, cause the said Trust to be released of record.

WITNESS the following signatures and seals this _____ day of_____ , 19_____

_____ (SEAL)
                                                                                    Borrower

_____ (SEAL)
                                                                                    Borrower

By _____

Title _____

CREDIT LINE DEED OF TRUST

THIS CREDIT LINE DEED OF TRUST, Made and entered into this _____ day of _____ , 19 _____, by and

between _____

_____

_____

parties of the first part; and   _____

_____

TRUSTEE, parties of the second part;

     Witnesseth: that for and in consideration of the sum of TEN DOLLARS, ($10.00), the said parties of the first part do hereby grant, bargain, sell and convey unto the said parties of the second part, WITH GENERAL WARRANTY OF TITLE, certain real estate in the

_____ , State of _____ , more particularly described as follows:

     Also including (but not excluding any fixtures which would ordinarily be construed as a part of the realty) any and all storm sashes, storm doors, vestibules, wire screens, wire doors, window shades, awnings, trees, shrubs, oil burner or other furnace equipment, domestic hot water boiler and equipment, and refrigerators, and stoves, used in the building upon said premises at the time of the execution of this deed of trust, or hereafter erected thereon, including, as well, all apparatus and fixtures of every description for watering, heating, ventilating, air conditioning, and screening said premises, together with all and singular the improvements, ways, easements, rights, privileges, and appurtenances to the same belonging, or in anywise appertaining.

     As further security for the debt hereby secured and the interest thereon and all of the sums authorized to be expended by the Trustees or the noteholder, the first parties hereby also sell, transfer and assign unto the noteholder, prior and superior to any and all other claims or demands thereto, the rents, issues, and income of and from the above described property accrued and hereafter to accrue, with full power and authority, at such holder's election, to collect and give receipts in full for the same and to apply all sums so collected, less a reasonable commission thereof which is hereby authorized to be paid to any agent employed by the noteholder to execute the provisions of this paragraph, and after deduction also of expenditures for repairs and upkeep of said property, to the payment of the indebtedness described in and secured by this Deed of Trust. There shall be no duty upon the said noteholder, however, to exercise such election and the noteholder may permit the first parties at any time and from time to time to collect said rents, issues, and income to their own use in which event the same shall in no way be deemed a waiver by, or to work an estoppel upon, the said noteholder thereafter to assert such holder's full rights and authority hereunder, provided, further, that no prepayment of any said rents, issues, or income for the whole or any portion of the said property, shall be procedured, or permitted, or valid, without the written consent of the noteholder. If, moreover, upon default in the payment of any amount secured by this Deed of Trust, the first parties, or their successors in title to the property herein conveyed, shall be or remain in possession thereof, or any part thereof, they shall be obligated to pay to the noteholder a fair and reasonable rental for the premise so occupied so long as they remain or are allowed to remain in such possession.

IN TRUST, HOWEVER, TO secure the prompt payment of certain negotiable promissory Notes to be executed in accordance with that certain Credit Line Collateral Loan Agreement, dated _____ , in an amount not to exceed

$_____ , and payable to the order of_____

_____ , at the office of the
which is the address to which any
Notices permitted to be given to the Noteholder under Section 55-58.2 of the Code of Virginia may be mailed or delivered, or at such other place as the holder of the Note, or Notes, may from time to time designate in writing, without offset, with interest at the rate provided in said Note, or Notes, until paid.

It is understood and agreed that the proceeds of the loan evidenced by the Note, or Notes, secured hereby will be advanced from time to time by the Holder of the Note, or Notes, in accordance with the provisions of a certain Credit Line Collateral Loan

Agreement, dated _____ , by and among FIRST AMERICAN BANK OF VIRGINIA, and the Parties of the First Part, which is incorporated herein by reference and made a part hereof to the same extent as if fully set forth herein, and which, together with this Deed of Trust are hereinafter sometimes collectively referred to as the Loan Documents, and it is further understood and agreed that the Parties of the First Part shall have the privilege, from time to time, of making repayments on account of the principal sum and the holder of the Note, or Notes, shall thereafter make additional advances including re-advances of sums previously repaid, as provided by the provisions of the Loan Documents, but at no time shall the aggregate amount of such additional principal advances, plus the then unpaid balance of the Note, or Notes, secured hereby including all additional advances previously

màde, exceed the sum of $_____ ; it being understood and agreed that the Holder of the Note, or Notes, does not intend to make any unsecured loans to the Parties of the First Part and that each and every advance made at the present or hereafter to the Parties of the First Part shall be deemed to be an advance made on account of the Note, or Notes, to be secured hereby.

In the event the title to the herein described property, or the ownership of any part thereof, or of any interest therein, is transferred in any manner, the entire indebtedness hereby secured shall immediately become due and payable at the option of the holder, or holders, of the Note secured by this Deed of Trust. In the event the ownership of said property, or any part thereof, or of any interest therein, becomes vested in a person other than the Grantor, with the consent of the Noteholder, the holder of said indebtedness may, without notice, to the Grantor, deal with such successor or successors in interest with reference to this instrument and the indebtedness secured hereby, in the same manner as with the Grantor and may extend time for payment of said indebtedness without disturbing or in any way affecting the liability of said Grantor hereunder, or under the indebtedness hereby secured; and for every such transfer of ownership so occurring a service charge not to exceed One Percent (1%) of the unpaid principal balance may be made by the holder of said indebtedness to defray the expense incident to such transfer.

Any default in the payment of any lien or encumbrances senior hereto shall give the holder of the note secured hereby the option to call the loan regardless of payment status on this trust.

Said Note, or Notes, will waive the Homestead Exemption as to the Makers and Endorsers thereof; and waive notice of maturity, presentment, demand, protest and notice of protest, notice of non-payment and dishonor of the Note, or Notes.

In case the Note, or Notes, are collected through an attorney-at-law, or under the advice thereof, the undersigned agree to pay all costs of collection, including reasonable attorneys' fees.

ALSO IN TRUST, to secure the payment of any renewals or extensions of said debt as and when the same shall become due and payable, and of all costs and expenses incurred in respect thereto, and of all costs and expenses, including reasonable counsel fees incurred or paid by the Trustees or by any party hereby secured, on account of any litigation at law or in equity which may arise in respect to this trust or the said property while this trust continues, and of all moneys which may be advanced as herein provided,

with interest at the rate of _____ PERCENT per annum on all such costs and sums so advanced from the date of such advance; and also in trust to secure the performance of all the covenants on the part of the grantors herein covenanted to be performed.

Except as herein otherwise provided, this Deed of Trust shall be construed in accordance with the provisions of Section 55-59 of the 1950 Code of Virginia, as amended.

Should one of the Trustees herein named die or decline or fail to execute this trust then the other Trustee shall have all the title, rights, powers and authority, and be charged with all the duties that are hereby conferred or charged upon both, unless and until a co-Trustee be appointed; but in any such event, or if both Trustees so die or decline or fail to execute this trust, (or for any other reason) if the Holder of said Note, or Notes, shall so desire, the said Noteholder is hereby authorized and empowered to appoint by an instrument recorded where this Deed of Trust is recorded, another or two other Trustees in the place and stead of either or both of those herein originally named or in the place and stead of any other Trustee or Trustees later substituted therefor, all of whom successively shall while so acting have all the title, rights, powers, and authority, and be charged with all the duties that are conferred or charged upon the Trustees herein originally named. Such power to appoint a substitute Trustee or Trustees shall not be deemed exhausted by any one or more such appointments, but rather shall continue unimpaired regardless of the number of prior appointments, and the recitals in every appointment shall be conclusive of the facts therein stated.

The said Parties of the First Part covenant: to pay the indebtedness hereby secured as and when the same shall become due and payable; to pay all taxes and assessments on said premises when due and immediately thereafter exhibit the official receipts to the Holder of the said Note, or Notes; to keep the improvements now on said property or any that may hereafter be erected thereon insured, for such coverage including Fire, Extended Coverage and War Damage, in an approved insurance company for such amount and in such company or companies as may be required by or acceptable to the Noteholder, and to assign the same with loss payable to the

Noteholder, and any amount received from said insurance shall be applied in reduction or payment of the debt hereby secured or to the repair or rebuilding of the improvements, as the Noteholder may direct; to pay promptly any and all sums which have or may at any time hereafter become due for labor and materials furnished in or about the construction of any improvements on said land, and to satisfy forthwith any indebtedness for which a notice of intention to claim Mechanics' or Materialmen's Liens may at any time be filed against said land and premises; to make all payments on prior encumbrances when due; not to do nor suffer to be done anything to depreciate or impair the value of the said property; and upon default or neglect in the performance of any of said covenants the Holder of said Note, or Notes, may at its option, declare the entire indebtedness hereby secured due and payable immediately, and may also pay such taxes and assessments, and have the said improvements insured, and pay and satisfy any debt for labor and materials furnished in, on, or about the said premises, and take steps to prevent depreciation or impairment of the value of the said property; make any payment on prior encumbrances that is past due and to bring said prior encumbrances current; and all expenses thereof shall be secured hereby, repayable upon demand, and shall bear interest at the rate of _____ % per annum from the date of any such payment or payments.

The First Parties hereby agree, at the option of the Noteholder, to make an additional payment to the Noteholder monthly during the time that the indebtedness remains unpaid, of an amount equal to one-twelfth of annual taxes and assessments and/or premiums on insurance on the property on which the Note, or Notes, is secured or any other insurance policies, the premiums for which are collected by the Noteholder.

In the event of default in the payment of said Note, or Notes, or any installment of principal or interest as and when the same shall become due and payable, or upon default in any respect in any of the covenants herein contained, or upon default in any

of the covenants contained in the Credit Line Collateral Loan Agreement, dated_____

_____, the Trustees herein named, or the Trustee or Trustees acting in the execution of this trust shall, upon being requested by the Holders of the Note, or Notes, hereby secured, sell the property hereby conveyed at public auction for cash upon the premises, or at the front door of the courthouse of the County or City wherein the said property is located or at some other place in the said County or City selected by the Trustees (and a bidder's deposit of as much as 10% of the principal then due on the Note, or Notes, may be required), after advertising the time, terms and place of sale in at least two weekly issues of some newspaper either published or having a general circulation in the said County or City, at the discretion of the Trustees, and shall convey the same to, and at the cost of, the purchaser thereof, who shall not be required to see to the application of the purchase money, and from the proceeds of said sale, shall pay, FIRST, all proper costs, charges and expenses, including a Trustees' commission of 5% of the gross amount of sale, or the sum of $750.00, whichever is greater; SECOND, all taxes, levies and assessments, with costs and interest, against the said property hereby conveyed due on date of sale; THIRD, the total amount of principal, including any advances thereon, unpaid on said indebtedness, with interest to date, whether the same be due or not; and the balance, if any, shall be paid to the owner of the said property hereby conveyed at the time of said sale upon delivery of possession of the said property hereby conveyed, less the cost, if any, in obtaining possession thereof; provided, however, that the Trustee, or Trustees, as to such residue, shall not be bound by any inheritance, devise, conveyance, assignment or lien or upon the grantor's equity, without actual notice thereof prior to distribution.

AND IT IS FURTHER COVENANTED AND AGREED, that if the said property shall be advertised for sale as herein provided, and not sold, the Trustee or Trustees acting herein shall be entitled to one-half of the commission herein provided, plus attorney's fees incurred by the Trustee, to be computed on the amount of the unpaid debt hereby secured at the time of the first advertisement.

IT IS UNDERSTOOD AND AGREED, that upon payment of all of the said principal and interest, and the fulfillment and performance of all of the covenants and agreements of the said Note, or Notes, and of this Deed of Trust, then upon the request and at the cost of the Parties of the First Part a proper release and discharge of this Deed of Trust shall be executed as to so much of the property hereby conveyed as has not been sold but any right to demand a marginal release is hereby waived. Until then the First Parties and their successors in title to the said property expressly waive all rights they may have to demand interim partial or protanto releases of this Deed of Trust. If a sale is had hereunder, the persons in possession of the property so sold shall be deemed to be tenants at will of the purchaser or purchasers.

NOTICE: THE DEBT SECURED HEREBY IS SUBJECT TO CALL IN FULL OR THE TERMS THEREOF BEING MODIFIED IN THE EVENT OF SALE OR CONVEYANCE OF THE PROPERTY SECURED HEREBY.

WITNESS the following signature and seal

THIS MODIFICATION AGREEMENT, made this .... day of .... ,

by and between .... ,
parties of the first part; and
...., party of the second part:

WHEREAS, by Deed of Trust dated .... and recorded in Deed Book ....

page.................. of the .... land records,

conveyed to the Service Corporation of Alexandria certain real estate described as ....

.... in trust to secure the party of the second

part, an indebtedness in the principal amount of .... plus interest at .... ,

payable in .... , evidenced by one (1) note more particularly described in said Deed of
Trust; and

WHEREAS, it is the desire of the parties hereto to amend and modify the terms of the Deed of Trust

Note as to its provisions set forth therein in Deed Book .... page .... of the ....

.... land records, and to modify the rate of
interest and the monthly payments.

NOW, THEREFORE, THIS AGREEMENT WITNESSETH: That for and in consideration of the
premises and the payment of the current interest due on the obligation secured by the said Deed of Trust

recorded in Deed Book..............page...........among the..
land records. The note therein recited is hereby amended as follows:

(a) The original amount of the said note being .... with the balance as of

.... of ...., is modified as follows to take effect .... :

(1) the interest rate is changed to ....

(2) monthly installments are changed to .... payable the first of every

month for a period of .... months.

All other terms and conditions of this note shall remain in full force and effect.

NOW, THEREFORE, THIS AGREEMENT FURTHER WITNESSETH: That the parties of the first
part do, by joinder herein, consent to this amendment and modification as provided above.

NOW, THEREFORE, THIS AGREEMENT WITNESSETH: That the party of the second part does, by
its joinder herein, consent to this modification as provided herein.

WITNESS the following signatures and seals and IN WITNESS WHEREOF, the said
                                                    caused this Modification Agreement to be signed by its
appropriate officer and its corporate seal to be hereto affixed, pursuant to due and proper authority duly
heretofore had.

STATE OF VIRGINIA:
                              to-wit:
CITY OF ALEXANDRIA:

I, the undersigned, a Notary Public in and for the.. ,

Commonwealth of Virginia, do hereby certify that.. ,

whose names are signed to the foregoing and hereto annexed Agreement, bearing date on the .... day of

.... have acknowledged the same before me in my City and State aforesaid.

Given under my hand this.............. day of ....

....
                                                                                          Notary Public

My commission expires:

STATE OF VIRGINIA:
                              to-wit:
CITY OF ALEXANDRIA:

I, the undersigned, a Notary Public in and for the.. ,

Commonwealth of Virginia, do hereby certify that.. ,

whose name is signed to the foregoing and hereto annexed Agreement, bearing date on the .... day of

.... , has acknowledged the same before me in my .... and State aforesaid.

Given under my hand this..............day of.. .

....
                                                                                          Notary Public

My commission expires:

(Lender)

MORTGAGE LOAN APPLICATION DISCLOSURE
(Fixed Rate/Fixed Term)

This Mortgage Loan Application Disclosure will explain how your mortgage loan from this lender will work. Your mortgage loan consists of two primary documents. One is the NOTE or loan contract. The other is the MORTGAGE or DEED OF TRUST that places a lien on your property. Once signed, both you and the lender are bound by the terms and conditions of these documents. It is very important that you become familiar with these documents and understand them before you sign on the dotted line. Modifications to your mortgage may be requested by either you or the lender at any time, although neither you nor the lender has to agree to any such request.

Your mortgage loan will have a term of _____ year(s). This means that it will mature or be due and payable, at the end of the term. The initial interest rate on your mortgage loan is either _____%, or will be established by the lender and disclosed to you at loan commitment based on market conditions at that time.

Your initial payment is either $_____, or will be disclosed by the lender at loan commitment based on market conditions at that time. An example is provided below to demonstrate how the lender establishes an amortization schedule for your loan as well as determines the amount of your payment and the portion of the payment that is credited to interest.

In this example the loan amount is $50,000.00 with a term of 30 years and an initial interest rate of 13%. The payment on this example would be $553.10 the amount required to reduce the principal balance to zero by the end of the term of your loan (amortization). Given the example above, the interest portion of the payment would be calculated by multiplying the loan amount ($50,000) by the interest rate (13%) and dividing the result by 12 to get a monthly interest figure of $541.67. Subtracting the interest ($541.67) from the payment ($553.10) leaves $11.43, or the amount the principal balance is reduced in the first month of the loan. Using the new principal amount ($49,988.57) repeating the steps above will produce an interest of $541.54, a principal of $11.56 and a new balance of $49,977.01. Continued repetition of these steps will result in the complete amortization of this loan example by the end of 30 years.

There are some contractual contingencies under which your loan may become due or which may result in a forced sale of your home. Generally, these contingencies would involve your defaulting on the terms of your mortgage. Examples of default are: not making your payments; failure to pay real estate taxes, liens or assessments on your property; abandonment of your property; condemnation of your property; your selling or transferring the property without the consent of the lender (due-on-sale); your failure to preserve or maintain your property; and any action that materially affects the lender's security (your property) such as: your bankruptcy, insolvency, code enforcements, death, or any legal proceedings or actions against you.

Your mortgage loan contract ☐ will ☐ will not provide for escrow payments. An escrow account spreads out, on a monthly basis, the cost of some substantial payments that occur either semi-annually or annually. By splitting these large payments into smaller monthly payments, they are not only easier to budget, but are also paid by the lender when they are due. These payments may include all amounts necessary to pay for taxes, assessments, ground rents and hazard insurance on your property. You will have to pay these amounts to the lender unless the lender tells you, in writing, that you don't have to do so, or unless the law requires otherwise. You will make these escrow payments on the same day that you make your payments of principal and interest. Generally, the amount of your escrow payments will be one-twelfth of any of the following that apply: estimated yearly taxes, assessments and ground rents on the property; estimated yearly premium for hazard insurance covering the property; and the estimated yearly premiums for mortgage insurance or credit life/disability insurances. The lender has the right to hold a one-sixth (2 month) reserve balance for real estate taxes to help cover anticipated tax increases on your property.

You acknowledge receipt of a completed copy of this Mortgage Loan Application Disclosure.

Signature

Signature

FEDERAL HOME LOAN BANK BOARD DISCLOSURE
ADJUSTABLE RATE MORTGAGE
(Annual Adjustments)
Mortgage Loan

This Disclosure is for informational purposes only to ensure full understanding of the operation of the loan for which you are applying. The Disclosure does not constitute a commitment on the part of the Lender to make a loan to you and, further, does not affect your obligations or those of the Lender with regard to any loan you now have with, or may obtain in the future from the Lender.

GENERAL INFORMATION REGARDING LOAN OBLIGATIONS

While the Disclosure does not obligate either you or the Lender, once the Promissory Note, Deed of Trust and other documentation required by the Lender evidencing the loan has been signed by you, both you and the Lender will become bound by the terms of all documents. Since such documents normally establish your rights, you should become familiar with and understand the provisions of those documents. Even though either you or the Lender may subsequently request a modification of any of the loan documents, neither party is bound to agree to such a request.

KEY LOAN PROVISIONS

This summary is intended for reference only. Important information relating specifically to your loan will be contained in the actual loan documentation, which alone will establish your rights.

1. **Loan Term:** _____ years.
2. **Interest Rate:** The initial interest rate on your loan will be dislosed to you prior to the time you obligate yourself to repay the loan, and will be established by market conditions at the time Lender commits itself to make the loan.
3. **Initial Payment and Amortization:** The Lender shall establish an initial payment schedule for the loan by calculating the monthly installment amount necessary to pay the loan off in full (principal and interest) at the end of the loan term based upon the initial principal amount of the loan and assuming that the initial interest rate will remain in effect throughout the loan term. At the time of each interest rate adjustment that occurs on or near the anniversary date of the Note, a new payment schedule shall be established providing for a monthly installment amount necessary to pay the loan off in full at the end of the loan term based upon the then outstanding principal balance of the loan and assuming that the new rate will remain in effect throughout the loan term.
4. **Changes In Interest Rate and Payments:**
   A. **Index:** The interest rate on your loan may be increased or decreased by the Lender based on the increase or decrease in the interest rate paid by the United States Government on one year obligations. From time to time, the U.S. Treasury Department conducts a sale of obligations which the Federal Government must repay in approximately one year. The weekly average yield on U.S. Treasury Securities adjusted to a constant maturity of one year, which is the result of the sales, may be obtained weekly from the Federal Reserve Statistical Release H.15(519). This publication may be obtained by writing the Board of Governors of the Federal Reserve System, Publication Division, Washington, DC 20551.
   B. **Substitution of Index:** In the event that the FEDERAL RESERVE BOARD ceases to publicly announce this Index, the Lender will select a substituted Index and notify you of the new Index. The new Index shall be publicly announced and shall not in any way be under the control of the Lender.
   C. **Rate Changes:** Twelve months after the first day of the month after the date of the Note, and annually thereafter, Lender shall adjust the interest rate up or down to an amount which is _____ % in excess of the Index figure (rounded to the next highest one-eighth of one percent) in effect 45 days before the end of each twelve month period. The dates on which these annual adjustments are made are called "Change Dates."
   D. **Minimum and Maximum Rate Change:**
      1. Regardless of the changes in the Index, the interest rate on this loan at any Change Date will not be increased, nor decreased, as the case may be, more than two (2) percentage points per Change Date.
      2. Regardless of the changes in the Index, the interest rate on this loan will not at any time be less than the original rate minus five (5) percentage points nor greater than the original rate plus five (5) percentage points.
   E. **Payment Changes:** Effective as of each Change Date on which there is an interest rate change, your monthly payment will be changed to an amount necessary to pay off the loan (principal and interest) in equal installments by the end of the loan term, assuming that the interest rate taking effect on such Change Date will remain in effect throughout the remainder of the loan term. Your monthly payment may also change annually if it includes amounts estimated by Lender to be needed for an "ESCROW" Account as described below.
   F. **Negative Amortization:** This loan does not include provisions that provide for negative amortization.
5. **NOTICE OF PAYMENT AJUSTMENTS:** Lender will send notice of each adjustment to your monthly payment at least thirty (30), but not more than forty-five (45) days before the adjustment becomes effective. The notice will be addressed to the then Borrower according to Lender's records and will contain at least the following infomation:
   A. The loan number.
   B. The new interest rate on your loan as of the Change Date, the Index value on which that rate is based, the next following Change Date.
   C. The outstanding balance of your loan on the adjustment date, assuming timely payment of the remaining payments due by that date.
   D. The amount of your new monthly payment.
   E. The title and telephone number of a person who will answer any question you may have regarding the notice.
6. **HOW THE LOAN MAY BECOME DUE:** Subject to applicable law, the Note and Deed of Trust will provide that Lender will have the right to require that your loan be paid in full prior to the maturity for certain reasons. If Lender exercises this right and you do not pay the loan off in full, a forced sale and loss of your home and your investment in it could result. Included among these reasons are the following:
   A. Failure to make any monthly payment on Lender's loan when due.
   B. Failure to pay real property taxes or assessments secured by the home or to pay escrow payments.
   C. Failure to keep the home insured.
   D. Failure to obtain Lender's express consent before selling or transferring the title.
   Your loan also may have to be paid in full if the security property is condemned, destroyed by fire or other casualty or you file or have filed against you proceedings in bankruptcy.

7. **PREPAYMENTS:** You may pay the loan before it is due in whole or in part at any time without fee or penalty. A partial prepayment will not change your monthly installment amount unless Lender agrees to do so in writing. If you make a prepayment, you must advise the Lender in writing at the time of the prepayment.

8. **LATE CHARGE:** Your monthly payment will be due on the first day of each month. Notwithstanding the due date, your payment will not be considered late if Lender actually receives the full payment by the fifteenth (15th) of the month. A late charge will be added to your account in the event full payment is not received by that date. The late charge will be specified in your Note and will be a fixed percentage of the amount due.

9. **DUE ON SALE:** The Promissory Note and Deed of Trust which you sign will contain a provision which will require full payment to Lender, at Lender's option, of the entire amount of principal and interest due in the event you sell or transfer the property which is security for the loan without the Lender's prior written consent. This means that the loan is not ''Assumable'' unless the Lender makes a separate agreement with you. Certain transfers to family members and other related parties are exempt from the due on sale provisions under Federal law.

10. **ESCROW PAYMENTS:**

    ☐ NO ESCROW PAYMENTS WILL BE REQUIRED

    ☐ ESCROW PAYMENTS WILL BE REQUIRED

The purpose of Escrow payments is to assure Lender of the payment of all taxes and assessments which may constitute a lien on your property and payment of insurance premiums required of you. You will be required to pay monthly with your monthly installment of principal and interest, an amount equal to 1/12th of the yearly amount of these items after the settlement of your loan. Each year Lender will recalculate your monthly Escrow payment based on the current tax or other assessments and the balance in your Escrow Account. Upon payment in full of your loan, Lender will promptly refund to you any funds held by Lender. Even though Lender may not require an Excrow Account established at time of loan settlement, Lender reserves the right to require that you begin making Escrow payments immediately upon receipt of notice from Lender.

11. **Example of this Adjustable Rate Loan:** The following example shows how this Adjustable Rate Mortgage Loan would operate using assumed Index Values. The example is based on $100,000.00, thirty (30) year loan made at a twelve percent (12%) initial interest rate. This example is hypothetical and does not reflect your actual loan amount or interest rate:

PAYMENTS	INDEX VALUE	(1) INTEREST RATE	MONTHLY PAYMENT	OUTSTANDING BALANCE
1-12	10%	12%	$1,028.61	$99,637.15
13-24	9%	11%	953.16	99,134.49
25-36	13%	13% (2)	1,103.50	98,758.08
37-48	16%	15% (2)	1,256.93	98,469.33
49-60	18%	17% (2) & (3)	1,412.52	98,241.68
61-72	19%	17% (3)	1,412.52	97,972.15
73-84	14%	16%	1,335.74	97,591.17
85-96	12%	14%	1,186.88	96,973.32
97-108	11%	13%	1,115.41	96,146.81
109-120	10%	12%	1,046.75	95,065.23
121-132	8%	10%	917.40	93,492.15

(Adjustments continue - this is a 30 year loan.)

1. Interest rate is the Index value at each Change Date plus 2% rounded upwards to the nearest .125%.
2. Maximum 2% adjustment per annum.
3. Maximum 5% adjustment based on initial interest rate.

APPLICANT'S CERTIFICATION

I/We certify that I/we have received a copy of this Adjustable Rate Disclosure, have reviewed it and understand the basic operation of this type of mortgage loan, and that I/we have received a copy of this disclosure form.

_____

(Borrower)

_____

(Borrower)

Date: _____

Loan Officer: _____

NOTICE TO CUSTOMERS
FEDERAL TRUTH-IN-LENDING
DISCLOSURE STATEMENT

ANNUAL PERCENTAGE RATE The cost of your credit as a yearly rate	FINANCE CHARGE The dollar amount the credit will cost you	Amount Financed The amount of credit provided to you or on your behalf.	Total of Payments The amount you will have paid after you have made all payments as scheduled.
%	$	$	$

Your Payment Schedule will be:

Number of Payments	Amount of Payments	When Payments Are Due
	$	
	$	

Variable Rate: The annual percentage rate may increase during this transaction if the monthly median annualized cost of funds for FSLIC INSURED Savings & Loan Associations, published by the FHLBB increases. Any increase will take the form of higher monthly payment amounts. See your FHLBB adjustable mortgage loan disclosure for the full details of this possible change and for an example.

Assumption: Someone buying your house

☐ may, subject to conditions, be allowed to assume the remainder of the mortgage on the original terms.

☐ cannot assume the remainder of the mortgage on the original terms.

Security: You are giving a security interest in the property being purchased.

Late Charge: If a payment is late, you will be charged $_____/_____% of the payment.

Prepayment: If you pay off early, you

☐ may ☐ will not   have to pay a penalty.

☐ may ☐ will not   be entitled to a refund of part of the finance charge.

Insurance: Credit life insurance and credit disability insurance are not required to obtain credit, and will not be provided unless you sign and agree to pay the additional cost. No such insurance will be in force until you have completed an application, the insurance company has issued the policy, the effective date of that policy has arrived and the required premium has been paid.

Type	Premium	Term	Signature
Credit Life	$		I want credit life insurance Signature _____
Credit Disability	$		I want credit disability insurance Signature _____
Credit Life and Disability	$		I want credit life and disability insurance Signature _____

You may obtain property insurance from anyone you want that is acceptable to this institution. If you get the insurance from

you will pay $ _____ _____ for a term of _____.

See your contract documents for any additional information about nonpayment, default, any required payment in full before the scheduled date, and prepayment refunds and penalties.

_____
e means an estimate

FHA/VA APPLICANTS STATEMENTS

PROPERTY_____   DATE_____

_____   FHA/VA CASE NO_____

I/We, the undersigned, are making the following statements for the purpose of inducing either the Federal Housing Administration or Veterans Administration, as appropriate, to issue its commitment on the mortgage secured by the captioned property:

1. AUTHORIZATION TO VERIFY INFORMATION

The undersigned authorize the Federal Housing Administration, U.S. Department of Housing and Urban Development, or the Veterans Administration to check and verify any information furnished on our loan application, or credit report, to include our employement, assets, and trade accounts.

2. RIGHT TO FINANCIAL PRIVACY ACT

I/We, the undersigned applicants, acknowledge receipt of a copy of the following Notice:

NOTICE TO APPLICANTS

This is Notice to you as required by the Right to Financial Privacy Act of 1978 that the [Veterans Administration Loan Guaranty Service or Division -or- Department of Housing and Urban Development, whichever is appropriate] has a right of access to financial records held by a financial institution in connection with the consideration or administration of assistance to you. Financial records involving your transactions will be available to [VA or HUD] without further notice or authorization but will not be disclosed or released to another Government agency or department without your consent except as required or permitted by law.

3. NAME STATEMENT (VA Loans Only)

This is to certify that I, _____, am the same person whose name appears on the Report of Transfer or Discharge from Military Service (DD Form 214 or equivalent) as _____, and I am making this certification for the purpose or establishing my identity as the same person in both the discharge mentioned above and the mortgage papers to be executed in connection with the subject property.

4. VA EDUCATIONAL ASSISTANCE INFORMATION (VA Loans Only)

A. Are you currently indebted to the Veterans Administration as a result of an overpayment of educational assistance?

☐ No   ☐ Yes   (If you indicate "Yes", please detail, on a separate sheet, the terms of your repayment agreement with VA, and furnish your VA "C" number below)**

B. Have you ever had a VA education loan? (Direct loan from the VA)

☐ No   ☒ Yes   If "Yes", please check the applicable statement:)

☐ (1) All such education loans have been fully repaid to the Veterans Administration.**

☐ (2) I am currently repaying the loan to the VA, and the payments on the loan are current and not delinquent.** My VA "C" number and/or loan number(s) are listed below.

☐ (3) I currently have an outstanding loan to the VA, and the payments on the loan are not current. (Please attach an explanation and furnish "C" number and/or loan number(s) below.

"C" Number: _____

Loan Numbers: _____

**NOTE: The Veterans Administration requires us to verify that the prior debts have been paid and/ or that the payments on any outstanding loan or obligation are current.

I (We) acknowledge receipt of the items, notices and/or warnings listed or contained herein.

1   The HUD Guide for Homebuyers, 'Settlement Costs and You', required by the Real Estate Settlement Procedures Act.

2.   The Good Faith Estimates of settlement services as required by the Real Estate Settlement Procedures Act.

3.   The Association's Loan Underwriting Standards are available upon request.

4.   NOTICE: The Federal Equal Credit Opportunity Act prohibits creditors from discriminating against credit applicants on the basis of race, color, religion, national origin, sex, marital status or age. The Federal agency which administers compliance with this law concerning this savings and loan institution is the Federal Home Loan Bank Board, Washington, D. C.

5.   NOTICE: You may apply for the loan in your own name or you may wish your spouse (if any) to be a co-applicant. There is no requirement for your spouse (if any) to apply or otherwise become obligated to repay the debt except to the extent that your spouse's income and/or assets are necessary to qualify you for the loan.

6.   NOTICE: You may use your birth-given first and surname, or a birth-given first name and a combined surname.

7. WARNING: Information about any co-applicant need not be revealed unless the co-applicant will be contractually liable on the debt or the co-applicant's income and/or assets are to be relied upon.

8. WARNING: No person is required to reveal income from alimony, child support or maintenance unless the applicant(s) chooses to disclose the same. Neither is any person required to designate a title such as Mr., Ms., Mrs., or Miss.

9.   NOTICE: Public Law 93-579, entitled the Privacy Act of 1974, requires that all applicants be informed of the purposes and uses to be made of the information which is solicited. The following is furnished to explain the reason why the information is requested and the general uses to which that information may be put.

      Purpose: The information requested in the loan application is considered relevant and necessary to determine your credit-worthiness for the loan applied.

      Use: The information will be used in evaluating your loan application.

      Effects of Non-Disclosure: Disclosure of the requested information is voluntary. No penalty will be imposed for failure to respond. However, the decision as to loan approval you are requesting must then be made on the basis of the information supplied. This may result in a delay in the processing of your application or denial of credit.

Form Approved
OMB No. 2900-0086

Veterans Administration	TO	VETERANS ADMINISTRATION ATTN: LOAN GUARANTY DIVISION

REQUEST FOR DETERMINATION OF ELIGIBILITY AND AVAILABLE LOAN GUARANTY ENTITLEMENT

NOTE: Please read instructions on reverse before completing this form. If additional space is required attach separate sheet.

1. FIRST - MIDDLE - LAST NAME OF VETERAN	2A. ADDRESS OF VETERAN (No., Street or rural route, City or P.O., State and ZIP Code)
2B. VETERAN'S DAYTIME TELEPHONE NO. (Include Area Code) 3. DATE OF BIRTH	

4. MILITARY SERVICE DATA (ATTACH PROOF OF SERVICE – SEE INSTRUCTIONS ON REVERSE (Paragraphs F and G.1))

PERIOD OF ACTIVE SERVICE		NAME (Show your name exactly as it appears on your separation papers (DD214) or Statement of Service)	SERVICE NUMBER (Enter Social Security No., if appropriate)	BRANCH OF SERVICE
DATE FROM	DATE TO			
A.				
B.				
C.				
D.				

5A. WERE YOU DISCHARGED, RETIRED OR SEPARATED FROM SERVICE BECAUSE OF DISABILITY OR DO YOU NOW HAVE ANY SERVICE-CONNECTED DISABILITIES?	5B. VA FILE NUMBER	6. IS A CERTIFICATE OF ELIGIBILITY FOR LOAN GUARANTY PURPOSES ENCLOSED?
☐ YES ☐ NO (If "Yes," Complete Item 5B)	C-	☐ YES ☐ NO (If "No," Complete Items 7A and 7B)

7A. HAVE YOU PREVIOUSLY APPLIED FOR A CERTIFICATE OF ELIGIBILITY FOR VA LOAN PURPOSES?	7B. HAVE YOU PREVIOUSLY RECEIVED SUCH A CERTIFICATE?	7C. THE CERTIFICATE OF ELIGIBILITY PREVIOUSLY ISSUED TO ME HAS BEEN LOST OR STOLEN. IF RECOVERED IT WILL BE RETURNED TO THE VA (Check if applicable)
☐ YES ☐ NO (If "Yes," give location of VA office(s))	☐ YES ☐ NO (If "Yes," give location of VA office(s))	☐

8. HAVE YOU PREVIOUSLY ACQUIRED PROPERTY WITH THE ASSISTANCE OF A GI LOAN?	9. ADDRESS OF REGIONAL OFFICE(S) WHERE LOAN WAS OBTAINED (City and State)
☐ YES ☐ NO (If "Yes," complete Items 9 through 18. Please attach a separate sheet if more than one loan is involved. If "No," skip to Items 19 through 21.)	

10. STATE TYPE(S) AND NUMBER OF LOAN(S) (Home, Mobile home, Condominium, Direct, Farm, Business, etc.)	11. ADDRESS(ES) OF PROPERTY PREVIOUSLY PURCHASED WITH GUARANTY ENTITLEMENT	12. DATE YOU PURCHASED THE PROPERTY(IES)

13. DO YOU NOW OWN THE PROPERTY DESCRIBED IN ITEM 11?	14. DATE(S) THE PROPERTY WAS SOLD	15. IS THERE ANY UNDERSTANDING OR AGREEMENT WRITTEN OR ORAL, BETWEEN YOU AND THE PURCHASERS THAT THEY WILL RECONVEY THE PROPERTY TO YOU?
☐ YES ☐ NO (If "Yes," do not complete Items 14 through 18)		☐ YES ☐ NO

NOTE: It will speed processing if you can complete Items 16, 17, and 18.

16. NAME AND ADDRESS OF LENDER(S) TO WHOM LOAN PAYMENTS WERE MADE	17. LENDER'S LOAN OR ACCOUNT NUMBER
	18. VA LOAN NUMBER(S)

I certify that the statements herein are true to the best of my knowledge and belief.

19. SIGNATURE OF VETERAN	20. DATE SIGNED

FEDERAL STATUTES PROVIDE SEVERE PENALTIES FOR FRAUD, INTENTIONAL MISREPRESENTATION, CRIMINAL CONNIVANCE OR CONSPIRACY PURPOSED TO INFLUENCE THE ISSUANCE OF ANY GUARANTY OR INSURANCE BY THE ADMINISTRATOR.

THIS SECTION FOR VA USE ONLY

DATE CERTIFICATE ISSUED AND DISCHARGE OR SEPARATION PAPERS AND VA PAMPHLETS GIVEN TO VETERAN OR MAILED TO ADDRESS SHOWN BELOW	TYPE OF DISCHARGE OR SEPARATION PAPERS RETURNED	INITIALS OF VA AGENT	STATION NUMBER

VA FORM 26-1880, JUN 1982   DO NOT DETACH

IMPORTANT - You must complete Item 21 since the Certificate of Eligibility along with all discharge and separation papers will be mailed to the address shown in Item 21 below. If they are to be sent to you, your current mailing address should be indicated, or if they are to be sent elsewhere, the name and address of such person or firm should be shown in Item 21.

Form Approved
OMB No. 2900-0406

| **Veterans Administration** | **VERIFICATION OF VA BENEFIT—RELATED INDEBTEDNESS** |

PRIVACY ACT INFORMATION: This information is to be used by the agency collecting it in determining whether you qualify for the VA loan benefit. This information request is authorized by Title 38, U.S.C., Chapter 37. Responses may be disclosed outside the VA only if the disclosure is authorized under the Privacy Act, including the routine uses identified in VA system of records, 55VA26, Loan Guaranty Home, Condominium and Manufactured Home Loan Applicant Records and Paraplegic Grant Applicant Records - VA published in the Federal Register.

TO: NAME AND ADDRESS OF LENDER

**INSTRUCTIONS
TO LENDER**

Complete Items 1 through 4. Have veteran complete Items 5 and 6. Forward to the Finance Officer (24) at the local VA office to determine whether the veteran has any VA benefit-related indebtedness. If a debt is found to exist, the home loan must not be closed until the veteran presents evidence showing that the debt has been cleared or an acceptable repayment plan has been established with VA. After completion by the Finance Officer, this form will be returned to the lender at the address shown. VA Form 26-8937 is a required exhibit to accompany reports of home or manufactured home loans closed on the automatic basis.

1. VETERAN'S NAME *(First, Middle, Last)*

2. DATE OF BIRTH

3. VA CLAIM FOLDER NUMBER *(C – File No.)*

4. SOCIAL SECURITY NUMBER

I HEREBY CERTIFY THAT I ☐ DO ☐ DO NOT have a VA benefit— related indebtedness to my knowledge. I authorize the VA to furnish the information listed below.

5. VETERAN'S SIGNATURE

6. DATE SIGNED

FOR VA USE ONLY

☐ The above named veteran does not have a VA benefit—related indebtedness.

☐ The veteran has the following VA benefit—related indebtedness:

VA BENEFIT— RELATED INDEBTEDNESS *(If any)*

TYPE OF DEBT(S)	AMOUNT OF DEBT(S)
	$

TERMS OF REPAYMENT PLAN *(If any)*

☐ Veteran is exempt from funding fee due to receipt of compensation in the amount of $ _____ per month. (Unless checked, the funding fee must be remitted to VA with the certification of Loan Disbursement or Automatic Loan Report.)

☐ Insufficient information. The VA cannot identify the veteran with the information given. Please furnish more complete information, or a copy of a DD214 or discharge papers.

SIGNATURE OF AUTHORIZED AGENT	DATE SIGNED

VA FORM 26-8937
APR 1984

MORTGAGE LOAN RATING SHEET

(THIS FORM MUST BE COMPLETED IN ITS ENTIRETY
FOR EACH RESIDENTIAL APPLICATION)

Applicant_____ Sale
Price_____ Loan
Amount_____ Application
Number_____

Interest
Rate_____ Term_____Years Type of
Financing_____

1. ANNUAL INCOME
    Borrower (Base).........................$_____
    Co-Borrower......................... ....$_____
    Other Income (Bonus, Part Time, etc.)...$_____

        TOTAL ANNUAL INCOME...........................$_____

2. GROSS MONTHLY INCOME (Annual Income divided by 12)......$_____

3. PROPOSED MONTHLY MORTGAGE PAYMENT

    Principal and Interest..................$_____
    Taxes...................................$_____
    Insurance...............................$_____
    Private Mortgage Insurance..............$_____
    Condominium Fees (when utilities are
        included in this fee only state one-
        half of the charge)...................$_____

        TOTAL MONTHLY PAYMENT..............$_____

4. INCOME RATIO (#3 divided by #2)..............$_____

5. OUTSTANDING MONTHLY DEBTS (List only those that have 8 remaining
                        payments)

    _____$_____
    _____$_____
    _____$_____

        TOTAL MONTHLY INDEBTEDNESS..............$_____

INCOME DEBT RATIO (#3 + #5 divided by #2)....$_____

REMARKS

If line #4 exceeds 28% or is line #6 36%, please indicate the
circumstances that you feel would substantiate approval of the
requested loan.

RESIDENTIAL LOAN APPLICATION

| MORTGAGE APPLIED FOR | ☐ Conventional ☐ VA ☐ FHA | Amount $ | Interest Rate % | No. of Months | Monthly Payment Principal & Interest $ | Escrow/Impounds (to be collected monthly) ☐ Taxes ☐ Hazard Ins. ☐ Mtg. Ins. |

Prepayment Option

SUBJECT PROPERTY

Property Street Address | City | County | State | Zip | No. Units

Legal Description (Attach description if necessary) | Year Built

Purpose of Loan: ☐ Purchase ☐ Construction-Permanent ☐ Construction ☐ Refinance ☐ Other (Explain)

Complete this line if Construction-Permanent or Construction Loan ☞ | Lot Value Data | Original Cost | Present Value (a) | Cost of Imps. (b) | Total (a + b)
Year Acquired $ | $ | $ | $

ENTER TOTAL AS PURCHASE PRICE IN DETAILS OF PURCHASE.

Complete this line if a Refinance Loan
Year Acquired | Original Cost | Amt. Existing Liens | Purpose of Refinance | Describe Improvements [ ] made [ ] to be made
$ | $ | Cost: $

Title Will Be Held In What Name(s) | Manner In Which Title Will Be Held

Source of Down Payment and Settlement Charges

This application is designed to be completed by the borrower(s) with the lender's assistance. The Co-Borrower Section and all other Co-Borrower questions must be completed and the appropriate box(es) checked if ☐ another person will be jointly obligated with the Borrower on the loan, or ☐ the Borrower is relying on income from alimony, child support or separate maintenance or on the income or assets of another person as a basis for repayment of the loan, or ☐ the Borrower is married and resides, or the property is located, in a community property state.

BORROWER

Name | Age | School Yrs

Present Address | No. Years _____ ☐ Own ☐ Rent

Street
City/State/Zip
Former address if less than 2 years at present address
Street
City/State/Zip
Years at former address

Marital Status: ☐ Married ☐ Separated ☐ Unmarried (incl. single, divorced, widowed)

DEPENDENTS OTHER THAN LISTED BY CO-BORROWER
NO. | AGES

Name and Address of Employer | Years employed in this line of work or profession? _____ years
Years on this job _____
☐ Self Employed*

Position/Title | Type of Business

Social Security Number*** | Home Phone | Business Phone

CO-BORROWER

Name | Age | School Yrs

Present Address | No. Years _____ ☐ Own ☐ Rent

Street
City/State/Zip
Former address if less than 2 years at present address
Street
City/State/Zip
Years at former address

Marital Status: ☐ Married ☐ Separated ☐ Unmarried (incl. single, divorced, widowed)

DEPENDENTS OTHER THAN LISTED BY BORROWER
NO. | AGES

Name and Address of Employer | Years employed in this line of work or profession? _____ years
Years on this job _____
☐ Self Employed*

Position/Title | Type of Business

Social Security Number*** | Home Phone | Business Phone

GROSS MONTHLY INCOME

Item	Borrower	Co-Borrower	Total
Base Empl. Income	$	$	$
Overtime			
Bonuses			
Commissions			
Dividends/Interest			
Net Rental Income			
Other† (Before completing, see notice under Describe Other Income below.)			
Total	$	$	$

MONTHLY HOUSING EXPENSE.**

Rent	Present	Proposed
	$	$
First Mortgage (P&I)		
Other Financing (P&I)		
Hazard Insurance		
Real Estate Taxes		
Mortgage Insurance		
Homeowner Assn Dues		
Other:		
Total Monthly Pmt	$	$
Utilities		
Total	$	$

DETAILS OF PURCHASE.

Do Not Complete If Refinance

a Purchase Price	$
b Total Closing Costs (Est.)	
c. Prepaid Escrows (Est.)	
d Total (a + b + c)	$
e. Amount This Mortgage	( )
f Other Financing	( )
g Other Equity	( )
h. Amount of Cash Deposit	( )
i. Closing Costs Paid by Seller	( )
j. Cash Reqd. For Closing (Est.)	$

DESCRIBE OTHER INCOME

NOTICE: † Alimony, child support, or separate maintenance income need not be revealed if the Borrower or Co-Borrower does not choose to have it considered as a basis for repaying this loan.

B—Borrower C—Co-Borrower	Monthly Amount
	$

IF EMPLOYED IN CURRENT POSITION FOR LESS THAN TWO YEARS COMPLETE THE FOLLOWING

B/C	Previous Employer/School	City/State	Type of Business	Position Title	Dates From/To	Monthly Income
						$

THESE QUESTIONS APPLY TO BOTH BORROWER AND CO-BORROWER

	Borrower Yes or No	Co-Borrower Yes or No
If a "yes" answer is given to a question in this column, explain on an attached sheet.		
Have you any outstanding judgments? In the last 7 years, have you been declared bankrupt?		
Have you had property foreclosed upon or given title or deed in lieu thereof?		
Are you a co-maker or endorser on a note?		
Are you a party in a law suit?		
Are you obligated to pay alimony, child support, or separate maintenance?		
Is any part of the down payment borrowed?		

If applicable, explain Other Financing or Other Equity (provide addendum if more space is needed)

*FHLMC/FNMA require business credit report, signed Federal Income Tax returns for last two years, and, if available, audited Profit and Loss Statements plus balance sheet for same period.

**All Present Monthly Housing Expenses of Borrower and Co-Borrower should be listed on a combined basis.

***Neither FHLMC nor FNMA requires this information.

FHLMC 65 Rev. 8/78

FORM NO. 023

FNMA 1003 Rev. 8/78

STATEMENT OF ASSETS AND LIABILITIES

This Statement and any applicable supporting schedules may be completed jointly by both married and unmarried co-borrowers if their assets and liabilities are sufficiently joined so that the Statement can be meaningfully and fairly presented on a combined basis; otherwise separate Statements and Schedules are required (FHLMC 65A/FNMA 1003A). If the co-borrower section was completed about a spouse, this statement and supporting schedules must be completed about that spouse also.

☐ Completed Jointly ☐ Not Completed Jointly

ASSETS

Description	Cash or Market Value
Cash Deposit Toward Purchase Held By	$
Checking and Savings Accounts (Show Names of Institutions/Acct. Nos.)	
Stocks and Bonds (No./Description)	
Life Insurance Net Cash Value Face Amount ($	
SUBTOTAL LIQUID ASSETS	$
Real Estate Owned (Enter Market Value from Schedule of Real Estate Owned)	
Vested Interest in Retirement Fund	
Net Worth of Business Owned (ATTACH FINANCIAL STATEMENT)	
Automobiles (Make and Year)	
Furniture and Personal Property	
Other Assets (Itemize)	
TOTAL ASSETS	A $

LIABILITIES AND PLEDGED ASSETS

Indicate by (*) those liabilities or pledged assets which will be satisfied upon sale of real estate owned or upon refinancing of subject property

Creditors' Name, Address and Account Number	Acct. Name if Not Borrower's	Mo. Pmt. and Mos. left to pay	Unpaid Balance
Installment Debts (include "revolving" charge accts)		$ Pmt./Mos.	$
		/	
		/	
		/	
Other Debts Including Stock Pledges		/	
Real Estate Loans			
		✕	
Automobile Loans		/	
Alimony, Child Support and Separate Maintenance Payments Owed To		/	✕
TOTAL MONTHLY PAYMENTS		$	✕
NET WORTH (A minus B) $		TOTAL LIABILITIES	B $

SCHEDULE OF REAL ESTATE OWNED (If Additional Properties Owned Attach Separate Schedule)

Address of Property (Indicate S if Sold, PS if Pending Sale or R if Rental being held for income)	Type of Property	Present Market Value	Amount of Mortgages & Liens	Gross Rental Income	Mortgage Payments	Taxes, Ins. Maintenance and Misc.	Net Rental Income
		$	$	$	$	$	$
TOTALS →		$	$	$	$	$	$

LIST PREVIOUS CREDIT REFERENCES

B—Borrower C—Co-Borrower	Creditor's Name and Address	Account Number	Purpose	Highest Balance	Date Paid
				$	

List any additional names under which credit has previously been received

AGREEMENT: The undersigned applies for the loan indicated in this application to be secured by a first mortgage or deed of trust on the property described herein, and represents that the property will not be used for any illegal or restricted purpose, and that all statements made in this application are true and are made for the purpose of obtaining the loan. Verification may be obtained from any source named in this application. The original or a copy of this application will be retained by the lender, even if the loan is not granted. The undersigned ☐ intend or ☐ do not intend to occupy the property as their primary residence.

I/we fully understand that it is a federal crime punishable by fine or imprisonment, or both, to knowingly make any false statements concerning any of the above facts as applicable under the provisions of Title 18, United States Code, Section 1014.

_____ Date _____   _____ Date _____
Borrower's Signature   Co-Borrower's Signature

INFORMATION FOR GOVERNMENT MONITORING PURPOSES

The following information is requested by the Federal Government if this loan is related to a dwelling, in order to monitor the lender's compliance with equal credit opportunity and fair housing laws. You are not required to furnish this information, but are encouraged to do so. The law provides that a lender may neither discriminate on the basis of this information, nor on whether you choose to furnish it. However, if you choose not to furnish it, under Federal regulations this lender is required to note race and sex on the basis of visual observation or surname. If you do not wish to furnish the above information, please initial below

BORROWER: I do not wish to furnish this information (initials) _____

RACE/ NATIONAL ORIGIN   ☐ American Indian, Alaskan Native   ☐ Asian, Pacific Islander
☐ Black   ☐ Hispanic   ☐ White   ☐ Other (specify) _____
SEX: ☐ Female   ☐ Male

CO-BORROWER: I do not wish to furnish this information (initials) _____

RACE/ NATIONAL ORIGIN   ☐ American Indian, Alaskan Native   ☐ Asian, Pacific Islander
☐ Black   ☐ Hispanic   ☐ White   ☐ Other (specify) _____
SEX: ☐ Female   ☐ Male

FOR LENDER'S USE ONLY

(FNMA REQUIREMENT ONLY) This application was taken by ☐ face to face interview   ☐ by mail   ☐ by telephone

_____   _____
(Interviewer)   Name of Employer of Interviewer

FHLMC 65 Rev. 8/78   FNMA 1003 Rev. 8/78

REVERSE

(Lender)

BALLOON MORTGAGE LOAN APPLICATION DISCLOSURE

This Balloon Mortgage Loan Application Disclosure will explain how your balloon loan from this lender will work. Your balloon loan consists of three primary documents. One is the NOTE or loan contract. The second is the BALLOON PAYMENT NOTE RIDER that explains the special characteristics of a balloon loan. The third document is MORTGAGE/DEED OF TRUST that places a lien on your property. Once signed, both you and the lender are bound by the terms and conditions of these documents. It is very important that you become familiar with these documents and understand them before you sign on the dotted line. Modifications to your balloon mortgage loan may be requested by either you or the lender at any time before maturity, although neither you nor the lender has to agree to any such request.

Your balloon mortgage loan will have a term of _____ year(s). This means that it will mature, or be due and payable, at the end of the term. You must repay the entire principal balance and any unpaid interest at this time. The lender is **not** obligated to refinance your loan at that time. You will be required to repay your loan from other assets you may own, or find another lender willing to lend you the money at prevailing market rates — which may be considerably higher or lower than the interest rate on this loan. If you refinance this loan at maturity, you may have to pay some, or all, closing costs normally associated with a new loan even if your balloon loan is refinanced by the same lender.

The initial interest rate on your balloon mortgage loan is either _____ %, or will be established by the lender and disclosed to you at loan commitment based on market conditions at that time. Your initial payment is either $_____, or will be disclosed by the lender at loan commitment. An example is provided below to demonstrate how the lender establishes an amortization schedule for your balloon loan. The example below determines the amount of your payment, what portion of the payment is credited to interest and what the final "balloon" payment will be.

> In this example the balloon loan amount is $50,000.00 with a term of 1 year and an initial interest rate of 13% amortized over 30 years. The payment on this loan would be $553.10, the amount required to reduce the principal balance to zero at the end of 30 years. Given the example above, the interest portion of the payment would be calculated by multiplying the loan amount ($50,000) by the interest rate (13%) and dividing the result by 12 to get a monthly interest figure of $541.67. Subtracting the interest ($541.67) from the payment ($553.10) leaves $11.43, or the amount the principal balance is reduced in the first month of the loan. Using the new principal balance ($49,988.57) repeating the steps above will produce an interest of $541.54, a principal of $11.56 and a new balance of $49,977.01. Continued repetition of these steps will result in a "balloon" balance of approximately $49,854.32 at the end of 1 year.

A maturity notice must be sent to you by the lender at least 90, but not more than 120, days prior to the maturity of your balloon mortgage loan. This notice will state the final balloon amount and the date payment is due.

There are some contractual contingencies under which your loan may become due or which may result in a forced sale of your home. Generally, these contigencies would involve your defaulting on the terms of your mortgage. Examples of default are: not making your payments; failure to pay real estate taxes, liens or assessments on your property; abandonment of your property; condemnation of your property; your selling or transferring the property without the consent of the lender (due-on-sale); your failure to preserve or maintain your property; and any action that materially affects the lender's security (your property) such as: your bankruptcy, insolvency, code enforcements, death, or any legal proceedings or actions against you.

Your balloon loan contract ☐ will ☐ will not provide for escrow payments. An escrow account spreads out, on a monthly basis, the cost of some substantial payments that occur either semi-annually or annually. By splitting these large payments into smaller monthly payments, they are not only easier to budget, but are also paid by the lender when they are due. These payments may include all amounts necessary to pay for taxes, assessments, ground rents and hazard insurance on your property. You will have to pay these amounts to the lender unless the lender tells you, in writing, that you don't have to do so, or unless the law requires otherwise. You will make these excrow payments on the same day that you make your payments of principal and interest. Generally, the amount of your escrow payments will be one-twelfth of any of the following that apply: estimated yearly taxes, assessments and ground rents on the property; estimated yearly premium for hazard insurance covering the property; and the estimated yearly premiums for mortgage insurance or credit life/disability insurances. The lender has the right to hold a one-sixth (2 month) reserve balance for real estate taxes to help cover anticipated tax increases on your property.

You acknowledge receipt of a completed copy of this Balloon Mortgage Loan Application Disclosure.

_____
Signature

_____
Signature

5
Loan Extensions

Loan Entension. If you have a fixed rate / fixed term mortgage you can count yourself among millions of individuals who have gotten loan extensions. You may have a good many more options than you thought when you are facing Foreclosure. Foreclosure can be very useful to you and a very costly experience for your lender. Unfortunately, when a person gets in a serious financial bind and is several payments behind on his mortgage debt, he is inclined to take the key to his house down to his lender and hand it to him. The lender will be happy to have the key, but unhappy to have his cash flow interrupted and to have to process a foreclosure. He would he happy to see that you don't know how to use the fact that credit is not money. He will be unhappy to find out that you do.

Institutional lenders do not like to take back property even if you make easy for them to do so by handing them the key. If you have an FHA-insured mortgage, your lender can turn the mortgage over to the FHA, get his money and you can deal directly with the FHA / HUD. Actually, the FHA doesn't like foreclosure any more than your lender, simply because it is a governmental organization. Usually, it will try to help you in any way it can to give you a loan extension and prevent foreclosure.

If you have a fixed rate mortgage loan, and no one will refinance it for you, you have little choice but to take a new kind of loan that may be very much to your disadvantage. There are lenders who are primarily interested in getting all the money they can get under various types of mortgage loans. It may be necessary for you to act immediately to save your property from foreclosure by going to a lender with a proposal he cannot refuse. Time and maneuverability are going to be your greatest allies, as you will need to know not only the most dangerous weapons in your opponent's arsenal, you will have to learn what your rights are in your state and how to use those rights legally to defend yourself, your credit, and your property. However, make whatever sacrifices you have to make and buy yourself the time you need. If Foreclosure is upon you, and you have no time to take out an FHA loan, or talk a lender into giving you variable rate mortgage with extra points to himself, then you will have to commence a lawsuit against your lender before he can bring an action against you. As pointed out before, have your attorney file a COMPLAINT, and become the Plaintiff. If you cannot stop foreclosure any other way, you still have two avenues of advantage. You can bid your property in at Sale, using silver dollars and insisting you have made the high bid with legal tender. And you can stop the sale from occurring by declaring Bankruptcy. These legal karate techniques will be taught to you elsewhere in this book.

The FHA Extension. The FHA does not want to take back property by Foreclosure. Rather, it strives to help the borrower. When there are a lot of foreclosures going on, due to a recession or a depression, the FHA fund becomes heavily burdened. The FHA is in a situation of taking thousands of properties with a resulting drain on its funds, or it can extend loans and avoid foreclosure for both the borrower and the organization.

The FHA Plan. The parent organization, the Department of Housing and Urban Development (HUD) has a plan available to you by asking for it, to aid you if you have an FHA-insured mortgage, when you get into financial trouble. Unfortunately, not many people know about it. Basically, if you are in default on your FHA mortgage, you can apply to the Department of Housing and Urban Development to take over your mortgage.

The fact that your mortgage is FHA insured does not automatically operate to provide you with such an umbrella. Taking over your mortgage is not automatic. If you have not made regular payments on your mortgage and are seriously in arrears, your lender will undoubtedly start to foreclose. Since you are not yet a legal karate expert, you may panic and let it happen. You need not. If you do not know the techniques of using Foreclosure procedures to your advantage you will learn them elsewhere in this book. Meanwhile, as a matter of avoidance, you can and you must ask HUD to take over the mortgage. If you don't, the foreclosure procedure will continue and you will ultimately lose your home, farm or business. Once the lender has taken title to your property, he will transfer to the FHA (HUD).

To avoid losing your home or property, the moment you are in Default and see no way of catching up, request an immediate transfer of title from your bank lender to the FHA (HUD) insurer.

Once the FHA becomes your lender, you can apply for loan extension, for changing the nature of your loan, for relaxed terms, whatever. Go for it. It is a bail-out program.

How to Apply. FHA (HUD) is located in every major city and a good many lesser urban areas. The head office, of course, is in Washington, D.C. Apply to the office nearest you. Be fully prepared to reveal your full financial situation. To meet FHA requirements:

1. You must be seriously in default, due to arrears of **three or more payments.**
2. You must present a very sound reason for such default. A reason beyond your control and preferably not your fault. Serious injury and loss of work from which you have now recovered, may be a good excuse. But,
3. You must provably show that you can reassume and repay your obligation. You must be able to show that you have returned to work or are taking special training for a job that will enable you to meet the payments

required of you. Sincerity and honesty are basic to favorable action. The FHA (HUD) allows up to a year for the training you may need, especially if you become disabled through injury or illness.

The BAIL-OUT PLAN IS A LOAN EXTENSION. The loan extension usually covers a period of three years. The HUD counselor will expect you to be able to catch up with the payments you missed within that time period. The plan is flexible, as you may also arrange to repay the loan in such a manner that it will become current within three years. The actual terms of an extension of your loan usually depends on each borrower's financial situation. You may be able to make partial payments over a period of several years, then resume higher payments or payments in excess of the original monthly sum until the mortgage is current; again, you may be allowed to make no payments for up to eighteen months. After that you would have to double up on your payments for an additional eighteen months until you have brought your mortgage into a current payment condition.

HUD has counselors and also gives you the borrower a list of FHA (HUD) approved agencies that do nothing but specialize in financial counseling, and sometimes financial aid, to help you avoid any further threat of foreclosure.

Refinancing Payments. Your lender bank may act much the same as the FHA (HUD) if you can present a creditable base for him to refinance your mortgage for you.

However, if you have an FHA mortgage and are threatened with foreclosure, immediately contact FHA (HUD) and request mortgage transfer.

Two. Prepare your request well, based on FHA / HUD criteria for Bail-Out.

Three. You must be three or more payments behind, facing foreclosure;

You must have a sound reason for not making payments (illness, injury, without your fault and beyond your control, same with loss of your job, etc.).

You must have and be able to show reasonable expectation of overcoming your financial problems within a period of 36 months.

You must be able to work out a creditable bail-out plan with this organization. OR THEY

WON'T LISTEN TO YOU.

Now, there are some considerations you must take into account. To save your property, you may have to rent it out. You know that is a no-no with a bank lender. Not so with HUD. The requirement that you maintain residency is waived. You must be able to show the FHA / HUD that the mortgagee has taken steps to foreclose.

If you are a member of the Armed Services, Army, Navy, Marines or Air Force or Coast Guard and are in Default due to assignment to a post of duty that is away from your home, farm or other business, don't panic. You can get immediate help and relief under the Soldiers' and Sailors' Civil Relief Act.

If you have received a letter threatening foreclosure, contact your lender and tell him you have contacted counsel (an attorney working for whatever service you are in, Army Adjutant General's Office, Navy General Counsel). Such an attorney will be well aware of the Soldier's and Sailor's Civil Relief Act, and he can and will help you protect your property against foreclosure. The effect of this Act is to suspend temporarily all but judicial foreclosure. Your lender bank or institution or even a private lender cannot foreclose out of court on any kind of mortgage once you inform the lender you are away from home in the service on assignment and intend seeking relief under the Soldier's and Sailor's Civil Relief Act.

In order to foreclose, your lender would have to bring the matter into court, and it is unlikely that the lender will prevail with any judge who understands that you are on assignment for the Armed Services. Unless there are some extenuating circumstances, the likelihood is that you will be protected for as long as you are on duty in the service.

In this connection, it would be well to be able to show the court, through representation by your attorney, that your Default has occurred without your fault and beyond your control.

If you are about to lose your home, farm or business, and go down to a recruiting station and sign up in the hope of avoiding foreclosure, you will be facing an entirely different situation in court. It is possible that you can convince your lender not to foreclose on the basis that you are going into the Army or Navy and will be able to maintain a schedule of payment commensurate with your pay.

On the other hand, you may have a member of the family, a son, daughter, brother, sister, a cousin or nephew who is going into the service, and who would be willing to have you transfer a portion of your property into his / her name. He / she goes into the service owning a portion of your property? Wrong. If you are shrewd, you will have him / her execute a reconveying Deed and not record it. After all, something could happen resulting in death and you would lose your property, or a portion of it. The person to whom you make such a transfer must send a registered letter to the lender notifying him that he now owns a portion of the property and is in the armed services and protected under the Soldiers' and Sailor's Civil Relief Act. You will avoid foreclosure.

The lender will undoubtedly seek to negotiate new terms. It may begin Foreclosure, but you usually have time to find this out, get down to the Clerk of the Court and file a COMPLAINT. The foreclosure case will then probably be dismissed on your Motion to Dismiss, as both the judge and the lender are or should be well aware that there are severe penalties for the lender for pursuing a foreclosure when the Soldier's and Sailor's Civil Relief Act has been invoked.

The lender probably will back off as soon as he sees you know something about the effect of taking such action as seeking protection under this Act, as well as filing a COMPLAINT. He will very likely agree to delay while you or your co-owner are in the service. You will be in a position to negotiate terms of payment that you can meet—and should meet.

The Act itself is to be found in the appendix to volume 50 of the United States Code 50, App. U.S.C. paras. 501-590 and though it is entitled "Soldiers' and Sailors' Civil Relief Act," it protects members of any of the armed services, such as the members of the Air Force, Marine Corps and Coast Guard. Reference 50 App. U.S.C. paras. 464, 466(c) and 511.

IT IS UP TO YOU TO GET A COPY OF THE ACT.

The Act itself is highly legalistic and technical and your benefits under it are limited. It would be well for you to have your attorney analyze the Act carefully to determine its benefit to you, or discuss its application to your particular situation with a legal officer of the armed forces. If you need such services, go to the nearest military installation and ask for the help of a legal assistance officer. Of course, you will only get it if you are a member of the armed services, or if the member of your family or the friend to whom you transferred a portion of your property can show that he is a member of the armed services in good standing.

The Act only applies to persons in the military service and includes all persons on extended active duty, whether inductees, regulars, members of the National Guard, Reserves, or volunteers. It also covers all officers of the Public Health Service who are detailed for duty with any branch of the military; also, the Act includes any person or persons who are training ot studying under the supervision of a Service preliminary to induction; and veterans who saw active duty during wartime. Enlisted reservists and draftees are protected by the relief the Act affords as soon as they receive orders to report for active duty. Merely knowing that the Act exists and can afford immediate relief is no assurance that you are home free.

You are faced with a lawsuit. Foreclosure. Your lender who brings the suit will be known as the "plaintiff" unless you get your complaint in first. The person against whom the suit is filed (with the Clerk of the Court in which the case is to be heard) will be known as the "defendant." Whichever one of you files his Complaint first will become the "plaintiff." In the Complaint you must state why the suit has been started. Statement should contain documentation of any error you have found in your mortgage documents. Recite facts as to any threats you have received, verbal or written and back them up with Affidavits or statements of witnesses. After you have filed your Complaint as a Plaintiff you must give the defendant lender notice that you have started a suit against him. This is accomplished by means of a Summons, a formal written form of Notice to the defendant to the effect that suit has been filed and has commenced against him and that unless he contests the suit, "judgment" may be entered against him.

Normally, the defendant will file an answer, stating why the Plaintiff should not prevail.

If the defendant does not file an answer or appear in answer to the summons within the time frame specified in the summons he will be held in default and the court will enter a "judgment by default" in favor of the Plaintiff.

In a suit for money, the judgment will order the defendant to pay or upon full examination of the facts, it may state he owes nothing. A judgment for money is collectible over the years.

Protection under the Civil Relief Act is provided and is applicable to all lawsuits in any court of law in the United States, from a Justice of the Peace Court to the U.S. Supreme Court. If you are a member of the armed forces on active duty or on reserve, a court will not enter default judgment against you unless the lender is able to state that he doesn't know and has not been able to find out whether or not you are in military service. He had better be able to prove his sworn statement. He will also be required to put up a security deposit, which will protect you in the event the judgment is set aside. The security deposit can be used for damages you may have suffered as a result of judgment incorrectly entered against you.

If the lender has falsely sworn that you are not in the military service, knowing that you are, he can be sent to prison or fined, or both.

If all these things happen, and you are away in military service you can, upon returning, ask the court to reopen your case, provided: (you must meet all three requirements)

1. You make application to the court within 90 days from date of your discharge.
2. You have suffered damages, were harmed, a cloud has been cast on your record, on your credit and the case is prejudiced by reason of your military service so that you could not properly present your side of the case to the court; and
3. You have a valid, legal defense you wish to present to the court.

The Act and Stays. While the Act provides general relief in almost any situation of merit, you may ask the court to stay the proceedings, as the Act requires the court to grant your request unless the judge decides conduct of the suit would be affected by your ability to prosecute or defend suit, by reason of your military service.

Once a lawsuit has begun, you must stay abreast of proceedings, or you will run into the time limit known as "Statutes of Limitations." If you permit time for filing certain motions to pass you will lose out under these Statutes.

In any court matter involving an installment contract, a mortgage, or a trust deed you will be asking the judge to act fairly in your behalf. Where you have received something of value for the note you have given, such as an automobile, household appliances, furniture or furnishings, you will not prevail in using court room karate techniques if you are trying to cheat your lender out of payment for goods valued and received. On the other hand, if your lender has merely loaned your credit and has created in your mind the assumption that he has given you something of value in exchange for your farm, or home or business, you are entitled to go into court and fight for your rights on the basis of the money issue, fraud, usury and deception. See to it that you are on the side of right. Pay what you honestly owe. Where you are liable for an obligation or money debt created to enable you to buy a home, home appliances, personal items of jewelry, clothes or animals or an automobile and you signed a contract to pay what you owe in monthly installments, do not expect a judge or any attorney to go along with you in using methods to deny your creditor what you honestly owe him.

Refinancing Balloon Payments. FHA / HUD will refinance whatever you have to refinance, provided you can show it a reasonable prospect that you will be able to resume full repayment of your mortgage loan after a period of time not exceeding 36 months. If you have a balloon payment at the end of a second term three mortgage amounting to $10,000 and can show the FHA / HUD a five year lease under which you will receive $4,000 income per year for rent you will have presented a creditable base for repayment of the balloon. You may offer to assign such rent, or if that is refused, you may offer to have it paid into an escrow account with your attorney as Trustee, so that the FHA / HUD will be assured at the end of three years that the Balloon payment will be met.

Other sources of cash to consider. You may consider a home occupation as a source of extra income. A license to conduct an occupation in your home such as dressmaking, or making rubber stamps for local small businesses is easily obtained for $10 from your local county Board of Assessors and Licenses. You may be talented in painting, making small repairs, cabinet making, any and all of which can be done in your spare time in addition to a regular job.

To add to Your Income. Look into your inventory of talents and if you have a talent, or special skill that could be turned to profit with a bit of training, go after the training and assure your lender you are doing just that in order to provide for the needed extra in-

come to meet your payments. You may be able to help refinance yourself through a home improvement loan at your local credit union. You will have to meet their criteria and requirements to qualify. But, indeed you may be quite capable of doing just that.

You may be able to turn to a friend or relative, for temporary relief.

Better still, you may be able to improve your property by your own efforts or with the help of friends and relatives to the point where you have obviously increased your property value. Once you have increased your property's value, you will have increased your **equity**. Get that increased value appraised, and apply for refinancing on the basis of increased equity!

An Unsecured Loan. If your situation is desperate and time is of the essence and you think the sheriff will be at your door any day, wait a minute! Your credit may still be good in every respect except where your mortgage payments are concerned. You may indeed be able to get an unsecured bank loan merely by asking for it.

Liquidating Assets. You may have personal items of jewelry that are worth more than you think. Perhaps a friend of yours has always admired a ring that you possess and has often said ''I'd give a mint to have that ring or one like it.'' Find out how much is in the mint.

You may have acreage, or other property somewhere, that is not mortgaged, on which you can borrow or which you can quickly sell. If the property is valuable, you may avoid foreclosure by offering it as additional security to your lender. He may cover both pieces of property with a new mortgage called a blanket mortgage. You will be in a position to negotiate much better terms.

Life Insurance. You may be able to borrow money on your life insurance policy. Whole life policies are like bank accounts. You may have been paying to the company for years without a thought of ever borrowing against your policy. Find out from your insurance agent what the cash value or loan value is. Interest for a loan is always at current market rates.

Temporary help from a family member who lives with you. You may have a mother, mother-in-law or other member of your family who wants to help but doesn't work. By going to work, he or she could probably provide substantial help, financially. If he or she cannot work, perhaps a loan can be negotiated against a pension fund.

Other Sources. If you have a MasterCard or Visa or both you may be able to raise immediate cash if needed. Some individuals have dozens of such cards from lending institutions, each with a separate credit limit running up to as much as $5,000 immediate available cash. However, beware, as the rate of interest you will have to pay on such credit usage can be very high and run as much as 21% per annum. You would have to have a repayment plan that you could put into effect within 60 days. Money unwisely borrowed on credit cards could ruin your credit, and hasten you into bankruptcy. Be fully aware that you would have no defense in court if you obtained cash advances by using your credit cards. That is not the same as a bank lending you its credit instead of money. If and when you received something of value such as currency in exchange for a Deed of Trust, you cannot block foreclosure on the basis of the money issue, simply because you have received money.

6
Credit

Credit. Credit is the ability you have to borrow money, to obtain goods on time, in consequence of the favorable opinion held by a particular lender as to your solvency and reliability. Credit involves time allowed to the buyer of goods by the seller, in which to make payment for them.

Trust. Trust is the credit of an individual in whom trust is reposed by those who deal with him, who believe he has the ability to meet his obligations and commitments.

Line of Personal Credit. Personal credit is that credit which a person possesses as an individual and which is founded on the opinion entertained of his character and business standing, usually by a creditor.

Creditor. A creditor in the strict legal sense of the term is one who has the legal right to demand and recover from another a sum of money on any account whatever, which may include a right of action against another arising out of a contract or for a tort, a penalty, or a forfeiture. The term "creditor," within the common law and statutes includes everyone having a right ro require the performance of any legal obligation, contract or guaranty. It may also extend to a legal right to damages growing out of contract or tort and includes one entitled to damages for breach of contract to convey real estate.

Classifications. A creditor may be called a "simple contract creditor," a "specialty creditor," a "noncreditor," or other name, according to the nature of the obligation giving rise to the debt owed to him.

Attaching Creditor. An attaching creditor is one who has caused an attachment to be issued and levied on the property of his debtor.

A Creditor at Large. One who has not established his debt by the recovery of a judgment or has not otherwise secured a lien on any of the debtor's property is called a creditor at large.

A Domestic Creditor. A domestic creditor is one who resides in the same state or county in which the debtor has his domicile or his residence.

An Execution Creditor. The term is self-explanatory as one who having recovered a judgment against the debtor for his debt or claim has also caused an execution of judgment to be issued.

Petitioning Creditors. This term describes petitioning creditor as used in Bankruptcy. All creditors petitioning for adjudication or seeking relief consistent with original petition by supplemental or intervening petition, in view of section 59f, 11 U.S.C.A. para. 95.

Principal Creditor. A principal creditor is one whose claim or demand very greatly exceeds the claims of all other creditors in the amount owed him.

Your credit is one of your most valuable assets. Establishing your credit may be as easy as opening a savings account at your local bank. You may later go to your banker and ask for a small loan, offer your savings pass book as security, pay off your loan and in so doing establish a credit record. One of the best ways to avoid credit problems is to use your credit wisely. If you have used your credit wisely and have established a good credit record, you can bring the full impact of that good record to bear in avoiding foreclosure procedures.

Prompt payment of bills. Your credit may be established by the manner in which you pay your bills. If you have kept your living expenses under control and pay your bills promptly, you will have a good credit record. A good credit record is a very valuable asset. If you are one of those individuals who because he has seen it, he wants it and will do almost anything to get it you have a serious problem. A good rule for you to adopt would be to pay cash only. Charge nothing. Cut up your credit cards. Do without what you cannot pay for. If you cannot pay for it don't buy it.

If you have serious credit problems, it would be well for you to consult any one of several consumer financial aid organizations. You will find a number of such good organizations in the yellow pages of your local telephone book. The National Foundation for Consumer Credit is just such an outfit, and is open to all who need financial counseling, whether he is rich or poor. If you are living in a small town, you may find the NFCC is listed as the Consumer Credit Counseling Service. In Washington, D.C., the address is: The National Foundation for Consumer Credit, 1819 H Street, N.W. A similar organization is called the Family Service Association of America located at 44 East 23rd Street, New York, NY 10010. This organization also has offices nationwide.

When you are faced with threat of foreclosure on your home, farm or business, it would be well for you to start asking for help and counseling at one of these offices. Such organizations have been set up to help consumers get their financial affairs straightened out and to reestablish their credit. They help you help yourself. That of course, is what this book is intended to do, also. But, it is assumed that you will make every effort to seek every avenue of protection and good advice you can get once you are threatened with foreclosure.

As explained earlier in this book, it is not an obvious fact that 97% of consumer business is done with credit. As a result special safeguards have been set up at all levels of government (federal, state, and local), to protect the creditor as well as the consumer. The strongest lobby in Washington, D.C., is the banking lobby. About 18,000 laws are on the books for the protection of bankers! None of them supercedes the Constitution of the United States. The bankers' lobbyists have not been able to prevail on the Congress to re-write the Constitution, however.

Credit Rights. Credit rights are those which apply principally to credit cards and retail purchases. Some apply to mortgages (and may be used in legal court room karate).

The Federal Trade Commission has the consumer's best interests at heart; one of its chief goals is to protect you from unfair credit terms and practices. A creditor who gives you unfair terms when he lends you credit or practices unfair and deceptive methods of foreclosure may be subject to severe penalties. The FTC will protect a borrower from a lender who uses deception. For example, a lender may send important looking documents bearing some kind of false but official-looking seal on them to give them the semblance of an official paper. Or he may send letters that bear a resemblance to government documents, or look something like a summons. He may do this to intimidate you.

Rule. A lender may not threaten you with an action unless the lender intends to take that action. As a matter of fact, he had better back up his threat by taking some open step in that action. If he is going to take you to court and threatens to do so, act immediately, as your safe presumption must be that he will do so. If you have given your lender a Trust Deed Mortgage, no court action is necessary. He can foreclose without it. Therefore, you must go at once to the Court, find the Clerk of Court, find out how to file a **Complaint** and effectively stop him by initiating action. If you have any kind of active status with the armed services get hold of a legal services officer at once, at your nearest armed services installation, explain your situation to him, and have him send a registered letter to the lender warning him to cease in his action of foreclosures as you are under the protection of the Armed Services Soldiers' and Sailors' Civil Relief Act.

Solving the Problem of Avoidance of Foreclosure. Act immediately. Hire an attorney to write a registered letter to the mortgage lender and to file a COMPLAINT for you in court establishing you as the Complainant, or Plaintiff. That will put the lender on the defensive. Establish your rights from the outset.

You have many rights as a borrower. Most of these rights are applicable when you become a mortgagor. When you are faced with foreclosure, the Marquis of Queensbury rules may no longer apply. Your lender's attorney will undoubtedly know all the legal karate tricks there are in the book. Your advantage will be to employ and apply techniques that will make court room life miserable for him and his client.

The Equal Credit Opportunity Act. The Equal

Credit Opportunity Act is an Act that protects you from discrimination because of sex, marital status, age, race, color, religion or any combination of these. Your rights under this Act do not necessarily apply when you are facing foreclosure, as legal actions are in themselves impersonal, through they may not be impartial. However, if you learn that the lender routinely applies more stringent foreclosure policies to certain borrowers in a discriminatory fashion, you may wish to explore your rights under this Act.

Credit Bureaus and the Fair Credit Reporting Act. Credit bureaus may serve you or serve against you. The TRW Services Division is one of the largest credit reporting bureaus on the East Coast.

Under the Fair Credit Reporting Act you are protected against erroneous or unfair credit reporting. And if you are in financial difficulty, it would be well for you to keep your credit record straight. If you are faced with foreclosure, some reporting agency is bound to pick up the information and report it to such an agency as TRW. It is vital that you keep any cloud off your credit record. If the reporting agency reports that you are in foreclosure, when you are not, you will have to take definite action to have such a false report removed. Your lender may have gratuitously passed such damaging information on to your credit bureau. If so, you will be able to find out.

1. You have a right to know who reported such information affecting your credit.
2. You have a right to call up and ask the TRW or any local credit bureat for a full credit report on the current status of your line of credit.
3. You have the right to know the sum and substance and source of any derogatory information affecting your credit.
4. You should take a friend with you to the reporting agency and ask them to explain why they passed derogatory information about you on to credit bureau prior to any actual foreclosure action. This will provide you with an Affidavit that can be presented with your complaint, when you file it.
5. You have a right to tell your side of the story to the credit bureau and have it included in your file.
6. You have a right to notify those who received any deleterious information about you of the facts in the matter.
7. You have a right to ask them to change their records accordingly.

In most instances, you can get a copy of the bureau's credit report on yourself; you can also see your file and discuss it with the bureau's representative. Most credit bureaus do not evaluate your credit history or make decisions whether credit is granted or denied. They store credit data and information that is reported to them by credit grantors who subscribe to their service. The decision making process varies from one credit grantor to another, depending on their own policy guidelines.

In addition, there are a few areas of data you may not be permitted to see, such as results of investigative reporting or information of a medical nature.

However, should you have a bad credit report based on a foreclosure that did not happen or on a default that was cleared up with your lender creditor, you would take steps to clear up the matter. Have your lender notify the bureau of applicable and proper changes. You notify the bureau as well. Credit is a valuable asset, especially if used wisely.

What your credit means to you. Your credit is one of your most valuable assets in today's world of checks, credit cards, letters of credit, loans without security, loans without collateral, loans without co-signers. As mentioned, credit is not money, but it may serve in the commercial world as though it were.

Most lender banks are becoming so sophisticated they are setting up subsidiary mortgage companies which bear the brunt of defaulting debtors. Also, many lender banks and companies who extend credit through associated but independent branches or companies will employ collection agencies on an annual basis. The methods used by these agencies may stock your arsenal with tremendous strength when you begin to enlist the sympathy of the judge. You will perhaps be able to tell him that an agency called up your place of employment and spread the bad news about you all over the place. Your employer may have called you in and advised you to get your personal financial problems straightened out immediately or the firm would have to let you go. Severe consequences can result from loss of a job and from being called a deadbeat. Harassment causing emotional distress is actionable. In your Complaint get Affidavits from fellow workers who heard the bill collector threaten you with some serious consequence if you did not promptly pay your bill. You may have a cause for charging the lender with using methods known as extortion, depending on the kind of threats used.

You would do well to protect your line of credit at all cost. Act timely, wisely and well to keep yourself above reproach. You can hold your head high if you have unfortunately gotten yourself into a financial bind that is not your fault and beyond your control. If such is the case you should not have any serious trouble in convincing any reporting credit bureau or agency of the facts in the matter.

The Federal Trade Commission is not empowered to help individuals with a specific problem, but it can investigate and bring action against any agency for unfair reporting practices. Act before the credit report sets and hardens. A bad report can always be changed if you give your personal attention, and present a creditable finds of fact.

When a Foreclosure is not a Foreclosure. Technically, if you have gone through a foreclosure sale, you may feel you are out your property. Not so. If you have an equity that was greater than the amount you borrowed, you have an equity redemption.

Foreclosure Sale. Foreclosure sale is usually preceded by the typical letter of NOTICE OF DEFAULT. This is a procedure the lender calls ACCELERATION, and it is based on a standard clause in a mortgage that allows the lender to call in his mortgage if you are in arrears. Such a clause usually reads: "At the option of the mortgagee, the entire principal sum along with all the interest shall become due if the mortgagor is more than fifteen days late in making any payment of principal or interest, or if the mortgagor fails to maintain adequate fire insurance." The clause may go on in this vein naming many other conditions entitling the lender to foreclose.

At this point, if you can persuade the lender to accept back payments due plus interest, the lender would have to start his Acceleration procedure all over again at a later date if you again got in arrears. In any case, it is going to cost him a lot of money so you have a good chance to negotiate, and pay as much on the debt as you can get together.

Acceleration under Mortgage Foreclosure. Many lenders who have sent you a Notice of Default (acceleration) find it easy to do. But for them to proceed further means they will have to use an attorney and go to considerable expense to foreclose. It may initially cost a lender as much as $5,000 just to commence suit. In view of this expense, it is to your mutual advantage to try to refinance your loan.

Complaint for Non-Payment. A Complaint for Non-Payment may be filed by the lender's attorney if you let it occur. Under a threatened Mortgage Foreclosure, first try to negotiate, and if that fails, immediately take the same kind of legal action to stop foreclosure outlined in a Deed of Trust Foreclosure, given elsewhere in this chapter. Once you have received a Complaint for Non-Payment, you will have to answer as a Defendant. Usually you have to admit that you are in default and behind in payments. The mortgagee will immediately file a motion for summary judgment, ask for a referee to be appointed, a judgment sale time approved, and move ahead to sell the property to satisfy the mortgage debt.

If you deny the Complaint and file a countersuit, a trial date will be set several months down the road, which will give you time to save your property, if it is worth saving. If you can challenge successfully the mortgage documents, you may also succeed in having the Foreclosure dismissed. If you lost your case, you can Appeal the Foreclosure Verdict.

While the Appeal action is pending, the referee in charge of the sale of your property will be stopped and the sale postponed. Appeals can take a long time. However, if the mortgagee can show the court that the Appeal is without merit, your Appeal can be denied as a mere delaying tactic. Again, negotiate, or file bankruptcy, which of course will effectively halt all foreclosure proceedings.

Mortgages and Equity Redemption. A mortgage usually carries a clause with an equity of redemption, because it is recognized in common law that the borrower's property may be of greater value than money to him. The clause makes it possible that if the borrower repays the lender within a reasonable time, even after the lender has seized the property, he has to give it back. That is redemption. Equity or interest in redemption exists in most mortgage states. The right does not operate where a trust deed foreclosure occurs out of court. However, where a note for a Trust Deed is foreclosed through a judicial proceeding and not by the trustee, redemption may exist.

7

What You Should Do to Avoid or Prevent Foreclosure

What you Should Do to Avoid Foreclosure.

1. Act timely. Negotiate. Refinance your loan, with your lender or seek out a private lender. Failing all else,

- File a Complaint. Get into Court first. Be the Plaintiff. Then negotiate. Make an offer. Use your Fractional Reserve Check. Have a witness, especially if your lender only lent you credit and gave you no money, as such.

- Go down to your local county court house and get acquainted with the Clerk of the Court where your case is likely to be heard. Find out about the procedures (for your state).

- Go to the law library in the court house and ask the Librarian for help, ask for books giving you information as to how to file, what to file and when to file a Motion.

- If you are too unnerved, hire an attorney (a constitutional attorney). An attorney is also an officer of the court, and he, like the judge and the sheriff, is sworn to uphold the Constitution of the United States.

- Make sure of your rights under the Constitution and the Bill of Rights, and also your rights that your state gives you to halt a foreclosure.

- Have an expert realtor study your loan documents for error, typographical errors, errors in spelling names, addresses, anything on which you can challenge the documents.

- Have your attorney file a Challenge of the Documents.

- Continue to talk to your lender, always with a witness present, do you can file affidavits as to any threat he may have made, offer you make which he refused, etc.

- Start your court room karate by having your attorney file a complaint. These initial pleadings are of utmost importance.

- As a last resort file bankruptcy. (This will be discussed in a succeeding chapter.)

- And remember, if you act timely, almost all foreclosures can be avoided, faced and in many instances successfully fought and stopped.

- Whatever you do, do not lose your rights through default or fear. Fight for what you value.

PLEADINGS. There are three systems of Pleadings: Common law, equity and code pleading.

Territorial distribution of the three systems. Common law jurisdictions: Alabama, Delaware, Florida, Maine, Maryland, Massachusetts, Michigan, Mississippi, New Hampshire, New Jersey, Pennsylvania, Rhode Island, Tennessee, Vermont, Virginia, West Virginia. Louisiana is peculiar in that its pleading is derived from the civil law or modern Roman law.

Formerly, congressional statutes provided that in equity cases equity pleading should be used. However, there have been many changes in the statutes and it would be well for you to find out what kind of pleading applies in your particular state.

Federal Courts. Federal Courts form a jurisdiction of their own. The District Courts of the United States have Code Pleading.

Forms of Action. Whatever your pleading it will be called a form of action. Real actions are for the recovery of property. Trespass against that property is also called a form of action in a common law pleading.

Classification of Actions. The various forms of action are divided into real, personal and mixed. A real action is one to recover land. A personal action is one to recover personal property, chattels, or money. In addition, there are actions on contracts, tort actions, and other forms of personal actions, such as ejectment, general issues and the like. All defenses showing that there is now debt would come under general issue, such as debt on or under a contract.

In state courts, the most appropriate institutional challenges would be under the 14th amendment: denial of property without due process, denial of equal protection under the laws, and the 7th amendment, denial of trial by jury.

Foreclosure of mortgages in courts of equity. In such a case, the mortgagee lender sends a letter threatening foreclosure with a Notice of Default, or he may only give notice by publication if the mortgagor is non-resident. Actual seizure of the land is required in the case of attachment at law. The court will find the mortgagor's indebtedness owing and enter an order that, unless he pays the amount within a certain number of days, the property will be sold to satisfy the debt. Thus, actual service of process has been avoided. The law will assume that property is always in the possession of its owner, in person or by an agent; and it will proceed upon the theory that its seizure will inform him not only that it is taken into custody of the court, but that he must look to any proceedings authorized by law upon such seizure for its sale. Beware!

JUDICIAL OR NON-JUDICIAL PROCEEDINGS.

One of the first things you need to know is whether you live in a state that uses a judicial or non-judicial process in Foreclosures.

Judicial. A judicial state is one where the lender files a Summons and Complaint and takes you to court to get a judgment against you. This is usually followed by a redemption period, then if you do not redeem or file countersuit, a sheriff's sale will occur. Judicial states are usually those where mortgages and mortgage notes are used. The process is based on the mortgage lien theory. The owner retains his deed to his property while the lender has a mortgage note.

Non-judicial state. A non-judicial state is usually one where the borrower signs a Deed of Trust and there is a ''note'' signed by the borrower. In those states, there are third party Trustee sales. Basically,

the lender just advertises and sells. However, in the lending case of *Pennoyer* v. *Neff* (20) 95 United States 714, The Supreme Court restored possession of the property to Neff because the court recognized that a seizure of property before judgment was essential to its validity. The court said: ''Substituted service by publication may be sufficient to inform the parties of the object of proceedings taken, where property is once brought under the control of the court by seizure.'' In non-judicial states, the lender does not have to go to the court to foreclose. Title companies usually handle Trustee sales. In some nonjudicial states like Minnesota, trustee sales are done by the Sheriff's department.

Some states use either judicial or non judicial processes. In Wisconsin, a judicial state, they used to allow foreclosures by advertisement until some sheriffs refused to conduct the sales and testified before the legislature that foreclosure by advertisement was a violation of the 14th Amendment and was unconstitutional. The legislature repealed the law allowing this kind of foreclosure.

In judicial states, you have the option of filing Complaint and becoming the plaintiff as a defendant. **In all non-judicial foreclosures, you must go on the offensive and sue as the Plaintiff,** or you will lose your property by mere advertisement of the lender and by the Trustee title company holding a sale.

SKELETON OUTLINE OF A CIVIL SUIT.

In civil proceeding, the following will occur if the case goes on trial. First, there will be a Summons served on you and a Complaint. The Complaint will be filed in the court where the trial is to be held. The next step your lender's attorney will take is called Discovery. (See Discovery pg. 189.) Third step is called Pretrial and the last is the trial, either tried before a jury or tried before the judge. Most court cases never go to trial. It is a statistical fact that 90% or better of all cases are settled out of court. These are the cases that survive what is known as a Motion to Dismiss hearing (also, called Demurrer). It is also a fact that most cases that never go to trial or are settled out of court are settled through Motion hearings. A Motion to Dismiss, if presented by the defendant and granted by the judge, ends a case unless there is an appeal. A Motion for Summary Judgment, if presented by the Plaintiff, and if granted by the judge, also ends a case unless there is an appeal. Appeals may or may not stay execution of judgment. The defendant is often required to put up a bond to cover the value of the judgment to stop seizure and sale of property to satisfy judgment. Often, when appeal is based on jurisdictional challenge, no bond is required to stay execution of judgment. Jurisdictional challanges are used when a defendant challenges the authority of the court to hear a case. This may be because of some prejudice or conflict of interest, such as when a judge has a mortgage lien on his home or property he owns with the same lender bank suing the defendant. You can find this out through local records at the town clerk's office. Also, defendant may challenge the authority of the court to hear his case because of some violation of the U.S. Constitution, state or federal law or local court rule in conflict with same. In judicial states, jurisdictional challenges have been used in Motion to Dismiss hearings to tie up cases in the courts for months, even years. Many issues can be raised in jurisdictional challenges and they vary so widely it would be impossible to list all of them. But here are a few:

1. Art. 1, Sec. 10 (U.S. Constitution)—Plaintiff did not tender his filing fees to the Clerk of Courts in gold or silver coins thus violating Art. 1, Sec. 10.

2. Plaintiff does not have a Certificate of Authority as a Corporation to do business in the state (is not registered with the Secretary or State or the Attorney General's Office or the State Corporation Commission).

3. Plaintiff names the wrong defendant (misspellings, wrong address, etc.)

4. Insufficiency of Process. Plaintiff did not serve defendant in a manner prescribed by state statute.

5. Plaintiff did not file an Affidavit of Service in the Court of Record.

6. Plaintiff did not state all the conditions required by the state statute in writing and filing the Affidavit of Service.

7. Plaintiff did not put a notary seal on the Affidavit.

8. Plaintiff should have filed in a federal court instead of a state court or vice versa.

9. Plaintiff did not afford a chance to settle with defendant under the bylaws of his corporation and thus denied administrative relief.

10. Plaintiff has failed to state a legitimate claim upon which relief can be granted.

11. Plaintiff has shown no injury or law broken by defendant of adverse effect on him.

12. Plaintiff has a note, but due to lack of consideration, cannot prove that the total amount of money lent adds up to the note's total value.

13. There is another action pending between the same parties for the same cause, and Plaintiff has failed to join all parties in the action as required by statute.

The above list is far from complete. You or your attorney can list other defenses that can be used in Motion to Dismiss hearings. Such defenses can be used if you are a defendant in an action started by a Plaintiff (lender) or as a Plaintiff (borrower) to get a Counterclaim filed against you dismissed.

Motions to Dismiss. After you have received a Summons, let us say your statute requires you to answer within 20 days. However, let us also say that you filed suit in a Complaint against your lender bank, 30 days earlier. Instead of answering the Summons and Complaint, you now file a Motion to Dismiss because of item #7, cited above, i.e., there is already another action pending between the parties for the same cause. The judge will have to agree and he will dismiss the complaint against you. The lender is left with the alternative to file an answer and counterclaim in your case against him or to file a Motion to Dismiss your action. If he does the latter, you are both back to ground Zero. Meanwhile negotiations can resume.

Get started with this kind of court room karate. Practical experience has shown one basic rule to follow in all states, both judicial and non-judicial is: If no Complaint has been filed against you, but you know foreclosure is impending, go on the offensive immediately and file your form of action (a Complaint) first. Always try to be the Plaintiff, instead of the defendant. The reason for doing this is that many attorneys will have to answer your Complaint and then file a counterclaim against you. This means the issues are joined and must go to trial. And you can demand a jury trial. It is an advantage to be the Plaintiff under these circumstances.

Understand, that if you are the defendent and you have let matters coast along until you have to file a Counterclaim against the lender plaintiff, and the judge dismisses your counterclaim, the issues the lender has raised will go to trial and your issue will not be given a hearing.

How to Reply to Bad Case Law. In replying to an attorney who brings up bad case law, we should counter with a deluge of case law that supports our position on the 7th Amendment and then support our position with our jury trial rights cited in the state constitution and in the state statutes. We must point out that court decisions made contrary to the intent of the framers of the 7th Amendment (to the Bill of Rights) were made without jurisdiction and are unconstitutional. The Constitution is your Rock. Use it to stand on or to throw.

In arguing any position in court, start off with your weakest arguments first and finish with your strongest arguments last. Your opponent may raise the argument that the proceeding is in equity and is therefore, triable only to the court. Your counter argument must be that your Complaint or Counterclaim is a "Suit at Common Law" and that this is the jurisdiction you invoked in your Complaint and that therefore, the attorney's arguments are without merit. It should be further pointed out that even in equity proceedings, jury trials are granted where there are material facts in dispute and that even though this proceeding is taking place in chancery or equity, there are material facts in dispute.

If the judge says that the proceeding is in equity, then you must state: "Your Honor, the term Equity is just another word for a suit at common law. Applying a different name here does not give justification to deny my right secured by the Constitution for a trial by jury."

Emergency Motion for a Court Determination of Jury Trial Demand. Be prepared. Have on hand and immediately file an Emergency Motion for a Court Determination of your Jury Trial Demand. Your Motion should contain arguments that focus on violations of your 5th, 7th and 14th amendment rights as well as violations of applicable sections of your state constitution. If the judge refuses to declare where he stands on your jury trial demand, then ask him this question: "What would be the earliest date, your Honor, that the court could schedule a jury trial?"

You will find out rather quickly where the judge stands. If the judge refuses to rule or decides against you, then seek advice of counsel as to how to get him off your case.

MEMORANDUM ON THE CREDIT ISSUE AND VOIDABLE CONTRACTS

This is a documentary, with exhibits in support, which will establish the following facts: 1. Privately owned banks are making loans of "credit" by writing checks with the intended purpose of circulating them as "money." 2. Other financial institutions are "laundering" checks which they receive directly or indirectly from commercial (privately owned) banks. 3. All this collective activity is unconstitutional, illegal, and a violation of common law, and the principles of natural equity.

This memorandum will, first of all, show that "money creation" by these privately-owned corporations is not really "money creation" at all, but the trade specialty and artful illusion of the law merchant who uses the trade secrets of the goldsmiths to entrap the borrower, as well as unjustly enrich himself. Issues based on both law and the principles of natural equity will be addressed in this memorandum.

THE GOLDSMITHS

In his book, *Money and Banking,* by Professor David R. Kamerschen, he writes: "The first bankers in the modern sense were the goldsmiths, who frequently accepted bullion and coins for storage...One result was that the goldsmiths temporarily could lend part of the gold left with them...These loans of their customers' gold were soon replaced by a revolutionary technique...When people brought in gold, the goldsmiths gave them notes promising to pay that amount of gold on demand. The notes, first made payable to the order of the individual, were later changed to bearer obligations. In the previous form, a note payable to the order of Harold Wait would be paid to no one else unless Wait had endorsed the note...But notes were soon being used in an unforeseen way. The noteholders found that, when they wanted to buy something, they could use the note itself in payment more conveniently and let the other person go after the gold, which the person rarely did...The specie, then, tended to remain in the goldsmiths' vaults...The goldsmiths began to realize that they might profit handsomely by issuing somewhat more notes than the amount of specie they held...These additional notes would cost the goldsmiths nothing except the negligible cost of printing them, yet the notes provided the goldsmiths with funds to let at interest...And they were to find that the profitability of their lending operations would exceed the profit from their original trade. The goldsmiths became bankers as their interest in manufacture was replaced by their concern with credit policies and lending activities...They discovered early that, although an unlimited note issue would be unwise, they could issue notes up to several times the amount of specie they held...the key to the whole operation lay in the public's willingness to leave gold and silver in the bank's vaults and use the bank's notes...This discovery is the basis of modern banking.''

In Ch. 5, Professor Kamerschen explains the evolution of the credit system further when he says: ''Later the goldsmiths learned a more efficient way to put their credit money into circulation. They lent by issuing additional notes, rather than by paying out in gold. In exchange for the interest-bearing note received from their customer, they gave their own noninterest bearing note. In effect, each was borrowing from the other...The advantage of the later procedure of lending notes rather than gold was that... more notes could be issued if the gold remained in the vaults...Thus, through the principle of bank note issue the banks learned to create money in the form of their own liabilities.''

Another publication which explains modern banking as derived from the goldsmiths is called *Modern Money Mechanics,* and is published by the Federal Reserve Bank of Chicago. On page 3 of the book, *Modern Money Mechanics,* it says: ''At one time, bankers were merely middlemen. They made a profit by accepting gold and coins brought to them for safekeeping and lending them to borrowers. But they soon found that the receipts they issued to depositors were being used as a means of payment... Then, bankers discovered that they could make loans merely by giving borrowers their promises to pay (bank notes). In this way, banks began to create money...Demand deposits are the modern counterpart of bank notes. It was a small step from printing notes to making book entries to the credit of borrowers which the borrowers, in turn, could 'spend' by writing checks.''

HOW BANKS CREATE MONEY

In the modern sense, banks create money by creating ''demand deposits.'' Demand deposits are merely ''book entries'' that reflect how much lawful money the bank owes its customers. Thus, all deposits are called demand deposits and are the bank's liabilities. The bank's assets are the vault cash plus all the ''IOUs'' or promissory notes the borrowers sign when they borrow either money or credit. When a bank lends its cash (money), it loans its assets, but when a bank lends its ''credit,'' it lends its liabilities. The borrowing of credit is, therefore, the exact opposite of the borrowing of cash (money).

At this point, to prevent confusion from entering the picture, we need to define the meaning of certain words like ''money,'' ''lawful money,'' and ''legal tender money.''

The term ''lawful money'' had its origin in Article 1, Sec. 8 and Article 1, Sec. 10 of the U.S. Constitution and under 12 USC 152 refers to ''gold and silver coin.'' The term ''legal tender'' was originally cited in 31 USCA 392 and is now recodified in 31 USCA 5103 and says: ''United States coins and currency... are legal tender for all debts, public charges, taxes, and dues.'' The common denominator in both lawful money and legal tender money is that they both are issued by the United States Government. However, we now come to the term ''money'' and find that there are now a whole range of definitions. We find that there are two forms of money—one is government issued and the other is privately issued. Since we have already discussed government issued forms of money, we need to look at privately issued forms of money.

All privately issued forms of money today are liabilities of the issuer. There are three common terms to describe privately created money. They are ''credit,'' ''demand deposits'' and ''checkbook money.'' For example, in the 5th edition of Blacks Law Dictionary, under the term ''Bank Credit,'' the word ''credit'' is described as follows: ''Money bank owes or will lend individual or person.'' It is quite clear from this definition that ''credit'' which is ''money bank owes'' is the bank's liability. The term ''check-book money'' is described in the book *I Bet You Thought*, published by the Federal Reserve Bank of New York, as follows: ''Commercial banks create checkbook money whenever they grant a loan, simply by adding deposit dollars to accounts on their books in exchange for the borrower's IOU...'' The word ''deposit'' and ''demand deposit'' both mean the same thing in bank terminology and refer again to the bank's liabilities. For example, the book, *Modern Money Mechanics* says: ''Deposits are merely book entries...Banks can build up deposits by increasing loans...Demand deposits are the modern counter-part of bank notes. It was a small step from printing notes to making book entries to the credit of bor-rowers which the borrowers, in turn, could 'spend' by writing checks.'' Thus, it can be seen that under the practice of fractional reserve banking, a deposit of $5,000 in cash could result in a loan of credit / check-book money / demand deposits of $100,000 at re-serves of 5%.

In a practical application, here is how it works. If a bank has ten people who each deposit $5,000 in cash (lawful money) and the bank keeps its reserves at 5%, then it will write out and lend twenty times this amount, or $1,000,000 in ''credit'' money. What the bank has actually done, however, is to write a check with the intended purpose of circulating it as ''money.'' The bank knows that if all the people who receive the check go to the bank and demand the cash, the bank will have to close its doors. It doesn't have the cash to back up its check. The bank's check will, however, pass as money as long as the people have confidence in it and they don't all run to the bank and demand the cash. When there are panics and people line up outside the bank and demand the cash, many banks will fold.

The process of passing checks as money is done quite simply. A deposit of $5,000 in cash by one person results in a loan of $100,000 to another person at 5% reserves. The person receiving the check or line of credit for $100,000 takes the check and deposits it in the same bank or in another bank. The check goes to the bookkeeping department where a book entry of $100,000 is added to that person's checking account. The person then spends these book entries (called demand deposits) by writing checks to others, who in turn deposit them and have book entries transferred to their checking accounts from the checking account of the person who wrote the check. The bank's origi-nal check that created the loan is then stamped ''Paid'' when the checking account of the person who de-posited the check is credited the dollar amount of the check. However, two questionable acts have now oc-curred. The first was when the bank wrote the check with insufficient funds to back it up, and the second is when the bank stamps its own check paid after merely crediting some person's account with some book entries they now call dollars. Ironically, the check seems good and passes as money—unless an emergency occurs.

DIFFERENT KINDS OF MONEY

The book called, *I Bet You Thought*, published by the Federal Reserve Bank of New York, says: ''Money is any generally accepted medium of ex-change, not simply coin and currency. Money doesn't have to be intrinsically valuable, be ISSUED BY A GOVERNMENT or be in any special form.'' Thus we see that privately issued forms of money only require public confidence to pass as money. Counterfeit money passes as money as long as nobody knows it is counterfeit. So likewise, checks pass as money as long as no one finds out they are bad. Yet, once the fraud is discovered, the value of such ''money,'' like bad checks, ceases to exist. There are, therefore, two kinds of money—government issued money and privately issued money.

DIFFERENT KINDS OF DOLLARS

The dollar once represented something real. In 1792, Congress defined the dollar as a silver coin con-taining 371.25 grains of pure silver. Since June 24, 1968, the dollar has ceased to exist and is now a fiction of law. The dollar today represents nothing more than a unit of measure like the ounce. An ounce must be an ounce of something, like an ounce of milk or an ounce of paper. The dollar is likewise a unit of meas-ure of different kinds of money. There is a dollar of pennies, a dollar of cash (lawful money), a dollar of debt, a dollar of credit and a dollar of checkbook money or demand deposits or a dollar of ''checks.'' When someone refers to a dollar spent or a dollar loaned, he must indicate what kinds of dollars he is talking about, since there are now so many different kinds. After all, a dollar of a ''promise to pay lawful money'' is the exact opposite of a dollar of ''lawful money.'' While the latter is an asset, the former is a liability. Thus, it can be seen from the earlier statement quoted from *I Bet You Thought* that money can be privately issued or, to quote from *I Bet You Thought*: ''Money doesn't have to...be issued by a government or be in any special form.'' (It should be noted here that those who issue and lend privately created money ask to be paid with government issued money.) Payment in like kind under natural equity indicates that a debt created by a loan of privately created money can be paid off with other privately created money, without regard for any special form, since there are no statutory regulations to indicate how private citizens can create money.

BY WHAT AUTHORITY

By what authority do banks as private corporations create money by lending their credit or more simply put—writing and passing checks as ''money''? Nowhere can a law be found that gives banks the authority to create money by lending their liabilities; so the next question is if they are in fact creating monies this way by passing checks, then where is their authority to do so? From their literature, they claim that their techniques were learned from the goldsmiths. It is evident, therefore, that money creation by private banks is not the result of powers conferred upon them by government, but rather the use of a long held trade secret. Thus, money creation is not being done by banks as corporations, but by bankers.

In addition, Article 1, Section 10, para. 1 of the U.S. Constitution specifically states that no state shall ''coin money, emit bills of credit, make anything but gold and silver coin a tender in payment of debts, pass any bill of attainder, ex post facto law, or law impairing the obligations of contracts.''

Obviously, the people never delegated to Congress or to any state government or agency the power to create, issue and pass credit off as money in the form of checks or any other form as a bill of credit. The Federal Government today does not authorize banks to emit, write, create, issue and pass such checks off as money. But banks do, and get away with it. Banks call their ''checks'' nicer names, like credit,

demand deposits, or checkbook money. However, credit money in the form of a check(s) really does not change the nature of what it is regardless of the terminology used. Such money though in common use is illegal under Art. 1, Sec. 10, para. 1 of the Constitution of the United States.

Rights Reserved. The various states have powers not delegated to the national (federal) government. Under the 9th Amendment, to the Constitution, the people have reserved certain rights, as inalienable.

THE ULTRA VIRES ISSUE

The courts have long held that when a corporation executes a contract beyond the scope of its corporate powers, it is void or ultra vires.

1. ''When a contract is once declared ultra vires, the fact that it is executed does not validate it, nor can it be ratified, so as to make it the basis of suit or action, nor does the doctrine of estoppel apply.'' *F & P R* v. *Richmond*, 133 SE 888; 144 SE 501, 151 Va 195.

2. ''Act is ultra vires when corporation is without authority to perform it under any circumstances or for any purpose. By doctrine of ultra vires a contract made by a corporation beyond the scope of its corporate powers is unlawful.'' *Community Fed S & L* v. *Fields*, 128 F 2nd 705.'' from Blacks Law Dictionary —5th edition.

3. ''A national bank...cannot lend its credit to another by becoming surety, indorser, or guarantor for him, such an act is ultra vires...'' *Merchants' Bank* v. *Baird*, 160 F 642.

THE ISSUE OF CONSIDERATION RECEIVED

The issue of who has the claim for relief when bad checks pass as money is easy to answer once the fraud is discovered, providing the check then ceases to circulate as ''money.'' It is the person holding the check at the time the fraudulent scheme collapses that without doubt has a claim for the money which the check represents. He has, no doubt, a claim for relief as the seller (holder in due course), as he gave value to the buyer (the borrower of credit from a bank).

The issue of whether the lender who writes and passes ''bad'' checks has a claim for relief against the borrower is also easy to answer providing the lender can prove that he gave a lawful consideration. Did the lender give a lawful consideration? To give a lawful consideration, the lender must prove that he gave the borrower lawful money such as coins or currency. Failing that, he can have no claim for relief in a court at law against the borrower as his actions were ultra vires.

The next question that will be raised is that because the borrower passed the "bad" check on to someone else and received goods and services from another party, this gives the lender his claim for relief against the borrower. The lender will argue that because the borrower had "confidence" in the check and the person who accepted the check from the borrower had "confidence" in the check, he should be allowed to take the borrower's property as payment for the debt. The lender will also argue that because his check passed as money, it was a valuable consideration, whether or not the check was good.

There can be no doubt that bad checks that pass as money are valuable; so are counterfeit coins and currency that pass as money. However, would a court of law allow a counterfeiter to foreclose against a person's home or farm because the borrower was late in his payments? If the court were to do so, it would be contrary to all principles of law. The question of valuable consideration does not depend on any value imparted by the lender, but by false confidence instilled in the "bad" check by the lender. In a court at law, the lender has no claim for relief. The final argument that because the borrower received property for his check, the lender has a claim for relief is not valid, unless the lender can prove that he is the party that gave real property such as goods and services. It is the holder in due course who is holding the bad check that has the claim for relief against either the borrower or the lender or both.

Since we have established that the holder in due course has a claim for relief, and the lender of counterfeit money has no claim for relief, the last question is, does the borrower have a claim for relief against the lender? First of all, it must be established that if the borrower has made no payments to the lender, then he has no claim for relief against the lender for money damages, but he may have a claim for relief to void the debts he owes to the lender for debts, notes and obligations unlawfully created. Also, the holder in due course has a claim for relief against the borrower and can demand the return for property given as a

consideration for the bad check he received. It is the, holder in due course, and not the lender that has the right to foreclose against the borrower. The borrower in turn has as a claim for relief against the lender to have the notes, security agreements, and mortgages notes he signed declared null and void. In addition, he may also have a claim for relief for breach of contract, for not lending lawful money, and for usury for charging an interest several times greater than the amount agreed to in the contract for the lawful money actually risked by the lender. He may also have a claim for relief under Federal Racketeering laws (18 USC 1964), as the lender may have established a "pattern of racketeering activity" by using U.S. Mail more than twice to collect on an unlawful debt in violation of 18 USC 1341, 1343 and 1961 and 1962. These are some of the claims for relief which the borrower has against a lender of "credit" and / or checks; and he may have more if he can prove there was or is a conspiracy to deprive him and other Americans of property without due process of law. Such additional claims for relief would be under 42 USC 1983 et seq.

The following excerpts address the definition of money.

1. "A check is merely an order on a bank to pay money." *Young* v. *Hembree*, 73 P 2nd 393.

2. "Both notes and checks are acknowledgments of indebtedness and promise of payment. *Hegeman* v. *Moon*, 131 NY 462, 30 NE 487." *Smith* v. *Treuhart et al.*, 223 NYS 481.

3. "In the federal courts, it is well established that a national bank has not power to lend its credit to another by becoming surety, indorser, or guarantor for him." *Farmers and Miners Bank* v. *Bluefield Nat'l Bank*, 11 F 2nd 83, 271 US 669.

4. "checks, drafts, money orders, and bank notes are not lawful money of the United States." *State* v. *Neilon*, 73 Pac 321, 43 Ore 168.

5. "Neither, as included in its powers not incidental to them, is it a part of a bank's business to lend its credit. If a bank could lend its credit as well as its money, it might, if it received compensation and was careful to put its name only to solid paper, make a great deal more than any lawful interest on its money would amount to. If not careful, the power would be the mother of panics, . . . Indeed, lending credit is the exact opposite of lending money, which is the real business of a bank, for while the latter creates a

liability in favor of the bank, the former gives rise to a liability of the bank to another. 1 Morse, Banks and Banking, 5th Ed, Sec 65; Magee, Banks and Banking, 3rd Ed, Sec 248.'' *American Express Co. v. Citizens State Bank*, 194 NW 429.

6. Justice Marshall wrote: ''The doctrine of ultra vires is a most powerful weapon to keep private corporations within their legitimate spheres and to punish them for violations of their corporate charters, and it probably is not invoked too often...*Zinc Carbonate Co. v. First National Bank*, 103 Wis 125, 79 NW 229'' *American Express Co., v. Citizens State Bank*, 194 NW 430.

7. ''A bank can lend its money, but not its credit.'' *First Nat'l Bank of Tallapoosa v. Monroe*, 135 Ga 614, 69 SE 1123, 32 LRA (NS)f 550.

8. ''It is not within those statutory powers for a national bank, even though solvent, to lend its credit to another in any of the various ways in which that might be done.'' *Federal Intermediate Credit Bank v. L' Herisson*, 33 F 2nd 841. (1929)

9. ''A national bank, under federal law being limited in its powers and capacity, cannot lend its credit by guaranteeing the debts of another, and all such contracts entered into are ultra vires.'' *Howard & Foster Co. v. Citizens Nat'l Bank of Union*, 133 SC 202, 130 SE 758.

10. ''A bank may not lend its credit to another, even though such a transaction turns out to have been of benefit to the bank, and in support of this a list of cases might be cited, which would look like a catalog of ships.'' *Norton Grocery Co. v. Peoples Nat. Bank*, 144 SE 501, 151 Va 195.

11. ''There is no doubt but what the law is that a national bank cannot lend its credit or become an accommodation endorser.'' *National Bank of Commerce v. Atkinson*, 55 Fed Rep 465.

12. (A national bank has no power to lend its credit; *Bowen v. Needles Nat. Bank*, 94 F 925, 36 CCA 553, certiorari denied in 20 S.Ct 1024, 176 US 682, 44 LED 637)

13. (A national bank has no power to lend its credit by guaranteeing a letter of credit; *Seligmaa v. Charlottesville Nat. Bank*, 3 Hughes 647, Fed Case No. 12,642)

14. ''In *Parsons v. Fox*, 179 Ga 605, 176 SE 642, the court said: (A loan may be defined as the delivery by one party to, and the receipt by another party of, a sum of money upon an agreement, express or implied, to repay the sum with or without interest.)'' *Kirkland v. Bailey*, 155 SE 2nd 701. (Also see *United States v. Neifert White Co.*, 247 Fed Supp 878)

15. ''The word 'money' in its usual and ordinary acceptation means gold, silver, or paper money used as a circulating medium of exchange...'' *Lane v. Railey*, 280 Ky 319, 133 SW 2nd 74.

16. ''A promise to pay cannot, by argument, however ingenious, be made the equivalent of actual payment...'' *Christensen v. Beebe*, 91 P 129, 32 Utah 406.

17. ''A bank is not the holder in due course upon merely crediting the depositors account.'' *Bankers Trust v. Nagler*, 229 NYS 2nd 142.

18. ''A holder who does not give value cannot qualify as a holder in due course.'' Uniform Commercial Code 3–303:1

19. ''It has never been doubted that a note given on a consideration which is prohibited by law is void. It has been determined, independent of the acts of Congress, that sailing under the license of an enemy is illegal. The emission of bills of credit upon the books of private corporations for the purpose of private gain is not warranted by the Constitution of the United States and is unlawful. (See *Craig v. Mo*, 4 Peters 912). This court can tread only that path which is marked by duty.'' *First Nat'l Bank of Montgomery v. Jerome Daly*, Credit River, Minnesota, 1968. Honorable Martin Mahoney, Justice of the Peace.

20. ''Each Federal Reserve Bank is a separate corporation owned by commercial banks in its region...'' *Lewis v. United States*, 680 F 2nd 1239. (1982 case)

21. ''If any part of the consideration for a promise be illegal, or if there are several considerations for an unseverable promise one of which is illegal, the promise, whether written or oral, is wholly void, as it is impossible to say what part or which one of the considerations induced the promise (Cases Cited)...The contract is void if it is only in part connected with the illegal transaction and the promise single or entire.'' *Menominee River B Co. v. Augustus Spies L & C Co.*, 147 Wis 559, 572; 132 NW 1118. (Also see *Guardian Agency v. Guardian Mut. Savings Bank*, 227 Wis 550; *Ebenreiter v. Freeman*, 274 Wis 290)

22. ''It is not necessary for recision of a contract that the party making the misrepresentation should have known that it was false, but recovery is allowed

even though misrepresentation is innocently made, because it would be unjust to allow one who made false representations, even innocently, to retain the fruits of a bargain induced by such representations." *Whipp* v. *Iverson*, 43 Wis 2nd 166.

23. "Any false representation of material facts made with knowledge of falsity and with intent that it shall be acted on by another in entering into contract, and which is so acted upon, constitutes 'fraud,' and entitles party deceived to avoid contract or recover damages." *Barnsdall Refining Corp.* v. *Birnamwood Oil Co.*, 92 F 2nd 817

24. "Where principal's assent is induced by creditor's fraudulent or material misrepresentation, contract is voidable by principal if he is justified in relying on misrepresentation." *Baumgarten* v. *Bubolz*, 104 Wis 2nd 210.

25. "Any conduct capable of being turned into a statement of fact is representation. There is no distinction between misrepresentations effected by words and misrepresentations effected by other acts." *Leonard* v. *Springer*, 197 Ill 532, 64 NE 299.

Fractional Reserve Checks. The author does not subscribe to the use of Fractional Reserve Checks as payment in kind for the check a borrower received from a lender using such a check as "credit money." Two wrongs do not make a right. And it is an axiom of equity that you come into court with clean hands, or you will not prevail. Stand above every appearance of wrong-doing when you stand in court and wish to elicit the sympathy as well as the fairness in trial given you by a judge. An example of a Fractional Reserve check has been given you; if you choose to use it as payment in kind for what you have received from a lender, you must be prepared to accept full responsibility for the issues it may raise.

Legal Karate

INSTRUCTIONS: HOW TO USE FRACTIONAL RESERVE CHECKS*

Dec 7, 1984: Fractional Reserve Checks are designed for the sole purpose of paying off unlawful debts, which were based on credit or checkbook money created by private banks or FR Checks are to be used

---

*An FRC is nothing but an I.O.U.

to pay off debts when there is probable cause to believe that the financial institution that made the loan obtained the credit or checkbook money from a bank who in turn had created it. Types of debts where F R Checks may be used are as follows: any bank loan or bank credit card, providing you did not receive cash from the use of the credit card or check you received from a bank. In that case, you must deduct the cash you received from the total debt. However, if you have paid off more of the debt than cash you received, then you may use a F R Check to pay off the balance of the loan. F R Checks may also be used to pay off Federal Land Bank, Production Credit Association and FmHA loans as there is probable cause to believe that all their credit that they loaned out had previously been created and transferred to them by a bank. Finance companies and mortgage companies and S & L's may also be paid with F R Checks as in many instances, the bulk of their credit was also created by a private bank and transferred to them through the vehicle of loans or purchases of mortgage notes, security agreements or deeds of trust. F. R. Checks are not to be used to pay off Gas or Department Store credit cards or to purchase any goods or services or to pay taxes. For example, a Sears credit card is different from a bank credit card, in that you receive a valuable consideration in the form of a tool or other item. Sears did not lend you their credit, but the right to use their goods. Sears accepted your credit in return. No money was created in this type of transaction. A bank loan is different. The bank accepts your credit and then gives you a check which is the bank's credit. There is no lawful consideration tendered as credit and checkbook money are not legal tender. The bank writes checks beyond its customers' deposits and intends these checks to circulate as money as people deposit these checks and write more checks which transfer book entries from one bank account to another. Now, people can create their own credit and checkbook money, as banks do, with the mere stroke of a pen, by using FR Checks and Certificates of Credit and pay off all these illegal loans.

It is recommended that you type or rubber stamp your name and address in the lower right corner of the check. Sign it and date it and fill out the dollar amount. Mail the check to the bank or other credit lender with a cover letter. There are two samples enclosed, one for banks and another for other financial institutions. When the bank comes to you to redeem the F R Check, then you take it and write out a Certificate of Credit. You hand them the Certificate of Credit and then stamp the FR Check ''Paid,'' for your records. If they want to cash the Certificate of Credit, then you hand them another F R Check and this can go on and on. The F R Checks do not promise lawful or legal tender money, but only credit and the Certificate of Credit only promise checkbook money in the form of F R Checks. So, you see, it is a closed loop. There is also a Memorandum on our inalienable right to make payments in a like kind of money. This material should be useful to defend your position in the courts. After you have paid off your mortgage, if the lenders refuse to accept your F R Check and try a court action against you, then you should file a Motion to Dismiss and challenge jurisdiction as they lack capacity to sue. (See model motion to dismiss enclosed). When and if the judge rules against you, file an Answer and Counterclaim. Support it with an Affidavit. A sample one is enclosed. In your Counterclaim, demand a trial by jury and pay for one at the clerk of courts office. Study the oral arguments paper.

By using the FR checks and by answering the complaint and denying that we are delinquent or by simply stating that we have paid off the entire debt, we have created a fact in dispute. This is especially true if we support our answer by affidavit. This is like throwing a gauntlet down before the king. We simply say: either give us a trial by jury so we can prove our credit is just as lawful as the bank's or charge us with perjury. Be careful how the Affidavit is worded—a sample is enclosed that I believe, in good faith, is safe to use. Our arguments are based on the common law principle of natural equity—payment in like kind of money.

While anyone can get a jury trial in a criminal proceeding, the courts grant jury trials in civil proceedings at their discretion, even though this is contrary to our 7th amendment right to a trial by jury and these judges are sworn under oath to uphold our 7th amendment rights and all other rights enumerated in the U.S. Constitution. The courts tell us that there must be facts in dispute before they will give us jury trials in a civil proceeding. With the use of F R Checks, and an Affidavit that we have paid the debt off, we now clearly have a fact in dispute. If the courts

ignore our Affidavits and jury trial demands and still grant judgments, we may claim reversible error, and we should appeal all such decisions. We can claim that the debt is paid and that since we support that statement with an Affidavit and no one has charged us with perjury, this case should have gone to trial. We should ask the Appellate Courts to order a new trial, consistent with all of our Constitutional rights.

Another recommended use for F R Checks is to outbid the banks or credit lenders at the sheriff or trustee sales, and again to demand a jury trial at the hearing on completion of the sheriff sale. Another party should bid 21 silver dollars at the same time. The person bidding the silver should then sue the sheriff and file a lis pendens on the land and property and, of course, demand a jury trial to determine who made the high bid in lawful money. The person bidding silver should name the bank and the party using the F R Checks as defendants and ask that a jury strike both of their bids as being contrary to Art. 1, Sec. 10, U.S. Constitution. The defendant who uses the F R check should file a Cross Complaint and ask for a jury trial to prove that the bank's bid was pure credit like his and that they had written a bad check as they did not have the cash to back up the check. That is a fact. If the banks and credit lenders had to bid cash at all the foreclosure auctions, many banks would fold up, as the cash doesn't exist. This concludes the instructions. One last note: if you live in a deed of trust state or have a state where non-judicial foreclosures are allowed, that is, they just advertise and sell; then you must pay off the debt with a FR Check and then sue the bank or credit lender for not giving you a clear title. Use Affidavits to support the fact you paid off the debt by returning payment in a like kind of money. An alternative plan to stop a sheriff or trustee sale is described below.

HOW TO USE FRCs TO STOP A SHERIFF OR TRUSTEE SALE

To stop a sheriff's sale in a state that has judicial foreclosures (that is, they go to court and get a judgment against you which is followed by a redemption period), do the following:

1. Pay off your credit lender per Cover letter #1 or #2 (see p. 102).

2. Send a copy of this cover letter to the sheriff by Certified Mail with an Affidavit in support and attach to this a Constructive Notice (Sample on page

SAMPLE COVER LETTER #1

(DATE)

Dear (BANK):

   Enclosed is a check for the sum of $. as full payment,
in like kind of money, for property located at:_____.
Please send me a receipt. A stamped self addressed envelope is
enclosed for your convenience.

Sincerely yours,

(NAME)

SAMPLE COVER LETTER #2

(DATE)

Dear (MORTGAGE COMPANY/FLB/PCA/ETC.):

   Enclosed is a check for the sum of $. as full payment,
in like kind of money, for the existing debt for a loan of credit made
to me on (DATE OF THE LOAN). Kindly send the (MORTGAGE NOTE, NOTE,
SECURITY AGREEMENTS, ETC.) back to me stamped "Paid".

Sincerely Yours,

(NAME)

P.S. If you choose not to present this check to me for redemption, you
can simply endorse the check "Pay to the Order of" any bank that you
have previously borrowed or received "credit" from as a tender for
that debt. If you have any further questions, contact me per the above
address. Thank you.

103). If the sheriff still won't stop the sale, then hand him a Title 42, U.S.C. 1983 lawsuit in Federal Court for depriving you of property in violation of your 14th amendment Constitutional rights. Present your lawsuit to the sheriff as soon as it is written and no later than the morning of the sale.

3. Another option is to remove the existing case to Federal Court just before the sheriff's sale and file a motion for consolidation of cases in Federal Court.

HOW TO STOP TRUSTEE SALES IN NON-JUDICIAL FORECLOSURE STATES

1. Send an FRC and a cover letter to your credit lender per Cover #1 or #2 above.

2. Send an Affidavit and a constructive Notice worded similar to the sample shown below and mail it or have it personally delivered to the Title Co. conducting the sale. That should stop it. Otherwise, file your Title 42 suit against the Title Co. and use the credit issue and sue the credit lender and file a lis pendens in court.

3. Since you have no existing case to remove to Federal Court, unless they start an action in ejectment against you, there is something else you can do to cloud the title even more. Write up a Quit Claim deed and deed some portion of your interest in the property to another party. Quit Claim Deed forms are available from your local Legal Blank Co. To fill it out, you simply state something like this: "Seller conveys, grants and deeds to [name of buyer] one half / one quarter / one tenth / etc. undivided interest in the following described property":

Follow this with the address and a legal description. Have it notarized and have the buyer (a friend or relative or neighbor) file it in the register of deeds office at your county courthouse. After it is filed, send a photocopy to the title company that won't stop the sale. Don't do this, however, until after you have first mailed them the FRC. It doesn't matter what they do with the FRC or even if they mail it back. Once you mail the FRC, payment in a like kind of money has been made and you can sell a partial interest in your property to anyone you please.

SAMPLE LETTER/AFFIDAVIT/ACTUAL NOTICE TO THE SHERIFF

Dear Sheriff (NAME):

Reference: pending sheriff sale for property located at:

_____.

Please take notice that the creditor, the (NAME OF LENDER FORECLOSING) has been paid in full on (DATE OF MAILING FRC). A check for the full amount of credit on the loan/judgment has been sent by Certified Mail. I affirm that this statement is true and correct. This letter is notarized and is to be construed as an affidavit. If you have any further questions, do not hesitate to contact me.

(DATE)   Sincerely yours,
                           (NAME)
                           (Add Notary Public's Seal and signature here)

(If the sheriff refuses to cancel the sale because of some behind the scenes maneuvers from the lender, send him this Constructive Notice.)

SAMPLE ANSWER TO COMPLAINT

Now comes the defendant,...and Answers the Complaint as follows:

1. Defendant admits that his name is...as stated in paragraph 1 of the Complaint.

2. Defendant admits he lives at....

3. Defendant denies he was loaned dollars of either legal tender or lawful money of the United States. Defendant admits he was loaned credit and checkbook money for the sum of $..., but that said credit and checkbook money was created by a private corporation.

4. Defendant admits he signed a [mortgage note or deed of trust] on ....

5. Defendant denies that he is delinquent in his payments as he has paid off the entire loan by returning payment, in like kind of money, for the sum of $... which payment was made on... (check #...).

Date ....   X...

SAMPLE AFFIDAVIT IN SUPPORT OF ANSWER

State of   )
) SS
 ?   County   )

I, ...[your name], being duly sworn on oath, deposes and states the following:

1. I am the defendant in this cause of action in Case #....

2. I am a layman and without any law school training.

3. I wrote the Answer to Complaint and Counterclaim which was filed with the court on....

4. The contents of the Answer and Counterclaim are true and correct, to the best of my knowledge and belief.

5. As of this date,...the [mortgage or deed of trust] has been paid in full with check #...sent on...which check has returned payment in like kind of money.

6. The debt that was paid off was based on a consideration of credit or checkbook money, created by a private bank, and did not consist of either lawful or legal tender money of the United States. This [mortgage note or deed of trust] has been paid in full by tendering credit and checkbook money to the lender for the full value remaining on the debt.

7. This Affidavit in not done for the purposes of delay and further; I am a competent witness and can testify to the above.

X...

Subscribed and sworn to before me, a Notary Public for the State of...on this...day of..., 19....

Notary Public...My Commission expires....

From:

FACSIMILE OR ACTUAL NOTICE supported by AFFIDAVIT

To Sheriff:

This letter is in reference to Case No._____ and a sheriff sale which is pending on property located at _____. The judgment / mortgage note / deed of trust note has been paid in full. Payment in full in like kind of money was made on [date] for the sum of [$?]. Since this property is scheduled to be sold on the courthouse steps on [date], I am notifying you that the debt has been paid in full so that this sale will be cancelled. I would apprecate it if you would send me a letter confirming cancellation of the sale.

This letter is notarized and is therefore an affidavit. The contents of this letter are true and correct, to the best of my knowledge and belief.

If there is any communications from the attorney for the lender that contradicts any statements made in this letter, I am requesting that you ask the attorney for an affidavit to support any position contrary to the facts stated in this letter, as the lender has thus far refused to stamp the notes ''paid'' and return them to me as I have requested. A civil action against the lendet is currently being drafted [or was filed on ?]. Should you have any questions concerning this letter, feel free to call me at [your phone No.] or write to me per the above address.

sincerely yours,
[your name and address]

Add Notary statement and seal here

MUTUAL RELEASE AND COVENANT NOT TO SUE

This mutual release and covenant not to sue is entered into this 7th day of December, 1984, by and between JOHN DOE and JANE DOE, his wife, and the FARMERS NATIONAL BANK.

WHEREAS, JOHN DOE and JANE DOE are currently indebted to the FARMERS NATIONAL BANK in the amount of $536,161.48 including principal and interest and overdrafts, by virtue of various loans made by the FARMERS NATIONAL BANK to JOHN DOE and JANE DOE all as evidenced by copies of said notes attached hereto and made a part hereof by reference.

WHEREAS, JOHN DOE and JANE DOE have pledged as security for said promissory notes certain livestock, farm machinery, equipment and motor vehicles and as further security executed a mortgage on certain of their real estate, all as evidenced by copies of security agreements, inventories and mortgages attached hereto and made a part hereof by reference.

WHEREAS, JOHN DOE and JANE DOE are unable to pay said indebtedness to the FARMERS NATIONAL BANK but desire to make some compromise of said debt to avoid litigation.

NOW THEREFORE IN CONSIDERATION of their mutual releases, promises and covenants not to sue the undersigned hereby agree as follows:

1. JOHN DOE and JANE DOE, his wife hereby agree to voluntarily transfer to the Farmers National Bank, Osborne, Kansas, any and all personal property which is now pledged as security for various loans made by the FARMERS NATIONAL BANK to JOHN DOE and JANE DOE. Property to be transferred will be as set out in the various security agreements and inventories attached hereto and made a part hereof by reference. All property to be removed in the presence of either JOHN DOE or JANE DOE, or with the verbal consent of either of them.

2. JOHN DOE and JANE DOE will assist the FARMERS NATIONAL BANK in every way possible, including providing the use of their hog facilities for a period not to exceed 90 days from December 7, 1984, on the unit, and 110 days on the feeding floor with the joint goal of all parties being to market said hogs at the most profitable time possible. The feeding, care and marketing of said hogs would be at the expense of the FARMERS NATIONAL BANK. JOHN DOE and JANE DOE further agree to not interfere or do anything to hinder the sale of the farm machinery and equipment transferred pursuant to this agreement. In the event said Bank shall exceed the 90 day limit on the use of the unit it agrees to pay as rental to JOHN DOE and JANE DOE the sum of $74.63 per day. In the event said Bank shall exceed the 110 day limit on the use of the feeding floor, it agrees to pay JOHN DOE and JANE DOE the sum of $30.00 per day.

At such time as the Bank shall sell all the hogs in place in either the unit or the feeding floor then its responsibility for rent shall cease. In the event of damages to the unit or feeding floor during the tenure of the Bank, then said Bank shall be responsible for payment of damages to JOHN DOE and JANE DOE. Damages shall not mean ordinary wear and tear.

3. The FARMERS NATIONAL BANK agrees to release any and all real estate mortgages which it now holds against real estate owned by JOHN DOE and JANE DOE and to return all outstanding promissory notes in favor of FARMERS NATIONAL BANK signed by JOHN DOE and JANE DOE with same being shown as paid in full.

4. JOHN DOE and JANE DOE and the FARMERS NATIONAL BANK hereby release, acquit and forever discharge each other from any and all actions, causes of action, claims, demands, costs, losses, expenses, compensation and deficiencies, whether known or unknown, on account of, or in any way growing out of the relationship between said parties as Borrower and Lender, said relationship having been in existence from since 1964.

This release binds the heirs, executors, administrators, successors and assigns of each of the parties hereto.

Witness our hands and seal this 7th day of December, 1984.

FARMERS NATIONAL BANK
Osborne, Kansas

By: _____

Title: _____

_____

John Doe

_____

Jane Doe

STATE OF KANSAS, OSBORNE COUNTY, SS:

Be it remembered, That on this 7th day of December, 1984, before me, the undersigned, a Notary Public in and for the County and State aforesaid came Stephen Banker, Vice President of Farmers National Bank, a corporation duly organized, incorporated and existing under and by virtue of the laws of the State of Kansas, who is personally known to me to be the same person who executed, as such officer, the within instrument of writing on behalf of said corporation, and such person duly acknowledged the execution of the same to be the Act and deed of said corporation.

In Testimony Whereof, I have hereunto set my hand, and affixed my official seal the day and year last above mentioned.

[Seal]   _____

Notary Public

Note: In an exclusive interview, the real "John Doe" told me that all the bank got was $165,000 worth of equipment and hogs in exchange for cancelling the $536,161.48 debt! Jan-85-C.E.L. Editor-P.I.N.

SAMPLE AFFIDAVIT IN SUPPORT OF MEMORANDUM OF LAW ON CONSTITUTIONAL MONEY.

JOHN DOE DOES HEREBY AFFIRM AND STATE THE FOLLOWING:

1. That I am the petitioner in this cause.
2. That I am a layman without any law school training.
3. That the contents of the Petition for Judicial Reviww and this MEMORANDUM are true and correct, to the best of my knowledge and belief.
4. That this Petition and Memorandum are not presented for the purposes of delay but presented in good faith as a challenge to the Defendant of Record's complaint or cross complaint.
5. That I truly believe that this Petition and Memorandum are proper legal challenges to the Respondent's complaint.
6. That I am a competent witness and can testify to the above, if called.

X _____

John Doe

(L . S .)

State of _____

County _____) ss.

Subscribed and sworn to before me,
this _____ day of July, 1984.

_____

Notary Public, State of
My Commission expires _____

MEMORANDUM ON CONSTITUTIONAL MONEY

The writer of this brief will establish through historical evidence as well as decisions of the U.S. Supreme Court and other courts all of the following points.

1. The Constitution and the intent of our founding fathers mandated a monetary system based on the precious metals of gold and silver coin.

2. This brief will establish the difference between a DOLLAR, A NOTE AND A BILL OF CREDIT.

3. This brief will establish the difference between "lawful money" and "legal tender."

4. This brief will establish that irredeemable Federal Reserve Notes are not "legal tender" for States to use, when objected to, in the nature of taxes or involuntary contributions.

5. This brief will establish that HJR 192, passed on June 5th, 1933 and 31 U.S.C. 405(a-3) which became fully effective on June 24, 1968 do not invalidate the provisions of Article 1, § 10 which say: "No State Shall Make any thing but Gold and Silver Coin a Tender in Payment of Debts."

6. This brief will establish that the Constitution of U.S. cannot be legally amended by changing the rules through executive, legislative and judicial fiat.

7. This brief will establish that only the States have the power to declare what is to be a legal tender subject to the prohibitions of Art. 1, § 10.

HISTORICAL EVIDENCE

At the drafting of the U.S. Constitution at the Federal Convention in Philadelphia on Aug. 16, 1787, the following is excerpted from the writings of James Madison when a discussion arose as to the wording or Art. 1, § 8. The proposed wording was as follows:

"The Legislature of the United States shall have the power to . . . coin money . . . and emit bills on the credit of the United States."

After this, a hot argument ensued on the power to "emit bills on the credit of the United States." In his diary, James Madison wrote:

[Mr. G. Morris moved to strike out "and emit bills of credit." If the United States had credit such bills would be unnecessary; if they had not, unjust and useless.

MADISON: Will it not be sufficient to prohibit the making them a tender? This will remove the temptation to emit them with unjust views. And promissory notes in that shape may in some emergencies be best.

MORRIS: Striking out the words will leave room still for notes of a responsible minister which will do all the good without the mischief. The Monied interest will oppose the plan of Government, if paper emissions be not prohibited.

COL. MASON: Though he had a mortal hatred to paper money, yet as he could not foresee all emergencies, he was unwilling to tie the hands of the Legislature.

MR. MERCER: It was impolitic to excite the opposition of all those who were friends to paper money.

MR. ELLSWORTH thought this was favorable to shut and bar the door against paper money. The mischiefs of the various experiments which had been made, were now fresh in the public mind and had excited the disgust of all the respectable part of America. By withholding the power from the new Government more friends of influence would be gained to it than by almost anything else . . . Give the Government credit, and other resources will offer. The power may do harm, never good.

MR. WILSON: It will have a most salutary influence on the credit of the United States to remove the possibility of paper money. This expedient can never succeed whilst its mischiefs are remembered, and as long as it can be resorted to, it will be a bar to other resources.

MR. READ, thought the words, if not struck out, WOULD BE AS ALARMING AS THE BEAST IN REVELATION.

MR. LANGDON had rather reject the whole plan than retain the three words "and emit bills."]

—The motion for striking out carried—   .

The court is asked here to take judicial notice that even as Art. 1, § 8 was drafted, the intent of our founding fathers who wrote the Constitution was that in granting Congress the power to "coin money," the power to emit or print irredeemable money was never granted.

"The intent of the legislators constitutes the law" *Stewart* vs. *Kahn*, 11 Wall (78 U.S.) 493.

On Aug. 28, 1787, the proposed working of Art. 1, § 10 was as follows:

"No state shall coin money; nor grant letters of marque and reprisal; nor enter into any Treaty, alliance, or confederation; not grant any title of Nobility.''

James Madison's account of the reaction to this is as follows:

[MR. WILSON & MR. SHERMAN moved to insert the words "coin money" the words "nor emit bills of credit, nor make any thing but gold and silver coin a legal tender in payment of debts" making these prohibitions absolute, instead of making the measures allowable with the consent of the Legislature of the U.S.

MR. SHERMAN thought this a favorable crisis for crushing paper money. If the consent of the Legislature could authorize emissions of it, the friends of paper money would make every exertion to get into the Legislature in order to license it.]

Roger Sherman was a delegate and was a JUDGE from the State of Connecticut. The court is asked to take a judicial notice here that the intent of Art. 1, § 10 is self evident as is written in the notes on the Federal Convention of 1787, by James Madison.

MINT ACT OF 1792

On April 5th, 1792, when the Congress assembled, they passed "An Act establishing a Mint, and regulating the Coins of the United States."

In part they established the Dollars as follows: "each to be of the value of the Spanish milled dollar as the same is now current, and to contain three hundred and seventy-one and four sixteenths grains of pure...silver." The act also established for half dollars and quarters and dismes (dimes) and half dismes all of which contained a proportional amount of pure silver. Also, there were eagles, half eagles and quarter eagles all made of pure gold, the eagle having a value of ten dollars. It was further enacted that "all gold and silver coins which shall have been struck at, and issued from the said mint, shall be a lawful tender in all payments whatsoever."

It further stated: "That if any of the gold or silver coins which shall be struck or coined at the said mint shall be debased...every such officer or person who shall commit any or either of the said offenses, shall be guilty of felony, and shall suffer death."

According to the mint act of 1792, a dollar looks as follows:

The above pictures are of a 1923 silver dollar and this dollar or its equivalent in two half dollars of silver or four quarters or ten dimes represents a dollar's worth of "lawful tender" as defined by the mint act of April 2, 1792.

CIVIL WAR LEADS TO PAPER MONEY

The war between the States in 1860 under the administration of President Abraham Lincoln led to the first issuance of United States Notes as the Government's first irredeemable paper money. A shortage of money to finance the war led President Lincoln to make a crucial decision. The bankers offered to lend Lincoln their privately issued Notes, and there was a shortage of gold and silver coin to finance the war. Lincoln told the bankers, we can print up that stuff ourselves and he did. United States Notes (greenbacks) were issued by the Government and the war was financed without creating a national interest bearing debt due to the banks. Sometime after the war, the U.S. Notes were made redeemable in gold coins at a New York office of the U.S. Treasury Dept. These United States Notes were declared to be "legal tender for all debts, public and private."

The decision of the Lincoln administration to print United States Notes not redeemable at the time they were issued in specie ran contrary to earlier Supreme Court decisions, some of which are as follows:

"The prohibitions not to make anything but gold and silver coin a tender in payment of debts, and not to pass any law impairing the obligations of contracts, were inserted to secure private rights." *Calder* v. *Bull*, 3 Dall 20 (1798)

"Was the general prohibition intended to prevent paper money. We are not allowed to say so because it is expressly provided that no state shall 'emit bills of credit' neither could these words be intended to restrain the states from enabling debtors to discharge their debts by the tender of property of no real value to the creditor because for that subject also particular provision is made. Nothing but gold and silver coin can be a tender in payment of debts.'' *Sturges* v. *Crowninshield,* 4 Wheat. 122, 17 U.S. 122 (1819)

It declares that 'no state shall coin money, emit bills of credit, make any thing but gold and silver coin a tender in payment of debts.' These prohibitions, associated with the powers of Congress to 'coin money, and to regulate the value thereof'...most obviously constitute members of the same family, being upon the same subject and governed by the same policy.

''This policy was to provide a fixed and uniform standard of value throughout the United States... should be regulated. For it might well be asked, why vest Congress the power to establish a uniform standard of value by the means pointed out, if the states might use the same means, and this defeat the uniformity of the standard and, consequently, the standard itself? And why establish a standard at all, for the government of the various contracts which might be entered into, if those contracts might afterwards be discharged by a different standard, or by that which is not money, under the authority of tender laws.'' *Ogden* v. *Saunders,* 12 Wheat. 213, 25 U.S. 213 (1827)

''The Constitution, therefore, considers the emission of bills of credit and the enactment of tender laws as distinct operations, independent of each other which may be separately performed. Both are forbidden.'' *Craig* v. *Missouri,* 29 U.S. 410 (1830)

''If the medium which the government was authorized to create and establish could immediately be expelled, and substituted by one it had neither created, estimated nor authorized—one possessing no intrinsic value—then the power conferred by the Constitution would be useless—wholly fruitless of every end it was designed to accomplish. Whatever functions Congress are, by the Constitution, authorized to perform, they are, when the public good requires it, bound to perform...'' *United States* v. *Marigold,* 50 U.S. 560 (1850)

On Dec. 5th, 1836, President Andrew Jackson made the following statement in reference to this:

''It is apparent from the whole context of the Constitution, as well as the history of the times which gave birth to it, that it was the purpose of the Convention to establish a currency consisting of the precious metals. These, from their peculiar properties which rendered them the standard of value in all other countries, were adopted in that as well to establish its commercial standard in reference to foreign countries by a permanent rule as to exclude the use of a mutable medium of exchange, such as certain agricultural commodities recognized by the statutes of some states as a tender for debts, or the still more pernicious expedient of paper currency.''

In addition to the above, the Supreme Courts of several States recognized that only gold and silver coins were the Constitutional currency. The following are a list of some of the cases:

STATE CASES

''the best Bank paper passes as money by consent only, and it cannot be otherwise so long as the inhibition of the Federal Constitution upon the rights of the States to dispense with gold and silver as the only lawful tender continues in force.'' *Carter and Carter* v. *Penn,* 4 Ala. 140 (1812)

''Bank issues are not, in the constitutional sense of the term, lawful money or legal coin. Gold and silver alone are a legal tender in payment of debts, and the only true constitutional currency known to the laws.'' *Dillard* v. *Evans,* 4 Ark. 175 (1842)

''The judgment was for dollars, and the payment so far as the facts are before us, could only have been made in gold or silver, the constitutional coin.'' *Bone* v. *Torry,* 16 Ark. 83 (1855)

''The result from an examination of all the cases is that money, in its strict legal sense, means gold and silver coin, and that an obligation for money alone can not be satisfied with any thing else.'' *Sinclair* v. *Piercy,* 28 Ky. 63. (1830)

''If Congress can create a legal tender, it must be by virtue of the 'power to coin money,'' for nowhere in the constitution is the power to make a legal tender expressly given to them, nor is there any other power directly given, from which power to make a legal tender can be incidently deduced.

''At common law, only gold and silver were a legal tender...In this State, where the common law has been expressly adopted, anterior to all legislative and constitutional provisions on the subject, gold and silver were the only legal tenders.'' *Clarin* v. *Nesbitt,* 2 Nott. and McC. (11 S.C. 519) (1820)

''By the Constitution of the United States nothing

can be a tender in payment of debt but gold and silver coin." *Lowry* v. *McGhee and McDermott*, 16 Tenn 242 (1835)

"The note calls for four hundred dollars, lawful funds of the United States. What is the plain meaning of 'lawful funds'? Gold and silver is [sic] the only lawful tender in the United States. It must therefore mean payment in gold' or silver. By equivalent, the parties must have meant paper currency as passed at par with gold and silver." *Ogden* v. *Slade*, 1 Tex 13. (1846)

"No state is authorized to coin money or pass any law whereby anything but gold and silver shall be made a legal tender in payment of debt. . .This conventional understanding that bank bills are to pass as money is founded upon the solvency of the bank and upon the supposition that the bills are equivalent in value to specie and are at any time convertible into specie at the option of the holder." *Wainwright* v. *Webster*, 11 Ver. 576 (1839)

Prior to the civil war, there was consistency in both the state courts and in the Supreme Court as to what was a lawful tender and there was no doubt that this consisted of coins issued by the Mint made of the precious metals. After the legal tender act of 1862, the U.S. Supreme Court did not address its constitutionality until 1870 in the case of *Hepburn* v. *Griswold*, 75 U.S. 603. This case had been earlier decided by the Kentucky in the case *Hepburn* v. *Griswold*, 63 KY. 20 (1865) and the Supreme Court of Kentucky had found the act unconstitutional. The U.S. Supreme Court upheld the decision of the KY S.Ct. in its decision which said:

"We are obliged to conclude that an Act making promises to pay dollars a legal tender in payment of debts previously contracted, is not a means appropriate, plainly adopted, really calculated to carry into effect any express power vested in Congress; that such an Act is inconsistent with the spirit of the Constitution; and that it is prohibited by the Constitution." *Hepburn* v. *Griswold*, 75 U.S. 603.

The majority decision of the high court was written by Salmon P. Chase, who during Lincoln's administration had been Secretary of the Treasury. It was Salmon P. Chase who had originally written the legal tender act of 1862. Chief Justice Salmon P. Chase clearly reversed himself in the decision of *Hepburn* v. *Griswold*.

After this decision, one of the justices resigned for health reasons and Congress passed legislation to increase the number of justices to nine. President Grant named two justices who were friends of paper money. A year later, in the case of *Knox* v. *Lee*, 79 U.S. 457, the Supreme Court reversed itself and declared that Congress had the power to make U.S. Treasury Notes a legal tender. In its decision, the court affirmatively stated that it did not intend to make paper a standard of value. Thirteen years later, the Supreme Court reaffirmed *Knox* v. *Lee* in the most famous of all legal tender cases—*Juilliard* vs. *Greenman*, 110 U.S. 421.

In this decision, the high court ruled:

"Congress is authorized to establish a national currency, either in coin or in paper, and to make that currency lawful money for all purposes, as regards the national government or private individuals."

In a dissenting opinion in the *Juilliard* v. *Greenman* case, Justice Fields wrote:

"The clause to coin money must be read in connection with the prohibition upon the States to not make anything but gold and silver coin a tender in payment of debts. The two taken together clearly show that the coins to be fabricated under the authority of the general government, and as such to be a legal tender for debts, are to be composed principally, if not entirely of the metals of gold and silver."

IT IS IMPORTANT TO NOTE THAT EVEN IN THE MAJORITY DECISION OF *JUILLIARD* V. *GREENMAN*, 110 U.S. 421, THE SUPREME COURT MADE NO MENTION OF DEBTS OR INVOLUNTARY CONTRIBUTIONS EXACTED UNDER STATE AUTHORITY IN THE NATURE OF TAXES, FINES OR FEES.

AFTER THE *JUILLIARD* V. *GREENMAN* CASE, THE SUPREME COURT RULED IN THE *HAGAR* V. *REC. DIST #108* AS FOLLOWS:

"The acts of Congress making the Notes of the United States a Legal Tender DO NOT apply to INVOLUNTARY contributions in the nature of TAXES or ASSESSMENTS exacted under State laws, but only to DEBTS in the strict sense of the terms; that is, to obligations founded on contracts, express and implied, for the payment of money." *Hagar* v. *Rec. Dist. #108*, 111 U.S. 701 (1884)

In the *Hagar* v. *Rec. Dist. #108,* 111 U.S. 701, the high court also said:

"that it was the right of each State to collect its taxes in such material as it might deem expedient, either in kind, that is to say, by a certain proportion of products, or in bullion, or in coin, the court observing that the extent to which the power of taxation of the State should be exercised, the subjects upon which it should be exercised, and the mode in which it should be exercised were all equally within the discretion of the legislature, EXCEPT AS RESTRAINED BY ITS OWN CONSTITUTION AND THAT OF THE UNITED STATES...and second, that legal tender acts had no reference to taxes imposed by State authority."

THE COURT IS ASKED HERE TO TAKE JUDICIAL NOTICE THAT *HAGAR* V. *REC. DIST. #108,* WAS THE LAST WORD FORM THE U.S. SUPREME COURT ON WHAT SHALL BE A LEGAL TENDER EXACTED UNDER STATE AUTHORITY IN THE FORM OF TAXES OR OTHER INVOLUNTARY CONTRIBUTIONS.

In 1913, when the Federal Reserve Act was passed, it was incorporated into the act that Federal Reserve Notes shall be "obligations of the United States" (12 U.S.C. Sec. 411) and that they shall be redeemable in "lawful money."

LAWFUL MONEY is defined in 12 U.S.C. Sec 152 which says: "The terms 'lawful money' and 'lawful money of the United States' shall be construed to mean gold and silver coin of the United States."

Thus the early Federal Reserve Notes issued said in the upper left corner: "REDEEMABLE IN GOLD ON DEMAND AT THE UNITED STATES TREASURY, OR IN GOLD OR LAWFUL MONEY AT ANY FEDERAL RESERVE BANK." On the bottom of the note, it said: "WILL PAY TO THE BEARER ON DEMAND" ONE DOLLAR OR FIVE DOLLARS OR TEN DOLLARS.

WHAT IS THE DIFFERENCE BETWEEN A DOLLAR, A NOTE AND A BILL OF CREDIT?

*A Dollar is defined by the Mint Act of 1792 ans is a coin containing 371.25 grains of fine silver—hence the expression—a Silver Dollar.

*A Note is the specimen above. On the bottom it says "Will Pay to the Bearer on Demand—TEN DOLLARS." It does not claim to be TEN DOLLARS. The Dollars this note offers to pay to the bearer each contain 371.25 grains of fine silver. This note also offers to redeem the bearer in lawful money (silver coins) or in gold coins denominated in dollar units. This note does not claim to be lawful money.

*A Bill of Credit is the specimen below. It offers not dollars and does not offer the bearer lawful money as does the note above. Rather, this specimen claims that it is TEN DOLLARS. This specimen is an unredeemable Bill of Credit. It is not a Dollar; it is not a Note. It is not lawful money. It is legal tender only for the Federal Government and for private individuals, BUT IS NOT LEGAL TENDER FOR STATES WHEN INVOLUNTARY CONTRIBUTIONS ARE EXTRACTED. See *Hagar* v. *Reclamation #108;* 111 U.S. 701 (1884).

The law which declares Federal Reserve Notes to be obligations of the United States and which are also to be redeemable in lawful money is 12 UCS 411 which reads:

[§411. Issuance to reserve banks; nature of obligation; redemption. Federal reserve notes, to be issued at the discretion of the Board of Governors of the Federal Reserve System...are authorized. The said notes shall be OBLIGATIONS OF THE UNITED STATES...THEY SHALL BE REDEEMED IN LAWFUL MONEY ON DEMAND...at any Federal Reserve Bank."

Let the court take judicial notice that the above statute remains on the books, but is apparently not being enforced, at least not since June 24, 1968.

After HJR 192 was passed by Congress on June 5th, 1933, Federal Reserve Notes were no longer redeemable in lawful money in the form of silver coins. The wording on the Federal Reserve Notes was changed as you will note below:

The bottom of each of these Federal Reserve Notes continued to say as did the Silver Certificates "WILL PAY TO THE BEARER ON DEMAND" so many dollars in silver coin. Through lobbying pressure from the American Bankers Association, the redemption of Silver Certificates and Federal Reserve Notes in silver coins ended on June 24, 1968 with the passage of 31 U.S.C. 405a-3. With this ended the last connection of our present money system with the one intended by our founding fathers. Throughout this evolution in our money system, no attempt was ever made to amend, alter or repeal Art. 1, § 10 of the U.S. Constitution. The prohibitions on the States in 1:10:10

remain as they were intended by the delegates to the Federal Convention of 1787 who wrote our Constitution. The last change in the Federal Reserve Notes occurred in 1963 when new notes issued removed the promise to redeem them in "lawful money" and the words "Will Pay to the Bearer on Demand" were removed. These new notes were first introduced to the banks on the day of President John Kennedy's funeral in 1963.

It is my belief that the force that led to the abrogation of the constitutionality of our money system came from the financial centers of Wall Street, who had already concentrated most of the power to create money into their own hands through a process known as "fractional reserve banking" wherein banks create "credit and checkbook money" by making bookkeeping entries.

THE CONSTITUTION AND THE COURT'S DILEMMA

The following are some court citations on the Constitution:

"Disobedience or evasion of a constitutional mandate may not be tolerated, even though such disobedience may, at least temporarily, promote in some respects the best interests of the public." from *Slote* v. *Board of Examiners,* 274 N.Y. 367

"In arriving at the proper construction of any part of the Constitution, the courts must consider the reason for the provision and the purpose of the convention in adopting it, and no part of the Constitution is to be construed so as to defeat its substantial purpose of the reasonable intent in adopting it." from *Runyon* v. *Smith,* 308 KY. 73

"The courts cannot rightly prefer, of the possible meanings of the words of the Constitution, that which will defeat rather than effectuate the constitutional purpose." from *United States* v. *Classic,* 313 U.S. 299

"The Constitution is a written instrument. As such, its meaning does not alter. That which it meant when it was adopted, it means now." from *South Carolina* v. *United States,* 199 U.S. 437, 448.

STATE OF NORTH CAROLINA

County of _____

File # _____

In the General Court of Justice
District Court Division
SMALL CLAIM

_____

First   Middle   Last Name

_____

Plaintiff's Address

vs.

_____

First   Middle   Last Name

_____

First   Middle   Last Name

JUDGMENT
in
Action for Summary Ejectment

_____

First Defendant's Address

_____

Second Defendant's Address if different

This action for summary ejectment was tried this date before the undersigned upon due and timely notice to the defendant of the nature of the action and the time and place of trial, as is shown in the record. THE COURT FINDS:

☐ That the plaintiff has proved his case by the greater weight of the evidence.

☐ That the plaintiff has failed to prove his case by the greater weight of the evidence.

☐ See reverse.

IT IS, THEREFORE, ADJUDGED

☐ That the defendant be removed from the plaintiff and be put in possession of the premises described in the complaint.

☐ That the plaintiff recover of the defendant at the rate of $_____ per _____ from the _____ day of _____, 19_____, to the present, a total principal sum of $_____, plus costs and interest at 6% on said principal sum from this day until this judgment is paid.

☐ That this action be DISMISSED, it being brought upon a forfeiture for nonpayment of rent and defendant having paid the rent due and costs.

☐ That this action be DISMISSED.

This _____ day of _____, 19_____.

NOTE: Disregard all paragraphs not checked.
See over for appeal entries.

_____
Magistrate

G.S. 7A–210(2), –223, –224, Ch. 42, Art. 3
AOC–L Form 314
10 / 71

"To disregard such a deliberate choice of words and their natural meaning would be a departure from the first principle of constitutional interpretation." *Wright* v. *United States,* 302 U.S. 583

"When any court violates the clean and unambiguous language of the Constitution, a fraud is perpetrated and no one is bound to obey it." *State* v. *Sutton,* 63 Minn. 147

"If the legislature clearly misinterprets a constitutional provision, the frequent repetition of the wrong will not create a right." *Amos* v. *Mosley,* 74 Fla. 555

"It is clear, of course, that no act of Congress can authorize a violation of the Constitution." *Almeida-Sanchez* v. *United States,* 413 U.S. 266

"Undoubtedly what went before the adoption of the constitution may be resorted to for the purpose of throwing light on its provisions." *Marshall* v. *Gordon,* 243 U.S. 251

SUMMARY

In concluding this brief, I believe that I have documented and substantiated most of the goals outlined on page 1. More could have been written about States rights under the 10th amendment which reserves to the states and to the people any powers not delegated to the U.S. Government. This clearly prevents the U.S. Government from declaring what the States are to use as a legal tender, especially so when the Constitution mandates what that legal tender shall be. Many erroneous case law citations claiming that Federal Reserve Notes are legal tender for the States are based on cases between individuals or between the Federal Government and an individual. These types of cases are a spin off of the *Juilliard v. Greenman* decision of 1884.

However, the *Juilliard* v. *Greenman* decision did not address the issue of what a State may declare to be a legal tender. This was done a few months later by the same court in the case of *Hagar* v. *Rec. Dist. #108,* 111 U.S. 701 in which the high court ruled:

"The acts of Congress making Notes a legal tender DO NOT apply to INVOLUNTARY contributions in the nature of taxes or assessments exacted under State laws..."

While this was the last word from the high court on this issue, the Constitution itself clearly says in Article 6: "This Constitution...shall be the supreme Law of the Land, and the Judges shall be bound thereby, any Thing in the Constitution or Law of any State to the Contrary notwithstanding."

Thus we are bound to those memorial words added to our Constitution on Aug. 28, 1787 by that delegate and judge from Connecticut—the Honorable Roger Sherman: "No state shall..."

Date _____   X _____

Additional Findings of the Court:

1. Defendants fuled a Notice of Jurisdictional Defect, alleging that the monies used to file the action and to pay the fees to serve the "Magistrate Summons" and "Complaint in Summary Ejectment" violated Article I, Section 10 of the United States Constitution and also the Coinage Act of April 2, 1792, as amended to date.

2. The Defendants also asked the Court to rule concerning the validity of House Joint Resolution #192 of June 5, 1933, in relation to Article I, Section 10 of the United States Constitution.

3. This COURT finds that:

   a. House Joint Resolution #192 of June 5, 1933, cannot be construed to invalidate the provisions of Article I, Section 10 of the United States Constitution with respect to the proceedings of the COURT.

   b. Monies used to pay fees were not in accordance with Constitutional requirements.

4. THEREFORE, this COURT allows Defendants' Motion to Dismiss this action because it lacks jurisdiction over the persons in this matter.

8
Defenses Against Foreclosure

Foreclosure Impending. When foreclosure is impending, you should act right away to commence suit against your lender, especially in states where foreclosure can occur by a mere advertisement or some other form of public notice and sale take place under third party Trustee Sale.

Model Lawsuits. In the following pages, you will find five model lawsuits, any one of which may be applicable to your particular situation.

Model #1. If you are suing a bank use Model lawsuit #1.

Model #2. If you are suing a mortgage company or a financial institution other than a bank, use Model Lawsuit #2.

Model #3. If you are filing a lawsuit after a sheriff or Trustee sale, use the information given in #4 with either #1, or #2, to make up model lawsuit #3.

Model #4. If you are going to a sheriff or trustee sale to buy in your property with constitutional money, then use Model Lawsuit #4 and combine it with information given in Model Lawsuit #5.

Model #5. If you use a check to pay off an unlawful debt (created by the lender bank by mere bookkeeping entry), then combine the information in Model #3 with either #1 or #2 and file it in court before a sheriff or Trustee sale can take place.

When using model Lawsuits. When you use a model lawsuit, omit any data not pertinent to your case and add any material that is new or particularly applicable to your case.

FRAMING YOUR LAWSUIT

The biggest challenge that anyone will have is to have his attorney frame a good lawsuit. We want a lawsuit that will survive a Motion to Dismiss hearing or Demurrer and finally reach a jury trial. **The key parts of a lawsuit are (1) The caption**—the first page, usually the top of which lists the plaintiffs and defendants, the court, Case # etc. **(2) Jurisdiction**—the first part of the body of the complaint or counterclaim that invokes part of the Constitution and state or federal laws applicable and states whether this is a Complaint at law or in equity. **(3) The Parties to the Action**—this is the section where you list the names and addresses of the defendants and the plaintiffs. **(4) Factual Background** this is the most important section of the lawsuit. Here, you must plead with particularity and state the facts chronologically. Avoid any mention of law here, avoid theory and conclusionary statements. **Case law is never cited in a complaint.** In framing a lawsuit on the credit issue, you must first list every loan of credit made, from the last one to the first one. Many debts are based on refinancing of existing debts, thus you must go all the way back to the original loan, regardless of how many years were involved. **You must then state the lender failed to lend you "legal tender" or "lawful money" as promised for all the loans involved, but that he did deliberately issue a "bad" check and passed it on to you to circulate as "money" and that he did deliberately to your detriment and damage. You must also state that you did not become aware of his fraudulent activity until after the date of your last loan,**

otherwise you are a party to fraud and have waived your claim for relief. If you have a note that has been sold by the original lender to several other lenders, then you must sue the original lender and name all the other parties to whom the note was assigned as defendants. You will have no claim for relief against the assigns (lenders who bought the note), but you can use your lawsuit to challenge jurisdiction of any action they bring against you based on #7 mentioned earlier—that there is an existing action pending between the same parties on the same cause of action. In your factual background section, you should add any other issues that are relevant to your case such as **"breach of oral promises,"** any demands made on you regarding **financial decisions** that were detrimental to you, and any other things done to injure or violate your rights under the law. **(5) The Counts.** This is a section where you will restate the allegations of your factual background section and then apply the law to the facts and state which laws they violated. Breach of Contract is a violation of the common law as well as Art. 1, Sec. 10, U.S. Constitution. Fraud is a violation of the common law and voids any contract. Usury is a violation of the contract based on the amount of lawful money or coins and currency actually risked in the loan. Racketeering is a violation of federal law and some state laws. Fraud can also involve a violation of state securities laws—that is when the lender obtains a note (a security) for a fraudulent or insufficient consideration. **Check your State Statutes on Securities. (6) Relief Requested—** here is where you ask for any relief that was not mentioned in the Counts section. You demand your trial by jury and ask for empanelment of a grand jury so you can present criminal charges against the defendants or ask to be directed to an existing grand jury so you can present testimony concerning violations of various state or federal criminal laws. This is the basic structure of a well written lawsuit. Reread this section before writing your lawsuit. Once you have written your lawsuit, you must make enough copies to serve one on each defendant. All copies must be signed. Then you will need a Summons form. While you can write up your own in many states, copies of a standard Summons form are available from the clerk of courts in your state or federal court or bankruptcy court, if you are filing a lawsuit there. Another form you will need is a Notice of Lis Pendens. This is a notice of a

lawsuit pending and must include the legal description of your property. You prepare this form yourself—a sample one is enclosed. This is filed usually in the register of deeds and clouds title to the property while the lawsuit is in progress. It is very important that you use all these forms to protect your interests.

After your lawsuit is written and filed, then you will need someone to serve it. You can get the sheriff's department to do this of you can hire a process server. To locate a process server, look up "Process Servers" in your yellow pages phone directory. Also, a friend or neighbor can serve the Summons and Complaint also. As a party to the action, you cannot serve any Summons and you cannot serve any other pleadings either, except for Motions, which in most areas can be served by mail, along with a Certificate of Service usually signed by someone other than yourself who did the actual mailing of the Motion. Once the defendants have been served, you must have the party serving it fill out an Affidavit of Service, which you must file with the court.

DEFAULT JUDGMENTS

If a defendant does not Answer your Complaint or does not file a motion to Dismiss within the time allowed in the Summons, you can then get the clerk of court to enter a Default Judgment for you. You will need four separate forms which you can prepare yourself or you can get preprinted forms from the clerk of courts. These forms are usually called (a) Request to clerk of courts to enter default judgment (b) Affidavit of no answer and amount due (c) Affidavit of non military service (d) Default judgment. Once the default judgment is entered, a copy is sent to the defendant. After their appeal time has run out, you have a judgment that can be collected by requesting the clerk of courts to issue a Writ of Execution to the sheriff. It should be noted here that a default judgment can be removed by a judge based on good cause presented by the defendant such as newly discovered evidence or insufficiency of service and for other reasons. If you were the defendant, you could file a Motion to Set Aside Default Judgment. In this motion, you could ask the court for permission to answer the complaint and / or file a Counterclaim based on newly discovered evidence. ("Newly discovered evidence" must be evidence which the defendant *could not,* in the exercise of diligence, have discovered prior to judgment.) Support your motion with an affidavit. If the judge does not grant it, then you must file a new lawsuit against the lender. After doing this, you can then file a Motion to Consolidate Cases—that is, to combine their case against you with your case against them. This will stop the clock on their execution of the judgment against you. Other options to stop them from seizing your property are to file a Petition for a Temporary Restraining Order (TRO) or to file a Chapter 11 or Chapter 13 bankruptcy plan. An automatic stay of execution goes into effect upon the filing of any bankruptcy plan.

IMPORTANT PRINCIPLES TO REMEMBER

1. The best defense is a good offense. 2. By What Authority? Always challenge the authority of the adversary to do what they do when you cannot find their authority for doing something. Challenge the authority of the court when your Constitutional rights are violated. 3. Use arguments based on natural equity and combine them with arguments in law in your pleadings. 4. If possible, go after your adversary criminally as well as civilly. 5. Always use Affidavits to support your motions and always use Affidavits to oppose their motions that you are opposed to. 6. Use all Discovery aggressively. Use Depositions for your most effective results to trap your adversary. 7. As a plaintiff or defendant, your very first motion should be a "motion for a Court Ruling on Jury Trial Demand." Support your motion by arguments based on the Constitution and case law. The best set of books to find supporting case law are called "Supreme Court Digests" and these can be found in your local law library, usually in the courthouse or at a college. When using case law, use Supreme Court cases primarily as these override all lower court decisions. Case law is always used in supporting briefs that are supported by affidavits.

COURTROOM PROCEDURE

In a court room, the party making a motion speaks first and the other party then responds. To present your arguments, make a sketch or outline of the points you will raise. Any surprise arguments you raise will throw your opponent off track. If the op-

posing attorney baffles you with a lot of legal mumbo jumbo, then ask the court to make him explain in plain English just what each of his words means. If you are not confident of yourself, then tell the court that you are standing by your written pleadings as being a person not trained in law, you are not qualified to debate the opposing attorney. ONE VERY IMPORTANT THING TO REMEMBER IS THAT AT A MOTION HEARING, STICK TO THE ISSUES IN THE MOTION AND DO NOT GET INTO A DISCUSSION ON THE MERITS OF THE CASE. Otherwise, you will get thrown off track. To get back on track, if the other attorney or the judge gets off track, you must point out that the new issues raised are not in the motion, but are part of the merits of the case which is not before the court today. By getting them back on point and to the issues before the court in the motion hearing, you will spare yourself a verbal debate on the merits of the case. Memoranda and briefs are always presented at the pretrial hearing, but may be used to oppose a Motion to Dismiss or a Motion for Summary Judgment.

SERVING MOTIONS

While the complaint is always served directly on the party you are suing, "motions" written afterwards are served on the attorney for the other party and this constitutes service on the other party. If any paper is served on the other party directly such as interrogatories or a Notice of Deposition, the other party's attorney must always get a copy. A Certificate or Affidavit of Service is then always filed with the court, usually the judge's secretary. While motions may be served by mail, usually certified, return receipt requested, a Notice of Deposition or Subpoena must always be personally served on the party affected.

QUESTIONS AND ANSWERS ABOUT TRIAL PREPARATION

Q: Where can I get a book on the rules of civil procedure for my state?

A: *Your State, Court Rules and Procedures* can be obtained from West Publishing Co., P.O. Box 3526, St. Paul, MN 55172. The fastest way is to call them on the cost and shipping charges at 612-228-2500.

Otherwise, send them $20 and ask them to send you this book and to refund the difference. Give them the name of your state that you want the court rules and procedures on. If you plan on being in Federal Court, send for a copy of Federal Rules of Civil & Appellate Procedure. Then go to the state court or the federal court and ask for a copy of the local court rules. If you are planning on being in bankruptcy court, see the Legal Karate packet for the names of the books you will need there.

Q: When can a case be removed to federal court?

A: Within 30 days after a federal issue is raised. Only defendants can remove a civil case to federal court.

Q: How do you gather evidence for a case?

A: It is vitally important that you have a pocket tape recorder with you at all court proceedings, all interviews with your lenders to record all verbal promises made, and at all sheriff or trustee sales. A tape recorder can provide evidence that will be invaluable to you in going after your adversaries both civilly and criminally. A Polaroid camera may be helpful to photograph the high bidder's check or other monetary instrument. Use a tape recorder when going into a bank to find out if a cashiers or certified check from the lender at a sheriff or trustee sale is any good— that is, if the bank has the cash to redeem it. Believe it or not, about half of them don't. See model lawsuits #4 and #5. If no check is tendered, then amend model #4 or #5 accordingly and charge the sheriff with failure to comply with the Constitution and state statutes by not requiring any money from the high bid that he accepted. You can also sue as an assigns to a land patent as this is the best and paramount title at law. These issues can be combined.

Also, when you call someone on the phone, have a telephone pickup device which you can obtain from Sears or Radio Shack connected to a cassette recorder to record any advice that you receive from someone on any legal questions you may ask them. A tape recording is better than most people's memories and can always be played back.

Getting a trial. One of the most important actions goals you can achieve is getting a trial. Most lawyers and many lenders are not knowledgeable in the area of fractional reserve banking. Indeed, many who work for banks don't know exactly how banks create "credit" money; and they definitely do not know on what authority "credit" money is created. Most important is a well pleaded complaint, especially one that is based on the money and credit money issue. You will probably want help in drafting such a complaint and it is of vital importance if you want to win your case and have the help of a "constitutional lawyer" who will know how to get the lender's attorney to answer the complaint. Getting him to answer the complaint virtually guarantees that a case will go to trial. Your next objective is to get a trial by jury. No one likes to see his fellow man put out of his home and you may enlist the sympathy of the jury immediately if you are being foreclosed for reasons not your fault and beyond your control.

FIRST, A FEW MORE NOTES ABOUT DEFENSES AND COMMENTS WITH REGARD TO MODEL LAWSUIT #1.

Model Lawsuit #1. This lawsuit is designed for suing banks in Federal Court and includes the option of suing the Federal Reserve Bank(s) and their Board of Examiners (name all of them in your Complaint). For those who prefer to file their lawsuits in a state court, omit the Federal Reserve Bank by dropping the last two paragraphs from the "Factual Background" section of the Complaint and by modifying the Counts and Relief Requested sections accordingly. For those who want to sue the Federal Reserve Banks along with their local bank, there is little to do except plug in the names and dates of loans and dollar amounts on the model form given herein. There may be other factors than those cited on the "Model" form to be considered in documenting your lawsuit, which may require the addition of extra parties and the adding of more facts to the "Factual Background" section of your Complaint. Here is a list of those possible additional factors:

Holder in Due Course. Who is a holder in due course? Let us say you took out a loan of credit from Bank A and Bank A sold it to Bank B. Bank B in turn sold it to Bank C. Now Bank C is foreclosing you. The question is: Whom do you sue? What you do is name Bank A, Bank B and Bank C as Defendants in your lawsuit. However in the last section of the "Factual Background" section of your complaint add another paragraph and state: Bank B and Bank C are not HOLDERS IN DUE COURSE under the

Uniform Commercial Code. Bank B and Bank C purchased the mortgage, the mortgage note, or deed of trust, security agreement etc., which was first obtained by Bank A, under conditions of Fraud and Misrepresentation. The documents which Bank B and Bank C have obtained from Bank A do not provide them with any claim whatsoever for relief, in either a court of law or equity.

If you live in a state where Bank C is foreclosing on you and they have already filed a suit against you in court, then as Defendant, name Bank A and Bank B as "Third Party Defendants" which will make you both Defendant and Third Party Plaintiff. If you live in a non-judicial state such as Virginia, which permits the lender merely to advertise and sell your property under foreclosure of a deed of trust and Trustee Sale, then you must take the offensive prior to such action, and sue all of the Holders in Due Course, naming all of them as Defendants and yourself as Plaintiff.

MODEL LAWSUIT #1

[your name],
    Plaintiff,

vs.

Bank of [   ], and
[Bank President or officer] and
Federal Reserve Bank President [name] and
John and Jane Does (1 to 25),
    Defendants.

Case # . . . .
Complaint at Law

Now Comes the plaintiffs, in propria personna, and relying on the decisions in *Haines* v. *Kerner,* 404 U.S. 519 and show their Complaint against the defendants as follows:

JURISDICTION

1. FOR STATE COURTS / (Jurisdiction in this action at law is based on the Constitution of the United States and in particular the 7th amendment as this is a suit at common law. Jurisdiction is further invoked under the Constitution of the state of [   ] and in particular by the. . .amendment which preserves the right to trial by jury in an action at law and jurisdiction is further invoked under 18 U.S.C. Sec. 1964.

FOR FEDERAL COURTS, use the following —

(Jurisdiction is invoked under 28 U.S.C. Sec. 1332 and involves diversity of citizenship and more than $10,000 in controversy and jurisdiction is further invoked under 42 U.S.C. 1983 et seq. and 18 U.S.C. Sec. 1964 as well as the Constitution of the United States and in particular the 7th amendment as this is a "suit at common law." This Complaint is filed in propria personna pursuant to Haines vs. Kerner, 404 U.S. 519).

PARTIES TO THE ACTION

2. The plaintiffs in this action are citizens of the United States and residents of the state of [   ]. The plaintiffs names and addresses are as follows: . . . . The defendants in this Complaint are the [name of bank] whose business address is as follows: . . .and a bank employee [President or loan officer] whose name is. . .and who lives at. . .and John and Jane Does (1 through 25) whose names and addresses are unknown at this time. (For Federal Court, add: "and other defendants include the President of the Federal Reserve bank of [your district] whose name is. . .and whose address is [use address of F. R. Bank here] and all members of the Board of Examiners whose names and addresses are unknown at this time.")

FACTUAL BACKGROUND

3. On or about [month, date, year], the [bank of   ] through its loan officer (or President) did verbally represent to the plaintiffs that it had approved a loan to them for the sum of [$ amount of loan] in lawful money of the United States and at annual interest rate of ?%.

4. The [Bank of   ] and its loan officer [insert name] knew or should have known that the verbal statement that they would lend the plaintiffs "lawful money of the United States" at an annual interest rate of ?% was a false representation that was made recklessly and with deliberate and intentional disregard for the rights of the plaintiffs.

5. Relying on these false representations, the plaintiffs were induced into signing a [mortgage, mortgage note, deed of trust, note, security agreement etc.] on or about [month, date, year]. Since the date of the loan, the plaintiffs have made payments of principal and interest totaling [total $ amount paid].

6. After the plaintiffs had signed the [mortgage,

deed of trust, note, etc.], the bank and its officer [name] did fail to lend the plaintiffs lawful money of the United States for the full value of the loan. For the actual lawful money which the bank risked for the loan, estimated to be no more than 5% of the loan's face value, the bank did charge an interest rate that was 20 times greater than what was authorized in the contract, and did this deliberately to the detriment and damage of the plaintiffs.

7. In carrying out their commitment to lend lawful money of the United States, the bank did write a check for the sum of [$ amount of loan]. The bank in writing this check, did deliberately make a loan beyond its customers' deposits.

8. The check (or checks) which the bank and its officers wrote were not backed by or redeemable in Federal Reserve Notes, coins or lawful money of the United States for their full face value.

9. The bank and its officers did use the U.S. Mails more than twice since the date of loan to collect money on this debt. Plaintiff did not become aware of the fraudulent activity of the defendants until on or around [month, date, year].

10. The only consideration which the bank provided for this loan was a book entry demand deposit which the bank itself created effortlessly and at virtually no cost to itself. The bank in stamping its own check "Paid," did make a false representation as it merely transferred some book entries and never intended to redeem this check in lawful money of the United States.

(Note: to sue the Federal Reserve Banks, add the following sections—)

11. The averments of the previously numbered paragraphs are restated by reference herein. The Federal Reserve Bank President, whose name is...and the Board of Examiners for this bank knew or should have known that the [name of bank] made a loan to the plaintiffs by writing a check on or around [date pf loan] and that the bank was charging interest on nonexistent funds. The Federal Reserve Bank President and the Board of Examiners for the F. R. Bank are a party to these false representations as they were a party to the transfer of book entries with the full knowledge that the bank did not have in its possession lawful money to redeem its check and they did all this to the detriment and damage of the plaintiffs. Their collective activities in passing this check is part of a planned scheme.

12. In addition to this, the Federal Reserve Bank President [name] and the Board of Examiners along with John and Jane Does, whose names are unknown at this time, are a party to a conspiracy to do all of the following: keep interest rates artificially high, contract credit to create unemployment and depress farm prices, and to select and pressure the bank to foreclose on the plaintiff's property all as part of a preplanned conspiracy to eliminate 2.3 million American farmers and to set up 100,000 corporations to own all the farm lands in the nation. All of this illegal activity is being done in violation of Federal Racketeering laws, Federal Antitrust laws, and in violation of the plaintiffs Constitutional rights, particularly the 5th, 7th, 9th and 14th amendments.

COUNT ONE

1. BREACH OF CONTRACT. The averments of the previously numbered paragraphs are restated by reference herein. The [Bank of] and its officer, [name], failed to lend the plaintiffs lawful money of the United States and instead substituted a check with the intended purpose of circulating it as money.

COUNT TWO

1. FRAUD AND RACKETEERING. The averments of the previously numbered paragraphs are referred to by reference herein. The [name of bank] and its officer, [name], and the president of the Federal Reserve Bank of [your district], whose name is... and the Board of Examiners are all parties to the writing and processing of a check written by the [name of bank] on or about [date of loan]. All these parties are in collusion in using the U.S. Mails and Wire Services to collect on this unlawful debt in violation of 18 U.S.C. 1341 (mail fraud) and 18 U.S.C. (wire fraud) and 18 U.S.C. 1962 in establishing a "pattern of racketeering activity." Plaintiffs ask for triple damages for actual and compensatory damages sustained pursuant to 18 U.S.C. 1964 from each and every defendant on all counts.

COUNT THREE

1. USURY AND RACKETEERING. The averments of the previously numbered paragraphs are restated by reference herein. By virtue of the bank's activities in creating an unlawful debt by passing a bad check, the [name of bank] has collected an annual interest rate estimated to be twenty times greater than the amount of interest the plaintiffs agreed to in

the note they signed. This violation of contract law and usury laws is due to the fact that the actual amount of lawful money risked by the bank in making the loan was less than 5% of the loan's face value.

RELIEF REQUESTED

1. The plaintiffs ask the court to empanel a Grand Jury to investigate the [name of bank], the Federal Reserve bank of [your district], and its President as well as the Board of Examiners for violations of Federal Antitrust laws and the Federal Racketeering laws including 18 U.S.C. 1341 (mail fraud) and 18 U.S.C. 1343 (wire fraud) and 18 U.S.C. 1962 (pattern of racketeering activity) and 18 U.S.C. Sec. 241 for conspiracy to violate the plaintiffs and other citizens Constitutional rights.

2. Plaintiffs ask for actual damages for the sum of [?$ paid on loan] and compensatory damages to be determined as well as three times this amount in punitive damages against each defendant convicted on any count.

3. Plaintiffs demand a trial by jury to be comprised of 12 members to determine all issues of facts in dispute and to determine and award all damages.

4. Plaintiffs ask for a court order declaring the [mortgage, mortgage note, note, deed of trust, security agreement, etc] to be null and void.

5. An injunction against the [name of bank] and the Federal Reserve Bank to divest themselves of any assets they have unlawfully gained and to return the same to the plaintiffs and all other debtors or injured parties.

Date . . . .   [Your Name] . . . .
                             Plaintiff—in propria personna.

Note: No statement claiming actual damage to the plaintiff except usury charge, which is questionable. Court will want to know exact nature of the damage suffered.

MODEL LAWSUIT #2 (for financial institutions other than banks)

CAPTION (See Model Lawsuit #1)

                             Case # . . . .
                             Complaint at Law

Now Comes the Plaintiffs, in propria persona, and relying on the decisions in *Haines* v. *Kerner,* 404 U.S. 519 and show their complaint against the defendants

as follows.

JURISDICTION
   1. (See Model Lawsuit #1)

PARTIES TO THE ACTION
   2. (See Model Lawsuit #1)

FACTUAL BACKGROUND

3. On or about [month, date, year], the [FLB / PCA / Mortgage Co., etc.] did verbally represent to the plaintiffs that they had approved a loan to them for the sum of [$ amount of loan] in lawful money of the United States at an annual interest rate of ?%.

4. The [FLB / PCA / Mortgage Co., etc.] and its loan officer, [name], knew or should have known that the verbal statement that they would lend the plaintiffs "lawful money of the United States" at an annual interest rate of ?% was a false representation that was made recklessly and with deliberate and intentional disregard for the rights of the plaintiffs.

5. Relying on these false representations, the plaintiffs were induced into signing a [mortgage, mortgage note, note, deed of trust, security agreement, etc.] on or about [month, date, year]. Since the date of the loan, the plaintiffs have made payments of principal and interest totaling [total amount paid].

6. After the plaintiffs had signed the [mortgage, mortgage note, note, deed of trust, etc.], the [PCA / FLB / Mortgage Co., etc.] did fail to lend the plaintiffs lawful money of the United States for the full value of the loan.

7. In carrying out their commitment to lend lawful money of the United States, the [PCA / FLB / etc.] did write a check for the sum of [$ amount of loan] on or about [date of loan]. The [PCA / FLB / Mortgage Co.] and its loan officer knew or should have known that they were accepting, lending checks which they had received either directly or indirectly from a commercial bank. They knew or should have known that the bank upon which the check for this loan was drawn had insufficient funds to redeem this check in lawful money of the United States.

8. The [PCA / FLB / Mortgage Co. etc.] and its loan officer, [name], did use the U.S. Mails more than twice since the date of the loan to collect money on this debt. The plaintiffs did not become aware of

the fraudulent activity alleged in this complaint until on or around [month, date, year].

9. The check(s) which [PCA / FLB / Mortgage Co. etc.] wrote for the sum of [$ amount of loan] was / were not backed by or redeemable for their full face value in Federal Reserve Notes, coins, or lawful money of the United States.

10. The [PCA / FLB / Mortgage Co.] knew or should have known that the checks they deposited in the bank account to cover the check they wrote for this loan was a bad check. Subsequently, the bank, against whom [PCA / FLB / Mortgage Co.] wrote the check never did redeem this check in lawful money of the United States, nor did the bank have in its possession the cash to redeem that check. The bank merely laundered the bad check by transferring some book entries.

11. The defendants, [PCA / FLB / Mortgage Co. etc.] and their loan officer, [name] knew or should have known that they were a party to a check kiting scheme by laundering bad checks which they had received either directly or indirectly from one or more commercial banks that originated the scheme.

12. The defendants, [PCA / FLB / Mortgage Co. etc.] and their loan officer, [name] knew or should have known that they were violating usury laws by charging interest on non-existent funds. The interest rate charged for the actual lawful money risked for this loan is estimated to be twenty times greater than that agreed to in the note signed by the plaintiffs. The interest rate charged should have been applied only to the lawful money risked in making this loan and instead was applied against the entire check even though this check is estimated to have been backed by only 5% of its face value in lawful money. The bank against whom this check was drawn was a party to this check kiting scheme.

(Note: Paragraph 11 and 12 of Model Lawsuit #1 can be substituted for paragraph 11 and 12 of Model Lawsuit #2.)

COUNT ONE

1. BREACH OF CONTRACT. The averments of the previously numbered paragraphs are restated by reference herein. The [PCA / FLB / Mortgage Co. etc.] and its officer [name] failed to lend the plaintiffs lawful money of the United States and instead substituted a bad check with the intended purpose of circulating it as money.

COUNT TWO

1. FRAUD AND RACKETEERING. The averments of the previously numbered paragraphs are restated by reference herein. The [PCA / FLB etc.] and its officer, and one or more unknown banks are parties to the writing and laundering of a bad check(s) written by [PCA / FLB etc.] on or around [date of loan]. All these parties are in collusion in using the U.S. Mails and Wire Services to collect on this unlawful debt in violation of 18 U.S.C. 1341 (mail fraud) and 18 U.S.C. 1343 (wire fraud) and 18 U.S.C. 1962 in establishing a "pattern of racketeering activity." Plaintiffs ask for triple damages for actual and compensatory damages sustained pursuant to 18 U.S.C. 1964 from each and every defendant.

(Note: if you have previously named the Federal Reserve Bank President and the Board of Examiners as defendants and have used paragraph 11 and 12 from the Factual Background of Model Lawsuit #1, then you should use Count Two from Model Lawsuit #1 as well.)

COUNT THREE

1. USURY AND RACKETEERING. The averments of the previously numbered paragraphs are restated by reference herein. By virtue of John and Jane Does who were the banks that were writing and passing bad checks to [PCA / FLB etc.] and by virtue of [PCA / FLB etc.] depositing these bad checks and passing them on to borrowers by writing checks against non existent funds, and by virtue of the fact these checks were only backed by 5% or less of their face value in cash, [PCA / FLB etc.] did knowingly charge an interest rate on lawful money actually risked that was about 20 times greater than the interest rate agreed to in the note signed by the plaintiffs. They did this in violation of 18 U.S.C. 1341 (mail fraud) and 18 U.S.C. 1962 by engaging in this pattern of racketeering activity.

RELIEF REQUESTED

1. Plaintiffs ask for actual damages for the sum of [total $ amount paid on loan] and compensatory damages to be determined as well as three times this amount in punitive damages against each defendant on any count.

2. Plaintiffs demand a trial by jury to be comprised of 12 members to determine all issues of facts in dispute and to determine and award all damages.

3. Plaintiffs ask for a court order declaring the

[mortgage, mortgage note, note, deed of trust, security agreement, etc.] to be null and void.

Date........   [Your Name]..............
                    Plaintiffs—in propria personna.

(Note: if you sued the Federal Reserve Bank President and the Board of Examiners, then use the 5 point Relief Requested material from Model Lawsuit #1 as a substitute for the Relief Requested section of Model Lawsuit #2.)

(To be added to Count 2 of Model Lawsuit #2)

FRAUD AND RACKETEERING

The plaintiff / defendant (strike one), restates the allegations of Counts 1 through 5. PCA / FLB (strike one) created an "unlawful debt" by requiring the Plaintiff / Defendant to purchase "stock" from them in the sum of [dollar value of stock purchased] on [date of loan or stock purchase]. PCA / FLB and its loan officer, _____, knew or should have known that the stock sold to me, the _____ in this case does not exist. The plaintiff / defendant in this action has never voted at any stockholders meeting and has never been invited to one. Furthermore, we allege that this stock does not exist and never did exist and the amount required for the stock purchase is nothing more that concealed interest rate charge. However, there is a failure of consideration as there is no stock and no actual ownership in PCA / FLB by me or other farmers as they claim. Because the stock does not exist, there is a failure of consideration, a breach of contract and fraud. PCA / FLB has, through these fraudulent actions created an unlawful debt and has more than twice used the U.S. Mails to collect on this debt, all in violation of 18 USCS 1341, and 18 USCS 1961 and 1962. Our actual damages in the payment of principal and interest on this non existent stock has been the total sum of $_____ which is the total amount we estimated we paid for this non existent stock since the first loan was taken out which was on [date of first loan]. Pursuant to 18 USCS 1964, we therefore are for treble damages or the sum of [insert triple damages here] plus punitive damages in the sum of [3 times the damages just quoted] for a total of [add actual and punitive]. In addition we ask the court for the following relief:

a. That the entire debt be declared null and void

and

b. That the damages awarded us be applied against all existing delinquent payments and future payments until paid in full and that the foreclosure action against us be dismissed.

Feb. 1985: Update insert—Because of a number of lawsuits filed against PCAs and FLBs on this issue, stock certificates starting showing up for the first time in February of 1985 in the state of Washington. The issue of fraud for requiring borrowers to buy non-existent stock can still be in any area where stock certificates have not been issued as other allegations added to Model Lawsuit #2.

THE PRIME RATE CASES
and
HOW TO ADD RACKETEERING CHARGES TO SUITS AGAINST BANKS AND OTHER LENDERS.

APRIL 4, 1984, *The Wall Street Journal* reports the following:

"When First National Bank of Atlanta agreed recently to settle a 3½ year old lawsuit for as much as 12.5 million, other banks took notice...At issue is a hallowed banking tradition: the prime rate, which for years has been described as the rate banks charge their best corporate customers...Angry non-prime borrowers, however, say banks have been overcharging them, often for years, because the prime rate their loans were tied to, wasn't the real prime, or best, rate ...The central figure in the burgeoning litigation is Jackie Kleiner, a 51 yr. old lawyer and business professor who started the Atlanta case in 1980. Since then, he says, he has been involved at one time or another in 38 of the estimated 50 prime rate suits. Currently, he says, suing banks is 'my main occupation'...In one case, for example, Mr. Kleiner says a client, Milwaukee Cheese Co., settled with a West German and two U.S. banks for about 10.5 million. He says Milwaukee Cheese paid the banks about $3 million, and the banks forgave about $13.5 million in loans. A banking source confirms that the settlement was for 'several million' dollars, but Milwaukee Cheese officials won't discuss the terms...Meanwhile, the controversy has prompted many banks to redefine the prime rate in lending documents..."

AFFIDAVIT AND NOTICE OF HIGH BID IN LAWFUL MONEY

THIS IS TO CERTIFY THAT David G. White made the high bid of $21.00 in lawful money of the United States at the foreclosure sale on January 17, 1985 at 10:15 o'clock A.M. at the south door of the Stearns County Courthouse in the City of St. Cloud. David G. White did bid twenty one (21) dollars in silver coins, and each dollar of silver contained 371.25 grains of pure silver and was minted by the United States government prior to 1965. Each dollar is as lawfully defined by the Coinage Act of 1792.

The silver coins were bid in compliance with Article I, Section 10 of the United States Constitution which states: "NO STATE SHALL MAKE ANY THING BUT GOLD AND SILVER COIN A TENDER IN PAYMENT OF DEBTS."

This foreclosure sale was for property described as follows:

S½NE¼, the E. 6 acres of SW¼NW¼ and SE¼NW¼, except: commencing at the N¼ corner of said Sec. 1; thence S. along the North–South ¼ line of said Sec. 1, a distance of 2017.57 ft. for point of beginning; thence S. along said line 145.20 ft.; thence W. at right angles 300 ft.; thence N. at right angles 145.20 ft.; thence E. at right angles 300 ft. to the point of beginning and there terminating, all in Sec. 1; AND EXCEPT that part of the S½NE¼ of Sec. 1, described as follows: Beginning at a point on the west line of said S½NE¼ of Sec. 1, distant 33.00 feet southerly of the northwest corner of said S½NE¼ of Sec. 1, distant 33.00 feet southerly of the northwest corner of said S½NE¼; thence easterly, parallel with the north line of said S½NE¼ a distance of 470.16 feet; thence southerly, parallel with the west line of said S½NE¼ a distance of 276.19 feet; thence northwesterly a distance of 486.74 feet to a point on the west line of said S½NE¼, distant 150.00 feet southerly of the point of beginning, thence northerly along said west line a distance of 150.00 feet to the point of beginning, containing 2.30 acres; all in Sec. 1, T125N., R32W.

The NE¼SW¼, except tract desc. as follows: Beginning at the NE corner thereof; thence W 53 rods to the center of the road; thence S. along said road 3 rods; thence E. to the E. line thereof; thence N. 3 rods to the place of beginning, Also Govt. Lots 1 & 2, except parcels:

Parcel A: That part of Govt. Lot 1 and Govt. Lot 2 desc. as follows: Commencing at the S¼ corner of said Sec. 35; thence N 89°57'W (assumed bearing) along the S. line of said Govt. Lot 2 for 1497.22 ft. to the centerline of a public road; thence along said centerline N 3°21'27"W for 1160 ft. to the point of beginning of the land to be described; thence continuing along said centerline N 3°21'27" W for 260 ft.; thence S 86°38'33" W for 152 ft. more or less to the shore of Freeport Lake; thence SW'ly along said lake shore to its intersection with a line draw S 86°'38"E for 462 ft. more or less to the point of beginning.

Parcel B: That part of Govt. Lot 2 desc. as follows: Beginning at a point in the S. line thereof 53 rods 3.05 ft. W of the SE corner thereof, said point being the center of the road; thence W 41 rods; thence N 9 rods; thence E 41 rods to the center of said road; thence S 9 rods to the place of beginning and also except that part of said Lot 2 lying W. of County Highway #11, as now constructed and travelled.

S½SE¼, also a part of the NW¼SE¼ desc. as follows: Beginning at the SE corner thereof; thence N 1 rod; thence W parallel to the S line thereof 67⅓ rods; thence NW'ly to a point on the W line thereof which is 66⅓ rods S of the NW corner; thence S along said W line to the SW corner; thence E to place of beginning, all in Sec. 35, T126N., R32W.

[signed] David G. White
Rt. 2, Box 286
Avon, MN 56310
THIS INSTRUMENT WAS DRAFTED BY
David G. White
Rt. 2, Box 286
Avon, MN 56310

Subscribed & sworn to me this
18th day of January, 1985
[signed] Jean A. Trunk

Even the new definitions don't bother Mr. Kleiner. He says the banks' new language is 'more deceptive' than before. He wants to challenge it in court.''

The above statements are excerpts from the article which appeared in The Wall Street Journal on April 4, 1984. The article was titled: CHALLENGES TO PRIME RATE AS BASE FOR LOANS STIR FEARS AMONG BANKS.

When the above article came to my attention, having been sent to me by a resident here in Milwaukee, I called the Milwaukee Cheese Co. and they provided me with the Case number. I went to the Federal Courthouse and looked the case up. A copy of this case that was apparently worth $10.5 million to the Milwaukee Cheese Co. is part of this packet, so you as a reader can see for yourself how it was placed together.

The issues in the prime rate cases are essentially this: breach of contract for charging an interest above the Prime Rate; fraud for doing it deliberately; and third racketeering for using U.S. Mails to collect on an unlawful debt. My interest in learning about the racketeering charges is because suits against banks on the ''credit'' issue involve the same fundamental issues which are breach of contract and fraud, for creating and lending ''credit'' which is not lawful money. Since the banks create an unlawful debt because of their failure to provide a ''lawful consideration,'' and because they use the U.S. Mail to collect on this debt, they are engaging in mail fraud, a violation of 18 USCS 1341, which is incorporated in 18 USCS 1961 which defines a ''pattern of racketeering.'' 18 USCS 1961 defines a ''pattern of racketeering'' as ''two acts of racketeering activity, one of which occurred after the effective date of this chapter [Oct 15, 1970] and the last of which occurred within ten years after the commission of a prior act of racketeering activtity.''

In other words, if any bank or other lender creates an unlawful debt in whole or in part and they send you statement to collect on this bill two or more times within any 10 year period, they have established a ''pattern of racketeering,'' and under 18 USCS 1962, this is a prohibited activity. Now, Under 18 USCS 1964, section c, it says: ''Any person injured in his business or property by reason of a violation of section 1962 of this chapter may sue therefor in any appropriate United States district court and shall recover three-fold the damages he sustains and the cost of the suit, including reasonable attorney's fees.''

THAT'S POWERFUL STUFF! You can sue to collect triple damages against anyone who creates an unlawful debt and uses the U.S. Mails to collect it.

What about loans from the Production Credit Association and the Federal Land Bank?

Both PCA and the Federal Land Banks (FLBs) require farmers to but ''stock'' when they take out an agricultural loan as a condition for the loan. The farmer usually borrows from 5 to 10% more in order to buy the stock, however, every farmer who has subpoenaed the stock from either the PCA of the FLB have never received any. Why? The answer is obvious —the stock doesn't exist! This is a Breach of Contract and because they are doing it deliberately, it is fraud and because they are using U.S. Mails to collect on an unlawful debt, they are engaged in a ''pattern of racketeering'' and are potentially liable to the borrowers (the farmers) for triple damages. Now, I am told that several years ago, the PCAs and the FLBs paid some interest to the farmers on this stock and then discontinued the practice. Also, that this year, one farmer received a check which amounted to 3% interest on the stock. Is this the same rate of return the other stockholders of PCA and FLBs receiving? I doubt it.

Consider that a farmer may have taken out several loans from either PCA or FLB for the last several years, you can sue to recover triple damages on this 5 to 10% of the loans value from the very first loan you took out. It is possible that much of your mortgage loan or deed of trust could be wiped out or repudiated.

Here is how you would calculate the amount of actual damages:

1. Get copies of all your original loan papers. Look up the original figures. Check your new loans or notes and you may find this amount already included in the loan that is refinanced. If you cannot locate the papers, then send PCA or FLB a ''Notice of Written Interrogatories'' and a ''Notice to Produce Documents'' OR send then a Notice of Deposition and a Subpoena Duces Tecum and ask them to appear before a Court Reporter and to bring the ''stocks'' with them and all figures of records showing the amount of ''stocks'' you were required to purchase in dollar values. The following is a list of questions for the interrogatories or for the deposition:

a. What was the dollar value of all stock I was required to buy from PCA / FLB for all loans I took out since [date of first loan]?

b. What percent of all loans that I took out constituted money which was used to purchase the stocks referred to in the above question?

c. What is the dollar amount of all payment (principal and interest) that I made to PCA / FLB since [date of first loan]?
(NOTE: An official of PCA whom I recently talked to indicated that PCA charges 8% of the loan value to stock and that Federal Land Bank charges 5%. There are no stock certificates!)

TO PCA or FLB:

You are required to bring to the deposition a copy of all stocks sold to [your name] which were a condition for the loan or loans executed on [date of loan].

NOTICE TO PRODUCE DOCUMENTS:

TO PCA or FLB:

Along with the answers to the interrogatories above, you are further required pursuant to Discovery statutes to send a copy of all "stocks" sold to [your name] which were a condition for the loan or loans executed on [date of loan].

As you can see from the above, you have two methods of obtaining the information and document you need through Discovery procedures. You can use the interrogatories with the notice to produce documents or you can use a deposition along with a subpoena duces tecum. I prefer the latter method myself, as you can grill them and ask them several questions, some of which you will only think of at the time of the deposition. (To set up a deposition, read the instructions in the book *Discovery Made Simple*, available from PIN.)

HOW TO CALCULATE ACTUAL DAMAGES

Once you know what percent of each loan you were required to purchase for the stock and you know the total dollar value of all payment you made to PCA or FLB, it is easy to calculate actual damages. Let's take an example: Let's say that on all your loans from PCA or FLB, you were required to buy 10% of the loan's value as "stock," and let's say that in 5 years on this loan you paid $50,000 in payments for both principal and interest. To calculate the actual damages is simple. All you do is multiply the percent of the loans that went for the stock purchase against the total payments you made to PCA or FLB. Take 10% (amount of stock purchase) times $50,000 (total amount of payments). This equals $5,000 ($50,000 × .10 = $5,000).

Now, under the RICO (Racketeering) laws, 18 USCS 1964, you are entitled to triple damages. So three times $5,000 equals $15,000.

$15,000 is the amount federal law requires the court to grant to you in damages. On top of this, you can ask for punitive damages of 3 times $15,000 or $45,000 or a total of $60,000 ($15,000 plus $45,000). Now we are talking about a sum to potentially wipe out the entire loan.

Now when you hit PCA or FLB in Federal Court with one of these suits, and you must sue them on this issue in Federal court, then they may call you and want to settle out of court. If you decide to settle out of court, I suggest that you ask for these three things:

a. That they drop the foreclosure action against you.

b. Refinance the loans you have with them at 6% interest, and not escalator clauses.

c. You will dismiss your suit against them.

JURISDICTIONAL CONSIDERATIONS

Since State Courts have jurisdiction to hear all foreclosure actions and because the racketeering laws (RICO) are Federal, so the State Courts have jurisdiction to hear the RICO cases? According to Attorney Carla Struble of Columbus, Ohio, they have used RICO in the state courts and jurisdiction has not been challenged. This is good news. However, if the plaintiff challenge the court's jurisdiction to hear the RICO part of your Counterclaim, then you should file a Petition for Removal to Federal Court. Be sure your Counterclaim mentioned, under Jurisdiction, 28 U.S.C. Sec. 1332 and that the amount in controversy exceeded $10,000.

If you live in a state where they foreclose against you without going to court, write up your suit on the credit issue and any and all other issues you can think of that apply to your case and add the racketeering charges and file it in the Federal District Court nearest you. Either way, you will need a book called *"Federal Rules of Civil Procedure."* You can obtain one by sending 15.00 to *West Publishing Co., P.O. Box 43526, St. Paul, Minn. 55164.* Send for this book as soon as possible. The amount ($15.00) is sufficient to cover the cost of the book as well as postage. They may give you a slight refund that will vary from state to state.

Q: What do I do if I have already filed a Complaint or a Counterclaim in State Court?

A: File an Amended Complaint or an Amended Counterclaim and add the charges. If the time to file an Amended Complaint or Counterclaim has expired under State statutes, then write up a whole new lawsuit and file it in Federal Court. After doing this, then file a Petition for Removal to Federal Court of the existing case in the State court, after which you file a Motion to Consolidate Cases in Federal Court. (Instructions on How to remove a case from state court to federal court are available from PIN for $3.00.)

WRITING A SUIT OR AMENDING ONE

Be sure the following information gets in under: (add the following to Model lawsuit #2)

JURISDICTION

Jurisdiction in this action is based, in part on 28 U.S.C. Sec. 1332, and involves more than $10,000 in controversy. Jurisdiction is also based on 18 U.S.C. 1964.

MODEL LAWSUIT #3

Note: (This model lawsuit contains information that should be added to Model Lawsuit #1 or #2 and should be filed before a sheriff or trustee sale. The purpose of this lawsuit is to stop a sheriff or trustee sale after an FRC was used to pay off a debt or judgment. For purposes of this suit, it is assumed that you have already sent an affidavit to the sheriff/trustee that the debt/judgment has been paid in full and that you have returned to the lender the full amount

of credit you owed him. If you lacked the time to use the information in Model #3 before the sheriff/trustee sale, then go directly to Model #4 and file this after the sheriff/trustee sale as soon as possible. Model lawsuit #5 is designed to be used if you go to a sheriff sale and bid 21 or more dollars in silver and gold coins on another person's property. In all these lawsuits, omit what is not applicable to your situation and add whatever else is applicable. These lawsuits may be filed in either state or federal court.)

MODEL LAWSUIT #3

[your name],
    Plaintiff,

vs.
                    Case # . . . .
                    Complaint at Law

Bank of [? / PCA / FLB etc.], and
Federal Reserve Bank President [name] and
Sheriff [name] and
John and Jane Does (1 to 25),
    Defendants.

Now Comes the plaintiffs, in propria personna, and relying upon the decisions in *Haines* v. *Kerner,* 404 US 519, and show their complaint against the defendants as follows:

JURISDICTION

   1. See Model Lawsuit #1.

PARTIES TO THE ACTION

   2. See Model Lawsuit #2, and add: (Sheriff [name], who is the sheriff of ? county and whose address is [address of sheriff's department or his home].

FACTUAL BACKGROUND

   3 through 12. See Model Lawsuit #1 or #2 and add the following paragraph:

   13. (On "day-month-year," the plaintiff sent a check to "bank, FLB, PCA etc." for the sum of $... The plaintiff did pay off the debt/judgment dollar for dollar by returning to [name of lender] the same amount of credit they had loaned us. The plaintiffs have discharged the debt/judgment by returning full payment in like kind of money. On or about "month-day-year," the plaintiff sent an affidavit to the sheriff attesting to the fact that the debt/judgment had been paid in full and requested that the sheriff sale be cancelled. The sheriff knows or should have

known that the contents of the affidavit are true. Yet, I have recently been informed by the sheriff's department that they plan to sell my property on "planned date of sale." The plaintiff's right not to be denied property without due process under the 5th and 14th amendments will be violated if the sheriff sale goes through as planned and the title to the plaintiff's property will be clouded by said sale. Furthermore, the plaintiff is not aware of any counter affidavit signed by the [lender] which says that "the debt has not been discharged in a like kind of money." In the absence of such an affidavit, the sheriff is bound by all the principles of our legal system to honor the plaintiff's affidavit and cancel said sheriff sale. The plaintiff believes that the sheriff sale will place the sheriff in violation of 42 USC 1983 and with an unknown party may also be in violation of 18 USC 241.

Counts 1 and 2 and 3 (See Model Lawsuits #1 or #2)

Relief Requested (See Models #1 or #2) and add the following:

#? Plaintiffs restate by reference all the averments of this complaint. Plaintiffs ask the court for a Temporary Restraining Order to stop pending sheriff sale and to suspend it for a minimum of 6 months until the merits of their case has been adjudicated before a jury. This request is made pursuant to their right to trial by jury under the 7th amendment to the Bill of Rights as well as their right not to be denied property without due process of law under the 5th and 14th amendments. Plaintiff also ask the court to order the sheriff to show cause why the plaintiff's affidavit is not being honored in the absence of a counter affidavit from the lender.

Date. . . . .   X . . . .

Exhibits: A copy of the Affidavit sent to the sheriff is attached hereto.

MODEL LAWSUIT #4

Note: (Model lawsuit #4 is filed shortly after a sheriff or trustee sale. If you have previously filed Model lawsuit #3 and if for some reason, it did not stop the sheriff or trustee sale, then you simply file an "Amended Complaint" and add the new material from Model lawsuit #4. If you did your homework, you should have plenty of exhibits to attach to Model lawsuit #4. If you did not file Model lawsuit #3, then #4 provides material to be added to Model Lawsuit #1 or #2 that can be found in the instructions that go with the Memorandum of Law on Bank Credit and Voidable Contracts. Although Model #4 can be used in state court, there are several reasons to believe that it will be more effective to file it in federal court. Model #4 is designed on the assumption that you placed a bid of 21 or more dollars in silver coin at the sheriff or trustee sale and that you also challenged the lender bid in credit money as described in the complaint. If these later conditions are not applicable, then omit them or modify the complaint accordingly.)

IN THE UNITED STATES DISTRICT COURT FOR THE. . .DISTRICT OF. . .

Caption—See Model Lawsuits #1, #2 or #3.

Under the defendants, add:
[name of bank against whose account the high bid in credit money was drawn at the sheriff sale]

Now Comes the plaintiffs, in propria personna, and relying upon the decisions in *Haines* v. *Kerner*, 404 US 519, and shows their complaint against the defendants as follows:

JURISDICTION
1. See Model Lawsuits 1, 2 or 3.
PARTIES TO THE ACTION
2. See Model Lawsuits 1, 2 or 3 and add the sheriff's name and the name of the bank against whom the check was drawn that the sheriff accepted for the high bid.
FACTUAL BACKGROUND
3 through 12. See Model Lawsuits 1, 2 or 3 and add the following:
#? Prior to the sheriff/trustee sale and on or about [month/day/year], the plaintiff sent a check to the [lender] for the sum of $. . . and paid the debt/judgment in full by returning payment in like kind of money. After this, the plaintiff did send to the sheriff whose name is. . .an affidavit that attested to the fact that the debt/judgment had been paid and discharged. Also, no counter affidavit was filed

by the [lender] that stated that "the debt had not been discharged in a like kind of money." The sheriff knew or should have known that the contents of my affidavit were true as there was no counter affidavit provided by the [lender]. In the absense of a counter affidavit, the sheriff violated all the principles of our legal system by selling the plaintiff's property on [month / day / year] to [name of highest bidder in credit money]. The sheriff did cloud and slander the title of the plaintiff's property and did deny him property without due court process which is the plaintiff's inalienable right under the 7th and 14th amendments to the U.S. Constitution. The sheriff sold the plaintiff's property deliberately to the detriment and damage of the plaintiff. The property the sheriff sold is located at. . . .

#? At the sheriff sale which occurred on [month / day / year], the plaintiff, [your name], in order to protect his interest in said property, felt compelled to place a high bid in lawful money of the United States. The plaintiff, [your name] did place a high bid in lawful money as required by Article 1, Section 10 of the U.S. Constitution. Article 1, Sec. 10 of the U.S. Constitution which says: "No State shall make anything but gold and silver coin a tender in payment of debts." Since the sheriff's department and his position is created under the jurisdiction of the state of. . . , the sheriff is bound by Art. 1, Sec. 10. He is further bound by his oath of office to uphold and defend the Constitution of the United States. The meaning of Art. 1, Sec. 10 is very clear on its face and the sheriff was aware of this prohibition and the sheriff [his name] is aware of its clear and unambiguous meaning. The plaintiff, [your name] did place the high bid in lawful money of the United States by offering the sum of $. . .dollars in silver coins. This bid was witnessed by the following persons: [insert names of witnesses present]. The sheriff did refuse to accept the high bid in silver coins and instead awarded the sale to [name] for a [Cashiers / Certified Check] which was offered by [name] for the sum of $. . . .

#? The plaintiff having knowledge that many "bad" checks are being submitted by financial institutions at sheriff sales and suspecting that this had happened here, asked the sheriff for a photocopy of the check submitted. This check was drawn on the bank of. . . . The plaintiff, with a tape recorder and with witnesses, went to the bank against whose funds this check was drawn and placed a tape recorder on the counter at the bank and proceeded to show the clerk behind the counter a photocopy of the check. (Note: if the sheriff won't give you a copy of the check, ask him the bank it is drawn against and the name on the corporation listed on the check.) The plaintiff then asked the clerk at the bank after showing the clerk a photocopy of the check (or verbally telling her the amount of the check) if they have sufficient cash in their vault to cash this check today. The clerk told us that the bank did not have enough cash to cash this check for the sum of $. . . . When asked what her name was she said it was [name of clerk]. (Note: in writing this part of the complaint, describe exactly what happened as it occurred at the bank.)

#? Upon learning that the bank has written / certified a bad check, we returned to the sheriff's department and played the tape recording to him. Yet, in spite of what evidence we showed him, the sheriff still insisted he would accept the cashier's / certified check. We also informed the sheriff that the bank had committed a fraud and that this was illegal. We also pointed out that the state statutes under [statute] requires bids at sheriff's sales to be placed in "cash and lawful money of the United States." We also showed the sheriff sale Art. 1, Sec. 10 of the U.S. Constitution and reminded him of his oath of office. The sheriff did accept a bad check written by [name of bidder] and drawn against the bank of. . . . The sheriff also committed perjury by failing to grant the sheriff's deed to the plaintiff, [your name], and instead gave the sheriff a bad check which was not redeemable in Federal Reserve Notes or coins, let alone gold and silver coin. The sheriff did this deliberately to the detriment and damage of the plaintiff(s).

Counts 1, 2 and 3 (See Model Lawsuits 1 or 2) and add the following:
Count 4
The averments of the previously numbered paragraphs are restated by reference herein. The sheriff violated the plaintiff's Constitutional rights under the 5th and 14th amendments and thus violated 42 USC 1983. The sheriff knew from the affidavit that the plaintiff, [your name] had paid the debt in full, in like kind of money. Yet, the sheriff did deliberately sell the plaintiff(s) property to the detriment and damage of the plaintiff. The sheriff accepted a

bad check from [name of bidder] as lawful money and knew that this was not lawful money and the sheriff [name] did this deliberately to the detriment and damage of the plaintiff. The sheriff violated his oath of office by not accepting the high bid in silver coins as he is required to do by his oath of office and then even violated the legal tender laws of Congress by not requiring actual coins or currency issued by the U.S. Government, but instead accepted a bad check from [high bidder]. Plaintiff asks as damages the costs of this action and a verdict from a jury trial voiding the deed issued at the sheriff sale and awarding the sheriff's deed to the plaintiff as well as reasonable compensatory damages to the plaintiff as determined by the jury.

Count 5

The averments of the previously numbered paragraphs are restated by reference herein. For not having cash to redeem the Cashiers check / Certified check, the plaintiff charges the bank and the person who signed or certified the check with Fraud. Plaintiff asks for a jury verdict to determine the fraud charge against the bank and for the costs of this action and for reasonable compensatory damages for the plaintiff as determined by the jury. The person who certified the check / wrote and signed the cashiers check is...(or is unknown at this time).

Relief Requested

1 through 3 (See Model Lawsuits 1 or 2) and add this:

4. Plaintiff ask the court for an Order for the Arrest of the bank official who certified the check / wrote the cashiers check and that he be charged with fraud. Plaintiffs ask the court to issue a Writ of Quo Warranto to execute the same. Plaintiffs further ask the court to empanel a Grand Jury or to direct the plaintiff to an existing Grand Jury so as to allow the plaintiffs to present written and oral testimony to the Grand Jury concerning violations of Federal and State criminal law by one or more defendants named herein.

Date........   X ....

MODEL LAWSUIT #5

[your name],
    Plaintiff,

vs.

Sheriff [name] and,
[Name of high bidder in unlawful money] and,
John and Jane Does,
    Defendants.

Case # _____
Complaint at Law

Now Comes the plaintiff, [your name] and relying upon the decisions found in *Haines* v. *Kerner*, 404 U.S. 519, and shows their complaint against the defendants as follows:

JURISDICTION

1. Jurisdiction in this action is based on the 7th amendment to the Bill of Rights as this is a "Suit at Common Law" and the value in controversy exceeds twenty dollars. Jurisdiction is further based on Article 1, Section 10 of the U.S. Constitution which prohibits states from making any thing but gold and silver coin a tender in payment of debts. Jurisdiction is further based on the common law tort of fraud.

2. Article 1, Section 10 of the U.S. Constitution says in part: "No State shall...make any Thing but gold and silver coin a Tender in Payment of Debts" and the 7th amendment to the Bill of Rights says: "In suits at common law, where the value in controversy shall exceed twenty dollars, the right of trial by jury shall be preserved."

3. This suit is filed in a court of record and in an action at common law in contrast to a suit in equity or chancery jurisdiction. The plaintiff has the right to have the issues tried to a jury where the issues of law as well as fact can be determined. In contrast, a jury trial only allows issues of facts in dispute to be determined. In a suit at common law, Motions to Dismiss, Demurs and Motions for Summary Judgment are not allowed as these are equity proceedings and are tried to a judge rather than a jury. If the defendants invoke the court's equity jurisdiction, it will be a violation of the plaintiff's 7th amendment rights as well as his 5th and 14th amendment rights. The plaintiff(s) request that the court act as an impartial referee so as both plaintiff(s) and defendants are afforded "due process" and a fair trial.

PARTIES TO THE ACTION

4. The plaintiff(s) in this suit at common law are citizens of the United States and residents of the State of.... The Plaintiff(s) names and addresses are as follows:...and.... The defendants in this action are Sheriff [name] who is the sheriff for...county. His address is [either insert home address or the address of the sheriff's department]. The sheriff is an elected / appointed official who has taken an oath to uphold and defend the Constitution of the United States. Sheriff [name] is being sued in his capacity as an individual and not in his official capacity. The other defendant in this action is an employee or agent for [bank or other financial institution]. This person [insert name or declare it to be a John or Jane Doe if you don't know the name] is being sued in their individual and not in their official capacity under the common law. The address of the second defendant is....

FACTUAL BACKGROUND

5. On or about [month / day / year], the plaintiff(s) in this action learned that a sheriff sale for the property located at...would be held by the sheriff's department on [date of sale]. The property located at the above address is legally described as follows:

[Insert legal description here]

6. On the morning of [date of sheriff or trustee sale], the plaintiff(s), [your name], did appear at [describe location of sheriff / trustee sale; give address] for the purpose of placing a bid in lawful money of the United States for the property described in the preceding paragraph. At or about [time], defendant Sheriff [name] came to this location for the purpose of conducting a sheriff sale on the above referenced property. Persons known to the plaintiff who were present to witness the sale were [names of witnesses].

7. In this paragraph, describe what happened exactly as it happened. Have your tape recorder running so you can recall events as they occur.

8. Then I approached the sheriff and told him I had good cause to believe that the check may not be good and I asked him for a photocopy of it. [If the sheriff won't give you the photocopy, then ask for the name of the bank it is drawn against and the account number and the name of the organization or person issuing it.] The sheriff gave me a photocopy of the check.

Count One

9. The averments of the previously numbered paragraphs are restated by reference herein. Plaintiffs charge the [person who signed and certified the check] with fraud and misrepresentation. Since the bank did not have the coins and currency to cash the check, their Cashiers / Certified check was a fraudulent representation. Plaintiffs ask for a jury determination of this fraud charge. Plaintiffs also ask for the cost of this action plus reasonable compensatory and punitive damages against [name of person signing or certifying cashiers / certified check].

Count Two

10. The averments of the previously numbered paragraphs are restated by reference herein. Sheriff [name] has damaged the plaintiff, [your name], deliberately and knowingly by refusing to accept our / my high bid in lawful money of the United States, which is required by Article 1, Sec. 10 of the U.S. Constitution to be gold or silver coins. The sheriff has also violated his own oath of office to uphold and defend the Constitution of the United States. The plaintiff asks for a jury determination on which of the bidders placed the high bid in lawful money of the United States as required by our Constitution and for a verdict awarding the Sheriff's Deed to the plaintiff, [your name] as the one bid which was the high bid in lawful money. Plaintiff asks for the costs of this action to be assessed against the sheriff in his capacity as an individual.

Relief Requested

11. The averments of the previously numbered paragraphs are restated by reference herein. The Plaintiff(s) ask the court for an Order for Arrest of the bank official who signed / certified the cashiers / certified check and that he / she be charged with fraud for misrepresentation of the check. Plaintiffs ask the court to issue a Writ of Quo Warranto to execute the same. Plaintiffs further ask the court to empanel a Grand Jury or to direct the plaintiff to an existing Grand Jury so as to allow the plaintiff(s) to present written and verbal testimony to the Grand Jury concerning violations of Federal and State law including and not limited to 18 USC 241, 18 USC 1001, and 18 USC 1621 and other violations of law against the defendants named herein as well as any other parties that may have conspired with them to violate the

above named laws.

12. Plaintiff(s) demand a trial by jury under the 7th amendment on all issues including the issue of what constitutes "lawful money" for a sheriff department under state jurisdiction. Plaintiff(s) demand all their rights at all times and waive none of their rights at any time including their right to time.

Date.........   X ....

LEGAL KARATE: Additional Notes and Comments.

SAMPLE COPY OF DOCKET FILE (Foreclosure on a business shown below.)

```
0033325 S        PROPERTY      FORECLOSURE                              03-10-81
            SHOPPING   MALL
```

```
------------------------------------------------ -----------
                                    SOROKIN,S.H.W.RG          060113
                                       EDWARD JENNINGS             71
                                        81-03-04

                                    TRANTOLO & T.             064310
                                       PARTITION CONTRACTING CO.     64
                                        81-03-30

                                    UPDIKE, K.&S.             065040
                                       ANTONIO REALE              50
                                        81-03-04






                                         JA-0002    02/09/83       4
```

```
0033325 S          PROPERTY       FORECLOSURE                        03-10-81
CV 81
BANKING CENTER                    LITCHFIELD                         03-02-81
          VS.                                    COURT
REALE, ANTONIO         ET AL   DISTRICT OFFICE                       NON PRIV.
```

```
GAGER,H & N                   021257   NO APPEARANCE PARTIES
   BANKING CENTER                01    * COLONIAL .ELECTRIC INCORPORAT    57
   81-03-02                                 ED
                                        BANKING CENTER                   59
                                      * UNITED STATES OF AMERICA          61
                                        GRINNELL FIRE PROTECTION SYS      62
                                           TEMS COMPANY, INC.
                                        PELLETIER SHEET METAL CO., I      63
                                           NC.
                                        JAMES J. TORRANT, INC.           65
                                        JOSEPH SCHNIER, INC.             66

                                      ALCORN,B.&S.                   000362
                                        ASTRO LANES, INC.               67
                                        81-03-11

                                      BAI, P. & D.                   001440
                                        SAFECO INSURANCE CO. OF AMER    60
                                           ICA


                                            JA-0002    02/09/83          1
```

```
0033325 S          PROPERTY       FORECLOSURE                        03-10-81
```

```
                                      81-03-11

                                      HOND, L. & F.                  028211
                                        C. LAVIERI & SONS, INC.         52
                                        81-03-12

                                      BYRNE,S.&S.,P.C.               034579
                                        KING'S DEPT. STORE, INC.        58
                                        81-03-12

                                      MERRIAM,V.C.& H.               037468
                                        MANCHESTER STATE BANK           68
                                        81-03-11
                                        NEW JERSEY BANK N.A.            69
                                        81-03-11
                                        FLEMINGTON NATIONAL BANK & T    70
                                           RUST CO.
                                        81-03-11


                                            JA-0002    02/09/83          2
```

```
101-00      PTF                  REQUEST FOR DISCLOSURE OF DEFENSE
   03-16-81

102-01      PTF                  MOTION FOR DEFAULT FOR FAILURE TO
   03-25-81 APPEAR                          STOUGHTON, J.
            ORDER 04-20-81

102-02      PTF                  MOTION FOR DEFAULT FOR FAILURE TO DIS-
   03-25-81 CLOSE DEFENSE                    STOUGHTON, J.
            ORDER 04-06-81

102-03      PTF                  MOTION FOR JUDGMENT OF STRICT FORE-
   03-25-81 CLOSURE

103-00      DFD SAFECO INSURANCE DISCLOSURE OF DEFENSE
   03-26-81

104-00      DFD SAFECO INSURANCE OBJECTION TO MOTION FOR DEFAULT
   03-26-81

105-00      DFD SAFECO INSURANCE MOTION FOR JUDGMENT OF FORECLOSURE BY
   03-26-81 SALE

106-00      DFD                  DISCLOSURE OF DEFENSE
  :03-27-81

107-00      PTF                  REQUEST FOR DISCLOSURE OF DEFENSE
   03-30-81

108-00      DFD C. LAVIERI & SON DISCLOSURE OF DEFENSE
   03-31-81

108-50      DFD C. LAVIERI & SON REQUEST TO REVISE
   03-31-81

109-00      DFD SAFECO INSURANCE NOTICE OF INTENTION TO ARGUE OR
   04-01-81 PRESENT TESTIMONY

110-00      DFD KING'S DEPT. STO ANSWER SPECIAL DEFENSE & COUNTERCLAIM
   04-02-81

111-00      DFD KING'S DEPT. STO MOTION FOR PERMISSION FOR OUT OF STATE
   04-02-81 COUNSEL TO APPEAR

112-00      DFD KING'S DEPT. STO DISCLOSURE OF DEFENSE
   04-06-81
```

```
CV  KEY POINT STATUS  ASSIGNED                                          1
81  LITCHFIELD    SUPERIOR      04/06/83
DN 003 33 25 S   BANKING CENTER             V REALE, ANTONIO    ET AL
                                            JA-0003A
```

113-00
04-06-81   DFD KING'S DEPT. STO CROSS COMPLAINT

114-00
04-06-81   DFD   MOTION FOR TEMPORARY INJUNCTION

115-00
04-06-81   DFD CONNECTICUT BANK DISCLOSURE OF DEFENSE

116-00
04-06-81   DFD MONTEROSS ET AL DISCLOSURE OF DEFENSE

117-00
04-06-81   DFD CONNECTICUT BANK MOTION FOR STAY

118-00
04-08-81   DFD REALE   ANSWER

119-00
04-08-81   DFD REALE   DISCLOSURE OF DEFENSE

120-00
04-10-81   PTF   REQUEST FOR DISCLOSURE OF DEFENSE

121-00
04-10-81   DFD MANCHESTER STATE MOTION TO WITHDRAW APPEARANCE
            GRNTD 08-02-82   STOUGHTON, J.

122-00
04-13-81   DFD MONTEROSS ET AL ANSWER & SPECIAL DEFENSE

123-00
04-13-81   PTF   MOTION FOR DEFAULT FOR FAILURE TO
            PLEAD

124-00
04-16-81   DFD SAFECO INSURANCE NOTICE OF INTENTION TO ARGUE OR
            PRESENT TESTIMONY

125-00
04-16-81   DFD SAFECO INSURANCE ANSWER

126-00
04-20-81   WIT   AMENDED RETURN OR AMENDED OFFICERS
            RETURN

127-00
04-24-81   DFD REALE   REQUEST TO AMEND & AMENDMENT

CV KEY POINT STATUS ASSIGNED
81 LITCHFIELD   SUPERIOR   04/06/83
DN 003 33 25 S   BANKING CENTER   V REALE, ANTONIO   ET AL
                                   JA-C003A

128-00   DFD C. LAVIERI & SON REQUEST RE DISCLOSURE & PRODUCTION
04-24-81   REALE

129-00   DFD C. LAVIERI & SON REQUEST RE DISCLOSURE & PRODUCTION
04-24-81   BANKING CENTER

130-00   DFD SAFECO INSURANCE REQUEST FOR LEAVE TO FILE AMENDMENT
04-27-81   AND AMENDMENT

131-00   DFD   MOTION FOR STAY
05-01-81

132-00   DFD KING'S DEPT. STO AMENDED CROSS COMPLAINT
05-07-81   C. LAVIERI & SONS, I

133-00   PTF KING'S DEPT. STO MOTION FOR TEMPORARY INJUNCTION
05-07-81   C. LAVIERI & SONS, I

134-00   WIT   SHERIFFS RETURN
05-08-81

135-00   PTF   REQUEST FOR LEAVE TO FILE AMENDMENT
06-04-81   AND AMENDMENT

136-00   WIT   SUPPLEMENTAL RETURN
07-21-81

137-00   DFD C. LAVIERI & SON MOTION TO COMPEL
09-25-81   REALE
            ORDER 10-05-81   PICKETT J.

138-00   DFD C. LAVIERI & SON MOTION TO COMPEL
09-25-81   BANKING CENTER
            OVER 10-05-81   PICKETT J.

139-00   PTF   REQUEST FOR LEAVE TO FILE AMENDMENT
10-08-81   AND AMENDMENT

140-00   DFD KING'S DEPT. STO ANSWER & SPECIAL DEFENSE
11-06-81

141-00   PTF   MOTION TO STRIKE
11-19-81
            DEND 02-10-82   STOUGHTON, J.

142-00   PTF   BRIEF/CLAIMS OF LAW
11-19-81

CV KEY POINT STATUS ASSIGNED
81 LITCHFIELD   SUPERIOR   04/06/83
DN 003 33 25 S   BANKING CENTER   V REALE, ANTONIO   ET AL
                                            JA-0003A

143-00 11-19-81	PTF	MOTION TO STRIKE
	ORDER 02-10-82	STOUGHTON, J.
144-00 11-19-81	PTF	BRIEF/CLAIMS OF LAW
145-00 11-19-81	PTF	MEMORANDUM
146-00 11-19-81	PTF	AFFIDAVIT
147-00 11-19-81	PTF	MOTION TO STRIKE
	DEND 02-10-82	STOUGHTON, J.
148-00 11-19-81	PTF	MOTION TO STRIKE
	DEND 02-10-82	STOUGHTON, J.
149-00 12-01-81	PTF	MOTION TO STRIKE
150-00 12-01-81	PTF	BRIEF/CLAIMS OF LAW
151-00 12-04-81	DFD C. LAVIERI & SON	ANSWER & SPECIAL DEFENSE
152-00 12-04-81	DFD C. LAVIERI & SON	BRIEF
153-00 12-15-81	PTF	MOTION TO STRIKE
	DEND 02-10-82	STOUGHTON, J.
154-00 12-15-81	PTF	BRIEF/CLAIMS OF LAW
155-00 12-16-81	DFD	MEMORANDUM
155-50 12-21-82	DFD REALE	BRIEF/CLAIMS OF LAW
156-00 12-23-81	DFD	NOTICE OF FILING OF INTERROGATORIES

```
CV  KEY POINT STATUS  ASSIGNED                                                    4
81  LITCHFIELD       SUPERIOR      04/06/83
DN 003 33 25 S        BANKING CENTER                V REALE, ANTONIO      ET AL
                                            JA-0003A
```

157-00 12-28-81	DFD	REQUEST TO AMEND & AMENDMENT
158-00 01-05-82	DFD C. LAVIERI & SON	BRIEF/CLAIMS OF LAW
159-00 01-14-82	PTF	BRIEF
160-00 02-01-82	DFD KING'S DEPT. STO	BRIEF/CLAIMS OF LAW
161-00 02-10-82	CRT	MEMORANDUM OF DECISION
162-00 02-17-82	DFD MONTEROSSO	ANSWER TO COMPLAINT AS AMENDED
163-00 02-17-82	DFD MONTEROSSO ORDER 05-03-82	MOTION FOR DEFAULT STOUGHTON, J.
164-00 03-09-82	DFD REALE DEND 04-28-82	MOTION FOR SUMMARY JUDGMENT STOUGHTON, J.
165-00 03-09-82	DFD REALE	AFFIDAVIT
166-00 03-09-82	DFD REALE	BRIEF/CLAIMS OF LAW
167-00 03-11-82	PTF	REPLY TO SPECIAL DEFENSE
168-00 03-11-82	PTF	REPLY TO SPECIAL DEFENSE
169-00 03-11-82	PTF	REPLY TO SPECIAL DEFENSE
170-00 03-11-82	PTF	REPLY TO SPECIAL DEFENSE
171-00 03-15-82		CLAIM FOR TRIAL LIST

```
CV  KEY POINT STATUS  ASSIGNED
81  LITCHFIELD      SUPERIOR      04/06/83
DN 003 33 25 S     BANKING CENTER              V REALE, ANTONIO        ET AL
                                      JA-0003A
```

172-00 03-19-82	DFD REALE	CLAIM FOR JURY OF 6
173-00 03-25-82	PTF CLOSE DEFENSE GRNTD 04-12-82	MOTION FOR DEFAULT FOR FAILURE TO DIS- STOUGHTON, J.
173-50 03-25-82	PTF	MOTION FOR JUDGMENT
174-00 03-26-82	PTF	REQUEST RE INTERROGATORIES
175-00 03-31-82	PTF	OBJECTION TO MOTION
176-00 03-31-82	PTF AFFIDAVIT DEND 04-28-82	MOTION FOR SUMMARY JUDGMENT AND STOUGHTON, J.
177-00 03-31-82	PTF	MEMORANDUM
178-00 04-05-82	DFD MONTEROSSO	OBJECTION TO INTERROGATORIES
179-00 04-06-82	DFD MONTEROSS ET AL	REQUEST TO REVISE
180-00 04-08-82	PTF	REPLY TO SPECIAL DEFENSE MONTEROSSO
181-00 04-08-82	PTF	MOTION FOR SUMMARY JUDGMENT
182-00 04-08-82	PTF	BRIEF/CLAIMS OF LAW
183-00 04-08-82	PTF	AFFIDAVIT
184-00 04-08-82	PTF DEND 04-28-82	MOTION FOR SUMMARY JUDGMENT STOUGHTON, J.
185-00 04-08-82	PTF	BRIEF/CLAIMS OF LAW

```
CV  KEY POINT STATUS  ASSIGNED
81  LITCHFIELD      SUPERIOR         04/06/83
DN 003 33 25 S      BANKING CENTER                V REALE, ANTONIO          ET
                                         JA-0003A
```

186-00 04-08-82	PTF	AFFIDAVIT
187-00 04-08-82	PTF	EXHIBITS FILED
188-00 04-23-82	DFD ORDER 05-10-82	MOTION FOR EXTENSION OF TIME STOUGHTON, J.
189-00 04-26-82	DFD	MEMORANDUM
190-00 04-26-82	PTF TIME	OBJECTION TO MOTION FOR EXTENSION OF
191-00 04-26-82	PTF	REQUEST RE INTERROGATORIES
192-00 04-26-82	PTF OR PRODUCTION	REQUEST RE EXAMINATION INSPECTION
193-00 04-26-82	DFD	OBJECTION TO MOTION
194-00 04-26-82	DFD	REQUEST TO REVISE
195-00 04-19-82	DFD	BRIEF/CLAIMS OF LAW
196-00 04-19-82	DFD	AFFIDAVIT
197-00 05-03-82	PTF ORDER 05-05-82	OBJECTION TO REQUEST TO REVISE STOUGHTON, J.
198-00 05-07-82	PTF	DISCLOSURE & PRODUCTION
199-00 05-12-82	PTF GRNTD 06-21-82	MOTION TO STRIKE FROM JURY DOCKET MISSAL J
200-00 05-13-82	DFD REALE	OBJECTION TO INTERROGATORIES

```
CV   KEY POINT STATUS  ASSIGNED
01   LITCHFIELD       SUPERIOR        04/06/83
DN 003 33 25 S       BANKING CENTER              V REALE, ANTONIO       ET AL
                                         JA-0003A
```

201-00 05-13-82	DFD REALE	MOTION FOR EXTENSION OF TIME
	ORDER 05-24-82	HULL, J
202-00 05-13-82	DFD REALE	MOTION FOR EXTENSION OF TIME
	ORDER 05-24-82	HULL, J
203-00 05-17-82	PTF AND AMENDMENT	REQUEST FOR LEAVE TO FILE AMENDMENT
204-00 05-18-82	DFD	ANSWER TO INTERROGATORIES
205-00 05-19-82	DFD MONTEROSSO	ANSWER TO INTERROGATORIES
206-00 05-20-82	DFD	MOTION FOR EXTENSION OF TIME
	GRNTD 06-21-82	MISSAL J
207-00 05-20-82	DFD	REQUEST RE DISCLOSURE
208-00 05-21-82	PTF	BRIEF/CLAIMS OF LAW
209-00 05-28-82	DFD	MOTION FOR ORDER
	ORDER 06-21-82	MISSAL J
210-00 06-16-82	DFD MONTEROSSO	NOTICE OF FILING OF DISCOVERY REQUEST
211-00 06-16-82	DFD MONTEROSSO	REQUEST RE DISCLOSURE & PRODUCTION
212-00 07-09-82	DFD C. LAVIERI & SON	REQUEST TO AMEND & AMENDMENT
213-00 08-02-82	PTF	MOTION FOR DEFAULT MONTEROSSO
214-00 08-02-82	PTF	MOTION FOR DEFAULT REALE
215-00 08-04-82	DFD	OBJECTION TO MOTION FOR DEFAULT

216-00 09-04-82	DFD	MOTION FOR DEFAULT
217-00 09-07-82	DFD	MOTION FOR SANCTIONS
218-00 02-09-83	PTF PARTICULAR DEFENDANT	WITHDRAWAL OF ACTION AGAINST COLONIAL ELECTRIC IN
219-00 02-09-83	PTF PARTICULAR DEFENDANT	WITHDRAWAL OF ACTION AGAINST UNITED STATES OF AME
220-01 03-25-83	PTF PLEAD	MOTION FOR DEFAULT FOR FAILURE TO
220-02 03-25-83	PTF	REQUEST FOR DISCLOSURE OF DEFENSE
220-03 03-25-83	PTF CLOSURE	MOTION FOR JUDGMENT OF STRICT FORE-
221-00 03-30-83	DFD	OBJECTION TO REQUEST
222-00 03-30-83	DFD	OBJECTION TO MOTION
223-00 04-04-83	DFD SAFECO INSURANCE PRESENT TESTIMONY	NOTICE OF INTENTION TO ARGUE OR
224-00 04-06-83	PTF CLOSE DEFENSE	MOTION FOR DEFAULT FOR FAILURE TO DIS-
224-50 04-06-83	PTF	MOTION FOR JUDGMENT
225-00 04-06-83	PTF PLEAD	MOTION FOR DEFAULT FOR FAILURE TO

CV KEY POINT STATUS ASSIGNED   9
81 LITCHFIELD   SUPERIOR   04/06/83
ON 003 33 25 S   BANKING CENTER   V REALE, ANTONIO   ET AL
                                               JA-0003A

Refinancing debts or loans. If you have had occasion to refinance your debt or loan, you must list each and every loan amount from the first one you took out with the lender bank and if possible list the first loan as the original loan. Append this bookkeeping detail to your statement of factual background. If you have not kept track of the exact dates then state "On or around [month, date, year], and if you do not know the exact amount you borrowed, you should indicate the approximate amount. Further, if you don't know the exact amount you paid the lender, then add language to your complaint like "Payments totaling approximately $???,000 were made to the bank from 197? to 198?. Usually, Discovery takes care of resolving such questions. However, it is important to note that Complaints are not written under oath or penalties for perjury, so you are not going to suffer for a minor error.

Co-signing and Mortgage Deed of Trust Assumption. If you assumed a mortgage by co-signing for it, then you must proceed to attack the original loan that was made to the person you co-signed the note with or assumed the note from. Your position is much the same as that of someone who has co-signed on a bad note. Detail the facts in the statement of "Factual Background" in your Complaint. Try to get the person you assumed the note from to join with you in the suit, as a co-plaintiff. If he doesn't cooperate, then list him as a Defendant in your suit, serve him with a Subpoena, charge him with knowledge that he was aware of the bank's fraud, and condoned it even at the time you assumed the note.

Other issues. There are other issues that can be added to individual lawsuits and they vary from case to case. But among these issues, things the lender should not have done would be: 1. "Backdating the Truth and Lending Forms"; 2. "recisions forms executed when the loan was taken out"; 3. "your signature appearing on documents you never signed (such signature made by a duplicating machine)." You can and must learn of their existence through Discovery procedures, depositions and interrogatories; 4. "verbal or written promises that were made to you about refinancing the loan which the lender reneged on unexpectedly or for some hidden reason;" 5. "failure of a corporation to register with the Secretary of State or the State Corporation Commission;" 6. "failure to obtain a Certificate of Authority to do business in the state." This is a particularly useful issue to raise in foreclosure. You find out by writing to your Attorney General's office or to the State Corporation Commission for the foreign corporations status regarding a "Certificate of Authority." Do not overlook any jurisdictional challenge.

Stock Fraud Charges. If as a Defendant you file an Answer and Counterclaim to a corporation foreclosure, add stock fraud charges for requiring you to buy non-existent stock in their associations. If you send them a Notice to Produce Documents, you will find that their stock is nothing more than a book entry and a concealed interest charge.

To block sheriff or trustee sale, use silver dollars with an Affidavit and a Constructive Notice. (See sample instructions in the Models given.)

COUNTERCLAIMS. In states where judicial foreclosures are used, file an Answer and a Counterclaim to any Complaint that is filed against you. In using Model Lawsuits #1 and #2, you reverse positions with the lender, i.e., you are the Defendant counterclaiming against the lender who is the plaintiff. You call your pleading a "Counterclaim at Law" instead of a "Complaint at Law." Also, if you are a Defendant suing another defendant you file a Cross Complaint and you are the Cross Plaintiff. If you bring in a bank or other lender that was not originally mentioned in your lawsuit, you can sue them by filing a "Third Party Complaint." In this, you will be called the Defendant and Third Party Plaintiff and the bank called the Defendant.

Defenses. Today, our courts often become collection agencies for the nation's banks and mortgage companies. This is because people do not avail themselves of the Defenses provided by the courts. They permit Foreclosure by Default and the courts have no alternative.

The purpose of this work is to teach you how to use courtroom karate techniques (a) to banish your fear and to show you how to use your Constitutional rights, especially to keep possession of your property until your case is decided before an impartial jury. Although these instructions are written mainly for the benefit of the "pro se" or person who proceeds in the proper person or "in propria persona," the information in these instructions will undoubtedly be of interest to the licensed attorney as well. It is now recommended that an attorney use all the Constitutional and legal arguments contained in the pleadings which are made a part hereof.

While the rights to a trial by jury is always granted in a criminal proceeding, it is frequently denied in civil proceedings, where the only issue in controversy is an amount of money. Legislators, lawyers, judges, sheriffs, have all taken an oath to uphold the Constitution of the United States, yet most of them fail to carefully read the document they are sworn to uphold.

While the Constitution is the foundation of law in the United States, many Constitutional rights have since been abridged and denied through legislative and judicial fiat. As a result, there are today many laws and practices in conflict with one another. However, because each and every judge and attorney at law has taken such an oath, act and proceed on the premise that it is and remains the Supreme Law of the Land. *Insist on it.*

TRIAL BY MOTION versus TRIAL BY JURY.

Most court cases today are decided with Motion hearings. The most frequently used Motions are a "Motion to Dismiss" and a "Motion for Summary Judgment." If the judge grants either Motion, your case will never come to trial. There is nothing wrong with lawsuits being decided in this manner so long as both sides agree to this format. These types of suits are called "suits in equity or chancery jurisdiction."

However, there is another kind of lawsuit called a "Complaint at Law or Suit at Common Law," and you have a right to have this kind of case tried before a jury, under the 7th Amendment to the Bill of Rights, U.S. Constitution, which says: "In suits at common law, where the value in controversy shall exceed twenty dollars, the right of trial by jury shall be preserved." **That is a Legal Karate hold.** Use it.

The main difference between a "suit in equity" and a "Suit at law" is that the former is tried before a judge while the latter is tried before a Jury.

Chancery or Equity Jurisdiction. Chancery or Equity Jurisdiction occurs every time you present any Motion before a judge. It is practical and possible to file a "COMPLAINT AT LAW" and then file a Motion before the court for some reason as long as your Motion does not deny the other parties' right to a trial by jury or deny them "equal protection of the laws" under the 14th Amendment. A Motion for a Continuance or a Motion for Certification of the Question are all proper Motions to present to the court.

In a Complaint at Law or Suit at Common Law, a Motion to Dismiss for any reason given, such as lack of jurisdiction or failure to state a claim upon which relief can be granted, must be tried before a jury. INSIST UPON IT. When an attorney files any of these Motions or if you do, it is the right of either party to the lawsuit to have such motions tried before a jury. By using these motions you obtain two jury trials. The first will be to determine if the court has proper jurisdiction or if you have a claim upon which relief can be granted.

If the jury decides in your favor, then you proceed to the second jury trial which deals with the merits of the case. The same jury will probably preside in both trials. While the right to a trial by jury is a Constitutional right under the 7th Amendment, practical experience has shown us the courts don't grant jury trials in civil proceedings unless there are MATERIAL FACTS IN DISPUTE. See to it that you bring MATERIAL FACTS INTO DISPUTE.

ANOTHER DEFENSE. One facing a Foreclosure must frame a COMPLAINT or COUNTERCLAIM in a lawsuit. Your Complaint is when you as a Plaintiff sue the defendant. In a Counterclaim, the defendant who is being sued counter sues the Plaintiff or "Counterclaims." The basic elements of a lawsuit are:

1. **Jurisdiction.** Establish what authority under the Constitution or laws you are invoking, so that the court has the authority to act.
2. **Parties.** The names and addresses of each party to the lawsuit, whether plaintiff or defendant, or third party plaintiff or third party defendant must be spelled out. There are also Crosscomplaints, where one defendant sues another defendant.
3. **The Facts.** Be specific and show that the intent of the person you are suing was to defraud you or breach contract or injure you in some way. You must name dates, places and names of persons involved. You need evidence for exhibits, such as letter promising to renew your loan, or offers to lend you money, in writing, or verbally, shortly before the lender reneges and calls in his note.

If you are very smart and shrewd you will take a witness with you and go to your lender and make an offer, within your stated means, to settle your debt, refinance it or whatever. Every word of what your lender counterproposes should be noted as well as any threats he may make to foreclose. The event should be recorded in an Affidavit, signed by your witness, notarized, etc. and presented as an exhibit in evidence.

4. **Laws Violated.** Any laws violated must be cited. You will need the help of an attorney in this area.

5. **Money Damages Relief.** The Relief you are requesting in money damages must be stated in your "COMPLAINT." You will need an attorney to help you in this area.

MODEL LAWSUIT #1. Model Lawsuit number one is a basic lawsuit on the "Money and Credit Issue." It is the model lawsuit you will use to sue the lender bank or institutional lender.

You are strongly advised to get the help of an attorney to add more to it than what is given in the skeleton framework presented. The more issues of facts in dispute that you can set forth the more you will increase your chances of getting a trial by jury, even in today's "equity courts."

Examples of issues of facts in dispute to present in your Complaint.

1. Breach of Contract or Agreement. (Such as when the lender in writing or verbally promises to renew your loan and reverses himself.)

2. If the lender presents documents to the court that you do not remember signing, disclaim them. BE SURE TO DENY YOU SIGNED SUCH DOCUMENTS, EVEN IF THE SIGNATURE APPEARS TO BE YOURS. (Many banks and lending institution have your signature copied by machine and by this means place your signature on documents you never signed.)

Note: In practice this usage of your signature amounts to forgery, accomplished by "signature machines." When filing your Counterclaim, deny signing any and all documents that you do not remember signing. Have your attorney send the lender an Interrogatory or have him take a Deposition in which they are asked if they own a "signature machine," a machine that duplicates a handwritten signature. At a deposition, if they admit to owning such a machine, and most lender banks and institutions have just such a machine, then ask them for what purpose

they own such a machine and why was your signature duplicated as if you had signed documents you had never seen? The answer should be most interesting to the court and especially to a jury.

3. Charge the lender with Usury and violating title 15 of the U.S. Code by not accurately figuring the Annual Percentage Rate based on Regulation Z.

Note: This is strictly legal karate. Why? It so happens that Regulation Z is so complicated that almost no one can figure out how to use it, including lenders and attorneys. Charge that the Annual Percentage Rate the lender has used is higher than the figure he reported in the Truth in Lending Statement. Then in a written interrogatory or at a Deposition, ask the lender to explain in detail how he arrived at his figures for the Annual Percentage Rate used in the loan; further, demand that he show just how this complies with Regulation Z.

4. Add any other issues of facts you can think of including any and all defects in the lenders Complaint, like errors in names, addresses, dates, loan figures, etc.

Courtroom Karate.

WEAPONS IN YOUR ARSENAL OF DEFENSE (Especially as a PLAINTIFF)

• Use of Court Rules.

• Use of an impartial Constitutional lawyer who will present your case in front of an impartial Constitutional judge (one who conscientiously observes his oath to uphold the Constitution of the United States).

• Get your Complaint filed before your opponent brings his action to the court. Attack his complaint, which has to be entered as a counter-suit (as you have made him the Defendant!).

• Diplomatically challenge the Judge as to where he stands with regard to the Constitution being the "Supreme Law of the Land." Does he agree? If not, have your attorney politely request that he disqualify himself for prejudice.

• If the Judge refuses your request have your attorney enter a Motion for Trial by Jury.

• If denied, enter counterclaims and cross claims against your opponent. Bring up every issue of money and credit that you and your lawyer can think of. Attack the Trustee's Complaint.

- Find flaws in every document your opponent presents to the Court.
- Enter Motion for Discovery (see sample given on DISCOVERY in the Appendix).
- The Judge may have a mortgage of record with your lender bank!
- Enter as many Motions for Discovery of facts and evidence in preparation for Trial as you can.
- Enter a Motion to obtain written Interrogatories (Depositions) from every individual connected with the lender in his lending institution who might have performed some act in processing your loan. (At this point, your lender may drop his suit and no longer respond to your Motions. And the Judge upon your Motion to Dismiss may do that very thing.)
- Your best weapons of defense (as a Plaintiff) are Motions for Discovery of Facts and a demand for written Interrogatories.
- Such documentation when gathered over the months, possibly years, will serve you well at Trial.
- Get all the documents you can applicable to your case into production, and file a Request for Admission of Documents.
- Enter a Motion to Terminate Litigation without Trial.
- Hold a series of pre-trial conference. Invoke Court Rules.*

Answering a Complaint. If you use the Fractional Reserve check (example given elsewhere in this book, which the author does not recommend using*) you

---

(*The example has been given as well as the instructions for use as use of these FRCs is becoming better known and more and more successful. Use at your own risk! Better to come into court with clean hands. Author's note.)

may follow model answers in the instructions that go with its use. If you do not use an FRC, an effective way to answer a Complaint that was used by Bob Bennett from Wisconsin is as follows: He denied everything except his name and address. In other words, an Answer to Complaint is a separate paper with that heading. He worded it: ''Now comes the defendant, in his own person, and answers the Complaint as follows:

''1. Defendant admits his name is. . .and that he lives at. . . .

''2. Defendant denies each and every allegation of paragraph two of the Complaint and leaves the burden to prove such allegations to the plaintiff.

Note: Paragraph two of the bank's complaint said that Mr. Bennett had signed a mortgage not on April 1st, 1979. By denying he signed the paper (even though he did so), Bennett forced the case to trial and caused a delay in the case. Had he admitted he signed the note, the bank's attorney would have immediately filed a Motion for Summary Judgment, which would have wiped out all chance of the case going to trial.

Mr. Bennett's admission of having signed the note would also have wiped out any chance of getting a jury trial.

When you answer. When you answer a Complaint, file a Counterclaim against the lender, using every issue you can find that is reasonably available. Use every strategy to get a judge to grant you a trial by jury that he would otherwise deny, especially in an equity proceeding. Your Counterclaim moves the case from the ''equity'' side of the court to the ''at law'' side under the protection of the 7th Amendment to the Bill of Rights.

9
Legal Karate in the Courtroom

THE USE OF LEGAL KARATE. WHAT TO DO.

If you are not experienced in court procedure, you will need all the help you can get. There is a list of attorneys attached hereto. The names with an (*) beside them are most likely to give you help in writing your complaint and other pleadings. You may find a local attorney, in which case you should bring this entire book to him and ask him to assist you. Keep a copy for yourself for the inevitable conferences that will take place. I suggest you may want to avoid any attorney who wants a large amount of money down and who will not agree to represent you in court on the Lawful Money and Credit Money Issue.

Of course, time is of the essence and the question of where one starts depends on whether or not your creditors have taken action in court to get a judgment against you or to foreclose you your property.

Legal Karate: Your Options Before Judgment. You have two legal karate courses of action. One is to file an original COMPLAINT at LAW, or wait until the lender files a Complaint and Summons against you, at which time you respond with either a MOTION TO DISMISS or an "ANSWER" and "COUNTERCLAIM AND THIRD PARTY COMPLAINT AT LAW."

If you sue first, with a Complaint at Law, suspend payments and save your money in an account at another bank or in a shoebox at home to cover future payments in the event you lose or decide to abandon the lawsuit down the road. If you are the Plaintiff, demand a Trial by jury, and at once proceed to use interrogatories and admissions as are described in DISCOVERY MADE SIMPLE (see Appenices). If you find that the lender(s) refuse to answer your interrogatories, then serve them with a NOTICE OF DEPOSITION, and with a Subpoena and ask them questions in court. (An attorney with good cross examination would come in very handy.) However, you can prepare your list from the admissions and interrogatories that they have refused to answer. Procedure for taking Depositions is explained in the Discovery Book, Appendices.

Further, should your lender bank refuse to answer a Request for Admissions, you should then file a MOTION for Summary Judgment, as the law says that any Admissions not answered are deemed "admitted." At this point, however, you have moved from a proceeding "at law" to one in "equity," and the judge should grant your Motion for Summary Judgment as a matter of right under the law.

Because of the questionable behavior of some of our judges, you may not be granted your Motion for Summary Judgment. Your next step would be to file a Motion for Leave of Court to Appeal the judge's refusal to grant judgment. If the judge refuses this Motion, immediately file a Petition for Writ of Error in Appellate Court. You are the Petitioner and the Judge then becomes the Respondent. You then ask the Appellate Court for an Order reversing the lower court decision of not granting you your Summary Judgment and cite the Discovery rules under Admissions to support your petition.

Another option which can be carried out at the same time is to file a Third Party Complaint for violation of your 14th amendment rights of not giving you equal protection under the laws. The debtor is entitled to the same protection as the creditor under the law.

Court room Karate: To support your Complaint, ask your attorney to subpoena to a Deposition adversaries and ask them a number of questions which will clarify what the statute says. Then follow this interrogation up with more questions about the particulars of the case. Use your equitable discovery rights, without waiving your trial by jury rights. Since the other party to your suit will not be idle, you must demand your trial by jury rights, especially when he files a Motion for Judgment against you.

YOUR OTHER LEGAL KARATE OPTION. You may wait until the lender sends you a Summons and Complaint, which are usually filed in Superior or State Court. You have two options here, in reacting to that action they have taken. One is to file a MOTION TO DISMISS for lack of jurisdiction of the court over the subject matter. The other is to file an ANSWER and COUNTERCLAIM and Third Party Complaint at Law. If you are only dealing with a bank lender, you need only to file an ANSWER and COUNTERCLAIM as you can file a THIRD PARTY COMPLAINT against third party holders in due course, course, if necessary, or if your Constitutional rights are violated. The Answer and Counterclaim and Third Party Complaint is used as your response against financial institutions other than banks (may be holders in due course). In any case, it is used against Mortgage companies and other like institutions. Name a number of John and Jane Doe respondents as Third Party Defendants. These John and Jane Does are banks or lender officers of such institutions who loaned, or bought your note from the original lender mortgage company, with "checkbook money or check credit money." It is quite safe to assume that they did as it is common practice for these same banks to create money on their books with checkbook or credit money.

FAILURE TO TENDER A LAWFUL CONSIDERATION. In this second type lawsuit, charge the lender(s) with "failure to tender a lawful consideration," "illegality," and "Breach of Implied Contract." Even though they state they have acted in good faith, their contract with you is voidable because what they did was illegal. There is no legal authority under the sun that gives them the right to create "credit money" and demand lawful money in return. Congress has declared only coins and currency to be legal tender in payment of debts, not "credit" or "checkbook money," created by a private corporation.

Furthermore, you may then charge your lender(s) with "material representation of facts and "fraud."

An additional karate option. An additional courtroom karate option is your MOTION TO DISMISS. This Motion should be used as your first option and if your Motion is denied, you must immediately file your Answer and Counterclaim.

In any state court, when anyone is foreclosing you your property and has filed a Summons and Complaint, you have the right to challenge the court's jurisdiction to hear the case. A simple defense here is to use Article 1, Section 10 U.S. Constitution which says: "No state shall coin money, emit bills of credit (credit money, checkbook money, Ed.) or make anything but gold and silver coin a tender in payment of debts.

Filing Fees. Every court case requires the payment of filing fees to initiate a case, unless the lender (bank or mortgage company) pleaded they had no lawful money (and many of them have very little), and proceeded "in forma pauperis." The filing fees must be paid in either gold or silver coin (have a roll of Roosevelt silver dimes handy) in order to comply with Art. 1 para. 10. In almost every instance, filing fees will be paid by check, which is not even legal tender by act of Congress. Neither checks nor currency nor copper-nickel coins comply with the prohibition in Art. 1 Sec. 10 on the states to make nothing but gold and silver coin a tender in payment of debts. Thus, all filing fees paid to file the lawsuits are in violation of Art. 1 Sec. 10 when they are paid in something other than gold and silver coin! Indeed, this is your basis for challenging jurisdiction.

In your Complaint and Motion to Dismiss you must allege that the Defendant / Plaintiff has already violated the law, the U.S. Constitution, which is the Supreme Law of the Land. And immediately thereafter, use a Discovery procedure called a NOTICE OF REQUEST FOR ADMISSIONS. The five questions you must ask the lender to admit are listed in Discovery Made Simple (see Appendices, Discovery Made Simple).

When you file your Motion to Dismiss, ask the judge's clerk for a date AFTER the date the Admissions are due for a Hearing. Get your date set for the Motion to Dismiss hearing. Ask for a date two or three weeks away.

If you send in the Request for Admissions the day after you have received a Summons, your Admissions request response will be due BEFORE the date of the hearing. In that way you will put the Plaintiff / Defendant lender in a "Catch 22" situation. By doing so you will have proved he not only is violating the Constitution; he himself is proving to the court that you are right under Discovery laws. The law says: Any admissions not answered are "admitted." And in this situation, the lender cannot answer the Admissions without admitting that he violated the Constitution under Article 1 para. 10.

- USE THE FOLLOWING MOTIONS:
- Notice of Jurisdictional Defect.
- Advance Trial Order of The Judge.
- Motion (have witnesses present) of Demand for Trial by Jury. (Don't let the Judge deny your Right.)
- If Judge denies your right to trial by jury seek publicity. Serve a Complaint on him. Call in the media.
- Otherwise, prepare for Trial before a Jury.
- Voir Dire.
- Opening Statements to the Court, as to the Constitutional Money Issues and as to the invalidity of your debt contract.
- Direct Examination of the Plaintiff.
- Presentation of Exhibits:
    Copy of the Constitution.
    Copy of The Bill of Rights.
    Copy of Sec. 31 U.S.C.A. 392.
    Copy of The Coinage Act of 1792: Money of Account
- Exhibits of all laws passed by our United States Congress on The Money Issue in contravention of the Constitution of the United States, federal and state statutes (see example, Memoranda, Appendices).
- Point out that Congress has enacted no legislation on the Coinage of Money and the regulation of the value thereof that isn't in contravention of the Constitution.
- ENTER:
- Objections to Plaintiff's Exhibitions (Defendant).
- Objections to validity of any contract existing between yourself and Plaintiff.
- Point out need for lawful coins to provide base for lawful consideration to make a contract valid.
- Cross examination techniques should be skillfully applied by your attorney.

- Additional Motions for Discovery and Interrogatories.
- Motion for Direct Judgment of the Court.
- Motion for Verdict.
- Closing Arguments.
- Instructions to the Jury (the Judge should stick to the Constitution).
- Verdict. If you win, you can go home. If not:
- Post Trial Motions.
- Appeal Procedures explained, again, will be MOTIONS, MOTIONS, i.e.,
- Motion for Judgment notwithstanding the Verdict (non obstento veridicto).
- Motion for New Trial.
- Motion to Vacate or Amend Judgment.
- Motion for Relief from Judgment or Order.
- Independent Suit to Set Aside Judgment.
- Appeal.

COURT ROOM KARATE WEAPONS SUMMARIZED.

1. A well written Complaint or Counterclaim.
2. Request for Substitution of Judge or Motion for Disqualification of the Judge supported by an Affidavit of Prejudice or Conflict of Interest.
3. Affidavits in opposition to MOTIONS TO DISMISS.
4. Raise all kinds of Issues of Facts and law In Your MOTION to DISMISS.
5. DEMAND TRIAL BY JURY based on the 7th Amendment to the Bill of Rights, U.S. Constitution.
6. Submit Affidavits in Opposition to the lender's Motions for Summary or Default Judgment, by raising issues of fact and law in your Affidavits. State them or have your Attorney state them for you to the Judge. Your case will then have to go to trial.
7. Actual Notice. Use these often and attach each one you use to your lawsuit.
8. Use Affidavits in support of all your Motions.
9. Use Cross Complaints. Third party Complaints.
10. Use Motions for New Trial or a Motion for leave of Court to file Counterclaim, if a judgment has been entered against you.
11. File a Chapter 13, to block entry of Judgment or to stop the Sheriff or Trustee Sale; also file Adversary Proceedings in Bankruptcy Court. (See

Appendix for forms.) Present a Complaint before a Grand Jury against any adversaries who get together in a way that violates your Constitutional rights, as their actions are in violation of Title 8, Sec. 241, which could subject them to a $10,000 fine and up to ten years in prison.

12. Use Depositions to win your case throughout all of this.

THIS IS THE ESSENCE OF LEGAL COURT ROOM KARATE.

There is value in using the jurisdictional challenge. First, it is placed in the record and you can always bring it up on appeal. If the issue is not first brought up in trial court it cannot be raised in the future when you appeal. An important strategy in any court proceeding is to use all the defenses, which are valid, and waive none. This strengthens your overall case. In a recent case, it took a judge six months before he decided he had jurisdiction (in a case brought by Dan Palmer of Olmsted Twp., Ohio). Palmer filed an Answer and Counterclaim on the "credit" issue—that of banks lending their credit as money, when in fact they did NOT have the actual amount of cash involved in their safe deposit vaults to back it up.

Another winner on this issue is Walter Moore of Dover, North Carolina. Mr. Moore successfully fought a foreclosure. He had to educate the sheriff, but his position was legally correct and the sheriff refused to carry out the court's order to evict Moore.

The Answer and Counterclaim, Third Party Complaint Definitions. An Answer to a Complaint is exactly that. You answer the lender's complaint by admitting parts of it and denying other parts. You may admit your name and address and deny all the rest.

A Counterclaim, a Complaint at Law, and a Third Party Complaint are all basically the same Motions in the same basic lwsuit used in different situations.

In a Complaint, you are the Plaintiff and the original moving party bringing the action. And it is always best if you are. You start the Action. You file the Summons. After all, you are the injured party, as you have given the lender a mortgage note or a Deed of Trust and note on your property for a mere credit entry on his books, which he created out of thin air. And he has misrepresented to you that he is lending you lawful money of the United States.

Pay the filing fees in currency or silver coin, and get a receipt showing you have paid cash.

In Counterclaim and Third Party Complaint actions you are the Defendant who is countersuing the Plaintiff lender or some other party connected with him in the existing case that was started against you. In the Counterclaim you must write up a Complaint against the Plaintiff. Basic court procedure is that both the Complaint against you and your Counterclaim against the Plaintiff must be tried at the same time. The Third Party Complaint which either the plaintiff or defendant can file literally brings a third party into the case as a Third Party Defendant. The Plaintiff would call himself both Plaintiff and Third Party Plaintiff, whereas if the defendant filed a Third Party Complaint he would call himself "Defendant and Third Party Plaintiff." The action on paper would look like this:

National Bank,
    Plaintiff,
      vs.
[your name],
    Defendant and Third Party Plaintiff,
      vs.
[Name of the Judge who broke his oath
not upholding the Constitution],
    Third Party Defendant.

Even if a judge should dismiss your Complaint or Counterclaim, your Third Party Complaint will effectively drive him off the case, even if you file your action after the judge's dismissal.

Also, in support of your MOTION TO DISMISS, you should submit to the court a MEMORANDUM OF LAW ON CONSTITUTIONAL MONEY (See Appendices pg. 226).

Motion for Summary Judgment. If the lender submits a Motion for Summary Judgment, you submit a Motion to the couty called an Answer and Counterclaim. However, determine first if the judge has ruled on whether or not he has jurisdiction to hear the subject matter in your case. During oral arguments, when the judge says he has jurisdiction, then you say: Your honor I anticipated that the court might overrule me on this Motion for equity consideration, and I have brought with me an Answer and Complaint, with a fifty page brief in support, and I would like now to file a copy with the court and with the Plaintiff/Defendant (lender).

The important point to remember in all this is

that when you file a Motion to Dismiss for lack of Jurisdiction or for any other reason, you must not answer the Complaint until the judge rules he has jurisdiction.

Actually, you always have the right to challenge jurisdiction at any point in a trial proceeding, even if you asked for a new trial, or again, at the confirmation of the sheriff or Trustree sale.

Summary of Options Before Judgment.

1. File Motion to Dismiss and challenge jurisdiction of court based on Article 1 Sec. 10.

2. If denied: File Answer and Counterclaim and Demand Trial by Jury.

3. Against lender's Motion for Judgment, file a Third Party Complaint. The judge may violate your Constitutional Rights such as total denial of Discovery rights through a ''protective order'' or if he says you will not get a trial by jury, or if he dismisses your Counterclaim, file your Third Party Complaint and sue him as an adversary party.

4. If you cannot do any of these things, immediately file under Chapter 13 in Federal Bankruptcy Court or a Chapter 11. (See Appendices for forms.) This will effectively block all action in your case, even a Trustee Sale. If your secured debts are under $300,000 and your unsecured debts are under $100,000 file a Chapter 13 action.

5. If your debts are over the $300,000 mark file a Chapter 11 Action.

6. File your Demand for Jury Trial under Rule 9015.

7. Challenge the alleged debts you owe as loans having been made as ''credit'' loans. And file your Memorandum of Law on what is Constitutional money.

8. Complete the Chapter 13 statement carefully, with the help of a specialist attorney familiar with all aspects of current bankruptcy law.

9. File a Complaint at Law with a Summons just like any other lawsuit modeled after Bankruptcy Form 34. It is called an ADVERSARY PROCEEDING NUMBER (Abbr.: ADV. PRO. NO.)

10. Proceed with Discovery against the lender (and all other parties connected with your case just as you would in any court. Pay for your Demand for Trial by Jury papers at the Federal Bankruptcy Clerk of Courts Office. Use cash. Get a receipt for payment showing CASH.

10
Saving Your Home, Farm or Business by Use of Bankruptcy Proceedings

YOUR RIGHTS IN BANKRUPTCY COURT.

1. You have the right to challenge your creditor's claims that you owe them money.
2. File a lawsuit to have the loans voided on the "credit" issue.
3. According to applicable rule you can have a jury trial.

Your basic rights in Bankruptcy Court are the same as in any other court. The basic model for filing a Complaint is called Form 34 and looks like the one at the top of pg. 157.

Where it says: "In re Case No. _____," you place the Case Number you were assigned when you filed your original papers in Bankruptcy Court. In the section called ADV. PRO. NO. _____, the clerk of the Bankruptcy Court will assign an Adversary Proceeding Number. The body of your Complaint at Law should be the same as any other lawsuit that would be filed in Federal Court. IT IS IMPORTANT TO REMEMBER HERE THAT FILING A COMPLAINT IN AN ADVERSARY PROCEEDING WILL RE-QUIRE A SUMMONS AND SERVICE JUST LIKE ANY OTHER LAWSUIT AND YOU PAY AN-OTHER FILING FEE WITH THE CLERK OF THE BANKRUPTCY COURT. SO TO KEEP THINGS CLEAR IN YOUR MIND, YOU MUST PAY TWO SEPARATE FILING FEES. YOU MUST FILE THE CH. 13 or CH. 11 PAPERS FIRST, AND THE CLERK OF BANKRUPTCY COURT WILL THEN NOTIFY ALL YOUR DEBTORS. IN YOUR CH. 13 or CH. 11 STATEMENT, YOU MUST STATE THE AMOUNT THEY CLAIM YOU OWE THEM,

BUT IN THE NEXT COLUMN WHERE THEY ASK THE "amount you admit you owe," you MUST WRITE "NONE." You write "NONE" to all cred-itors whose debts you will then challenge by filing a Complaint at Law as per the above caption. WHEN YOU FILE YOUR COMPLAINT, PER FORM 34 ABOVE, THE MATTER OF WHETHER OR NOT THERE IS A DEBT MUST BE SETTLED BEFORE ANY PAYMENT PLANS CAN BE ARRANGED. A "SUMMONS" form can be obtained in the Federal Clerk of Courts office. Service of Summons and Complaint is the same as for suits in Federal District Court, which is to have a Process Server or person other than yourself serve it and file an Affidavit and Proof of Service statement or to send it by Certified Mail, Return Receipt Requested along with a Certifi-cate of Service signed and notarized by the person mailing the Summons and complaint. The Certifi-cate of Service statement or the Affidavit of Service statement, both of which must be notarized are then filed in the Federal Clerk of Courts office as proof of service. FROM THIS POINT ON, YOU SHOULD SERVE INTERROGATORIES, ADMISSIONS AND THEN TAKE A DEPOSITION. Be sure to check the correct timing of these in the Federal Rules as revised or in the Discovery Made Simple book. Attach a De-mand for a Jury Trial to your Complaint along with a Constructive Notice to the attorney not to file a Motion to Dismiss.

Your Ch. 13 or Ch. 11 action in Federal Court must be filed before the sheriff or trustee sale, even if is only the day before. Then your Complaint per Form 34 above is then written up and filed later in the same Bankruptcy Court. You then proceed to use

Discovery aggressively, because it is your most valuable legal weapon.

THE 10 DAY RULE

It is important to remember that in Federal Bankruptcy Court, any decision or order of the Bankruptcy judge to be appealed from must be done within 10 days according to the rule of Bankruptcy Court. This is done by following the model Form 35 which looks like the one at the bottom of pg. 157.

EMERGENCY RULES TO STOP JURY TRIALS

Because of a Supreme Court decision in the case of *Northern Pipeline Co.* v. *Marathon Pipe Line Co.*, 102 S.CT. 2858, on June 28, 1982, the Administrative Office of the United States Courts came up with a set of Model Emergency Bankruptcy Rules. This was done because powers of the Bankruptcy judges were curtailed in the Northern Pipeline Decision which had existed under 28 U.S.C. § 1471 (c). These rules are now in effect until Congress enacts new rules for the Bankruptcy Courts to follow which Congress has not yet done as of June, 1984. The new Emergency rules forbid the Bankruptcy judge from conducting jury trials. Now, what do you do.

1. Ask the Clerk of the Bankruptcy Court for a copy of the Emergency Rules and a copy of any local rules of court.

2. Use Discovery procedures aggressively to prove your case (interrogatories, admissions and depositions). When they obstruct Discovery by not answering your questions or admit to the truth of your allegations, then file a "Motion for either a Default or Summary Judgment" in the Bankruptcy Court. (Use Default Judgment if they obstruct Discovery and a Summary judgment if they provide enough answers to prove your allegations.)

3. If the Bankruptcy Judge turns down your Motion for Judgment, then make a verbal request for a trial by jury. (You must have made your trial by jury request in your original Complaint also.) Then when the judge turns you down because of the Emergency Rules, file a Motion to Transfer the ADV. PRO. CASE to the federal District Court for a trial by jury in your case. If he agrees, then you pay for a trial by jury in the Federal District Court. If the Bankruptcy Judge denies your Motion for a Jury Trial, whether the Motion was made orally or in writing, then file a Notice of Appeal to the District Court per Form 35 above.

YOU SEE, THE BANKRUPTCY JUDGE CANNOT DETERMINE ANY PLAN FOR REPAYING YOUR DEBTS UNTIL THERE IS FIRST A DETERMINATION THAT A DEBT EXISTS! Meanwhile, your case is now in Federal District Court and the first thing you should do there is to file a MOTION TO COMPEL ANSWERS TO INTERROGATORIES OR QUESTIONS YOU ASKED AT THE DEPOSITION. If the Federal Judge fails to grant your order or if he grants a totally protective order for the defendant (bank or other lender), then you file a Third Party Complaint against the Federal Judge and drive him off the case for denying your 5th amendment rights (denial of property without due process and / or denial of a trial by jury under the 7th amendment). Before suing the Federal Judge, you should make an oral request for a Ruling of your right to a jury trial in court at the hearing on your Motion to Compel Answers.

SUMMARY OF COURTROOM KARATE PROCEDURES

- How to Stop Foreclosure on Your Home, Farm or Business.
- Pre-trial information. Obtain from Clerk of Court.
- How to prepare for "Trial." Obtain from local counsel.
- Case information: Assemble all evidence of debt.
- How to fit your case into the total trial system.
- How the trial system works; learn from Clerk of Court.
- Prepare your Findings of Facts. Consult Law Librarian.
- Investigate applicable Court Rules and Proceedings. Same.
- Investigate applicable State Statutes. (Law Librarian)
- Familiarize yourself thoroughly with Court Rules.
- Familiarize yourself with the trial plan (your state).
- Pleadings: Present your defense on The Money Issue (example given). Do not reveal all. Merely indicate what your Defense is going to be; Statement as a Plaintiff if applicable. Ask Court for Trial by Jury.
- Present expert testimony. Affidavits of Witnesses. (Counsel)

FORM 34
UNITED STATES BANKRUPTCY COURT
...DISTRICT OF...

In re Case No._____

_____,
                          Debtor,

_____,
                          Plaintiff,

      vs.   ADV. PRO. NO. _____

_____,
                          Defendant.

                                             COMPLAINT AT LAW

FORM 35

In re Case No._____

_____,
                          Debtor,

_____,
                          Plaintiff,

      vs.   ADV. PRO. NO. _____

_____,
                          Defendant.   NOTICE OF APPEAL

_____, plaintiff [or defendant or other party] appeals to the district court [or the bankruptcy appellate panel], from the final judgment [or order or final decree] [describe it] of the bankruptcy court entered in this adversary proceeding on the _____ day of _____. The parties to the judgment [or order or decree] appealed from and the names and addresses of their respective attorneys are as follows: _____

Dated: _____   Signed: _____
                                           In Propria Persona
                                           [or Attorney for Appellant]
                                  Address: _____

- Motions requesting Time for Discovery. Depositions. (Counsel)
- Motions in rubuttal. (Counsel)
- Interrogatories, motions to take. (Counsel)
- Motions to Strike. (Counsel)
- Foreclosures: Case Examples, Strict and by Sale.
- Letter from Creditor. Basis of Civil Complaint.
- Civil Summons. Service: By Mail; By Marshal.
- Plaintiff files return of service, and complaint which is attached to Summons in local Superior Court.
- Answer Summons with appearance in Court, or:
- Plaintiff enters Motion for Default for Failure to Appear.
- Judge grants Motion for Default.
- Plaintiff files Affidavit of Debt.
- Plaintiff files Request for Strict Foreclosures.
- Plaintiff files Bill of Costs (taxed).
- Plaintiff files Motion for Judgment of Strict Foreclosure.
- Judge Grants Above Motions. (Case Strict Foreclosure Shown.)
- Foreclosure by Sale. Starting the case. Plaintiff's demand letters.
- Summons with Complaint attached comes by Post or Officer.
- Plaintiff files Summons and Complaint in local civil Court. Usually Superior Court.
- Files mortgage note secured by Mortgage on property.
- Files Lis Pendens.
- Files Affidavit as to Lis Pendens.
- Files Affidavit of Deputy Sheriff as to Original Writ, Summons and Complaint.
- Files Amended Complaint (original complaint if in generalities, Amendment if in detail).
- Appearance of parties to the suit in Court.
- Demand for Disclosure of Defense (gives Defendant 5 days to answer full complaint).
- Motion for Default for Failure to Disclose Defense.
- Motion for Order by the Court.
- Motion filed for Default if 5 days pass and Defendant fails to disclose Defense.
- Files Certification of Service Notice Demanding Disclosure.
- Motion for Defendant's Failure to Disclose a Defense.
- Motion requesting Order by the Court.
- Motion for Disclosure of Defense.

- Motion for Judgment by Foreclosure.
- Motion of Foreclosure by Sale.
- Plaintiff's Motion for Default for Failure to Disclose.
- Plaintiff's Motion for Judgment of Foreclosure by Sale.
- Plaintiff's Affidavit of Debt of Defendant.
- Plaintiff's Certification of Bill of Costs.
- Plaintiff's Certification of Service on Defendant.
- Appearance of Parties to the Suit.
- Judgment of Foreclosure by Sale so Ordered by the Court.
- Oath of Appraisers.
- At this point Defendant may notify Court he has gone into Bankruptcy (Federal District) Court. (Delay tactic)
- Otherwise case proceeds with Publisher's Affidavit.
- Motion for Approval of Committee of Sale.
- Committee Report to the Court.
- Bond for Deed Notarized.
- Registered Bidders list entered to file.
- Course of Bidding recorded.
- Committee Deed filed.
- Judgment of the Court. Disposal of Case as to all Parties and Counts.
- Plaintiff's Supplemental Letter of Complaint.
- Supplement Affidavit of Debt.
- Request for Supplemental Judgment for Foreclosure by Sale.
- Motion for Determination of Priorities and Further Supplemental Judgment.
- Final Supplement Judgment. Case example given in accordance with how it usually goes.
- How to Stop Foreclosure on Your Home, Farm or Business. Case examples. Similarity of Proceedings.
- Letter of Complaint received from creditor (bank) by Certified or Registered letter, with 10 days to reply.
- Defense (keep letter) answer the Complaint (see Sample letter given on the Money Issue, Appendices).
- Keep copies of all letters received and of reply.
- Plaintiff Files Complaint in local civil Court.
- Plaintiff files Motion for Judgment of Pleadings.
- Defendant Files Request for Judge to state where he stands with regard to whether he holds the Constitution of the United States to be the Supreme Law of the Land.
- Judge will demand your reasons for the challenge.

- Submit your reasons based on the Money Issue as to Article 1 Secs. 8 & 10 of the Constitution and as to Plaintiff's Breach of Contract by means of deceit and Fraud. Do not reveal all. File your Memorandum of Law.
- See Appendices for Memorandum of Law.
- Have Witnesses. If Judge agrees to the Constitution being the Supreme Law of the Land, proceed.
- If the Judge does not agree, have each Witness sign a notarized Affidavit stating what they heard him say.
- Pay for the Filing of these Affidavits in gold or silver coins, such as silver quarters minted prior to 1965.
- Demand a Trial by Jury, with Witnesses on your side.
- Again follow above procedures if denied. (Every U.S. Citizen has an inviolate right to a trial by jury.)
- File your Memorandum of Law.
- Plaintiff files motion to Lift Stay of Court Proceedings.
- Defendant appears and objects to Motion to Lift Stay Reasons: No trial has occurred. No evidence presented.
- Defendant requests Court to give Time for taking Depositions and for answering as to whether Court will grant or deny Motion for Trial by Jury. (Have Witnesses)
- File Motion to make Discovery and Take Depositions.
- Discovery explained. Depositions and Interrogatories explained. (See Appendix)
- Defendant files copy of list of Questions to be asked of Creditor money-lender. Additional Depositions taken and filed.
- File discovery and deposition papers with Answer to Complaint and attach Memorandum of the Court's decisions citing Statutes and cases prior decided on The Money Issue. (Appendices for Statutes and cases cited.)
- Defendant Files Motion to Dismiss Case.
- In view of your Challenges etc. (all must be done politely) Judge may dismiss your case, or only the Motion.
- If so, File again for Trial by Jury.
- Defendant File Affidavit of Merits in support of your request and right to have a Trial by Jury.
- Cite Constitutional law protecting your Right to

Trial by Jury. The Judge will begin taking you seriously, and not just another deadbeat.
- Plaintiff will file for Pre-trial hearing.
- File a Writ of Mandamus in Appeal's Court. State reasons. Submit copies of all papers so far submitted to the lower court.
- Attach Memorandum of Law and Statutes applicable to your right to have a Trial by Jury.
- Mandamus automatically stays proceedings in lower Court.
- Defendant. If appeal is denied, carry your plea to the State Supreme Court. Call in Newspapers, Radio, TV Reporters hawking for news and give them the story. You have been denied an inalienable right.
- File Motion in Civil Court again requesting the Judge to reconsider his decision and grant you a Trial by Jury.
- Defendant request Pretrial conference. Do not show all evidence on the Money Issue and on the fraud and deceit basis on which rests the breach of Contract.
- Submit evidence (Constitutional provisions as to what is lawful money). Cite Statutes pertinent to Money Issue Cases.
- State you received no valuable consideration, merely bank credit-money, which is a mere bookkeeping entry to your account and which amounts only to a Promise to Pay Money from the lender for which you signed a Note Mortgaging your Home, having real property value.
- If Judge rules against you and Orders Sheriff Sale, and Plaintiff Files Motion for Judgment by Foreclosure he will also:
- File an Affidavit of Debt
- A Bill of Costs.
- Court will Render Judgment v. Defendant.
- File Motion of Appeal in Higher Court.
- File Motion for Trial by Jury in Appeals Court with copies of all Motions filed in lower Court.
- File Additional Motion asking for more Time for making Discovery and for Taking Depositions (with additional lists of questions to ask of the money-lender, cashier of the bank, loan officer, etc.)
- File Motion to Stay Court Proceedings if Discovery Procedures have been granted.
- Defendant. Appears in Court.

- State your position and merits of Defense.
- Give reasons for asking for Time for making Discovery and for taking Depositions (Interrogatories).
- Defendant. Do not let Statute time for Appeal expire.
- File Motion in lower Court for Reconsideration of Judgment.
- Appear for Hearing of Motion for Reconsideration.
- What to do if Sheriff's Sale is Imminent.
- File Motion for Stay of Sheriff's Sale. State Money Issue reasons.
- Make Motion for Stay to give you more time to Prepare a proper Defense.
- File Motion for Right to Trial by Jury. State you are proceeding in forma pauperis because you have no gold or silver coins to tender as "lawful money" or "lawful tender." State that the only lawful money that can be used for filing fees for Trial by Jury is gold and silver coin. Therefore, Defendant is forced to tender as filing fees Federal Reserve Notes UNDER PROTEST AND DURESS.
- Decision. File Motion for Order of Decision of the Court. Decision of the Court must guarantee you your Right to Trial by Jury in Forma Pauperis, as such is required by every State Statute in the United States.
- Defendant: You now have effectively repudiated use of Federal Reserve Notes as "legal tender" or lawful money by proceeding in Forma Pauperis.
- Defendant: File a Complaint against the lender.
- Attach Complaint to Summons. Proceed with Service by Marshal or Sheriff.
- Complaint: Charge lender with Fraud, Deceit, Breach of Contract, Embezzlement. Fraudulent appropriation to his own use or benefit the mortgage note on your property intrusted to him, when he led you to believe he was acting in a fiduciary character. (4 Bl.Comm. 230,231) (A,. Life Ins. Co. v. U.S. Fidelity and Guaranty Co., 261 Mich. 221,246 N.W. 71).
- Attach Complaint to Summons and file copies with "Lis Pendens" (see example). Sale proceedings will be stopped.
- The Sheriff's Sale: If prejudice is apparent for you, have friend bid for you. Bid in silver coins. Have two or three witnesses.
- Pay silver dollar(s) (culls can be bought at a Coin Shop for current market price of troy silver). If Sheriff refuses to accept your money or bid, pay into Clerk of Court's Office. Obtain receipt, signed.
- Have each Witness make out an Affidavit of what happened at the Sale, and state what they heard you Bid and that they saw you offer lawful silver dollars to the Sheriff, who refused them.
- File Affidavit and Notice of High Bid in Lawful Tender.
- File Affidavits of each Witness attending the Sale with you. Be sure they are notarized.
- File Motion for Trial by Jury to determine Who made High Bid in "lawful money."
- If refused: File Motion for Stay of Proceedings on Completion of Sheriff's Sale.
- If refused and Court renders Judgment of Foreclosure by Sale:
- Quit Claim by Deed, your home to nearest and dearest to you, in exchange for similar Deed. Hold similar Deed.
- File Quit Claim Deed, but keep secreted Deed given you in exchange. This will cloud Title and prevent transfer of property to any new unlawful bidder or owner.
- Attach Memorandum of Law on Lawful Money on Motion for Trial by Jury. Cite your Constitutional rights. (See Appendix)
- Base Motion on Constitution Art. 6, Sec. 2. (Marbury v. Madison: and on 16 Am. Jur. 2nd Sec. 256: No one is bound to obey an unconstitutional Law and No Court is bound to enforce such obedience.)
- Effect of above: Clouds Title on your property and forces case back into Court.
- File Motion again for Trial by Jury.
- You now have a Case that can be appealed all the way up to the Supreme Court of the United States. Since you are your own attorney, you are costing the other side legal costs of thousands of dollars, and only at the personal cost of your own time and the relatively moderate cost of Forms.
- Caution: if friend bids in your property in silver dollars, have him file the Affidavit and Notice of High Bid in Lawful Money, as an Interpleader, or as an Intervenor; Be sure to check out (your State) Court rules of Procedure as to filing Affidavit etc.
- The case of the Interpleader: Use same case number as your own case number and that of Party Acting against you, i.e., case number of the lender.
- Add your name to that of the Interpleader on all

Motions filed. Complete with addresses of both parties.

- Again file request for Trial by Jury.
- Again file Motion for Stay of Court Proceedings.
- File Writ of Mandamus in Appeal Court, if refused Trial by Jury (you are now beginning to "practice law" as ably if not more so, than your unsuspecting adversary).
- Now file your Quit Claim Deed to reclaim your property:
    (1) To remove cloud on Title
    (2) To exercise all your rights under law as Defendant
- File Complaint against the alleged high bidder in paper money (it will be the moneylender, no doubt).
- File Lis Pendens (this again clouds Title).
- If the Judge refuses to grant you any Constitutional rights in above proceedings:
- Use of Court Rules
- How you (as defendant) can attack a Complaint.
- How, diplomatically, to challenge the Judge as to where he stands with regard to the Constitution being the Supreme Law of The Land. Does he agree? If not, how to politely request that he disqualify himself.
- What to do if the Judge refuses your request.
- Motion for Trial by Jury.
- What to do if denied.
- How to plead your counterclaims and cross claims.
- Third Party complaints.
- Motion for Discovery of facts and evidence in preparation for Trial.
- Motion to obtain written Interrogatories (Depositions).
- Your best Discovery weapons, at Trial.
- Production of Documents.
- Requests for Admission of documents.
- Motion to terminate litigation without Trial.
- Pre-trial conference.
- Invoking The Rule.
- Notice of Jurisdictional Defect.
- Advance Trial Order of The Judge.
- Motion (have witness present) of Demand for Trial by Jury. (Don't let the Judge deny your Right.)
- Opening Statements to the Court, as to the Constitutional Money Issues and as to the invalidity of your debt contract.

- Direct Examination of the Plaintiff.
- Presentation of Exhibits:
    Copy of the Constitution,
    Copy of The Bill of Rights.
    Copy of The Coinage Act of 1792: Money of Account
- Objections to Plaintiff's Exhibit.
- Objections to validity of any contract existing between yourself and Plaintiff.
- Cross examination techniques.
- Additional Motions for Discovery and Interrogatories.
- Motion for Direct Judgment of the Court
- Motion for Verdict.
- Closing Arguments.
- Instructions to the Jury.
- Verdict.
- Post Trial Motions.
- Appeal Procedures explained.
- Motion for Judgment notwithstanding the Verdict (non obstento veridicto).
- Motion for New Trial
- Motion to Vacate or Amend Judgment.
- Motion for Relief from Judgment or Order
- Independent Suit to Set Aside Judgment; seek counsel of attorney.
- Appeal.

Remember this: although given orally, a final order or judgment must be signed by the judge and entered in the file before it is final. By serving him while he sits on the bench and before he signs such a final order or judgment, you block its entry to file and the case must go before another judge. Also, you can appeal any adverse action taken against you. As a matter of fact you must appeal, as any action they take after they are sued is reversible error and the Court of Appeals will reverse the judge's decision.

You also have Grand Jury indictments to help you.

If your Constitutional rights continue to be violated, even after you have served the offending judges Constructive Notices, then you must proceed to get all the judges and attorneys who have conspired against you indicted by a Federal Grand Jury under Title 18, Sec. 241. Be sure to obtain the counsel of an attorney before you undertake these and/or any of the following actions.

Basic Procedure, to obtain help of a Grand Jury.

1. Go to the Federal Clerk of Courts and ask for the name of the Grand Jury Foreman. Write it down. Call him. Find out when the jury next meets, time and place, and tell him how much time you will need to present a Complaint before the Jury.

2. If you cannot get the Grand Jury Foreman's name from the Clerk, ask it of the U.S. Attorney.

3. If this tactic fails, place an ad in a legal publication or your daily newspaper as an OPEN LETTER TO THE GRAND JURY FOREMAN and ask him to contact you as you have evidence to present to the Grand Jury about a certain number of judges and attorneys who have conspired against you to deprive you of your Constitutional rights under the 7th and 14th amendments in violation of Title 18 para. 241. Mention no names. Finish your ad with your name and telephone number.

4. If you should find out where the grand jury meets, try to identify them as they park their cars. Get their license plate numbers. Go to your public library and find the numbers in the appropriate directory. This book also includes the names and addresses of all the vehicle owners in the state. Send each one your information and related information in the Money Issue.

5. Support all information you submit to the Grand Jury in a written testimony in Affidavit form.

6. The Grand Jury may subpoena the attorneys and judges involved to tell their side of the story. What possible defense can they offer for violating your 7th amendment right to trial by jury?

YOUR OPTIONS AFTER A SHERIFF OR TRUSTEE SALE

After a sheriff or trustee sale, you should file an original lawsuit in Federal District Court. Also, immediately file a Motion for A Stay of Proceedings in State Court, until the merits of your case are settled in the Federal Court. Your "STAY" should also request a "STAY" on any Writ of Assistance or Writ of Eviction. If your Motion is denied, you must file a MOTION FOR LEAVE OF COURT TO FILE AN APPEAL. Ask for leave of the court to appeal the decision. If our Motion for Leave of Court is denied, file a Third Party Complaint against him using your old Case number in the State court.

Never let your time to file any Motion expire under state Statutes. Keep your reason based on violation of your 14th amendment rights: DENIAL OF PROPERTY WITHOUT DUE PROCESS AND DENIAL OF ACCESS TO THE APPELLATE COURT, both of which are covered under the 14th amendment. Denial of access to the courts is denial of equal protection of the laws under the 14th amendment. Use it.

Always keep the Motions process going. Keep your appeals process going whenever necessary, until your case is finally heard and decided by a jury or won through the very effective use of Discovery procedures.

A Few Questions and Answers on Bankruptcy.

Q. How do I know if I should file a Chapter 11 or a Chapter 13?

A. If your total secured debts are under $350,000 and your unsecured debts are under $100,000, file a Chapter 13 plan. Note: The Legal Karate plan is to file the applicable plan, admit none of the debts that you want to challenge on the credit issue and work to void these loans in their entirety by filing a Complaint in bankruptcy court and then using DISCOVERY PROCEDURES or a TRIAL BY JURY to prove your case. A Chapter 11 plan is when your debts are higher than those listed and is essentially a one year reorganization plan. You stay in your home, your farm or business under either plan and can challenge the validity of debts under either plan.

Q. I am now in Ch. 11 or Ch. 13, as prepared by my attorney, and he has filled out the forms and in the section under Secured Debts and Unsecured Debts, he has "admitted" that I owe the banks or other lenders the amount they claim I owe them. What do I do now?

A. Have your attorney file an amended Statement and change your admission to NONE as to the amount that you owe. Also direct him to file a Complaint in the Court against the bank or other lenders on the credit money issue, then file a Notice of Dismissal and file it with the court. Hand him a copy. Find an Attorney who will cooperate with you in your best interest. Be sure that your Complaint at Law in the Bankruptcy Court is filed per form 34 and serve a Summons on the creditor(s). Your Summons can be mailed by Certified

Mail, Return Receipt Requested; include a Certificate of Mailing, Notarized and signed with a witness's signature to the Certificate of Mailing. This must then be filed with the court along with a photocopy of the Return Receipt as your Proof of Service. Your battle is now half won. Next, go after your adversaries with Interrogatories and Admissions and Depositions. Depositions under Federal rules can be taken anytime 30 days after service of Summons. Keep on trying always to be the Plaintiff.

Q. When should I ask for Trial by Jury in Bankruptcy Court and what should I do if it is denied?

A. The first step to take in Bankruptcy court is to use Discovery procedures to the maximum. Use Interrogatories, subpoenas, and depositions. When your creditors answer and admit enough allegations in the admissions, then file a MOTION FOR SUMMARY JUDGMENT. If the creditors obstruct and refuse to answer, file a MOTION TO COMPEL ANSWERS. If the judge refuses to grant your Motion to Compel Answers, then file a Motion for Trial by Jury. If denied, file a Motion to Transfer the Case to Federal District Court, for Trial by Jury. If the judge denies this motion, then file a Notice of Appeal to the Bankruptcy Appellate Panel, and if turned down there, file a Notice of Appeal to the Federal District Court. Keep your appeals going right on up to the U.S. Supreme Court, or until you get your Trial by Jury. Your determination will win. Meanwhile, the bankruptcy judge cannot set a schedule for repayment of your alleged debts, until a court of jurisdiction decides if in fact a debt exists! In a bankruptcy case from Nevada, 1983, West's Bankruptcy Digest for 1984, cites the following: ''Bankruptcy court's equitable power may be exercised to look behind prior judgment; and it may be collaterally attacked when it is the product of fraud, collusion, or duress, when prior court lacked subject matter or personal jurisdiction, or when the judgment was founded on NO· REAL DEBT or on a LEGALLY UNENFORCEABLE OBLIGATION. 28 U.S.C.A. para. 1481. In re A-1 24 Hours Towing Inc., 33 B.R. 281. This is an excellent case to cite when suing creditors for tendering an ''unlawful consideration'' in exchange for your mortgage note or Deed of Trust to your property. Include fraud and usury charges.

NOTICE OF MOTION

TO: [plaintiff or defendant]

    PLEASE TAKE NOTICE THAT the [defendant / plaintiff], [your name] will move the Court, presided over by the Honorable [judge's name] on the _____ day of [month], 19____, at _____ a.m. / p.m. for a Motion [describe Motion]. The place where this Motion will be presented is the [name of courthouse], which is located at [address of courthouse] in the city of _____, _____. A copy of said Motion is attached hereto.

Date _____   X _____

****

Note: The above Notice of Motion is filled in by the judge's secretary, whom you should contact either personally or by phone. Some courthouses have forms to use when setting dates for motion hearings. An alternative type of Notice is listed below when the court contacts you on the date for the hearing.

NOTICE OF MOTION

TO: [plaintiff or defendant]:

TO: JUDGE _____

[ADDRESS OF COURTHOUSE]:

PLEASE TAKE NOTICE that the [plaintiff or defendant] will move the court, presided over by the Honorable _____, at a time and date determined by the court, for a Motion to [describe Motion]. A copy of said motion is attached hereto.

Date _____   X _____

(Sample form for serving Motions by Mail)

CERTIFICATE OF SERVICE

I, [name of person mailing motion] hereby certify and affirm that on the [day] of [month], 1984, I mailed a true and correct copy of the following described Notice / Motion [describe Motion or Notice] by [1st class / Certified mail] to:

Name [name of person or attorney to whom motion was mailed]

Address _____

City _____ State _____ Zip _____

Dated this _____ day of _____, 1984.   X [signature of person who mailed motion]

Address _____

City _____ State _____ Zip _____

[Add Notary Seal here]

(This form to be used when challenging jurisdiction in a state court. This should be sent out after a Notice of Request for Admissions is sent out.)

_____,

Plaintiff,

    vs.

[Your Name],

Defendant.   Case #_____

MOTION TO DISMISS

Now Comes the defendants, _____, and files this Motion to Dismiss for lack of jurisdiction over the subject matter for the following reasons:

1. The Constitution of the United States is the Supreme Law of the Land
2. Article 1, Section 10 of the U.S. constitution says: "No state shall make any thing but gold and silver coin a tender in payment of debts."
3. Article 6 of the U.S. Constitution says: "This Constitution shall be the supreme Law of the Land; and the Judges shall be bound thereby, any Thing in the Constitution or laws of any State to the Contrary notwithstanding."
4. The laws of the State of _____ require every plaintiff to pay filing fees when a lawsuit or complaint is filed.
5. The plaintiff in this case did file a complaint against the defendant on _____ and was required to and did tender some thing as filing fees.
6. The defendant alleges that the plaintiff tendered filing fees in some form of paper money as a check or in Federal Reserve Notes. Said check or notes are not gold or silver coin and are not redeemable in either gold or silver coin.
7. Defendant asks the court to inquire to the Clerk of Courts office to determine the substance of monies used to pay filing fees and to determine if this form of money consisted of either gold or silver coin and complied with the requirements under Art. 1, Sec. 10 of the U.S. Constitution.
8. Will then the court determine if the monies paid as filing fees complied with the Constitutional requirements under Art. 1, Sec. 10, that "No state shall make any thing but gold and silver coin a tender in payment of debts?"
9. Does this Court have the authority to waive the payment of filing fees and has the plaintiff requested such waiver?
10. Did the plaintiff proceed "in forma pauperis" or otherwise claim to be unable to obtain lawful money?
11. This court must show that it has jurisdiction before it can render a judgment in this case: "A court is without power to render a judgment is it lacks jurisdiction of the parties or of the subject matter...." *O'Leary* v. *Waterbury Title Co.*, 117 Conn. 39, 43, 166 A. 673.
12. Defendants ask the court to justify jurisdiction if the plaintiff's filing fees were not paid in either gold or silver coin and thus did not comply with Art. 1, Sec. 10 of the U.S. Constitution and [your state] statutes which require the payment of filing fees.
13. Defendants ask that this case be dismissed without prejudice so as the plaintiff may refile this complaint and tender filing fees in either gold and silver coins and this comply with Constitutional requirements.

Date _____   X _____

NOTE: #13 to Dismiss without prejudice is an appeal to the courts equity side, to be fair and balanced and not to jeopardize any equitable interest of the plaintiff. If Art. 1, Sec. 10 is upheld, it will mean that at the sheriff sale, if there is one ever held, the bids will have to be placed in gold or silver coin. This will create a real logistics problem for the credit lenders. Where are they going to get all this gold and silver?

	CIRCUIT COURT	
STATE OF WISCONSIN	CIVIL DIVISION	MILWAUKEE COUNTY

FIRST SAVING ASSOCIATION OF WISCONSIN

A Domestic Corporation

Plaintiff,

JOHN DOE and JANE DOE his wife;
CN COMPANY; STATE OF WISCONSIN,
and UNITED STATES OF AMERICA

CASE NO. 635975

AFFIDAVIT IN SUPPORT OF NOTICE
OF MOTION AND MOTION TO DISMISS

JOHN DOE DOES HEREBY AFFIRM AND STATE AS FOLLOWS:

1. That he is one of the persons named as Defendant in the above-captioned cause.
2. That he is a layman and without any law school training.
3. That he has filed a Notice of Motion and Motion to Dismiss on July 24, 1984, has read and is familiar with its contents.
4. That the contents of said Notice of Motion and Motion are true and correct to the best of his knowledge and belief.
5. That said Notice of Motion and Motion is not presented for the purpose of delay but presented as a good faith challenge to Plaintiff's complaint.
6. That he truly believes that there are proper challenges to the Plaintiff's Complaint and to jurisdiction.
7. That he is a competent witness and can testify to the above, if called.
   And Further Affiant Saith Not.

_____
John Doe

SUBSCRIBED AND AFFIRMED before me, a Notary Public for and in the County of Milwaukee, State of Wisconsin on this _____ day of July, 1984.

_____   My Commission expires _____
Notary Public

*IMPORTANT NOTE:

An Affidavit in support of a "Motion to Dismiss" strengthens your case whether you are challenging jurisdiction or for any other reason. All Affidavits must be notarized. An Affidavit worded similar to the one above one is recommended to be served and attached to a "Motion to Dismiss" like the one on the preceding page. In this particular case, the defendant was successful in getting a foreclosure action dismissed as the attorney for the Savings and Loan had forgot to file a "Certificate of Service" of his original Summons and Complaint. As there was no "Certificate of Service" in the court file before the hearing on his "Motion to Dismiss." In this case, the defendant refused to admit to the judge that he had received "process" (Summons and Complaint). The judge then looked and was unable to locate a "Certificate of Service" in the court file and then dismissed the case. Be sure to write up and attach an "Affidavit in Support of your Motion to Dismiss" similar to this one.

John Doe
Box 1191
Duncan, Oklahoma 73533
Tele: 405 / 555-3752

State of Oklahoma   )
)   ss.

County of Stephens   )

AFFIDAVIT AND

NOTICE OF RECISSION
OF CONTRACT FOR
FRAUD, USURY AND
BREACH OF CONTRACT

COMES NOW the Affiant, John Doe, and hereby declares and states that the following is true and correct to the best of his belief and knowledge:

1) That on the 27th day of June, 1984, the affiant did confer with Mr. Thomas L. Banker of First Bank and Trust Company at 923 Main Street, P.O. Box 580, Duncan, Oklahoma concerning a loan of Seventy-five thousand seventeen Dollars and twenty-five Cents ($75,017.25) which affiant desired to obtain from said First Bank and Trust Company.

2) Mr. Thomas L. Banker did represent unto the affiant that the bank would lend to the affiant seventy-five thousand seventeen Dollars and twenty-five cents the bank was entitled to receive interest upon the whole seventy-five seventeen Dollars, and that the entire loan would be of and consist of seventy-five thousand seventeen Dollars and twenty-five Cents.

3) By the research and study performed by the affiant concerning the contract that was signed between the parties it has come to the knowledge and to the attention of the affiant that said bank, by and through its agent Mr. Thomas L. Banker, did misrepresent unto the affiant the true and correct total of the funds loaned to the affiant.

In reliance upon the representations by the representative of First Bank, Mr. Thomas L. Banker, the affiant did execute and deliver unto the First Bank a certain promissory note in the amount of seventy-five thousand seventeen Dollars and twenty-five Cents which stated collateral categories as a 1978 White Tractor Truck and Equipment.

4) The First Bank, by and through its agent Mr. Thomas L. Banker, knew, should have known, or had the responsibility of knowing that the amount actually loaned to the affiant was not seventy-five thousand seventeen Dollars and seventeen Cents, but in fact (the amount risked) was not greater than 10% (ten percent) of the seventy-five thousand seventeen Dollars and twenty-five Cents because that percentage is the reserve ratio that the bank is required to keep (to the best of the affiant's knowledge), and that in fact, the bank only loaned to the affiant an amount not greater than seven thousand five hundred one Dollars and seventy-three Cents ($7,501.73). The other sixty-seven thousand five hundred fifteen Dollars and fifty-two Cents ($67,515.52), or more, was nothing more than demand deposit credit creations.

5) The First Bank by and through its agent, Mr. Thomas L. Banker has represented unto the affiant that they are entitled to receive interest on the full seventy-five thousand seventeen Dollars and twenty-five Cents. The First Bank knew, should have known, or had the responsibility of knowing that the usury demanded of them from the affiant was unlawful and usurious and that they were charging interest on seventy-five thousand seventeen Dollars and twenty-five Cents when in fact they knew, should have known, and had the responsibility of knowing that they only risked an amount not greater than seven thousand five hundred one Dollars and seventy-three Cents ($7,501.73) and that they could only charge interest on the seven thousand five hundred one Dollars and seventy-three Cents ($7,501.73).

The First Bank knew, should have known, and had the responsibility of knowing that they IN FACT breached the contract with the affiant by declaring unto the affiant that they would lend to the affiant seventy-five thousand seventeen Dollars and twenty-five Cents when they had IN FACT only risked the sum of seven thousand five hundred one Dollars and seventy-three Cents.

The affiant understands that the reserve ratio requirement is no greater than ten percent (10%). Therefore the amount actually risked by the First Bank and Trust Company was no greater than seven thousand five hundred one Dollars and seventy-three Cents and interest thereon, said amount being the total debt to which First Bank and Trust Company is entitled to recover.

Affiant makes this timely notice to all parties concerned, having become aware of the fraud described above on or about the thirteenth day of December, nineteen eighty-four (12 / 13 / 84).

Dated this 21st day of December, 1984.

John Doe, Affiant

Subscribed and sworn to before me this 21st day of December, 1984.

NOTARY PUBLIC in and for Oklahoma residing in Stephens County, Oklahoma. My Commission Expires 10-30-85

ADDITIONAL CASE CITATIONS

ACTUAL NOTICE
Case #...

TO:

This Complaint at Law / Counterclaim at Law (strike one) is a "Suit at Common Law" under the 7th amendment to the Bill of Rights under the U.S. Constitution. The value in controversy exceeds twenty dollars and as a party to this action, I have demanded a trial by jury.

The 7th amendment to the Bill of Rights reads: "In a suit at common law, where the value in controversy shall exceed twenty dollars, the right of trial by jury shall be preserved."

"Motions to Dismiss" or "Demurrers" will have the effect of violating my 7th amendment rights if the result is I am denied a trial by jury in this case. The right to a trial by jury for a sovereign citizen and freeman is derived from the U.S. Constitution, and the Articles of Confederation and the Magna Carta which preceeded it. Beyond this, it is based on inalienable rights under Divine law. This action is filed for the purpose of pursuing justice and for no other purpose.

Federal Statutes to wit:

1. 42 USC 1983: "Every person who, under the color of any statute, ordinance, regulation, custom or usage, of any state, subjects or causes to be subjected, any citizen of the United States or other person within the jurisdiction thereof, to the deprivation of any rights, privileges, or immunities secured by the Constitution and laws, shall be liable to the party injured, in a civil action at law, suit in equity, or other proper proceeding for redress."

2. Title 18, U.S. Code 1001; Title 18, U.S. Code 1621: (False swearing and perjury).

3. Title 18, Sec. 241: "If two or more persons conspire to injure, oppress, threaten, or intimidate any citizen in the free exercise or enjoyment of any right or privilege secured to him by the Constitution or laws of the United States...They shall be fined not more than $10,000 or imprisoned not more than ten years or both."

The following quote is taken from the case of Miller v. Smith; W. Va. Sup. Ct. App., 12 / 18 / 81 as reported in the "Criminal Law Reporter" on Jan. 27, 1982 as follows: "To fulfill its functions of protecting citizens and providing them with a forum for bringing complaints within the criminal justice system, the grand jury must be open to the public for the independent presentation of evidence before it. If the grand jury is available only to the prosecuting attorney and all complaints must pass through him, the grand jury can justifiably be described as a prosecutorial tool...We therefore hold that, by application the circuit judge, whose duty it is to insure access to the grand jury, any person may go to the grand jury to present a complaint to it."

Date......... X ....

Case #_____*

ACTUAL NOTICE AND DEMAND

TO: **Waukesha County Sheriffs Dept.** and **Moving Company, name unknown** and all personnel & employees thereof:

NOTICE IS HEREBY GIVEN TO YOU AND EACH OF YOU that if you proceed to remove property and the family of John and Candice Kilroy from their home at S 89 W 22730 Milwaukee Ave. in the city of Big Bend, Wisconsin, that you will be a party to the violation of their constitutional rights under the 7th and 14th amendment to the U.S. Constitution as well as Article 1, Section 5 of the Wisconsin State Constitution.

PLEASE TAKE NOTICE that there is a lawsuit in this case which has not been brought to trial. Plaintiffs in this case have demanded a trial by jury and have paid for the same.

The plaintiffs who are adverse parties in possession of the above described property have filed a suit at common law per the 7th amendment of the U.S. Constitution which says:

"In suits at common law, where the value in controversy shall exceed twenty dollars, the right of trial by jury shall be preserved."

PLEASE TAKE NOTICE that the plaintiff's demand for a trial by jury was denied by Judge Willis J. Zick and that the Plaintiffs have amended their complaint and have sued the judge for violating his oath of office and the constitutional rights of the plaintiffs. Also, the attorney for Security Saving and Loan Assn. is being sued on perjury charges.

PLEASE TAKE NOTICE, that if you are a party to denying the undersigneds property without due process of law, that each and every one of you will be violating the following federal statutes and you will be LIABLE to the family of John and Candice Kilroy for civil damages.

THE FOLLOWING FEDERAL STATUTES WILL BE VIOLATED IF YOU REMOVE PERSONS OR PROPERTY FROM S 89 W 22730 Milwaukee Ave. in Big Bend, Wisconsin. The statutes you will be violating are as follows:

1. Title 42, U.S.C. 1983 et seq.
2. Title 18, Sec. 241 and 242.

TITLE 42, U.S.C. Section 1983 reads: "EVERY PERSON WHO, UNDER COLOR OF ANY STATUTE, ORDINANCE, REGULATION, CUSTOM OR USAGE, OF ANY STATE, SUBJECTS OR CAUSES TO BE SUBJECTED, ANY CITIZEN OF THE UNITED STATES OR OTHER PERSON WITHIN THE JURISDICTION THEREOF TO THE DEPRIVATION OF ANY RIGHTS, PRIVILEGES, OR IMMUNITIES SECURED BY THE CONSTITUTION AND LAWS, **SHALL BE LIABLE TO THE PARTY INJURED** IN A CIVIL ACTION AT LAW, SUIT IN EQUITY, OR OTHER PROPER PROCEEDING FOR REDRESS.''

TITLE 42, U.S.C. 1986 reads: "EVERY PERSON WHO, **HAVING KNOWLEDGE** THAT ANY OF THE WRONGS CONSPIRED TO BE DONE, AND MENTIONED IN THE PRECEDING SECTION (42 USCS 1985), ARE ABOUT TO BE COMMITTED, AND HAVING POWER TO PREVENT OR AID IN PREVENTING THE COMMISSION OF THE SAME, NEGLECTS OR REFUSES SO TO DO, IF SUCH WRONGFUL ACTS BE COMMITTED, **SHALL BE LIABLE TO THE PARTY INJURED** . . .''

TITLE 18, SECTION 241 reads: "If two or more persons conspire to injure, oppress, threaten, or intimidate any citizen in the free exercise or enjoyment of any right or privilege secured to him by the Constitution or laws of the United States. . .They shall be fined not more than $10,000 or imprisoned not more than ten years or both.''

UNDER STATE STATUTES, A JUDGE WHO IS SUED AND IS A PARTY TO A CASE MUST REMOVE HIMSELF FROM THE CASE AND THE CLERK OF COURTS HAS NO JUDICIAL POWERS.

ANY WRIT OF ASSISTANCE THAT YOU MAY HAVE IN YOUR POSSESSION IS UNLAWFUL AND ANY ACTIONS TO CARRY OUT AN UNLAWFUL WRIT SHALL CAUSE YOU TO BE IN VIOLATION OF THE ABOVE DESCRIBED STATUTES. SINCE EACH OF YOU HAVE TAKEN AN OATH TO UPHOLD THE CONSTITUTION OF THE UNITED STATES, YOU MAY FURTHER FOUND IN VIOLATION OF 18 U.S. Code 1001 and Title 18, Sec. 1621.

DATE: March 5, 1984 X_____

John Kilroy, plaintiff

X_____

Candice Kilroy, plaintiff

*Note: Make up a similar Notice and Demand and print up 15 or more copies. Serve it on the sheriff's department and on anyone who tries to move you out.

State of ?   (   ) (   )

(J. Freeholder),
    Plaintiff,

vs.   Case # . . . .

                             AFFIDAVIT IN
Bank of ? and,   OPPOSITION TO
John and Jane Does (1 to 50) MOTION TO
    Defendants   DISMISS

COMES NOW the plaintiff, J. Freeholder, and alleges and shows to the court the following:

1. PLAINTIFF ALLEGES THAT THE COURT LACKS JURISDICTION TO GRANT THE MOTION TO DISMISS FOR ALL OF THE FOLLOWING REASONS:

a. First, this is a COMPLAINT AT LAW as distinguished from a COMPLAINT IN CHANCERY OR EQUITY or a COMPLAINT UNDER ADMIRALTY or MARITIME JURISDICTION.

b. A COMPLAINT AT LAW is a COMPLAINT AT COMMON LAW.

c. PLAINTIFF DID ASK FOR A JURY TRIAL UNDER RULES OF COMMON LAW PURSUANT

TO THE 7th AMENDMENT TO THE BILL OF RIGHTS OF THE UNITED STATES CONSTITUTION.

d. A COMPLAINT AT LAW is a "SUIT AT COMMON LAW."

e. The 7th amendment to the U.S. Constitution says: "In suits at common law, where the value in controversy shall exceed twenty dollars, the right of trial by jury shall be preserved..."

f. This case involves a suit where the value in controversy does exceed twenty dollars; therefore, under the 7th amendment, the right to trial by jury is preserved.

g. The Constitution of the United States is the Supreme Law of the Land as stated in Article 6, paragraph 2, U.S. Constitution.

h. The Honorable Judge_____ who is presiding in this trial did take an Oath to uphold the Constitution of the United States, and is therefore bound thereby. Article 6: "and the Judges in every State shall be bound thereby, any Thing in the Constitution or Laws of any State to the Contrary notwithstanding."

i. In this SUIT AT COMMON LAW, the plaintiff did not waive his right to a trial by jury and has in fact demanded the same.

j. The court, therefore, has no jurisdiction to grant the Motion and Dismiss, until after the jury has rendered its verdict and then only if the verdict is in favor of the defendant and against the plaintiff.

k. The Doctrine of Absolute Immunity, as applied to judges, exists only when the judge acts within his jurisdiction. There are numerous Supreme Court decisions on this. See Randall v. Brigham, 74 U.S. 523, 19 L.Ed. 285 or 9 S CT Digest 746.

l. Judge_____, would therefore, become liable to the plaintiff for civil damages, if he acted without jurisdiction and dismissed this case without first having preserved the right of trial by jury under the 7th amendment he is sworn to uphold.

I, (J. Freeholder), being sworn on Oath affirm that all statements made herein are true and correct.

X_____

J. Freeholder, plaintiff
(pro se)

STATE OF (WISCONSIN)
(MILWAUKEE) (COUNTY) ss.
Subscribed and sworn to before me,
this _____ day of _____, 19_____.

_____

Notary Public, State of (Wisconsin)
My Commission expires _____.

═══════════════════════════════

UNITED STATES DISTRICT COURT
NORTHERN DISTRICT OF INDIANA
SOUTH BEND DIVISION

LARRY J. RYNEARSON,
    Plaintiff,
(Note, if you are defending Counterclaim, substitute the word "defendant" for the word "plaintiff.")
vs.   CAUSE # ......

FIRST NATIONAL BANK, et al.,
    AND
THE STATE EXCHANGE BANK, et al.,
    Defendants,
    AFFIDAVIT AND BRIEF IN OPPOSITION
    TO MOTION TO DISMISS.

Comes now Plaintiff, Larry J. Rynearson, and states as follows:

On April 18, 1984, Plaintiff filed his Complaint, JURY ACTION AT LAW, SUIT AT COMMON LAW, plainly setting out a demand for trial by jury under the 7th amendment to the Constitution of the United States.

"The phrase 'common law' found in this clause, is used in contradistinction to **equity**, and **admiralty**, and **maritime** jurisprudence.
Parsons vs. Bedford, et al., 3 Pet 433, 478-9.

In suits at common law, motions to dismiss, motions in limmine, protective orders and summary judgments are not allowed.

The common law is higher than statute law. There is only substance at the common law.

"By **common law**, they (framers of the 7th amendment) meant what the constitution denominated in the third article 'law,' not merely suits which the common law recognized among its old and settled proceedings, but suits in which legal rights were to be ascertained and determined, in contradistinction to those where equitable rights alone were recognized, and equitable remedies were administered; or where, as in the admiralty, mixture of public law and of maritime law and equity was often found in the same suit.''

Parsons vs. Bedford, 3 Pet 433, 479 (1930)

The common law jury had the right to determine the law as well as the facts. Under the common law one suffered the pains (imprisonment) as well as the penalty (monetary damages) as the jury could award both. Defendants frequently preferred to pay the civil damages rather than run the risk of a jail sentence if tried.

Under common law every individual knows his duties and responsibilities to the other individuals in the society. Unless he damages them by a violation of their right to life, liberty, and property, there is no action at law against that man.

Plaintiff did, prior to filing suit, give notice to defendants of the charges against them as per the common law. (See exhibit F.)

Defendants failed to answer or deny, or to even respond in the time designated. Therefore their omission is to be construed as an admission of the facts stated. This is a **fact** which cannot be denied.

Defendants either have no knowledge of the common law or choose to ignore it.

> ''If the **common law** can try the cause and give full redress, that alone takes away the admiralty jurisdiction.''

Ramsey vs. Allegrie, supra, p. 411.

Plaintiff has invoked jurisdictions under the common law, the 5th and 7th amendments of the Constitution as well as 28 USC 1331 and 1343, 42 USC 1983–1986, and 18 USC 241–242. Plaintiff has stated claims upon which relief can be granted and has been denied his property both real and personal under color of law.

> ''A Plaintiff need not pursue his state remedies before instituting a 1983 action.''

Monroe vs. Pape, 365 US 167 (1961)

''A claim under the civil rights act expressly gives the district court jurisdiction, no matter how im-

perfectly the claim is stated; . . . the judge's feelings that the case is probably frivolous does not justify by-passing the right to a hearing on the merits.''

Harmon vs. Superior Court of the State of California. 307 F 2d 796 (CA. 9, 1962)

''Pro se petitioners—In determining whether such constitutional rights were denied, we are governed by the substance of things, not by mere form.''

Louisville N.R. Co. vs. Schmidt, 177 U.S. 23 S Ct 620.

Title 28 USC 1343(3) and 42 USC read as follows:

''To redress the deprivation, under color of any state law, statute, ordinance, regulation, custom or usage, of any right, privilege or immunity secured by the Constitution of the United States or by any Act of Congress providing for equal rights of citizens or of all persons within the jurisdiction of the United States.''

''Every person who, under color of any statute, ordinance, regulation, custom or usage, of any State Territory, subjects, or causes to be subjected, any citizen of the United States or other person within the jurisdiction thereof to the deprivation of any rights, privileges, or immunities secured by the Constitution and laws, shall be liable to the party injured in an action of law, suit in equity or other proper proceeding for redress.''

It is at least a custom or usage that defendant banks lend their credit without any authority to do so while regulatory agencies of this state appear to look the other way, thereby increasing the supply of ''money'' in violation of federal law.

Such action damages Plaintiff by devaluing Plaintiff's property, by defrauding Plaintiff into paying interest on ''money'' that was never loaned.

By defrauding Plaintiff into believing that a real contract existed and enticing him to put up his home as collateral on a loan that was never made, Plaintiff was damaged.

Plaintiff alleges breach of contract, fraud and usury in Counts 1, 2 and 3 of the Complaint. Plaintiff's exhibits and Memorandum of Law together with the case law cited therein, clearly state the fact that Plaintiff's right to life, liberty and property were deprived under the regulation, custom and usage of the banking practices perpetuated on Plaintiff.

Further, Count 4, showing that conspiracy by all the defendants, has denied Plaintiff of his property without due process under color of state law.

"...statutes which would deprive a citizen of the rights of person or property without a regular trial, according to the course and usage of common law, would not be the law of the land."
Hoke vs. Henderson, 15 N.C. 15, 25 AM Dec 677.

"Law of the land" means "The Common Law." Justice O'Neal in **State vs. Simmon,** 2 Spears 761, 767 (1884); and Justice Bronson in **Taylor vs. Porter,** 4 Hill 140, 146 (1843).

FACTS ALLEGED:
(1) All defendants were given a COMMON LAW NOTICE of the charges against them.

(2) Said NOTICE with proof of service are attached to Plaintiff's pleading.

(3) Defendants, with the exception of T. Edward Ummel, have failed to answer or deny the charges.

(4) The Factual Background, as stated in the Complaint, along with the exhibits attached, show the fact that loans were executed, and that Plaintiff alleges the same were unlawful as the banks only loaned their credit. Plaintiff's Memorandum Of Law submitted with the Complaint, cites several cases where it has been well settled in law that a bank cannot lend its credit. This is a fact that defendants cannot deny. If there is only one fact that cannot be stipulated to, that is all that is required for a jury trial.

(5) The Complaint on page 8, item #23, states the fact that the defendant State Exchange Bank openly violated the full disclosure provision of the Federal Truth In Lending Act.

(6) Plaintiff set out in "Facts Of The Matter," pages 14 and 15, that a corporation is without authority to make a contract beyond the scope of its corporate powers. The courts have stated:

"Act is ultra vires when corporation is without authority to perform it under any circumstances or for any pupose. By doctrine of ultra vires, a contract made by a corporation beyond the scope of its corporate powers is unlawful."
Community Fed. S. & L. vs. Fields, 128 F 2d 705.

"When a contract is once declared ultra vires, the fact that it is executed does not validate it, nor can it be ratified, so as to make it the basis of suit or action, nor does the doctrine of estoppel apply."
F & PR vs. Richmond, 133 S E 888 as quoted in **Norton Grocery Co. vs. Peoples Nat'l Bank,** 144 S E 501, 151 VA 195.

It is a fact that all such action in conspiracy did deprive Plaintiff of his property culminating in an unlawful Sheriff's Sale (held under color of State Law). Defendants were put on notice in the Complaint to cease and desist from all unlawful activities directed against Plaintiff's person and/or property, as fraud had been exposed, and that Plaintiff laid claim to his property until his suit was adjudicated in the proper court. Since Plaintiff had no funds, he could not avail himself of injunctive relief as per Rule 65 FRCP; he could only exercise his common law rights to inform the parties involved not to sell his property as it was under litigation.

However, against Plaintiff's 5th amendment rights and under color of state law, defendant State Exchange Bank and their counsel, T. Edward Ummel, did participate in said Sheriff's sale, when they and he could have prevented it.

Further, in violation of Plaintiff's 1st amendment right to be left alone, and his 4th amendment right to be secure in his person, house, papers and effects, State Exchange Bank and their counsel, T. Edward Ummel, coerced the Fulton County REMC to shut off Plaintiff's electricity, although the contract with REMC was in Plaintiff's name and was being paid by Plaintiff. Such request did result in Plaintiff's electricity being shut off for several hours, causing Plaintiff and his family mental anguish, trauma, loss of work time and expense of unnecessary travel before electrical service was restored.

"Where **rights** secured by the Constitution are involved, there can be no rule making or legislation which would abrogate them."
Miranda vs. Arizona, 384 U.S. 436, 491.

"Defendants can be held in actions under 42

USC 1983, even though they did not act willfully. Even though they did not have a specific intent to deprive the plaintiff of a federal right, such defendants can be held to civil responsibility.''
Monroe vs. Pape, 365 U.S. 167, 1961.

The court should take note that all this action was taken by an officer of the court, T. Edward Ummel, who has taken an oath to uphold the Constitution of the United States of America. Although defendant T. Edward Ummel did answer Plaintiff's Complaint by denial, he failed to do so by affidavit. Plaintiff can understand why, when it is clear that several of his rebuttal statements are patently false.

(1) He states that Plaintiff has not made any house payments for two years, whereas Richard Smikle of Ice Miller Donadio & Ryan, on page 1 of his ''Memorandum In Support Of Motion To Dismiss,'' states:

''The note held by First National Bank of Rochester was not actually in arrears.'' (This was a note on Plaintiff's home.)

(2) He states the electricity was not turned off, whereas the fact is that the electricity WAS turned off.

Plaintiff will wait until Trial and allow defendants to defend their positions.

''Title 28 USCA Sec. 1343 expressly grants jurisdiction to the federal district courts in civil actions for violations of civil rights, that is, for any wrongs specified therein.''
U.S. Agnew vs. City of Compton, 239 F 2d 226.

''In a 42–1983 action, the allegations of the complaint and the inferences to be drawn therefrom, upon a motion to dismiss, must be taken most favorably to the Plaintiff.''
Nanez vs. Ritger (1969, DC Wis.) 304 F Supp. 354.

''Complaint may not be dismissed for failure to state a claim if there is a possibility that plaintiff could obtain some relief on the facts stated, even though plaintiff may not have prayed for the appropriate relief.''
12B:34, **U.S. vs. White County Bridge Commission.** 2 FR serv. 2d 107, 275 F 2d 529 CA 7 1950.

''A complaint will not be dismissed for failure to state a claim, even though inartistically drawn and lacking in allegations of essential facts, it cannot be said that under no circumstances will the party be able to recover.''
(12b: 34 FR Serv 29, 19 Fd 511 DCED Pa 1958)

Plaintiff wishes to inform the court that the case at bar which is at law, suit at common law, is of a very different status than the cases cited by the defendants in their Briefs In Support Of Dismissal.

''The language of the Constitution cannot be interpreted safely, except where reference to **common law** and to British institutions as they were when the instrument was framed and adopted. The statesmen and lawyers of the convention who submitted it to the ratification of conventions of the thirteen states, were born and brought up in the atmosphere of the **common law** and thought and spoke in its vocabulary. . . when they came to put their conclusions into the form of fundamental law in a compact draft, they expressed them in terms of **common law,** confident that they could be shortly and easily understood.''
Ex Parte Grossman, 267 U.S. 87, 108.

Plaintiff has supported all his pleadings by affidavit. Except for the defendant T. Edward Ummel, defendants have not answered Plaintiff's Complaint. There has been no action taken by defendants supported by affidavit.

''A complaint may not be dismissed on motion if it states some sort of claim, baseless though it may prove to be and inartistically as the complaint may be drawn. This is particularly true where the plaintiff is not represented by counsel. **Brooks vs. Pennsylvania R. Co.,** 91 F. Supp. 101 (DC SD NY, 1950).

Plaintiff has alleged a deprivation of constitutionally guaranteed rights.

''Any plaintiff who can allege deprivation of federal right by reason of action under color of law can maintain action under this sub-chapter. **Nationwide Amusements, Inc., vs. Nattin,** DC La. (1971), 325 F. Supp. 95.

"Civil action for deprivation of rights: This section making any person, who under color of state law, deprives U.S. citizens of his constitutional rights liable to party injured is to be construed literally."
Nanez vs. Ritger, DC Wis. 1969, 304 F. Supp. 354.

The courts are not at liberty to arbitrarily dismiss a Complaint alleging a deprivation of constitutionally guaranteed rights.

"When a judge exceeds his jurisdiction and grants or denies that beyond his lawful authority to grant or deny, he has perpetrated a 'non-judicial' action."
Yates vs. Hoffman Estates (1962, DC IL) 209 F. Supp. 757.

"It is well established that judges may be enjoined from interfering with citizens rights."
Bramlett vs. Peterson (1969, DC FL) 307 F. Supp. 1049; **Pierson vs. Ray** (1967) 386 U.S. 547.

The Constitution of the United States protects the citizens from unconstitutional laws to limit admiralty so that it:

"...could no longer prescribe its own limits in prejudice of the individual, and to the exclusion of the common law rights."
Ramsey vs. Allegrie, supra, p. 399.

"The **common law** is the standard by which to ascertain what are proper cases for a prohibition to a court of admiralty, and not the civil law..."
Bains, supra, p. 56.

"The trial of issues in fact, in the district courts, in all causes except civil causes of admiralty and maritime jurisdiction, shall be by jury."
Section 9, Judiciary Act of 1789, 1 State, 77.

Plaintiff, In Propria Persona, is to be held to less stringent standards in making his claim, than that of formal officers of the court.

"Pro se complaints, according to the Supreme Court, are held 'to less stringent standards than formal pleadings by lawyers,' and regardless of who represents the plaintiff a motion to dismiss is not to be granted unless it appears beyond doubt that the plaintiff can prove no set of facts which would entitle him to relief."
Haines vs. Kerner, 1972, 404 U.S. 519, 30 L Ed 2d 652, 91 S Ct 594, 496 Reh. Den., 405 U.S. 948, 30 L Ed 2d 918, 92 S Ct 963.

This court has jurisdiction in suits at common law.

"There are three classes of cases for which the Constitution grants power to the judiciary.
1. Cases in law, or suits at **common law,** wherein legal rights are to be ascertained, and legal remedies administered according to the old and established proceedings at **common law.**
2. Cases or suits in equity where equitable rights only are recognized, and equitable remedies administered.
3. Cases or suits in the admiralty, where there is a mixture of public or maritime law and of equity in the same suit."
Bains vs. The Scooner James and Catherine, Federal Cases 576.

SUMMARY

WHEREAS the Plaintiff has alleged specific facts of fraud, usury, illegality and conspiracy, establishing a deprivation of Constitutionally guaranteed rights, and

WHEREAS Plaintiff is entitled under the common law to a trial by jury to judge the law and the facts and to have damages determined,

THEREFORE, this court has proper jurisdiction over the subject matter.

[signed] Larry J. Rynearson
In Propria Persona
P.O. Box 1656
LaPorte, IN 46350

Date: July 25, 1984

CERTIFICATE OF SERVICE

This will certify that a true and correct copy of the foregoing BRIEF IN SUPPORT OF PLAINTIFF'S SECOND OBJECTION TO DEFENDANT'S MOTIONS TO DISMISS AND PLAINTIFF'S RESPONSE TO THE COURT'S ORDER OF JULY 13, 1984, was mailed, first class mail, on the date listed below, to the following:

R. Stanley Lawton
ICE MILLER DONADIO & RYAN
One American Square Box 82001
Indianapolis, IN 46282

William I. Kohn
BARNES & THORNBURG
Sixth Floor, 1st Source Bank Center
South Bend, IN 46601

Lawrence Brown
BROWN RAKESTRAW & KEHOE
227 E. 9th Street
Rochester, IN 46975

James S. Downing
KRIEG DeVAULT ALEXANDER & CAPEHART
2800 One Indiana Square
Indianapolis, IN 46204

Timothy W. Woods
JONES OBENCHAIN FORD PANKOW & LEWIS
1800 Valley American Bank Bldg.
South Bend, IN 46634

T. Edward Ummel
SOWINSKI EASTERDAY & UMMEL
300 East Jefferson St.
Plymouth, IN 46563

[signed] Larry J. Rynearson
In Propria Persona
P.O. Nox 1656
LaPorte, IN 46530

Date: July 25, 1984

Part 1.

Your name,
    Plaintiff,
    vs.
Judge Chancery,
    Defendant.

Case #_____

REQUEST TO CLERK OF COURTS
TO ENTER DEFAULT JUDGMENT.

    Pursuant to [Federal or State] statutes, the plaintiff, [your name], requests the clerk of courts to enter a Default Judgment on behalf of the plaintiff and against the defendant for the sum of $_____.

Date: _____

X _____

[Add Notary Public here]

Your name,
    Plaintiff,
    vs.
Judge Chancery,
    Defendant.

CASE #_____

AFFIDAVIT OF NO ANSWER
and AMOUNT DUE.

Part 2.

I, [your name], being dult sworn on oath state the following: 1. that the Summons and Complaint has been duly served on the above named defendant. 2. Proof of Service is now on file. 3. The time for answering in said action has expired. 4. No answer has been filed herein or has been served on the plaintiff or his attorney from the above named defendant. 5. The amount due plaintiff in this action is $ [enter amount you asked for in complaint]. Defendant is in Default.

X _____

[your name]

State of [   ])
[County   ) ss.

Subscribed and sworn to before me,
this _____ day of _____, 19_____.

_____
Notary Public, State of [   ]
My Commission expires _____.

Your name,
      Plaintiff,
  vs.
Judge Chancery,
      Defendant.

CASE #_____

AFFIDAVIT OF NON MILITARY
SERVICE.

I, [your name], being duly sworn on oath, deposes and says the following: 1. This Affidavit is made in accordance with the Soldiers and Sailors Relief Act. 2. Affiant knows of his / her knowledge that the above named defendant is not in the active service, active duty or military service of the United States.

X _____
                              [your name]

[Add Notary Public Here]

Part 4.
Your name,
      Plaintiff,
  vs.
Judge Chancery,
      Defendant.

Case #_____

DEFAULT JUDGMENT

The Clerk of Courts has examined the file and finds the following: 1. Proof of Service statement. 2. Affidavit of No Answer and Amount Due. 3. Request to Clerk of Courts to Enter Default Judgment. 4. Affidavit of Non Military Service.

The Clerk of Courts hereby enters a Default Judgment in favor of the plaintiff, [your name], and against the defendant, [his name], for the sum of $ [amount due].

This judgment is entered pursuant to [Wisconsin Statutes 806.02 / Federal Rule 55c].

Date: _____   X _____
                                         Clerk of Court

Note: Parts 1 through 4 are needed to enter a Default Judgment in the Clerk of Courts office, if no answer to Complaint is filed.

State of Wisconsin	Circuit Court	Milwaukee County

Marine Bank N.A.
1337 South 16th St.
Milw., Wis. 53204,

     Plaintiff,

  vs.

Christopher L. Niesl
3864 South 92nd St.
Milw., Wis. 53228,

     Defendant and Third Party Plaintiff.

  vs.

Thomas P. Doherty (individually)
901 N. 9th St.
Milw., Wis. 53233,

     Third Party Defendant and

John and Jane Does (1 to 50),
     Third Party Defendants.

Case # 622785

THIRD PARTY COMPLAINT
AT LAW

THIS IS A COMPLAINT AT LAW AND A SUIT AT COMMON LAW

1. Jurisdiction: Invoked in Case # _____, _____ statutes and Constitution, The United States Constitution, and in particular the 7th amendment, in reference to suits at common law, as well as rights of immemorial antiquity existing under common law.

2. Parties: Plaintiff is Marine Bank N.A.; Defendant and Third Party Plaintiff is Christopher L. Niesl, who are both the original parties in Case # _____. John and Jane Does (1 to 50) are persons whose names and addresses are unknown and against whom the defendant and third party plaintiff believes he has a cause of action. The Third Party Defendant named herein is Thomas P. Doherty, a circuit court judge in _____ County who presided in Case # _____.

3. Defendant, Christopher L. Niesl, hereby reaffirms all the allegations made against Marine Bank N.A. in his Counterclaim as amended to date.

4. Facts: On Sept. 30th, 1983, Christopher L. Niesl did pay for a 12 person jury trial and this was demanded in his Counterclaim against the Marine Bank N.A. filed on Sept. 30th, 1983.

5. On Jan. 16th, 1984, Judge Thomas P. Doherty did dismiss the Counterclaim and granted a Summary Judgment to the Marine Bank N.A.

6. On Feb. 20th, 1984, a Motion ofr Reconsideration was heard before Judge Thomas P. Doherty to vacate the judgment and to set a date for a jury trial pursuant to the defendants 7th amendment rights to the same in an "at law" proceeding or "suit at common law." Judge Doherty was given notice that if the defendant was denied a jury trial, that it would be a knowing and deliberate violation of his right to a trial by jury under the 7th amendment as well as a denial of property without due process under the 14th amendment.

NOTE: THIS IS THE APPROACH THAT IS THE MOST EFFECTIVE WAY FOR A DEFENDANT TO REMOVE A JUDGE FROM A CASE WHEN THE JUDGE HAS DISMISSED HIS COUNTER-CLAIM AGAINST THE BANK. USE A REGULAR *SUMMONS* HERE.

7. The main issues that were to be tried before a jury was whether or not the bank had tendered a lawful consideration using monies which the bank had created on its own books and whether for failure to tender a lawful consideration the security agreement and all other security agreements signed by the defendant were now a legal nullity and that the bank had no claim for relief having used a consideration forbidden by law.

8. On Monday, Feb. 20th, 1984, the defendant did give notice to Judge Doherty in an oral presentation in support of his Motion for Reconsideration that this was a SUIT AT COMMON LAW and that under the 7th amendment, he had the right to plead his case before a jury and Judge Doherty having taken an oath to uphold the Constitution of the United States was bound to uphold the defendants right to a trial by jury under rules of common law. Judge Doherty was also noticed that a denial of trial by jury would be a violation of the defendants 14th amendment rights.

9. On _____, 1984, Judge Thomas Doherty did dismiss the defendant's Motion for Reconsideration and did deny him a trial by jury. In so doing, Judge Doherty did violate his oath of office and did violate the defendants rights under the 7th and 14th amendments to the United States Constitution. In so doing, he did act without authority and jurisdiction and is now fully liable to the defendant for all civil damages which he has sustained. Defendant was damaged by Judge Thomas P. Doherty in the sum of $6,154.00, which is the actual damages which were listed in his Counterclaim against the bank. Also, Judge Thomas P. Doherty damaged the defendant by ordering a summary judgment against said defendant and this enabling the plaintiff, Marine Bank N.A. to repossess his property, a 1982 Oldsmobile Model: DRB Body Style: CPE ID # 1G3AY37NOCM181582. Defendant claims a value of his constitutional right to a trial by jury at $10,000.00 in the instant case, which Judge Thomas P. Doherty did deny the defendant.

10. By the actions of the third party defendant, Thomas P. Doherty, obstructed justice in this case and violated his oath of office and did knowingly, willingly and maliciously violate the defendants constitutional rights.

RELIEF REQUESTED

1. Wherefore, Christopher L. Niesl demands against the third party defendant, Thomas P. Doherty for actual damages in the sum of $16,154.00 and $30,000.00 in punitive damages.

2. Christopher L. Niesl hereby demands a trial by jury at common law pursuant to the 7th amendment to the Bill of Rights, U.S. Constitution.

Date: _____   X _____

                                                   Christopher L. Niesl, defendant
                                                   and third party plaintiff.
                                                   pro se.

State of Wisconsin	Circuit Court	Waukesha County

John A. Kilroy and
Candice L. Kilroy, his wife,

     Plaintiffs,

  vs.

Security Savings and Loan Assn.,
184 W. Wisconsin Ave.,
Milw., Wis., and,

                                          CASE # _____

Russell Scot Long,
184 W. Wis. Ave.,
Milw., Wis., and,

Willis J. Zick,
515 West Moreland Blvd.,
Waukesha, Wis., and,

                                       AMENDED SUMMONS

John and Jane Does (3 to 25),

     Defendants.

TO WILLIS J. ZICK:

    THE STATE OF WISCONSIN, TO SAID DEFENDANT, AND EACH OF YOU: YOU ARE HEREBY SUMMONED AND REQUIRED TO SERVE UPON, JOHN AND CANDICE KILROY, WHOSE ADDRESS IS S89 W22730 Milwaukee Ave., Big Bend, Wisconsin, 53103, an ANSWER TO COMPLAINT, which is herewith served upon you, within FORTY FIVE days after the service of SUMMONS upon you, exclusive of the day of service; and in case of your failure to do so, a judgment will be rendered against you according to the demand of the complaint.

DATE Feb. 21, 1984

                                      [signed] John A. Kilroy, plaintiff, pro se
                                      [signed] Candice L. Kilroy, plaintiff, pro se

STATE OF WISCONSIN   CIRCUIT COURT   WAUKESHA COUNTY

John A. Kilroy and
Candice L. Kilroy, his wife
S 89 W 22730 Milwaukee Ave.
Big Bend, Wis. 53103,

     Plaintiffs,

   vs.

Security Savings and Loan Assn.
184 W. Wisconsin Ave.
Milwaukee, Wis. 53203, and

Russell Scot Long,
184 W. Wisconsin Ave.,
Milwaukee, Wis. 53203, and,

Willis J. Zick,
515 West Moreland Blvd.
Waukesha, Wis. and
John and Jane Does (3 to 25),

     Defendants.

CASE # 84-CV-228

AMENDED COMPLAINT AT LAW
(SUIT AT COMMON LAW)

---

1. Jurisdiction is invoked in existing Case # 84-CV-228 and in the 7th amendment to the Bill of Rights to the U.S. Constitution which says: "In suits at common law, where the value in controversy shall exceed twenty dollars, the right of trial by jury shall be preserved...."

2. Two additional parties are added to this complaint at law and suit at common law and are removed from the list of John and Jane Does. They are: Russell Scot Long, an attorney employed by Security Savings and Loan Assn. whose work address is 184 W. Wisconsin Ave., Milwaukee, Wis. and Willis J. Zick, a Circuit Court Judge in Waukesha County at 515 West Moreland Blvd., Waukesha, Wis.

3. Plaintiffs allege that Attorney Russell Scot Long committed PERJURY by signing an Affidavit of Mailing and making false statements therein. This Affidavit of Mailing was for a NOTICE TO CONFIRM SALE AND ADD ADDITIONAL SUMS TO JUDGMENT. The letter which contained said NOTICE was mailed on Feb. 8, 1984. The CERTIFIED MAIL NO. was P593773217 to Candice Kilroy and P593773218 for John Kilroy. The date of the hearing was Feb. 6th, 1984. The NOTICE TO CONFIRM SALE AND ADD ADDITIONAL SUMS TO JUDGMENT was actually mailed out two days after the hearing took place. An Affidavit of Mailing for this notice is on file and is a perjured statement. John and Candice Kilroy have been damaged by this action for the sum of $20,496.72 and an additional amount for violation of their 14th amendment rights under the United States Constitution.

4. All allegations against Security Savings and Loan Assn. stated earlier are reaffirmed herein.

5. On Feb. 20th, 1984, Willis J. Zick dismissed our complaint at law against Security Savings and Loan Assn. and did violate the plaintiffs 7th and 14th amendment rights under the U.S. Constitution and did violate the plaintiffs rights under Art. 1, Sec. 5 of the Wisconsin State Constitution. In doing so, Willis J. Zick, circuit court judge, acted without jurisdiction, and is fully liable to plaintiffs for damages in the sum of $20,496.72 as well as additional damages for violation of the plaintiffs 7th and 14th amendment rights.

6. Judge Willis J. Zick has taken an oath to uphold the Constitution of the United States and the Constitution of the State of Wisconsin.

7. Judge Willis J. Zick knew that plaintiffs had filed a COMPLAINT AT LAW and SUIT AT COMMON LAW.

8. Judge Willis J. Zick knows that the Constitution of the United States is the Supreme Law of the Land.

9. Judge Willis J. Zick knows what the 7th amendment says.

10. Judge Willis J. Zick knows that the 7th amendment says: "In suits at common law, where the value in controversy shall exceed twenty dollars, the right of trial by jury shall be preserved...."

11. Judge Willis J. Zick knows that in this case the value in controversy does in fact exceed twenty dollars.

12. Judge Willis J. Zick knew that the plaintiffs had paid for a trial by jury, and had demanded the same.

13. Judge Willis J. Zick has violated the 7th amendment rights of the plaintiff in this case, KNOWINGLY, WILLINGLY AND WANTONLY.

14. Judge Willis J. Zick knows that the 14th amendment to the U.S. Constitution says: "nor shall any State deprive any person of life, liberty, or property, without due process of law...."

15. Judge Willis J. Zick knows that Article 1, Section 5 of the Wisconsin says: "The right of trial by jury shall remain inviolate, and shall extend to all cases *at law* without regard to the amount in controversy...."

16. Judge Willis J. Zick knew that this was a COMPLAINT *AT LAW* and did knowingly, willingly and wantonly violate the plaintiffs rights under the 14th amendment to the U.S. Constitution as well as under Art. 1, Sec. 5 of the Wisconsin State Constitution.

17. Judge Willis J. Zick knew that the issues raised om Case #84-CV-228 of illegality for failure to tender a lawful consideration and fraud charges had not previously been raised in Case #83-CV-1134 and that the defense of Res Judicata did not apply.

Relief Requested

1. From each defendant, plaintiff demands the sum of $20,496.72.

2. Trial by jury demanded pursuant to the 7th amendment and according to the rules under common law: no Motions in Limine and No Directed Verdicts.

DATE: Feb. 21, 1984

[signed] John A. Kilroy, plaintiff—pro se
[signed] Candice L. Kilroy, plaintiff—pro se

FREEDOM OF INFORMATION ACT REQUEST

TO SOFRON B. NEDILSKY

FEDERAL CLERK OF COURTS:

DEAR Mr. Nedilsky:

This is a REQUEST made under the FREEDOM OF INFORMATION ACT made pursuant to 5 USC 552.
The undersigned requests the following information:

1. The name and address of the foreman of the local Federal Grand Jury.

This request is made for the purpose of reporting to the foreman certain violations of Federal criminal law by certain persons in Waukesha county. Please provide this information as soon as possible.

Thank You for your cooperation,

sincerely yours,

John A. Kilroy
3864 South 92nd St.
Milwaukee, Wis. 53228

The information should be sent to the above address, which is my place of residence. My signature has been signed in the presence of a Notary Public.

An alternative way to obtain the name of the Grand Jury Foreman and from experience most effective than sending out a F.O.I.A. request is to do the following:

Go to the Federal Clerk of Courts office and tell them this:

"Do you know if the grand jury has indicted anyone recently?"

Could you check the file for me?

When the file is brought out, then ask them: "Could I take a look at it?"

If they ask you for what purpose you want to look at the file, tell them: Well, *I'm a news reporter* and I wanted to see if there was anything new to report. This is a public record, I believe. Are the court files public records?

They should tell you that it is a public record and when you get the file, look for the sheet signed by the grand jury foreman. Write down his or her name. Then look up their phone number and give the foreman a call and ask them when there next meeting is and where and if if would be all right for you to go before them and present a complaint.

State of Wisconsin) ss.

Subscribed and sworn to before me,

this _____ day of May, 1984

_____

Notary Public, State of Wisconsin.

My Commission expires _____

Appendices

Attorneys with Known Experience

The following list is of attorneys who are known to have had experience in foreclosure cases. The listing is not intended to represent all attorneys with experience in foreclosure. No endorsement of those listed is herein stated or implied.

Alabama:
Lowell Becraft, 110 Southside Sq., Huntsville, 35801 (205-533-2535)
J. L. Chestnut, 1405 Jefferson Davis Avenue, Selma, 36702 (205-875-9624)

California:
Brian C. Davis, Modesto, 95352 (209-527-3904)
Robert Winterbottom, Newport Beach, 92662 (714-851-7717)

Colorado:
Lawrence Griffin, Fairplay, 80440 (303-836-2442)
Richard Gonzales, 550 W. Colfax Avenue, Denver, 80206
Charles Booth, 180 Cook St. #404, Denver, 80206 (303-399-2256)

Connecticut:
Benson Snaider, 22 Trumbull St., New Haven, 06511 (203-777-6426)

Florida:
Howard Kusnick, 7770 W. Oakland Park Blvd., Sunrise, 33321 (305-235-3571)
George Heath, 321 21st Street, Suite #3 Vero Beach, 32961, (305-562-7708)
Bennett D. Fultz, 619 S.W. 12th Avenue, Miami, 33197 (305-858-4733)

Georgia:
Roy Allen, P.O. Box 355, Tifton, 31793 (912-382-2421)
Harold Miller, 116 E. Howard, Decatur, 30030 (404-373-5515)

Illinois:
Mitchell Edelson, Chicago, 60608 (312-772-6555)
Gerald Barringer, R.R. 1, Box 198A, Palmyra, 62474 (217-436-2332)
Bob Collins, 100 W. Roosevelt, Wheaton, 60187
Stanley J. Stewart, R.R. 1, Box 198A, Palmyra, 62474

Indiana:
John Hyde, 1224 Hoffman Street, Hammond, 46327

Iowa:
Ken Schoenauer, Clinton, 52753 (319-242-7613)
Howard Fisher, 3123 Jackson, Olin, 52320
Marilyn Jensen, Osceola, 50213 (515-342-3536)
Jay Schweister, Columbus Junction, 52738 (319-728-2219)
Greg Steensland, Ames, 50010 (575-233-2037)

Kansas:
Leonard Robinson, Rt. 1, Box 172B, Eskridge, 66423 (913-775-6450)

Kentucky:
Frank Yates, 1188 Starks Bldg., Louisville, 40217 (502-582-1845)
Richard Wilson, 515 W, Market St., 40402 (502-583-7513)

Louisiana:
Craig Hattier, 9608 Robin Lane, River Ridge, 70123 (504-821-3025)

Maryland:
John Welsh, 7422B Altoanna Blvd., Glen Burnie, 20161 (301-760-3300)
Robert Cohn, 414 Hungerford Dr., Rockville, 20850 (301-244-9650)

Minnesota:
Patrick Schemmel, Rte. 1, Pennock, 56279 (612-597-4738)
Bill Walker, Star Rte., Itasca (218-732-8812)
Bill Cowell, Gaylord, 55334 (612-237-2954)
Michael Haugerud, Rte. 3, Box 56, Harmony, 55439

Mississippi:
James Wing, Rte. #, Box 335, Blue Springs, 38828 (601-869-2038)

Missouri:
Jimmie Nix, 620 Edmond, St. Joseph, 64501 (816-233-7777)
Robert Clayton, 999 Broadway, Hannibal, 63401 (314-221-7333)

Montana:
Jeff Shrom, P.O. Box 7733, Missoula, 59807 (406-721-3257)
Neil Halprin, 422 W. Spruce, Missoula, 50806 (406-721-7738)
Laura Lee, Billings (406-256-8888)

North Dakota:
William S. Williams, P.O. Box 1681, Fargo, 58102 (701-235-4687)

Nebraska:
Daniel Winkel, 11212 Davenport, Omaha, 68154 (402-334-4110)

New Jersey:
Martin Burger, 232 Broad Avenue, Palisades Pk., 07650 (201-944-3600)

New York:
Jeffrey Werner, Box 769, Newburgh, 12550 (914-562-1154)
Theron Foote, 23 W. Court St., Warsaw, 14569

Ohio:
Charles McFarland, Newton Falls (216-898-5511)
Frank Phillips, 146 S. Main, Marion, 43302
F. L. Schenk, 106 E. Wyandot Ave., Upper Sandusky, 43351 (419-293-3315)
Charles Ewing, 3316 N. High, Columbus, 43202 (614-836-4582)
Rob Bradley, 7809 Laurel Lane, Cincinnati (513-561-3322)
Carla Struble, 3316 N. High, Columbus, 43202 (614-837-4582)

Oklahoma:
Ted Strickler, Gentry, 74544 (501-736-2278)

Oregon:
Everett Thoren, 410 N. 10th St., Elgin, 97827 (503-437-5155)

South Carolina:
Tony Ponds, 1211 Broughton St. S.E., Orangeburg, 29155 (803-823-2751)

South Dakota:
Richard Hoppell, Sioux Falls, 57101 (605-334-0982)

Tennessee:
Call Mid South Patriots, 3273 Hickory Hill, Memphis, 38115 (901-795-1502)

Texas:
Herbert Porras, El Paso (no address) (915-533-8948)
Robert Cowie, Houston (no address) (713-236-0361)
American Law Assn., Bryan (no address) (409-846-9210)
Thomas Priolo, 910 W. 7th St., Amarillo, 79105

Utah:
Gary Joslin, 7742 Mountain Estates Dr., Salt Lake City, 84121 (801-943-2440)

Virginia:
Edmund P. Shevlin, 1815 Henry Avenue, Winchester 22601 (703-667-7549)
Patsy Bickerstaff, Brandon Ladd Apts., Waynesboro 22980 (703-943-3509)

Wisconsin:
Russ Stewart (no address) (414-273-0200)

Discovery Made Simple

It should be noted that the author, having retired, is not a licensed attorney. He provides no legal services, such as writing "Discovery" questions for any particular case. All materials written here are presented solely for their informational and educational value in helping the reader better understand the judicial process. It is recommended that anyone going "Pro Se," which means acting as your own attorney, seek local counsel to examine your pleadings before you submit them to the court. They should be in proper form and submitted according to local court rules. While many attorneys will insist on taking the whole case or not getting involved at all, there are many who will provide counsel and charge you by the minute or hour for advice. It is recommended that the latter approach be used if you cannot afford the full time services of an attorney. By doing most of your own legal work, many of your legal expenses can be substantially reduced. As you read through this book, the magic of Discovery and what it can do for you will unfold in the simplicity of a layman's language.

Definitions of Legal Terms

*DISCOVERY—a word that means your right under the law to obtain information and evidence that will be of benefit to you in a court action.

*COURT ACTION—a word that generally refers to a lawsuit filed by a plaintiff or a counterclaim filed by a defendant. In statutes or codes or laws of a state, the word "action" refers to a court case in progress. In a civil proceeding for money damages, an action is started when a plaintiff serves a Summons and Com-

plaint on a defendant. In a criminal proceeding, an action is started when a Warrant is issued for someone's arrest.

*SUMMONS—a legal paper filed with a complaint that notifies the defendant that a lawsuit has been filed against him and that he must answer the complaint in a certain number of days or a judgment will be rendered against him.

*COMPLAINT—a legal paper, also called a pleading, wherein the plaintiff complains against one or more defendants as to how they either injured him or broke the law or both and which also asks for court relief in the form of money damages and / or other relief.

*PARTY—in legal terminology is not a place where people gather to have fun. A "party to the action" refers to either a plaintiff or defendant in a lawsuit, but can also refer to an intervenor or interpleader. For example, in a divorce action, both the husband and wife are "parties to the action." A relative or friend could then file a pleading with the court as an interpleader or intervenor for some cause of action affecting their own interests.

*INTERROGATORIES—a set of questions sent by one party to an action to another party to the same action. To interrogate means to question. In some states, interrogatories are required to be answered under oath. Interrogatories are frequently used as a first form of discovery to gather information for depositions that are taken later on.

*ADMISSIONS—a special form of discovery that is a set of questions that start off with the words: "Do you admit that...?" The questions are then followed by a set of facts that are answered as either "admitted" or "denied." Under Federal Rules and the rules of most states, a set of admissions that are not answered in the requested time are then deemed to be "admitted." The failure of the other party to answer a set of admissions can be used to support a "Motion for Summary Judgment" against the party that refused to answer them.

*NOTICE TO PRODUCE DOCUMENTS—a form of discovery in which a party to an action asks another party to produce copies of certain books, records, checks and other documents which are then sent to the requesting party's address.

*SUBPOENA DUCES TECUM—a form that can be written up that requires the party receiving it to actually deliver certain books, records and documents to a designated address for inspection and copying. Preprinted Subpoena Duces Tecums are often available from local "legal blank companies." Subpoena Duces Tecum forms are frequently used with Notice of Depositions to require the person being deposed to bring along books, records and other documents, which are then inspected and copied or are used as a basis for questioning at the deposition.

*SUBPOENA—a legal form that can be used to require the presence of a witness at a trial. These forms are available from your local clerk of courts office.

*WITNESS FEES—are paid by the person serving a subpoena on a person who is not a party to an action, but whose testimony is desired. Witness fees are not paid to any person who is a party to an action, but only to persons who are not party(s) to an action. In Wisconsin, witness fees are presently $16 minimum or 20 cents per mile, whichever is greater. Mileage costs are figured both to and from the site of the deposition to the witness's home.

*NOTICE OF REQUEST TO ENTER BUILDINGS AND INSPECT DOCUMENTS AND EQUIPMENT—a form of discovery used to enter the building or property of another party to the action to inspect and copy records or inspect equipment at a time and date requested by the party seeking this form of Discovery.

*DEPOSITION—a set of legal papers prepared by a Court Reporter that contain the testimony of a person who answered questions under oath.

*TO TAKE A DEPOSITION—means the person who will ask the questions which are to be answered

under oath or affirmation.

*DEPONENT—the person who is subpoenaed to a deposition to be questioned; the person answering the questions at a deposition.

*COURT REPORTER—a stenographer who is authorized by the state to administer oaths and who records the deposition and later types it up in a form to be submitted to the court. Court Reporters can be located in your yellow pages phone directory under "Reporters, Courts and Conventions."

*DISCOVERY AS OF RIGHT—a term that means you go ahead and start discovery under the authority of existing statutes. There is no need to file a motion with the court when discovery is of right. Defendants under Federal law and the laws of most states have immediate discovery rights as soon as they are served a Summons and Complaint. Discovery as of right means you can immediately file interrogatories, admissions, notices to produce documents, depositions, etc. without going to the court to get the judge's permission. Plaintiffs, however, under Federal law and the laws of many states must wait 30 days after service of a complaint to take the deposition of a defendant and cannot require answers to interrogatories or admissions until 45 days after service of the Complaint.

*DISCOVERY BY MOTION—when discovery is not an automatic right under the law, it may be had by filing a Motion for Discovery with the court. The motion would state the questions to be answered and / or the particular documents to be copied or inspected or the person to be deposed at a deposition. The motion should state that the discovery sought is designed to lead to admissible evidence for your defense or to support your complaint or counterclaim. In Wisconsin, you would also need to attach to your Motion for Discovery a Notice of Motion and an Affidavit of Service and an Order for the judge to sign if he approves your motion. Discovery by motion is usually used in Small Claims Courts, Inferior Courts and Municipal Courts and in Appellate Courts if additional evidence to support your case is needed.

*DISCOVERY IN CRIMINAL PROCEEDINGS —some discovery is allowed in criminal proceedings like examining all the evidence the District Attorney has against you in a case and a list of witnesses he will call at the trial. Depositions are usually not allowed in criminal proceedings until a motion is filed with the court. This would usually be done if a witness you needed for your defense would not be available at the trial to testify but would be able to make a deposition prior to the trial which could then be submitted as evidence. For information on discovery in criminal proceedings, see your state's court rules and procedures book.

*COURTS OF RECORD—a court which has a Court Reporter who records all conversation and testimony given at a court hearing or trial. Courts of Record are usually called by the following names: District Courts, Circuit Courts, Superior Courts, Courts of Common Pleas. Courts where no records are kept are called inferior courts, small claims courts, municipal courts and traffic courts. In Courts of no record, you may have to hire your own Court Reporter if you want a record. A less expensive alternative is to bring in a tape recorder.

*SERVICE OF PROCESS—in discovery, service of a set of interrogatories, admissions or notice to produce documents are usually sent by certified mail, return receipt requested and include an affidavit of service. After service, copies of your discovery questions and your affidavit of service are filed with the court. Subpoenas for witnesses to appear are always served by a person who is not a party to the action such as a process server, sheriff, friend or relative. A notice of deposition and a subpoena duces tecum is usually served by a person in the same manner as a subpoena is served although in some states, service by certified mail is allowed.

*REASONABLE TIME—a person seeking a deposition from another party must give a reasonable amount of time from the date of the deposition. Seven days is usually considered a reasonable amount of time, but 10 days or more is even more acceptable. In sending interrogatories or admissions, 30 days is usually the time frame in which they can be required to answer. You may ask for answers in a shorter amount of time, if a motion hearing or pretrial require answers in a shorter amount of time.

*MOTION FOR PROTECTIVE ORDER—a motion that a party from whom discovery is sought places before the court to stop or limit discovery. Reasons for asking for protective orders are the following: there are too many questions to be answered, many of the questions are for purposes of harrassment and are not designed to lead to admissible evidence and / or

will create an excessive economic hardship on the party required to answer them. A defendant may use a motion for a protective order and ask for a delay in answering the discovery requests if he has a motion to dismiss before the court. A party seeking discovery can usually prevent such motions from being filed if he keeps his discovery short and to the point. If he has too many questions to ask, the best way to avoid a protective order is to take a deposition where there is no limit on the amount of questions you may ask or even how long you may keep them answering questions at a deposition. If the questions and the subparts exceed 30 in number, then get a copy of your local court rules to make sure you are not over the limit.

*LOCAL COURT RULES—a set of rules on court procedure than vary from court to court. A copy of local court rules can be obtained from the clerk of courts in the court where the action is pending. Local court rules often set limits on the number of questions that can be sent out in interrogatories, admissions, etc.

*YOUR STATES COURT RULES AND PROCEDURES—a book that is an absolute must in any court. There is a chapter on discovery rules and procedures for your state and the rules often vary from state to state. It is absolutely necessary that you get a copy of this book and read the chapter on discovery rules for your state. These books are available from West Publishing Co., P.O. Box 3526, St. Paul, Minn. 55165. If you live in Wisconsin, you could call them and ask for ''Wisconsin Court Rules and Procedures'' and ask them for the cost including shippng charges to where you live. You may call them at 612-228-2500. If you are in federal court, you will need a copy of ''Federal Rules of Civil and Criminal Procedure'' which is also available from West Publishing Co. Other sources include the law library at your county courthouse or even your local library or a university bookstore.

*MOTION TO COMPEL ANSWERS AND TO PRODUCE DOCUMENTS—if the party from whom discovery is sought refuses to answer some or all of the questions and refuses to produce copies of documents or objects to questions at a deposition, etc., you may file a motion with the court to compel them to answer questions or produce copies of documents. You must give reasons why you need this information or evidence such as it is designed to lead to admissible evidence, etc. An Order for the judge to sign if he approves it must be prepared and attached to the motion.

*MOTION FOR SANCTIONS—sanctions or penalties may be sought in court against a party that willfully obstructs discovery. A list of sanctions allowed in your state are usually described at the end of the chapter on discovery in "your states, court rules and procedures" book. You can ask for a number of things such as actual cost of money damages sustained for setting up a deposition or other discovery that was not responded to or you may ask that all proceedings by stayed until the other side responds to your discovery requests or you may ask that his motions or portions thereof be stricken or you may ask for a dismissal of their suit against you or you may ask for a default judgment. If admissions are not answered, you may ask for a summary judgment.

BASIC INFORMATION ON USING DISCOVERY

Today, most court cases in civil proceedings never come to trial. First of all, 90% of them are settled out of court and many of them never get past a motion to dismiss hearing. Most court cases that get past a demurrer or motion to dismiss hearing can be won through the effective and creative use of Discovery. Depositions are your most powerful form of Discovery, although not necessarily the first type you use. Depositions have often been referred to as a trial outside the courtroom. They are the counterpart of cross examination of witnesses at a trial and just as effective.

By now, you should have looked through the sample discovery forms at the end of this book. If you haven't, stop now and review these forms so you will have a better idea of the terms I will be using in this chapter. Discovery procedures give you a method of controlling the direction your case takes as it moves toward trial or a motion for summary or default judgment hearing. As a defendant, discovery can also be used to strengthen your arguments challenging jurisdiction as well as strengthening other arguments you may have in a demurrer or motion to dismiss hearing. When discovery is used to support a demurrer or motion to dismiss, the questions asked must be framed and limited to the issues raised in your demurrer or motion to dismiss pleading. When using discovery in this manner, keep it short and to the point and do not get into issues involving the basic (meritorious) issues of the complaint. There is no requirement that discovery be used in any particular order. Discovery may be used in any order and all forms of discovery can be used at one time, if the party seeking discovery desires to do so.

All paperwork used in discovery is written up by the party seeking discovery, except for subpoenas for witnesses which can be obtained from the clerk of courts if you want to subpoena a witness for a trial. While a "Notice of Deposition" and a "Subpoena Duces Tecum" can be typed up by a party to an action, these forms are usually also available from local "Legal Blank" companies which you can locate in your Yellow Pages telephone directory. An important point to note here is that a "Subpoena" is used to obtain the testimony of a witness at a trial and a "Subpoena Duces Tecum" is used to compel a witness or party to a deposition to bring along materials and other written documents for inspection and copying or to be questioned about these materials and documents at a deposition.

Getting started with discovery is simple if you are a party to an action in a state or federal court. You simply look through the various forms of discovery, think up the questions you want answered and the documents you want produced and do your paperwork. If you are not a party to an action (no one is suing you and you are suing no one), then you do not have discovery as of right. Also, if you are in a small claims court or other inferior court of no record, you usually do not have discovery as of right, but you can file a Motion for Discovery and in your motion, you can name the party you want to depose for a deposition or name the documents you want produced or the questions you want answered. Under Wisconsin rules, you would need a Motion for Discovery, a Notice of Motion, an Affidavit of Service and an Order for the judge to sign. You will need at least 3 copies. The original is filed with the court, and one is served on the party from whom discovery is sought and the other is for your records. It is very important that any discovery sought be served on the attorney for the party if he has made his appearance. Service on the party(s) attorney is the same as service on the party. If the other party has an attorney, all interrogatories, admissions, notice to produce documents and notice of depositions must be served on the attorney for that party. Otherwise, the attorney will object to you introducing the answers or depositions into the court record as evidence. Copies of all papers used in discovery must be served on all parties to an action. If a party has an attorney to represent him, service must be made on the attorney. If the party has no attorney to represent him, service must be made on the party directly. Service of Notice of Depositions and Subpoenas are usually made personally by someone who is not a party to the action. Service of interrogatories, admissions, notice to produce documents are usually made by mail. I recommend using Certfied Mail with a Return Receipt signed by the person receiving the discovery pleading.

GETTING STARTED

Most people start using discovery by sending out a notice of written interrogatories and / or a notice to produce documents. These can then be followed up with more notices of written interrogatories and more notices to produce documents. In interrogatories, if you don't know the name of the documents you would like to examine or copy, it is best to ask general questions like "Would you name every paper or document in your possession and provide a general description of the contents of each as they relate to the following subjects: a, b, c, etc.?" Other basic questions should include questions about words and their meanings. Under Federal rules and Wisconsin rules, a defendant has immediate and unrestricted discovery rights, so you can begin right away any discovery you need. There is no order in which you must use discovery, so you could use all forms of it at one time, if you want to. Generally, however, it is more practical to use interrogatories and notices to produce documents first, and follow this with a notice of request for admissions and a notice of depositions.

TIME

As a defendant, the usual rule is to allow the other party 30 days to answer interrogatories or admissions or to produce copies of specified records and documents like photocopies of checks, etc. You can, however, ask for answers in less time than 30 days if you need the information to support your position at a motion or court hearing that is coming up within the

30 days. In this instance, you would ask for the answers or documents by a specified date that would be less than 30 days after serving them the interrogatories or notice to produce documents. In depositions, a reasonable amount of time is 7 days after serving a party with a notice of deposition, although the usual amount of time is 10 days to two weeks, although you could set a date later than this if it more convenient. As a matter of courtesy for the opposing attorney, it is recommended that you call him and tell him of your desire to take a deposition of his client and suggest a date and time when this can be done. If he is not agreeable to this, he may suggest another date and time. If this is agreeable to you, then you must call a Court Reporter and set up this date and time for a deposition. Court Reporters can be located in your Yellow Pages phone directory under "Reporters, Court and Conventions." Once you have set up the date and time with the Court Reporter, then write up your Notice of Deposition and have someone serve it on the party(s) attorney and then mail a copy to the party as a courtesy.

If you are a plaintiff in an action, you can send out interrogatories and admissions, but cannot require answers until 45 days after the service of the Summons and Complaint on the defendants. If you serve interrogatories and admissions 15 days after the Summons was served on the defendants, you can ask for answers in the usual 30 day time period (15 + 30 = 45 days). If you want to take the deposition of a defendant, you must wait 30 days after the Summons was served on the defendant. After these initial time periods have passed, there are no restrictions on the use of discovery by a plaintiff seeking information and evidence from a defendant.

ADMISSIONS

Admissions are a unique form of discovery as all questions start off this the words; "Do you admit that. . .?" Each admissions is followed by a set of facts which the party from whom discovery is sought must answer as either "admitted" or "denied." The thing interesting about admissions is that if they are not answered, the law deems them admitted and the failure of a party to answer can be used to support a Motion for Summary Judgment against the party that fails to answer. In contrast, the failure of a party to answer interrogatories or produce documents which are available can be used to support a Motion for a Default Judgment. A summary judgment means there are no facts in dispute, and is a more difficult judgment to remove, once it is entered. A default judgment can be vacated by motion if the party seeking to vacate it files a motion to vacate default judgment and supports it with an affidavit that raises material issues of fact and can explain why through no fault of his own, he did not answer a complaint, counterclaim or discovery requests. Failure to receive notice by being served the pleadings in question are a common reason for vacating default judgments.

ADVANCED PROCEDURES ON USING DISCOVERY

Let us suppose that you sent out a set of interrogatories and a notice to produce documents and the party failed to respond or responded by refusing to answer some questions and failed to produce some documents. What do you do? Your first response should be to file a "Motion to Compel Answers" or a "Motion to compel the production of documents" or "Motion to compel answers and produce documents." You should take note of the three different wordings, but there are more like a "Motion to compel attendance of [name] at a deposition" and a "Motion to compel [name] to allow [yourself] to enter building and inspect equipment and examine documents." Of course, with any motion, you will need a notice of motion, the motion itself, an affidavit or certificate of service and an "order" for the judge to sign if he grants your motion. In some states, a "notice of motion" is not required and the judge simply rules on the motion as it is presented. When a notice of motion is required, you must type it up and then call the judge's secretary and ask for a date and time to have the motion heard. This information is then filled in the notice of motion so the party that it is served knows when it will be heard in court.

AFFIDAVITS IN SUPPORT OF MOTIONS

I always recommend that you use an "Affidavit in Support of Motion" whenever you present any motion to the court as this gives your motion the equivalent of court testimony, since it is now under oath. While attorneys generally avoid the use of affidavits except when filing motions for default of sum-

mary judgment, the use of affidavits to support your motions will strengthen your case and will increase your chances of success.

MOTION FOR SANCTIONS

Let us say that the judge has granted your motion to compel answers and the party to whom discovery is directed has answered none of the questions or produced none of the documents even though the court has ordered him to do so. Your next step in view or total failure of the party to comply with the motion to compel is to file a "Motion for a Default Judgment." I am assuming for purposes of this example that the party either failed to show up for a deposition or failed to answer interrogatories or produce documents. A motion for a default judgment would be proper at this time to dispose of the case. If you are plaintiff, you will need a notion of motion, motion for default judgment, supported by affidavit, order for judgment, affidavit of service. In your motion for default judgment supported by affidavit, you must state the general facts regarding the discovery sought, the motion to compel presented to the court and granted by it, the amount due in your complaint, and that the party has failed to answer any interrogatories or produce any documents and the time for doing so has expired and that this party is not a full time active member of the armed forces. Your motion for default judgment should be granted to you as a matter of right unless the other party appears and gives good cause as to why he has failed to comply and asks for more time. Whatever he does, he must do so timely and by motion. By timely, I mean that most states require at least 5 days notice prior to a motion hearing and some states require 7 days notice. If he doesn't comply with these court rules and procedures, you can object. It is important to remember here that when you file a motion, that you comply with the required minimum amount of time to give notice of a motion hearing. Check your book of the court rules and procedures for your state. The best way to look up this information is to look in the general index in "Your State, Court Rules and Procedures" and look up the word "time" or look under "motions" first and then look up "time." The index will be your starting point to look up all kinds of information as the need arises. If you had served a notice of request for admissions and the time for answering had expired, you could then file a motion for summary judgment rather than a motion for default judgment. Your paperwork would be similar to filing a motion for default judgment except you would add in your motion for summary judgment that pursuant to your state statutes . . ., there are no material facts in dispute as all factual allegations of your complaint or counterclaim have been admitted since the statute says any admissions not answered are to be deemed as "admitted."

In a second example, the party from whom discovery is sought partially answers your interrogatories and partially produces the documents requested, what do you do? If you are a defendant in an action, you could make a "Motion to stay all proceedings" pending compliance by the other party with all your discovery requests. Again, support it by affidavit and state that the discovery sought is designed to lead to admissible evidence and that you absolutely must have this information and evidence for your defense. Other sanctions include making motions to strike all or part of their pleadings. A defendant who has filed a counterclaim may move that the plaintiff's motion to dismiss the counterclaim be stricken or be stayed until the discovery sought is provided by the plaintiff. On the other hand, a plaintiff may move that the defendant's counterclaim be stricken if he fails to comply with discovery. There are many options possible under sanctions and everyone should read the section of your state rules dealing with discovery, particularly the last section dealing with sanctions against the party that obstructs discovery. In theory, a party can move for sanctions against another party that obstructs discovery without seeking a motion to compel from the court. In practice, this is rarely done, unless the amount of money sought is relatively small. In a foreclosure proceeding, a defendant seeking sanctions against a plaintiff is more likely to get a stay of proceedings than either a default or summary judgment against a lender. This is because sanctions are up to the discretion of the court and a judge has considerable latitude in deciding just how far sanctions should go against an offending party. The judge, however, must grant you some relief for if the judge provided you no relief, he would be violating your 14th amendment rights. The 14th amendment guarantees all citizens equal protection under the law. Under the law, a debtor must be given the same rights and relief as a creditor.

MOTIONS FOR PROTECTIVE ORDERS

Everyone using discovery should, in addition to getting a copy of his state rules on civil procedure, get a copy of his "local court rules." This is a book or set of instructions available from the clerk of courts at your local courthouse. These rules vary from courthouse to courthouse. For example, some federal courts set an upper limit of 40 questions per set of interrogatories. The 40 questions include the subparts of a question. Other federal courts require that the maximum number of interrogatories be set at 30 per set. No more than one set can be sent out at any one time. Also, questions asked must be related to the issues raised in your complaint or counterclaim. Otherwise, the other party may file a "Motion for Protective Order" and refuse to answer any questions at all. Arguments presented in a motion for protective order include that the discovery sought is excessive and would create a great economic hardship on you, that the discovery sought is not designed to lead to admissible evidence and / or that it is being done for purposes of delay, and to harass the other party. In opposing a motion for a protective order, you must state by affidavit what discovery you need and state that it is not being done for purposes of delay (as a defendant), that it is designed to lead to admissible evidence, and that it absolutely necessary for your defense and your reasons why. A motion for protective order is a two edged sword. You too can file a motion for a protective order if the other party seeks excessive discovery not related to the issues in dispute or done for purposes of harassment. You can help prevent motions for protective orders from being filed by keeping your interrogatories short and not requiring answers that will take days of research to locate. Use your initial discovery to locate documents and save your more difficult questions for the deposition, your most powerful discovery tool.

DEPOSITIONS—YOUR MOST POWERFUL DISCOVERY TOOL

Depositions have been called a trial outside a courtroom. They provide you with a chance to come face to face with your opponents and to question them under oath. Other attorneys and parties to the same action have the right to cross examine the party or witness you depose after you have finished your questioning. You have the right to continue questioning after this cross examination. Depositions are not as expensive as you might be led to believe. While attorneys will charge several hundred to several thousand dollars to take a deposition, a pro se can usually accomplish the same thing for $35 to $100.

There are five basic questions to consider in setting up a deposition. First, have you obtained all the information you can through interrogatories and notices to produce documents? Second, what Court Reporter should you get to record the deposition? Third, where will the deposition be held? Fourth, who will you depose? and fifth, what questions will you ask him or her and what documents will you ask them to bring to the deposition for inspecting, questioning or copying?

Assuming that you have obtained most of the information you wanted up to this point through interrogatories and other notices, and having a lot of unanswered questions or having in your possession answers to interrogatories that you don't believe and you want to ask them further questions on, you now decide to set up a deposition. First of all, you need to locate a Court Reporter and a place to take the deposition. After calling several Court Reporters which you locate in the Yellow Pages under "Reporters, Courts and Conventions," you call them up an inquire as to the hourly rate and the charge for each written deposition they provide. You then find a court reporter who has a room in their office for taking depositions, so you pick a date and time. You then type up a notice of deposition and name the party you will depose. You may depose more than one person at a time. To one of the party(s), you can also serve a subpoena duces tecum along with a notice of deposition as you want them to bring along certain books and records for examination and copying. If you are serving a notice of deposition on a witness who is not a party to the action (neither a plaintiff nor defendant), you must include witness fees. In Wisconsin, these happen to be .20 per mile from their home to the place where the deposition is held. There is a $16 minimum fee. If you have any questions concerning witness fees, ask the Court Reporter as they should know. If you are deposing a party to the action, such as another plaintiff or defendant, there are no witness fees to pay. They must come at their own expense.

Prior to the deposition, you must prepare your list of questions to ask each deponent. You should prepare your questions so as to drop the unexpected question that is critical to your case at the moment the deponent least expects it and after he has made admissions that you can then join in one question like, if this is true and that is true, then how can you explain this? Getting the party to talk is very helpful to winning your case. Most people convict themselves with their own words. Anytime during a deposition, you can call for a 5 to 10 minute break to check over your questions and answers and to think of any new questions that might have just occurred as a result of the answers just given. If the other party is represented by an attorney and the attorney objects and they will, just say: "your objection is noted for the record, now will you answer the question?" If the deponent still refuses to answer, continue with your line of questioning. Never allow yourself to get into a debate with the attorney or allow the attorney to snow you or counsel you as to what questions you may or may not ask. Remember, this is your deposition, not his. Never allow yourself to be ordered around by an opposing attorney. Focus your eyes on the person you are questioning, not his attorney. Anytime a deponent uses words you do not fully understand, write them down and than ask him the meaning of those words.

Imagine deposing a state judge you are suing in federal court for violating your Constitutional rights (a title 42, USC 1983 action). You can ask him questions like how a replevin action gives you due process when you are not given a notice of hearing? Why he denied you property without due process of law? Why he denied you a trial by jury which is your right under the 7th amendment and under your state constitution? Why he refused to grant you sanctions when the other party obstructed discovery—a violation of the equal protection clause of the 14th amendment and why he denies you access to the courts by refusing to let you file pleadings, another violation of equal protection clause under the 14th amendment. The possibilities are endless. The judge may have had a conflict of interest if he owned stock in the financial institution you are suing. His relatives may be bankers or his employment in the past before he became a judge may have had him as an employee of the party you are suing.

If one deposition doesn't answer all your questions, you can depose them again. If they obstruct discovery by refusing to answer certain questions, you can file a motion to compel answers to specific questions or produce documents or you can file a motion for sanctions or for default judgment.

On a final personal note, the purpose of the court process is the pursuit of truth and justice, and the courts should not be an arena to impress others with our legal wizardry or lack of it. If you are having problems figuring out questions to submit, say a prayer and sleep on it. The next day more questions will then arise. Consult with others who are having similar problems and they may offer some helpful suggestions. Consulting with an attorney for some advice on even a part time basis can be most helpful to overcome logjams. Framing your questions in discovery procedures will always be your biggest challenge like framing your facts in a lawsuit. You can never ask too many questions at a deposition, but you can ask too many in a set of interrogatories and find your discovery obstructed with a protective order. Aggressive discovery procedures won't make up for a poorly written complaint, so be sure to consult with others to improve the quality of your pleadings.

QUESTIONS AND ANSWERS

Q: Where can I find a book on how to be my own lawyer in court?

A: A book called *How to Be Your Own Lawyer in Court* by Attorney John Cotton Howell is available from Citizens Law Library, Box 3408, Boulder, CO 80307. Price is $19.95.

Q: What are other good sources of information on books for anyone who wants more knowledge in specialized areas of law?

A: Write to Practicing Law Institute, 810 Seventh Ave., N.Y., N.Y. 10019. Ask for their latest catalog on books available. Also, write to NOLO PRESS, 950 Parker St., Berkeley, CA 94710. Ask for their latest catalog. They have an excellent selection on do it yourself bankruptcy procedures. Also write to America's Legal and Professional Bookstores, 725 "J" St., Sacramento, CA 95814. Ask for their latest catalog. Other legal pleadings are available from Barristers' Inn, P.O. Box 9411, Boise, ID 83707. Another organization that has a list of self help books for the pro se is called HALT, Suite 319, 201 Massachusetts Ave., N.E., Washington, DC 20002. Write and ask for a price list of their publications.

Q: Are there any other books on Discovery available?

A: Yes. One called *Discovery—Win Your Case Without a Trial* by Attorney John Demay. It is available from Prentice Hall, Inc., P.O. Box 505, West Nyack, N.Y. 10994. Price $34.95. A lot of discovery questions related to personal injury of accident cases are contained in this book.

FORM #1 SET #1:
DISCOVERY QUESTIONS TO BE USED ONLY WHEN CHALLENGING JURISDICTION

Plaintiff

vs.   Case No._____

Defendant

Notice of Written Interrogatories
and
Notice to Produce Documents.

To Bank / Mortgage Co. / PCA / FLB / Bank for Cooperatives / S & L etc.:
address, city, state, Zip:

Please take notice that the defendant [your name] serves upon you this notice for written interrogatories and to produce documents pursuant to Discovery rights under [Federal or State] statutes. Please answer all interrogatories and produce copies of all documents requested and mail or personally deliver them to the defendant [your name] within 10 days or by [date you want interrogatories answered and documents produced]. Send your answers and copies of documents to this address: [enter your address here]. Thank you for your cooperation.

Date: _____   X _____

1. Do you have a Certificate of Authority to do business in the state of [your state]?
2. If you do not have a Certificate of Authority to do business in the state of [your state], then cite the laws that give you exemption from obtaining a Certificate of Authority and the legal basis for your doing business in this state? (Note: if your answer to interrogatory No. 1 is "yes," then skip question 2 and 3.)
3. If you do not have a Certificate of Authority to do business in this state and claim that your authority is that you are a federal instrumentality, then explain why this lawsuit was filed in state court instead of federal court and why you believe the state court has jurisdiction. In your answer, address the question of how this jurisdiction is compatible with the 10th amendment to the bill of rights under the U.S. Constitution which reserves to the states any powers not delegated to the U.S. Government? In particular, cite the section of the U.S. Constitution which allows federal instrumentalities to override the 10th amendment and cite the state law that exempts you from have a Certificate of Authority to do business in this state.
4. Did you pay filing fees to the clerk of courts when this lawsuit was filed and what was the amount?
5. Were the filing fees paid in either gold or silver coins or in a form of negotiable instrument redeemable in gold and silver coins?
6. If your filing fees were not paid in either gold or silver coins, can you explain how the type of monies used to pay said fees complied with Article 1, Section 10 of the U.S. Constitution which says: "No state shall make any thing but gold and silver coins a tender in payment of debts"? (Note: If your answer to interrogatory No. 5 is yes, then skip questions 6 and 7.)
7. Can you explain what section of the U.S. Constitution allows you the right not to comply with Article 1, Section 10?
Notice to Produce Documents
Please send a copy of your Certificate of Authority along with your answers. Thank You.

FORM #2 SET #2:
DISCOVERY QUESTIONS FOR PRODUCTION CREDIT ASSN. AND FEDERAL LAND BANKS AND BANK OF COOPERATIVES.

Plaintiff

vs.   Case No._____

Defendant

Notice of Written Interrogatories
and
Notice to Produce Documents.

To PCA / FLB etc.:
address, city, state.

Please take note that the defendant [or plaintiff], [your name], requests the following interrogatories be answered and copies of documents produced and mailed or delivered to the defendants [or plaintiffs] address at: [your address] by [date you want answers]. This request is made pursuant to Discovery rights under [Federal or State] statutes. Thank you for your cooperation.

Date: _____   X _____

1. Name and list all the class A or preferred stockholders of your Association or Corporation.

2. As consideration for the note signed by the [defendant or plaintiff], [your name], on [date you signed note, mortgage note, security agreement, etc.] did your association lend money that was issued by the United States Government or did it lend a privately created form of money?

3. In reference to interrogatory No. 2, if your association loaned a privately created form of money, would you name the individual or entity that created the money and would you describe what the privately created form of money looked like?

4. In reference to interrogatory No. 2, if your association loaned a form of money issued or coined by the government of the United States, would you list the serial numbers of the Federal Reserve Notes or United States Notes loaned to the [defendant or plaintiff] on or around [date of loan]?

5. Did you lend credit to the [plaintiff or defendant] on or around [date of loan?

6. If your answer to interrogatory No. 5 is yes, then would you describe a "credit" such as providing us with its length, width, thickness and color and any other characteristics it may have?

7. Did your association write a check or draft for the loan they made to the [plaintiffs or defendants] on or around [date of loan]?

8. Name the bank against whom this check was drawn and their address and the entire account number as written on the check.

9. Regarding the account number referred to in interrogatory No. 8, does your association ever deposit in this account checks or drafts which it receives from the Federal Intermediate Credit Bank? If your answer is yes, then give us the name and address of this FICB.

10. In reference to interrogatory No. 9, does your association ever deposit cash (coins or currency) into this account? If the answer is yes, then estimate what percentage of total deposits made 90 days prior to [date of loan] consisted of coins and currency.

11. Is your association audited by members of the Federal Reserve Board of Examiners?

12. Did the Federal Reserve Board of Examiners ever tell you to call in a loan or to increase the security and collateral backing a loan made to any borrower in the past year?

13. If your answer to interrogatory No. 12 is yes, give us the name of this official and his official address, if you have it and the names of the debtors he referred to.

14. Did any official of the Federal Reserve Board of Examiners or of the Farm Credit System other than one which works in your local office tell you not to renew or extend credit or call in the loan of the [plaintiff or defendant], [your name]? If this be so, give us the official's name and who he works for and his address, if you know it.

15. Has your association ever had any funds advanced to it by the Federal Reserve Bank of New York or any other Federal Reserve Bank? If the answer is yes, state the amount advanced, the date of the advancement and describe what the funds looked like and from whom they came.

16. Does your association own a machine that duplicates hand written signatures? If this be so, provide us with the make and address of the party from whom you purchased it and date of purchase.

17. Does your association have on file a complete set of bylaws of the farm credit system and about how many pages does it contain and can I stop in on any date with 24 hours prior notice and inspect or copy portions of said bylaws?

Notice to Produce Documents

1. Send a photocopy of all checks written by your association for the loan of credit to the [plaintiff or defendant] made on or around [date of loan]. Include both sides of the checks.

Notice to Inspect Documents

1. Please take notice that the [plaintiff or defendant]. [your name], will stop in your office located at [address] to examine and copy certain portions of the bylaws of the farm credit system and to examine records pertaining to my personal file. The date and time of this examination is [date and time].

SET #3:   DISCOVERY QUESTIONS FOR THE FEDERAL INTERMEDIATE CREDIT BANKS

Since Forms No. 1 and 2 show you how to submit interrogatories and notices to produce documents as well as inspect records, the following are discovery questions only for either interrogatories or to be asked at a deposition. These would be used if you as a defendant had filed a third party complaint against a FICB or filed an amended complaint as a plaintiff and named them as a John Doe defendant.

1. Within 6 months of the [date of your loan], how much money or credit did the FICB loan or transfer to the PCA / FLB etc. located at [address].
2. Does this FICB has an account at the Federal Reserve Bank of New York or at any other Federal Reserve Bank? Describe which Federal Reserve Banks you have accounts at and the account numbers and describe what purpose the account is for such as depositing book entry consolidated bonds etc. to act as collateral for funds advanced to you?
3. Has the Federal Reserve Bank of New York or any other Federal Reserve Bank ever advanced any funds to this Federal Intermediate Credit Bank. If so, how much was transferred to this FICB within 6 months prior to [date of your loan].
4. If any Federal Reserve Bank advanced or loaned money to you, would you list the serial numbers of the United States Notes or Federal Reserve Notes loaned or advanced to you?
5. If any Federal Reserve Bank advanced or loaned something other than actual money, would you describe what it looked like, such as a book entry deposit, a credit or a draft or a check or something else?

SET #4:   DISCOVERY QUESTIONS FOR FEDERAL RESERVE BANKS

The following are discovery questions that can be used on officials of the Federal Reserve Banks who are either named as John Does or defendants in a third party complaint.

1. Does the Federal Intermediate Bank of [address] have an account at your bank? If so, what is the account number and what do they deposit in this account.

2. Does the FICB of [address] deposit in this account Consolidated Bond, Debentures, notes, etc. as security for funds which you advance to them to be disbursed through the farm credit system?

3. What is the dollar value of such funds loaned or advanced to them within 6 months prior to [date of your loan]?

4. Do you have a record of the serial numbers of the United States Notes or Federal Reserve Notes you advanced or loaned to the FICB of [address] in the time frame mentioned above?

5. If you loaned or advanced the FICB or [address] something other than actual money, would you describe what it was you loaned or advanced them such as a book entry, a credit, a check, a draft or something else?

6. A few years ago, the Federal Reserve Bank of Boston wrote a book called *Putting It Simply—the Federal Reserve* and in which they say: "When the Federal Reserve writes a check, it is creating money."
Is that how the Federal Reserve Bank obtained the funds it used to loan or advance to the FICB of [address]. Did you literally create the money on your books?

7. Is it true that this Federal Reserve Bank is a privately owned corporation owned by the banks within this district? and second, can you cite the statute that says a book entry or promise to pay money is legal tender for the payment of debts, public and private?

8. Do you admit that you never really created the money you loaned or advanced to the FICB of [address], but that you merely wrote a bad check with the intended purpose of circulating it as money?

10. Do you admit that by writing and passing bad checks as money means you are intentionally involved in a check kiting scheme for your own benefit and the benefit of your stockholders?

Note: Sets Nos. 2, 3 and 4 are all connected to lawsuits filed against the farm credit system as complaints or counterclaims. Set No. 1 can be used by defendants against any lender in a foreclosure proceeding in a judicial state to challenge jurisdiction. Set No. 5 which follows can be used by either a plaintiff or a defendant who has filed a complaint or counterclaim against a regular commercial bank. The caption and introductory wording of a set of interrogatories are shown in Set Nos. 1 and 2 and are not repeated to conserve space.

SET #5:   DISCOVERY QUESTIONS FOR BANKS

1. Would the [name of bank] approve a loan to a customer who asked to borrow actual cash [coins or currency]?

2. Has the [name of bank] ever approved a loan since [date of your loan] to any customer who asked for actual cash? If your answer is "yes" then state the dollar amount involved in the transactions and the party you actually loaned cash to.

3. What is the total dollar value of all the outstanding loans of the [name of bank] [on the date of your loan]?

4. Are the outstanding loans referred to in interrogatory No. 3 considered the bank's assets?

5. What is the total dollar value of the bank's deposits on [date of your loan]?

6. Are the bank's deposits referred to in interrogatory No. 5 considered its liabilities?

7. What is the total dollar value of all the checking accounts held by your bank on [date of your loan]? (Your answer here is to include the total amount of personal and business checking accounts only and is not to include IRA or savings accounts or other types of accounts.)

8. What is the total dollar value of all loans made on [date of your loan] which figure is to include the loan made to [your name]? Note: The figures in your answer are to be only the loans actually made on [date of your loan] and are not to include loans made on any other date.

9. What is the total dollar value of all cash in actual coins and currency held by your bank on [date of your loan]? Your answer here must not include any forms of negotiable instruments such as money orders, checks, or accounts receivable or accounts held at the Federal Reserve Bank.)

10. What is the total dollar value of your reserve account at the Federal Reserve Bank on [date of your loan]?

11. Is it true that the figures given in your answer to interrogatory No. 5 are liabilities because they represent book entries that reflect how much the bank owes its customers?

12. Is it true that the figures given in interrogatory No. 5 do not reflect deposits of real money as they do not represent coins and currency held by the bank?

13. On [date of your loan], did the [name of bank] loan [your name] actual coins or currency? (Note: if your answer is "yes," then list the serial numbers of the Federal Reserve Notes or United States Notes actually loaned.)

14. On [date of loan], did the bank loan [your name] money which was derived from its customers' deposits at the bank?

15. Since the deposits at the bank are also the bank's liabilities, would it be correct to say that the bank loaned [your name] its liabilities in the sum of [dollar value of loan] on [date of loan]?

16. If your answer to interrogatory No. 15 was "yes," were the liabilities loaned to [your name] on [date of loan] taken from just one customer's accounts or was a little but taken from everybody's account? (Note: if your answer to No. 15 was "no," then skip this question and go on to No. 17, 18, 19, 20 and 21.) (Note: if your answer to interrogatory No. 15 was "yes," then go on to No. 17 and skip Nos. 18, 19, and 20.)

17. Would it be correct to say that liabilities represent "debts owed?"

18. If your answer to interrogatory No. 15 was "no," then is it correct to say the bank loaned an asset to [your name] on [date of loan]?

19. If your answer to interrogatory No. 18 was that the bank loaned an asset to [your name] on [date of loan] and if your answer to interrogatory No. 6 indicates that the bank's deposits are its liabilities, then is it not also true that the bank could not nave loaned out its deposits as these are the bank's liabilities?

20. Would you explain how the bank loaned out its assets to [your name] on [date of loan] if it did not loan out vault cash and did not loan out its customers' deposits, the latter of which are liabilities of the bank? What precisely did the bank lend [your name] on [date of loan] if it did not lend out its vault cash and did not lend out its customers' deposits?

21. Is it true that if a check is drawn on [name of bank] and its records show that the dollar value of the check is on deposit, that the [name of bank] will honor each and every such check presented?

22. Does your bank own a machine that duplicates hand written signatures? If this be so, then state the date

of purchase and the make and model and from whom it was purchased.

23. Define in plain English what the following words mean to the bank:

    a.   Dollar

    b.   Lawful Money

    c.   Legal Tender

    d.   Credit

    e.   Checkbook Money

    f.   Demand Deposit

    g.   Line of Credit

    h.   A Bad Check

24. Since money creation by your bank has been based on the trade secrets of the goldsmiths, provide us with the Patent Number and the date it was issued which gives you the exclusive right to create credit, demand deposits or checkbook money using the trade secret known as fractional reserve banking.

25. Would you agree that a check written by a bank without sufficient funds or money to back it up and redeem it would constitute a bad check?

FORM #3   SET #6:
NOTICE TO PRODUCE DOCUMENTS (FOR BANKS AND OTHER FINANCIAL INSTITUTIONS)

Plaintiff

vs.   Case No._____

Defendant

Notice to Produce Documents

To [lender]

address:

Please take notice that the plaintiff / defendant, [your name] serves upon you this Notice to Produce Documents pursuant to Discovery rights under State / Federal statutes. Please mail or deliver them to me by [date you want them] and send them to my address at: [your address]. Your cooperation will be appreciated.

Date: _____   X _____

1. Send a photocopy of all checks written by your bank to me on or around [date of loan], which is the date of the loan in question.

2. Send a photocopy of the bank's public financial statement that was released closest to this date: [date of your loan].

A COMMENTARY ON THE DISCOVERY QUESTIONS.

In your answers to the interrogatories, you will find the total dollar value of all the checking accounts held in the bank and the total dollar value of all the loans made on the date you took out your loan (Interrogatory No. 7 and 8). Then you add these two figures and subtract from this the total amount of actual vault cash (Interrogatory No. 9). In most instances, the vault cash will be less than the total dollar value of the checking accounts and the loans made on the date you took out your loan. This then provides you with bonafide proof that when the bank made its loan to you, it intentionally wrote a bad check to circulate as money since it already had insufficient cash to redeem the total dollar value of the checks and the loans if they had all been presented for payment on that day (the day you took out your loan). Following these interrogatories, you should send out a set of admissions such as those which follow or subpoena them to a deposition and ask them the interrogatories they refused to answer and again subpoena any documents they have previously failed to produce. Answers to these interrogatories will raise now questions that will result in a second or even a third set of interrogatories which you can send to the bank or ask at a deposition. The key here is that the bank did not lend you cash and if it still claims it loaned you its assets, it is going to have a difficult time to explain this since the bank's financial statement says its deposits are its liabilities, therefore it could not have loaned out its customers' deposits. If the bank loaned out its liabilities, then it has admitted it wrote a bad check to circulate as money and did not lend money. Just look at a bank's financial statement. They all claim that their vault cash is their assets and the deposits are their liabilities. If they had loaned you cash, they would have loaned you their assets. Since, they don't do this, they loaned you their liabilities and to loan a liability is the same thing as loaning a debt. It is the same thing as loaning money that doesn't exist. They simply cannot have their cake and eat it too. In other words, the bank never created any money and to claim that they did is to create another illusion. They simply wrote a bad check to circulate as "money."

NOTE: With regard to Admissions Questions for Banks you will want to obtain the following information:

Total dollar value of charge accounts i.e.	$2,000
Total value of loan accounts i.e.	$6,000
	$8,000
Total actual vault cash	$2,500
Shortage −	$5,500

Any bank should be able to show it had actual dollar cash in vault to cover dollar cash and checks amount it loaned out on any banking day, if not, the check given you as a loan was not a good check.

FORM #4   SET #7:   ADMISSIONS QUESTIONS FOR BANKS

Plaintiff

vs.   Case No._____

Defendant

Notice of Request for Admissions

_____

To [name of bank]
address:

Please take notice that the plaintiff / defendant, [your name], serves upon you this Notice of Request for Admissions pursuant to Discovery rights under the State / Federal statutes. Please answer each question as either "admitted" or "denied." Your answers, when completed should be mailed or delivered to me at [your address] within 30 days [or specify a different number of days] and no later than by [insert date you want admissions returned].

Date: _____   X _____

1. Do you admit that a bank's vault cash are its assets?

2. Do you admit that a bank's deposits are its liabilities?

3. Do you admit that a credit card or a check drawn against a bank are not lawful money?

4. Do you admit that the bank did not lend me actual cash on [date of your loan] for the sum of [dollar value of loan]?

5. Do you admit that a bank lends its liabilities if it lends its deposits?

6. Do you admit that when you lend credit to someone, you merely add numbers called "dollars" to their account in the bookkeeping department?

7. Do you admit that a "promise to pay money" is a liability of the party making the promise?

8. Do you admit that lending a liability is the same as lending a promise to pay money?

9. Do you admit that a bank's deposits are also known as "demand deposits"?

10. Do you admit that "demand deposits" are created by your bank whenever it makes a loan of credit and then exist in your bank or in another bank as mere book entries?

11. Do you admit that demand deposits as book entries are not legal tender for the payment of debts?

12. Do you admit that a check written by your bank is a liability on your bank?

13. Do you admit that a check written by your bank is supposed to be drawn against cash in the bank's vault?

14. Do you admit that if a check written by your bank is deposited by one of your customers in your bank that this increases the amount of the bank's demand deposits by the face value of the check?

15. Do you admit that if none of your customers would cash any checks and they would just use checks as "money," there would be virtually no limit on the amount of checks you could write or the amount of demand deposits you could create as "book entries"?

16. Do you admit that if every customer cashed every check you wrote, that you could not make them circulate

bad checks as money?

17. Do you admit that every check you write or line of credit you create that is not also the equivalent of cash by being fully redeemable in cash is a bad check?

18. Do you admit that lawful money or legal tender does not include any of the following: checks, credit cards, credit, lines of credit, letters of credit, checkbook money and demand deposits.

19. Do you admit that when your bank receives a check from another bank, it is "paid" by merely transferring some book entries from the bank against whom the check is drawn to your bank?

20. Do you admit that the check referred to in the preceding question is stamped "paid" by the bank against whom it is drawn even though no actual cash is transferred to your bank?

21. Do you admit that the check or checks you wrote to me or for my benefit on [date of loan] for the sum of [amount of loan] was a bad check designed to circulate as "money"?

22. Do you admit that the bank in writing the check or checks referred to in the previous question did deliberately create "demand deposits" to circulate as money?

23. Do you admit that the bank's charter does not give it the authority to write and circulate bad checks as money or to create money by lending their liabilities?

24. Do you admit that there is no law passed by Congress that gives banks the authority to create money, to circulate bad checks as money or to participate in a check kiting scheme?

25. Do you admit that since your corporation exists as a privilege of government, that you cannot act beyond the scope of the powers delegated to it and that if you act beyond the scope of the powers delegated to it, your actions are ultra vires—null and void?

26. Do you admit that more than 50% of all deposits held in your bank are owned either by the bank itself or are owned by other financial institutions?

27. Do you admit that the deposits referred to in the preceding question were either created by yourself or created by other financial institutions for deposit in your bank?

Note: in submitting these admissions, if you have assumed a loan from someone, you should substitute their name where yours would normally appear and use the date they took out the loan in the appropriate admissions.

SET #8: DISCOVERY QUESTIONS FOR USERS OF BANK CREDIT CARDS

1. On the total dollar value of credit cards loaned to [your name], how much of this amount consisted of coins and currency issued by the United States Government?

2. What was the total dollar value of credit loaned to me which consisted of demand deposits created by the bank as mere book entries?

3. If you loaned out your depositors' money in lending credit, did you take a little bit from evereyone's account or did you take it all from one person's account? Can you explain how this was done?

4. Is the lending of credit the lending of an asset or a liability?

5. Are the deposits in your bank the bank's liabilities?

6. Is the vault cash your bank's assets?

7. If you claim you loaned a bank asset when you loaned me credit, can you explain how this was done since you did not lend any cash and if you had loaned your deposits, you would have loaned a liability?

8. If you claim you loaned me credit which is a liability of the bank, then can you offer evidence to show that the credit was good credit and not bad credit? In other words, what kind of money or substance backed the credit?

9. Since your bank statements use dollar signs, would you describe a dollar as to its length, width, thickness, what it is made of and any other characteristics it may have?

10. Would you describe a unit of credit and what it looks like as to its width, length, thickness, what it is made of and any other identifying characteristics?

Note: possibly the above list of questions can be expanded by reviewing the interrogatories and admissions prepared for the banks. A shortened list of admissions can be derived from the set just furnished, simply by eliminating those admissions that refer to checks.

SET #9:   DISCOVERY QUESTIONS FOR FINANCE COMPANIES, MORTGAGE COMPANIES AND S AND L'S AND OTHERS.

1. Is the [name of creditor] owned by a bank? If so, would you give the bank's name and address?

2. Name and list the class A or preferred stockholders of your association or corporation?

3. As consideration for the [note, mortgage note, deed of trust, security agreement] signed by the [defendant or plaintiff] on [date you signed the papers], did your association or corporation lend money that was issued by the United States Government in the form of coins and currency?

4. If your association loaned lawful or legal tender money, would would list the serial numbers of the Federal Reserve Notes or United States Notes that you loaned to me on [date of the loan]?

5. Does your association or corporation borrow money or credit from other financial institutions? If this be so, name the institutions and the amounts borrowed and indicate if they loan you cash?

6. Did you lend credit to the [plaintiff or defendant], your name, on or about [date of loan] for the sum of [dollar value of loan]?

7. Would you describe what a dollar looks like as regards its physical characteristics such as its length, width, thickness, color and anything else that will help identify it.

8. Would you describe what a dollar of credit looks like such as its length, width, thickness, color, what it is made of and any other identifying characteristics?

9. Is vault cash on hand considered an asset or liability of your association or corporation?

10. Are your customers' deposits considered to be your assets or your liabilities?

11. If a check was written at the time of the loan to me, would you name the bank it was drawn against, the account number of the check and provide a photocopy of this check with your answer?

12. Does the Federal Reserve Board of Examiners examine your records?

13. Has the Federal Reserve Board of Examiners ever told you to increase the collateral for a loan for one of your clients or advised you to call in a loan or refuse to renew a note of loan? If this be so, would you provide us with the examiners name and when this happened and the name of the debtor he referred to? Was [your name] a debtor that a Board of Examiner official ever referred to as one you should call in or foreclose on or require additional security for?

14. Has your association or corporation ever borrowed any coins or currency from a Federal Reserve Bank?

15. Has your association or corporation ever assigned or sold deeds of trust, mortgages or mortgages notes to any other financial institution for either money or credit? If this be so, provide us details about any and all such transactions that occurred within 180 days prior to [date of your loan]? Name all the commercial banks involved and indicate if they ever advanced any cash [coins and currency] to you or if they advanced you lines of credit or checks?

16. Does your association have on file a set of bylaws that are available for inspection and copying?

17. Does your association or corporation own a machine that duplicates hand written signatures? If this be so, then give us the date you purchased it and the name of unit and the party from whom you made this purchase.

Note: When you get answers, prepare another set of interrogatories or a deposition to get more detailed answers or details on vague answers. Also, when you get a photocopy of the checks they wrote, set up a deposition of an officer of the bank they kept their account with and subpoena with a subpoena duces tecum copies of all deposit slips and checks or other monetary instruments deposited in that account within 90 days prior to the day of the loan. The object of this is to find out if any cash was deposited in this account or if only checks were deposited. The bank against whom the checks for the loan were made should be asked if they paid out any cash and several questions can be asked like, was the check stamped "paid" and other questions can be used derived from the Discovery questions for banks and the admission questions for banks. The bank should then be sued for fraud and for kiting a bad check if they stamped it "paid" and did not pay out actual cash or if the total of its customers checking accounts and loans for that day exceeded the bank's vault cash on the day the check was presented for payment.

FORM #5:   A NOTICE OF DEPOSITION

Plaintiff

vs.   Case No._____

Defendant

Notice of Deposition
_____

To Corporation and / or name of person:
Address:

   Please take notice that the [plaintiff or defendant], [your name] will depose and ask questions of [name of party you will depose] which questions are to be answered under oath. This is a Discovery request for the purpose of gathering informtaion and evidence related to issues in Case No._____. A Court Reporter will record all questions and answers during the deposition. The place, date and time of the deposition is as follows:
   Place: [name and address here]
   Date of Examination: [give month and date and year here]
   Time: [give hour of day and indicate if it is a.m. or p.m.]

Pursuant to [State / Federal] statutes, you are further required to bring along the following materials and documents:
   a.
   b.
   c.
Your failure to appear for this deposition may result in penalties at law.

Date: _____   X _____
                                          (your signature and address here)

FORM #6:   A SUBPOENA DUCES TECUM

Plaintiff

vs.   Case No._____

Defendant

Subpoena Duces Tecum

_____

THE STATE OF [WISCONSIN or your state] TO: [insert name of party]
PURSUANT TO SECTION (805.07) OF THE [WISCONSIN STATUTES], YOU ARE HEREBY COM-
MANDED TO APPEAR IN PERSON AS FOLLOWS:

> Before: [name of place or court reporter]
> Place: [address of place or court reporter's office]
> Time: [a.m. or p.m. and the hour]
> Date: [month / date / year]

to give evidence in an action between [your name] and [the other party].
You are further commanded to bring along the following:

> 1. [describe books, records or documents]
> 2.
> 3.

FAILURE TO APPEAR MAY RESULT IN PUNISHMENT FOR CONTEMPT OF COURT OR OTHER
PENALTIES AT LAW.

Date: _____   sent by _____
                                              (sign your name here)

Note: The above Subpoena Duces Tecum is usually served along with a Notice of Deposition if the production of documents is demanded. Copies of both are also served on all attorneys in the action or on the
parties themselves, if they are not represented by attorneys. This is done so the attorneys or the other
parties may make an appearance and cross examine the deposed party. If you fail to provide notice to all
the other party(s) to the action, your deposition may be prevented from being introduced into evidence
in the court record. After service, an Affidavit of Service is filed with the clerk of courts along with a copy
of the Notice of Deposition and the Subpoena Duces Tecum. If you are subpoenaing a witness who is not
a party to the suit, then you must attach witness fees and mileage fees to the subpoena or notice of
deposition.

FORM #7: AFFIDAVIT OF SERVICE

I, _____ did personally serve this Notice of Deposition and Subpoena Duces Tecum in Case No. _____ upon [name of person or party deposed or their attorney] at his residence at [address of where service was made] on [month / day / year] at [time a.m. / p.m.]. I also served a copy of these papers on the attorney for [the deposed party] at [address] at [time] on [date / month / year]. A copy of these papers was also served on [name] at [address] on [date / month / year] at time [a.m. / p.m.] who is also a party in this action.

Date: _____   X _____

(signature of process server)
address of process server

State of ?)
County of ?) ss.
Subscribed and sworn to before me,
this _____ day of _____ 19____.

_____

Notary Public, State of ?
My Commission expires_____

FORM #8: A NOTICE OF MOTION REQUIRED IN WISCONSIN AND SOME STATES

Plaintiff

vs.   Case No._____

Defendant

Notice of Motion

_____

To: [Plaintiff or Defendant], [name]
address:

Please take notice that the [plaintiff or defendant], [your name], will move the court presided over by the Honorable [judge's name] on [month / day / year] at [time a.m. / p.m.] for an Order Compelling Answers to Interrogatories and the Production of Documents. A copy of this motion is attached hereto. The motion will be heard in Room [?] at the [Name and address of the courthouse].

Date: _____   X _____

(your signature)
(your address)

Copy to Attorney [name], counsel for the [plaintiff or defendant]
address:

Note: A Notice of Motion is typed up or hand written and the date and times are left blank. When you are ready to file it, you call the judge's secretary and ask for a date and time and then you fill in the blank spaces. In some states, Notices of Motions are not required and the judge simply rules on it. Check with a local paralegal, attorney or your state rules of civil procedure.

FORM #9: A MOTION TO COMPEL ANSWERS TO INTERROGATORIES, ETC.

Plaintiff

vs. Case No._____

Defendant

Motion to Compel Answers to Interrogatories
and the Production of Documents

_____

To [plaintiff or defendant], [name]:

Now comes the [plaintiff or defendant], [your name], and relying on the rulings found in *Haines* vs. *Kerner*, 404 U.S. 519 and upon state statutes moves the court for an Order Compelling Answers to Interrogatories and the Production of Documents.

[Plaintiff or Defendant], has submitted a set of interrogatories and a request fir the production of documents on [date you sent them] and the time for answering them has expired. [Plaintiff or defendant] has submitted these interrogatories and requests to gain information designed to lead to admissible evidence. The [plaintiff or defendant] has [failed to answer any interrogatories and has failed to produce any documents / has answered some interrogatories and has failed to answer interrogatories Nos. ?, ?, ? and ? and has failed to produce the following documents:] [describe the documents requested]. [Plaintiff or defendant], [your name] needs these interrogatories answered and documents produced to as to [defend himself against the allegations of the other party(s) complaint / to prove the allegations of my counterclaim]. [Plaintiff or defendant] asks the court to order that the interrogatories be answered and documents produced by [date].

Date: _____ X _____
                                          (your signature)
                   address:

Copy to Attorney [name], counsel for the [plaintiff or defendant]
attorney's address:

FORM #10:   AN AFFIDAVIT OF SERVICE

Affidavit of Service by Mail

Case No._____

    I, [name], being duly sworn on oath, affirm that I personally mailed by [first class / Certified mail] a copy of this Notice of Motion and Motion to Compel Answers to Interrogatories and the Production of Documents to [name and address of party against whom motion is directed or to his attorney, if he has one] on this _____th day of _____, 19?

Date: _____   X _____

                                      (signature of person mailing process)

State of ?)
County of ?) ss.
Subscribed and sworn to before me,
this _____ day of _____ 19____.

_____
Notary Public, State of ?
My Commission expires_____

FORM #11:   AN ORDER FOR THE JUDGE TO SIGN

Plaintiff

vs.   Case No._____

Defendant

                                            Order

_____

Upon motion of the [plaintiff or defendant], [your name], the court orders the [plaintiff or defendant], [their name] to answer all interrogatories and to produce the documents requested by _____.

Date: _____   X _____

                                 The Honorable [judge's name]

FORM #12: A MOTION FOR A PROTECTIVE ORDER

Plaintiff

vs.   Case No._____

Defendant

Motion for Protective Order

_____

Now comes the [plaintiff or defendant], [name], and moves the court to grant a protective order to the [plaintiff or defendant], [name] for the following reasons:

1. The defendant in this case has a demurrer motion to dismiss before the court. If the defendant's motion before the court is granted, the discovery sought by the other party will have placed a burdensome and unnecessary expense on the defendant. The defendant requests an Order to stay discovery sought until after the court has ruled on our motion to dismiss.

or

1. The discovery sought by [name] is not designed to lead to admissible evidence and would be costly and very time consuming. The discovery sought is not related to the issues of the complaint or counterclaim is and done for purposes of harassment. The [Plaintiff or Defendant] seeks an Order striking interrogatories Nos. ?, ?, ? and striking their request for the following documents: [describe]. The documents requested are in no way related to the material issues in dispute in this case.

Date: _____   X _____

Note: Also include a Notice of Motion, an Affidavit of Service by Mail and an Order for the judge to sign. See forms Nos. 8, 10 and 11 to assist you.

FORM #13: THIS FORM IS USED WHEN DISCOVERY IS NOT OF RIGHT SUCH AS IN SMALL CLAIMS COURT OR IN A CRIMINAL PROCEEDING

Plaintiff

vs.   Case No._____

Defendant

Motion for Discovery

_____

Now comes the [plaintiff or defendant], [your name] and moves the court for an Order granting discovery rights to the [plaintiff or defendant] to require [name] to answer a set of interrogatories attached hereto and to produce the documents requested and to allow the [plaintiff or defendant], [your name] to take a deposition of [name of person you want to depose] at [name and address of court reporter] on [date / month / year] at [time a.m. / p.m.] for the following reasons:

1. This discovery is sought for the purpose of obtaining admissible evidence in this case.

2. The [plaintiff or defendant], [your name], requests answers to the following interrogatories:

     a.

     b.

     c.

3. The reasons why I need these interrogatories answered are as follows:

3. The [plaintiff or defendant], [your name] need the following documents produced:

     a.

     b.

     c.

5. The [plaintiff or defendant], [your name], need these documents produced for the following reasons:

6. We also need to take the deposition of [name] for the following reasons:

7. [Plaintiff or defendant], [your name], requests the court to grant this motion and any other relief that is in the interest of justice.

Date: _____   X _____

Note: include a Notice of Motion, an Order for the judge to sign and an Affidavit of Service. See forms Nos. 8, 10 and 11.

FORM #14:   A MOTION FOR PENALTIES OR SANCTIONS WHEN DISCOVERY IS OBSTRUCTED

Plaintiff

vs.   Case No._____

Defendant

Motion for Sanctions

Now comes the [plaintiff or defendant] and for a cause of action shows the court the following:

1. On [month / day / year], the [   ] sent a set of interrogatories and a notice to produce documents to [name], the [plaintiff or defendant] in this action.

2. The [plaintiff or defendant] refused to answer several of the interrogatories and produced none of the documents requested nor did the [plaintiff or defendant] seek a protective order from the court.

3. On [month / day / year], the [plaintiff or defendant], [your name] filed a Motion to Compel Answers to Interrogatories and to Produce Documents and the time for doing so has expired.

4. The defendant in this action therefore requests an order form the court dismissing the plaintiff's actions against him. This request is made pursuant to sanctions allowed under [your state] statutes, section ?

Date: _____   X _____

Affidavit in support of Motion

I, [your name], being duly sworn on oath affirm that all statements made in this motion are true and correct, to the best of my knowledge and belief.

Date: _____   X _____

[Add notary public seal and signature here]

> Note: In your motions for sanctions, you could also ask for a court order to stay all court proceedings until your discovery requests are answered. If you are a defendant in an action, this is a practical motion to file. If you are a plaintiff, you could file a motion for a default judgment, if the defendant obstructs discovery. It is not required that you have a court order compelling answers before moving for sanctions, but it helps. There are many more possibilities as well. Check out the penalties or sanctions section under the discovery chapter of your states court rules and procedures. Be sure to prepare an Order for the judge to sign, and of course, have your notice of motion, if required and an Affidavit of Service by Mail.

FORM #15:   A MOTION FOR DEFAULT JUDGMENT BROUGHT BY A PLAINTIFF AGAINST A DEFENDANT WHO OBSTRUCTS DISCOVERY REQUESTS

Plaintiff

vs.   Case No._____

Defendant

Motion for Default Judgment

Now comes the plaintiff, [your name], and for a cause of action states the following:

1. The plaintiff sent the defendant a set of 20 interrogatories and a request to produce 3 documents on [date].
2. The time to answer these interrogatories has expired and the defendant has only answered 3 of the 20 interrogatories and has failed to produce any of the documents requested.
3. The plaintiff took the deposition of the defendant, [name], before a court reporter, [name] at [address] on [date] at [time]. The defendant refused to answer the following questions:

     a.

     b.

     c.

4. The defendant, having willfully obstructed discovery and having failed and did not seek a protective order from this court. The plaintiff, therefore, pursuant to State statutes, Section ? moves the court to grant a default judgment in favor of the plaintiff and against the defendant for the sum of [$] together with court costs in this action.

Date: _____   X _____

Affidavit in Support of Motion for Default Judgment

I, [your name], being duly sworn on oath affirm that all statements contained in this motion are true and correct, to the best of my knowledge and belief.

Date: _____   X _____

Note: Add Notary Public Seal and Signature here.

FORM #16:   AN ORDER FOR A DEFAULT JUDGMENT

Plaintiff

vs.   Case No._____

Defendant

Order for Default Judgment
_____

On motion of the plaintiff, [your name], it is hereby ordered, adjudged and decreed that:

1. A Default Judgment is entered in favor of the plaintiff, [your name], and against the defendant, [his name], for the sum of [$?] together with court costs.

Date: _____   X _____
                                                            The Honorable [judge's name]

FORM #17:   A MOTION FOR A SUMMARY JUDGMENT WHEN ADMISSIONS ARE NOT ANSWERED

Plaintiff

vs.   Case No._____

Defendant

Motion for Summary Judgment
_____

Now comes the defendant, [your name], and for a causes of action states the following:

1. The defendant in this action sent the plaintiff, a bank a set of 27 requests for admissions on [date]. The time for the plaintiff to answer the admissions has expired and no answers have been sent to the defendant and the clerk of courts has verified that no answers to the admissions can be found in the court record.

2. Pursuant to discovery rules under [your state] statutes, section ?, any admissions not answered are deemed to be admitted. The defendants request for admissions, having not been answered, are, therefore entered into this court record as having been admitted.

3. A copy of this Motion for Summary Judgment was served on the Plaintiff's attorney, [name] on [date] at [time] at [address] as the attached Affidavit of Service will attest.

4. The admissions, having been deemed as admitted, there are no longer any material facts in dispute in this case. Defendants therefore request, as a matter of law, that the complaint filed against them by the plaintiff in this foreclosure action, be dismissed with prejudice. Defendants also ask for court costs.

Date: _____   X _____

Affidavit in Support of Motion for Summary Judgment

I, [your name], being duly sworn on oath, affirm that all statements made in this Motion for Summary Judgment are true and correct, to the best of my knowledge and belief.

Date: _____   X _____

(Add Notary Public seal and signature here)

Note: Prepare an Order for the judge to sign similar to the sample given in the Order for Default Judgment. Substitute the word Summary Judgment for the words Default Judgment.

[Name]
address,
        Plaintiff,

vs.   Case # _____

[bank or an official by name]
address,   NOTICE OF DEPOSITION
        Defendant.

TO: [Bank or official by name]
      address:
   PLEASE TAKE NOTICE that the [plaintiff or defendant], [your name] hereby deposes [name the bank or the bank official] to answer questions under oath. The [plaintiff] will ask the [defendant] questions in the presence of a Court Reporter who is authorized to administer an Oath as well as record all questions and answers. The name and address where the deposition will be taken is:

        PLACE: [Kempfer Reporting, 532 N. Water St., Milw., Wis.]
        Date of Examination: [Nov. 1, 1983]
        TIME: [9 a.m.]

(Optional)
You are further required, pursuant to [your state] statutes, to bring along the following materials and documents:

        1. a dollar
        2. a demand deposit
FAILURE TO APPEAR FOR THIS DEPOSITION MAY RESULT IN PENALTIES AT LAW.

Date: _____   sent by _____
                                                        (sign your name here)

***NOTE: While the right to take depositions remains for party(s) in all civil proceedings; in Wisconsin, in CRIMINAL proceedings, the right to take a deposition is taken away. See Wis. Statutes 972.11. Note, however, in 972.11, that the right to serve Interrogatories and Admissions in Criminal proceedings *is retained*. (from Wis. Court Rules—1982 ed.)
Note: Foreclosure actions are civil proceedings and all Discovery rights are available to use for plaintiff or defendant.

[Name]
address,

     Plaintiff,

vs.

                                             Case # _____

[Bank or official]
address,
                                  SUBPOENA DUCES TECUM

     Defendant.

THE STATE OF WISCONSIN TO: [NAME OF BANK OR OFFICIAL]

PURSUANT TO SECTION (805.07) of the [Wisconsin statutes], you are hereby COMMANDED to appear in person as follows:

     Before: [Kempfer Reporting]

     Place: [532 N. Water St., Milwaukee, Wis.]

     Time: [9 a.m.]

     Date: [Nov. 1, 1983]

to give evidence in an action between [your name] and [name of bank].

     YOU ARE FURTHER COMMANDED TO BRING WITH YOU THE FOLLOWING:

     1. a dollar

     2. a demand deposit

FAILURE TO APPEAR MAY RESULT IN PUNISHMENT FOR CONTEMPT OF COURT OR OTHER PENALTIES AT LAW.

Date: _____   sent by _____

                                                (sign your name here)

NOTE: THE **SUBPOENA DUCES TECUM** IS SERVED ALONG WITH THE **NOTICE OF DEPOSITION**. AFTER SERVICE, AN (AFFIDAVIT AND PROOF OF SERVICE STATEMENT IS FILED IN THE CLERK OF COURTS OFFICE).

_____

    Plaintiff,

vs.

_____   Case # _____

                                              NOTICE OF MOTION

    Defendant.

_____

TO: Defendant:

    NOTICE IS HEREBY GIVEN TO YOU, that the plaintiff, [your name], will present a MOTION FOR A DEFAULT JUDGMENT before the HONORABLE [name of judge] at [   ] a.m. / p.m. on [date-month-year] at the [name of courthouse], [address of courthouse] or as soon thereafter as Motion may be heard. A copy of Motion is attached hereto.

Date: _____   X _____

                                                (your signature)

_____
plaintiff,

vs.

_____
defendant.

Case # _____

MOTION FOR DEFAULT JUDGMENT

NOW COMES the plaintiff, [your name], and for a cause of action hereby states the following:

1. Plaintiff submitted interrogatories to defendant on Nov. 1, 1982, which were due on Dec. 1, 1982.

2. Interrogatories were received on Dec. 10, 1982 and 7 of 14 questions were unanswered.

3. Plaintiff subpoenaed defendant to a deposition on Jan. 5, 1983 subpoenaed document. Defendant appeared and brought none of the documents and refused to answer more than half of the questions.

4. Plaintiff filed a MOTION TO COMPEL ANSWERS TO INTERROGATORIES AND PRODUCE DOCUMENTS on Feb. 10, 1983 and did clearly specify in writing which questions were to be answered and which documents were to be produced. The court did sign this ORDER on Feb. 10, 1983.

5. Defendant has failed to answer 3 interrogatories and produce 2 documents that are crucial to plaintiff's case.

6. The failure of the Defendant to respond to the Order of the Court and their refusal to comply with State Statutes has damaged the plaintiff in the preparation of his case, and was done willfully and knowingly by the defendant.

7. Therefore, the plaintiff, [your name], respectfully requests the Court to enter a Default Judgment in favor of the plaintiff and against the defendant, [defendant's name].

Date: _____   X _____
(your signature)

Amount Requested $ _____

_____
      Plaintiff,

vs.

_____
      Defendant.

Case # _____

ORDER FOR A DEFAULT JUDGMENT

ON MOTION OF THE PLAINTIFF, [YOUR NAME], IT IS HEREBY ORDERED, ADJUDGED AND DECREED THAT:

1. A DEFAULT JUDGMENT IS ENTERED IN FAVOR OF THE PLAINTIFF, [YOUR NAME] AND AGAINST THE DEFENDANT, [HIS NAME] FOR THE SUM OF [DOLLAR AMOUNT].
2. Mortgage and Mortgage Note signed by plaintiffs on [date—month-year] are null and void and ultra vires.
3. Security agreement signed by plaintiff on [day-month-year] on loan for car and farm equipment is null and void.
4. Sheriff sale on [day-month-year] is null and void.

Date: _____   X _____

                                The Honorable [name of judge]

Case No._____

AFFIDAVIT AND PROOF OF SERVICE

I, _____, personally served this Notice of Deposition / Subpoena Duces Tecum to _____ at the following address: Street:_____ City:_____ State:_____ at _____ a.m. / p.m. on month _____ date _____ year 19_____.

I, _____, being duly sworn on oath, hereby affirm that the information on this document is true and correct, to the best of my knowledge and belief.

Process Server: X _____
Street: _____
City: _____
State: _____

STATE OF WISCONSIN)
                 COUNTY) ss.

Subscribed and sworn to before me,
this _____ day of _____ 19_____.

_____
Notary Public, State of Wisconsin.
My Commission expires_____.

Memorandum of Law on Constitutional Money

The Plaintiff herein is asserting, in support of this motion, an issue commonly referred to as the "money or specie" issue, which is based solely upon Article 1, section 10, clause 1 of the United States Constitution and which reads as follows, to wit:

> "No state shall...coin Money; Emit Bills of Credit; make any Thing but gold and silver Coin a Tender in Payment of Debts."

This memorandum, which the author recommends not be included in a sample brief by an attorney, is directed toward this issue and establishes the premise that all states are constitutionally compelled to operate on a specie basis. The Plaintiff contends that Article 1, section 10, U.S. Constitution (hereinafter referred to as "Art. 1, sec. 10") prohibits the use by the separate states of our Union of any irredeemable paper currency, issued by the Federal Reserve System, private banking institutions, or otherwise.

During the colonial times in our nation's history, paper money was issued by colonial governments with disastrous results. The first documented issuance of a fiat or paper currency occurred in 1690, when the colony of Massachusetts issued paper notes to pay soldiers returning from war in Canada; see *Craig Missouri,* 29 U.S. 410 (1830). This first paper money experiment was a success in most respects for the reason that the notes were limited in issue and were eventually redeemed. However, the other colonies noted this occurrence and its obvious benefits and implemented legislation necessary for issuance of such currencies. By the 1740s, several colonies, including Rhode Island, were profligately issuing "bills of credit" which resulted in the gradual deflation in the value of such bills, thus causing inflation.

For example, Rhode Island in 1743 issued bills of credit wherein 27 shillings were equal in value to one ounce of silver. But in 1751, the Rhode Island General Assembly devalued their notes to the point where the same were worth 54 shillings to an ounce of silver. Shortly after this devaluation, the Assembly again devalued its notes to the point where 64 shillings equalled an ounce of silver. These devaluations severely affected intercolony commerce as Roger Sherman, author of Art. 1, sec. 10 and delegate to the Philadelphia Convention, noted in his 1752 treatise entitled *A Caveat Against Injustice.*

This treatise of Roger Sherman, in addition to its value in noting the injustice and inequity of a fluctuating medium of exchange, is of immense value in determining the true intent and meaning of Art. 1, sec. 10. Sherman demonstrated that the viability of commerce was dependent upon traders and businessmen exchanging their goods and commodities for currency of intrinsic value. Such businessmen had surrendered property of specific value in order to accumulate the commodities they were selling. At the time of sale, the contract price for the goods sold included the cost of such goods as well as a return for the labors of the businessman. If the currency utilized to effect this commercial exchange was without intrinsic value, or its intrinsic value was being deflated by actions of a sovereign government, the businessman was being unfairly and unjustly deprived of his property and labor. Sherman's conclusion was as follows:

"But if what is us'd as a Medium of Exchange is fluctuating in its Value it is no better than unjust Weights and Measures, both which are condemn'd by the Laws of GOD and Man, and therefore the longest and mosr universal Custom could never make the Use of such a Medium either lawful or reasonable.

"And instead of having our Properties defended and secured to us by the Protection of the Government under which we live; we should be always exposed to have them taken from us by Fraud at the Pleasure of other Governments, who have no Right of Jurisdiction over us.

"But so long as we part with our most valuable Commodities for such Bills of credit as are no Profit; but rather a Cheat, Vexation and Snare to us, and become a Medium whereby we are continually cheating and wronging one another in our Dealings and Commerce...we shall spend great Part to our Labour and Substance for that which will not profit us.

Further discussion of the disastrous and ruinous effects of bills of credit (paper money) can be found in *Craig* v. *Missouri,* supra, and *Townsend* v. *Townsend,* 7 Tenn. 1 (1821), among many others.

It appears that the 1752 wisdom and prophesy of Roger Sherman went unheralded and unnoticed for a considerable length of time. Prior to the Revolutionary War, the colonial governments continued the use of their separate and divergent monetary systems, having currencies of fluctuating value, and thus causing inflation which wreaked havoc in the market place. Some colonial governments even utilized cattle, wampum, tobacco, valueless land, and other commodities as legal tender, but the passage of time proved the futility of such media of exchange.

Although the signs and indications of an unjust monetary system based upon a fluctuating medium of exchange were evident to the colonists at the time of the Declaration of Independence, the Continental Congress improvidently chose to continue this hazardous scheme by emitting Continental Notes. During the Revolutionary War, the Congress emitted the first issuance of such notes upon a promise that the same were redeemable in specie. However, the exigencies of the War necessitated further and larger issues which soon made it evident that the Continental

Congress would not be able to redeem all issues at par with either gold or silver coin. These additional and larger issues, which factually and truthfully could not be redeemed in any respect, caused inflation and the abundance of currency having a falling value not only caused creditors to avoid their debtors, but also caused vast portions of the population to avoid holding such notes. In response to this situation, legal tender acts were passed making it a treasonable and felonious offense for a citizen to fail to accept a Continental note in discharge of a debt. It is almost certain that the members of the Continental Congress were as wise and intelligent as any subsequent Congress of the United States, but these gentlemen were unable to make any laws which would effectively repeal the operation of natural economic laws. Greshman's Law, "bad money drives out good money," resulted in the hoarding of all valuable media of exchange, and the abundance of the "bad" money— Continental notes—caused severe inflation. In January, 1781, these notes were sold on the market at the rate of 100 dollar notes for one dollar of specie coin. But by May of the same year, these notes were so abundant that no sane person would exchange them for specie coin and thus the notes "died" in the hands of their possessors. Surely this period of time was more inflationary than any other time in our nation's history. This infatuation caused severe economic distress which in turn severely affected trade and commerce.

During the Revolutionary War as well as the period of time our nation existed under the Articles of Confederation, the states alone, and not Congress, possessed the power to declare what was to be a legal tender for the payment of debts. The Continental Congress, not having this power to declare a legal tender and desiring to give its notes legal tender quality, was compelled to enlist the aid of the separate states to give Continental Notes such quality. The states complied by enacting laws making Continental Notes a legal tender, and thus they aided and abetted the Continental Congress in an endeavor which, with the fall of the Continental Notes, resulted in the loss of fortunes, wealth, property, and business activity of state citizens, particularly those who had faith in such notes. The ravenous inflation of Continental Notes and various state bills of credit and the subsequent destruction of the same caused state citizens and their elected leaders to become seriously concerned with the powr and propriety to make valueless paper the equal of intrinsically valuable specie coin. Peletiah Webster in 1789 made the following remark in reference to the destructive effects of paper money:

> "Paper money polluted the equity of our laws, turned them into engines of oppression, corrupted the justice of our public administration, destroyed the fortunes of thousands who had confidence in it, enervated the trade, husbandry and manufacturers of our country, and went far to destroy the morality of our people."

In 1787, the citizens and leaders of the Confederation states realized that the Articles of Confederation had to be revised, so in the Spring of that year, the States sent delegates to Philadelphia to draft a new national constitution. One of the purposes of the Philadelphia Constitutional Convention was to address the causes and problems created by the issuance of bills of credit by both the states and the national government. The best source of information concerning the debates occurring at the Convention is James Madison's notes of the Convention. Madison reveals that on Thursday, August 16, 1787, the Convention was discussing the proposed Constitution's provisions contained in Article 1, section 8 wherein Congress was given the power to "emit bills on the credit of the United States." Gouverneur Morris on this date moved to strike this phrase from the Constitution. In response, Mr. Ellsworth stated that he "thought this a favorable moment to shut and bar the door against paper money." He further stated, "the mischiefs of the various experiments which had been made were now fresh in the public mind and had excited the disgust of all the respectable part of America. By withholding the power from the new government, more friends of influence would be gained to it than by almost anything else. Paper money can in no case be necessary. Give the government credit, and other resources will offer. The power may do harm, never good." Mr. Wilson commented that it will have a most salutary influence on the credit of the United States to remove the possibility of paper money. Mr. Read noted that he "thought the words, if not struck out, would be as alarming as the mark of the Beast in Revelations." Even more emphatically voiced was Mr. Langdon's remark that he "had rather

reject the whole plan than retain the three words, 'and emit bills.' " The motion to strike these words from the Constitution carried by a vote of nine states in favor and two opposed.

On Tuesday, August 28, 1787, the Convention was discussing the provisions contained in Article 1, section 10 of the proposed Constitution. Mr. Roger Sherman and Mr. Wilson moved to amend the proposed Article 1, section 10 to include the words "nor emit bills of credit, nor make anything but gold and silver coin a tender in payment of debts." The discussion concerning this proposed amendment concerned only the portion regarding "emit bills of credit." In support of his motion, Mr. Sherman stated that he "thought this a favorable crisis for crushing paper money." He stated that "if the consent of the Legislature could authorize emissions of it, the friends of paper money would make every exertion to get into the Legislature in order to license it." The voting concerned the power to emit bills of credit was eight states in favor and two opposed. The remainder of the proposed amendment concerning gold and silver coin passed with no opposition.

Thus, it had taken Roger Sherman some 35 years to obtain the consent of his fellow citizens to change the monetary system from one based upon bills of credit to one baed upon precious metals having intrinsic value. A medium of exchange having a fixed and unfluctuating value was secured by having Congress coin these precious metals. Since the value of such coins would be fixed by law, citizens would not suffer when exchanging the fruits of their labors for this coin, which was valuable in and of itself. However, in the event that a responsible federal minister was compelled in the future to emit bills of credit, Art. 1, sec. 10 insured that no state would compel its citizens to accept such bills except on a voluntary basis.

After submission of the proposed Constitution to the states for debate and ratification, the public discussion of the document drafted by the Convention was heated. In New York, Alexander Hamilton, James Madison, and John Jay came to the defense of the proposed Constitution by publication of a series of articles concerning the Constitution in New York newspapers. This series, now known as the *Federalist Papers,* contains virtually the best source of information concerning the interpretation of our

Constitution. In Article number 44, written by Madison, the following comments are made concerning the relevant portion of Article 1, section 10 with which we are concerned:

"The extension of the prohibition to bills of credit must give pleasure to every citizen in proportion to his love of justice and his knowledge of the true springs of public prosperity. The loss which America has sustained since the peace, from the pestilent effects of paper money on the necessary confidence between man and man, on the industry and morals of the people, and on the character of republican government, constitutes an enormous debt against the States chargeable with this unadvised measure, which must long remain unsatisfied, or rather an accumulation of guilt which can be expiated no otherwise than by a voluntary sacrifice on the altar of justice of the power which has been the instrument of it. In addition to these persuasive considerations, it may be observed that the same reasons which show the necessity of denying to the States the power of regulating coin prove with equal force that they ought not to be at liberty to substitute a paper medium in the place of coin. Had every State a right to regulate the value of its coin, there must be as many different currencies as States, and thus the intercourse among them would be impeded; retrospective alterations in its value might be made, and thus the citizens of other States be injured, and animosities be kindled among the States themselves. The subjects of foreign powers might suffer from the same cause, and hence the Union be discredited and embroiled by the indiscretion of a single member. No one of these mischiefs is less incident to a power in the States to emit paper money than to coin gold or silver. The power to make anything but gold and silver a tender in payment of debts is withdrawn from the States on the same principle with that of issuing a paper currency."

When the United States Constitution was finally adopted, Article 1, section 10 thereof had been divided into three separate clauses. Whereas the prohibition upon the states listed in clauses two and three were only conditional prohibitions in that they could be circumvented with the consent of Congress, the words "without the consent of Congress" were omitted from clause one, thus making the first clause in this section a mandatory prohibition upon the states. The reasons for the construction of Article 1, section 10 in this fashion are obvious. When the states possessed the unlimited power to declare a legal tender, they had taken the opportunity to declare the intrinsically valueless currency emitted by Congress to be a legal tender. Once so empowered, the Continental Congress did cause the emission of substantial quantities of its notes and in the process ruined the commerce and wealth of the country. The state participation in this Congressional scheme greatly damaged state citizens and the great object of Article 1, section 10, clause 1 of the U.S. Constitution was to forever prevent this activity again. The state governments, prior to the enactment of the Constitution, were the people's trustee of the power to declare a legal tender, but the states had committed a grievous sin by their improvident use and abuse of this power. Because of the exercise of this power in a ruinous fashion, the citizens by the Constitution limited the exercise of this power to only gold and silver coin. By the insertion of these 17 words into the U.S. Constitution, the states were compelled to be the guardians of the economic and property rights of their citizens and they were required to forever insure to them a specie currency.

With the enactment of the Constitution, the prohibition on paper currency had a most beneficial effect upon the economy of our new nation. The improvement of the economy can be discerned from an examination of letters written by our first President, George Washington. In 1786, George Washington wrote to James Madison a letter wherein he stated as follows:

"Blood running in the streets. Mobs of rioters and demonstrators threatening banks and legislatures. Looting of shop and home. Credit ruined. Strikes and unemployment. Trade and distribution paralyzed. Shortages of food. Bankruptcies everywhere. Court dockets overloaded. Kidnappings for heavy ransom. Sexual perversion, drunkenness, lawlessness rampant."

This letter most assuredly reflected the true state of economic affairs during the confederation period of our history and prior to the adoption of our Constitution. In contrast with the above statement, Washington, in letters written in 1791, stated as follows:

> "The United States enjoys a sense of prosperity and tranquility under the new government that could hardly have been hoped for."

> "Tranquility reigns among the people with that disposition towards the general government which is likely to preserve it. Our public credit stands on that high ground which three years ago it would have been considered as a species of madness to have foretold."

Not only did Washington make such observations, but other parties did so as well. For example, on December 16, 1789, an article in the *Pennsylvania Gazette* stated as follows:

> "Since the federal constitution has removed all danger of our having a paper tender, our trade is advanced fifty percent. Our monied people can trust their cash abroad and have brought their coin into circulation."

Thus, through the vehicle of Article 1, section 10, clause 1 of the U.S. Constitution and its mandate and command authorizing only a specie currency, our early nation's economy substantially improved and our destiny as a great nation was insured.

Following the adpotion of the U.S. Constitution, the state and federal courts of our nation were not reluctant in any respect to giving weight to the prohibitions of Article 1, section 10. To note the U.S. Supreme Court's adherence to the limitations, monetary powers, and disabilities of the U.S. Constitution, the following cases are cited:

1. *Calder* v. *Bull*, 3 Dall. 20 (1798):

> "The prohibitions not to make anything but gold and silver coin a legal tender in payment of debts, and not to pass any law impairing the obligations of contracts, were inserted to secured private rights."

2. *Sturges* v. *Crowninshield*, 4 Wheat. 122, 17 U.S. 122 (1819):

> "We are told they were such as grow out of the general distress following the war in which our independence was established. To relieve this distress, paper money was issued, worthless lands and other property of no use to the creditor were made a tender in payment of debts; and the time of payment, stipulated in the contract, was extended by law. These were the peculiar evils of the day. So much mischief was done, and so much more was apprehended, that general distruct prevailed, and all confidence between man and man was destroyed.

> "Was the general prohibition intended to prevent paper money. We are not allowed to say so because it is expressly provided that no state shall 'emit bills of credit'; neither could these words be intended to restrain the states from enabling the debtors to discharge their debts by the tender of property of no real value to the creditor because for that subject also particular provision is made. Nothing but gold and silver coin can be made a tender in payment of debts."

3. *Ogden* v. *Saunders*, 12 Wheat. 213, 25 U.S. 213 (1827):

> "It declares that 'no state shall coin money, emit bills of credit, make any thing but gold and silver coin a tender in payment of debts.' These prohibitions, associated with the powers granted to Congress 'to coin money, and to regulate the value thereof, and of foreign coin' most obviously constitute members of the same family, being upon the same subject and governed by the same policy.

> "This policy was to provide a fixed and uniform standard of value throughout the United States, by which the commercial and other dealings between the citizens thereof, or between them and foreigners, as well as the moneyed transactions of the government, should be regulated. For it might well be asked, why vest Congress the power to establish a uniform standard of value by the means pointed out, if the states might use the same means, and thus defeat the uniformity of the standard and, consequently, the standard itself? And why establish a standard at all, for the government of the various contracts which might be entered into, if those contracts might afterwards be discharged by a different standard, or by that which is not money, under the authority of tender laws."

4. *Craig* v. *Missouri*, 29 U.S. 410 (1830):

"The Constitution, therefore, considers the emission of bills of credit and the enactment of tender laws as distinct operations, independent of each other which may be separately performed. Both are forbidden."

Dissenting opinion of J. Johnson:

"The great end and object of this restriction on the power of the States, will furnish the best definition of the terms under consideration. The whole was intended to exclude everything from use as a circulating medium except gold and silver, and to give to the United States the exclusive control over the coining and valuing of the metallic medium. That the real dollar may represent property, and not the shadow of it."

5. *United States* v. *Marigold*, 50 U.S. 560 (1850):

"They appertain rather to the exclusion of an important trust invested by the Constitution, and to the obligation to fulfill that trust on the part of the government, namely, the trust and the duty of creating and maintaining a uniform and pure metallic standard of value throughout the Union. The power of coining money and of regulating its value was delegated to Congress by the Constitution for the very purpose, as assigned by the framers of that instrument, of creating and preserving the uniformity and purity of such standard of value.

"If the medium which the government was authorized to create and establish could immediately be expelled, and substituted by one it had neither created, estimated, nor authorized—one possessing no intrinsic value—then the power conferred by the Constitution would be useless—wholly fruitless of every end it was designed to accomplish. Whatever functions Congress are, by the Constitution, authorized to perform, they are, when the public good requires it, bound to perform; and on this principle, having emitted a circulating medium, a standard of value indispensable for the purposes of the community, and for the action of the government itself, they are accordingly authorized and bound in duty to prevent its debasement and expulsion, and the destruction of the general confidence and convenience, by the influx and substitution of a spurious coin in

lieu of the constitutional currency."

Not only did the U.S. Supreme Court acknowledge the proper monetary powers and disabilities contained in the U.S. Constitution, U.S. Presidents did so as well. On December 5, 1836, in President Andrew Jackson's Eighth Annual Address to Congress, he made the following statement in reference to this issue:

"It is apparent from the whole context of the Constitution, as well as the history of the times which gave birth to it, that it was the purpose of the Convention to establish a currency consisting of the precious metals. These, from their peculiar properties which rendered them the standard of value in all other countries, were adopted in this as well to establish its commercial standard in reference to foreign countries by a permanent rule as to exclude the use of a mutable medium of exchange, such as of certain agricultural commodities recognized by the statutes of some states as a tender for debts, or the still more pernicious expedient of a paper currency."

In addition to the supreme authorities in our national executive and judiciary, the Supreme Courts of many States acknowledged the fact that only gold and silver coin were the constitutional currency. In support hereof, the following cases are cited:

A. ALABAMA
Carter and Carter v. *Penn*, 4 Ala. 140 (1842):
"The note does not stipulate for the payment of a debt in Bank bills, but is an undertaking to pay 'current money of the State of Alabama.' It is true that an infinite variety of commodities have been used as money in different periods and countries... and in common parlance all these different representations of the common standard of value have been designated as money. But the notes of the Bank which are not redeemable in coin, on demand, cannot, with any propriety be regarded as such; in fact, the best Bank paper passes as money by consent only, and it cannot be otherwise so long as the inhibition of the Federal Constitution upon the rights of the States to dispense with gold and silver as the only lawful tender continues in force."

B. ARKANSAS

Dillard v. *Evans,* 4 Ark. 175 (1842):

"Bank issues are not, in the constitutional sense of the term, lawful money or legal coin. Gold and silver alone are a legal tender in payment of debts, and the only true constitutional currency known to the laws."

Bone v. *Terry,* 16 Ark. 83 (1855):

"The judgment was for dollars, and the payment so far as the facts are before us, could only have been made in gold or silver, the constitutional coin."

C. CONNECTICUT

Foquet v. *Hoadley,* 3 Conn. 534 (1821):

"A promissory note, payable in money, cannot be discharged, by the act of the debtor, without the co-operation of the creditor, unless in gold and silver coin. Const. U.S. art. 1 sec. 10. Bank notes are not a legal tender, if the creditor objects to receive them."

D. INDIANA

Prather v. *State Bank,* 3 Ind. 356 (1852):

"No clerk, nor sheriff, nor constable, as such, has a right, under the constitution and law, to receive payment of a judgment in anything but the legal currency of the country. *Griffin* v. *Thompson,* 2 How. 244."

E. KENTUCKY

McChord v. *Ford,* 19 KY. 167 (1826):

"But as bank notes are not money, it also follows that this note can not intend bank notes, but gold or silver."

Sinclair v. *Piercy,* 28 Ky. 63 (1830):

"The result from an examination of all the cases is that money, in its strict legal sense, means gold or silver coin, and that an obligation for money alone can not be satisfied with any thing else."

Pryor v. *Commonwealth,* 32 Ky. 298 (1834):

"Yet, that its true technical import is lawful money of the United States, in other words, gold or silver coin, and when used in judicial proceedings it is always to be taken in this technical sense."

F. MISSOURI

Bailey v. *Gentry,* 1 Mo. 164 (1822):

"Construing the Constitution, then, to prohibit the States from passing laws, the effect of which would be to induce the creditor to receive something else than gold and silver coin in payment of the debt due him, in order to avoid an inconvenience that would result on his failure to do so, we are lead to the conclusion that the act under consideration is repugnant to the provisions of the Constitution of the United States last referred to."

Cockrill v. *Kirkpatrick,* 9 Mo. 697 (1846):

"But if the note was 'payable in the current money of Missouri,' as the obligor subsequently stated, then all necessity for construction is absolutely excluded, for the terms explain themselves, and can only mean 'tender money,' gold or silver coin.

G. PENNSYLVANIA

Gray v. *Donahoe,* 4 Watts (Pa.) 400 (1835):

"No principle is better established or more necessary to be maintained than that bank notes are not 'money' in the legal sense of the word. . .Coins struck at the Mint or authorized by act of Congress are alone lawful money. They possess a fixed and permanent value or, at least, as nearly so as human affairs admit of. Bank notes are merely promissory notes for the payment of money—ordinarily, it is true, convertible into coin on demand at the bank where they are issued."

H. SOUTH CAROLINA

Clarin v. *Nesbitt,* 2 Nott. and McC. (11 S.C.) 519 (1820):

"If congress can create a legal tender, it must be by virtue of the 'power to coin money,' for no where in the constitution is the power to make a legal tender expressly given to them, nor is there any other power directly given, from which the power to make a legal tender can be incidentally deduced.

"At common law, only gold and silver were a legal tender. . .In this State, where the common law has been expressly adopted, anterior to all legislative and constitutional provisions on the subject, gold and silver were the only legal tenders.

"From the passage of this act to the adoption of the constitution of the United States, the only legal tenders in this State were gold and silver and those were so by virtue of the common law. Prior to the adoption of the constitution of the United States, the States, respectively, possessed and exercised jurisdiction over the 'legal tender.'

"If congress did not possess the power of creating a legal tender under the confederation, they do not possess the power under the constitution, for the grant in both instruments is the same, 'to coin money.' The States have been limited in their exercise of power over the legal tender to gold and silver, but it does not follow, because power has been taken from the States, it has been given to Congress.

"They have further said, that nothing but gold and silver coin shall be a legal tender for the payment of debts. The language of the 10th sec. of the 1st article, is, 'no State shall make any thing but gold and silver coin a legal tender in the payment of debts.' The language of the 5th clause of the 8th sec. of the 1st article, is, 'congress shall have power to coin money, and regulate the value thereof.' Construe the two sections together, and the constitution appears to intend to limit the power of the States over the legal tender, to gold and silver. This construction is further supported by the two following considerations. 1. One of the great objects which led to the adoption of the constitution, was the annihilation of a spurious currency, which had for years afflicted the people of this country. Give to congress the power of making a legal tender, and you but change the hand from which the affliction is to proceed; so construe the constitution as to restrict the legal tender to gold and silver, and one of the great objects for which it was ordained, is accomplished. 2. The constitution, no where gives to congress any control over contracts. It is indeed scrupulously avoided. If, however, they derive the power of making a legal tender from the power of coining money, they indirectly obtain that which was intended to be withheld."

I. TENNESSEE
Townsend v. *Townsend*, 7 Tenn. 1 (1821):
"With respect to the disorders produced by paper money and tender laws, both theory and experience present them to view. Who will be so imprudent as to give credit to the citizens of a State that makes paper money a tender, and where he can be told, take for a gold and silver debt depreciated paper, depreci-

ating still more in the moment it is paid. Who would trust the value of his property to the citizens of another State or of his own State, who can be protected by law against the just demands of creditors by forcing them to receive depreciated paper, or to be delayed of payment from year to year until the Legislature will no longer interfere?

"One of the most powerful remedies was the tenth clause of the first article, and particularly the two sentences which we are now considering. They operated most efficaciously. The new course of thinking, which had been inspired by the adoption of a constitution that was understood to prohibit all laws for the emission of paper money, and for the making anything a tender but gold and silver, restored the confidence which was so essential to the internal prosperity of nations."

Lowry v. *McGhee and McDermott*, 16 Tenn. 242 (1835):
"By the Constitution of the United States nothing can be a tender in payment of debt but gold and silver coin.

"The answer to this argument is that the Constitution of the United States is the supreme law, and that no law can be valid which, in violation of that instrument, shall attempt to make anything but gold and silver coin a tender."

J. TEXAS
Ogden v. *Slade*, 1 Tex. 13 (1846):
"The note calls for four hundred dollars, lawful funds of the United States. What is the plain meaning of 'lawful funds'? Gold and silver is [sic] the only lawful tender in the United States. It must therefore mean payment in gold or silver. By equivalent, the parties must have meant such paper currency as passed at par with gold and silver."

K. VERMONT
Wainwright v. *Webster*, 11 Ver. 576 (1839):
"No state is authorized to coin money or pass any law whereby anything but gold and silver shall be made a legal tender in payment of debt...This conventional understanding that bank bills are to pass as money is founded upon the solvency of the bank and upon the supposition that the bills are equivalent in value to specie and are at any time convertible into specie at the option of the holder."

In summary, the period of time in our nation's history between the Constitution's adoption and the Civil War saw the courts of our nation, both state and federal, giving full and complete attention to the requirements of Article 1, section 10. The Civil War is of immense importance to the "specie issue" for the reason that the actions of Congress during the war gave rise to the various legal tender cases which are used by the opponents of this issue, the paper money advocates, as authority that Article 1, section 10 no longer has any legal significance.

With the outbreak of the Civil War, the federal Treasury became depleted because of the vast expenditures necessary to conduct the war. In 1862, Congress considered the enactment of the Legal Tender Act which was to allow the U.S. Treasury to emit bills of credit carrying on their face a legal tender provision that such bills were "legal tender for all debts, public and private. Many members of Congress thought that the Act was unconstitutional, but in the end, the Act was passed out of desperation with an expedient motive. It was only natural and probable that the Legal Tender Act passed during the War would be challenged on constitutional grounds after the cessation of hostilities.

The passage of the Legal Tender Act of 1862 presented to the various state courts of our nation the horns of a dilemma. If such courts followed the plain letter of Article 1, section 10 as well as its known intent, they had to find the Act unconstitutional; however, by disregarding Article 1, section 10, the courts could find the Act to be constitutional. Either alternative was unsettling and disturbing to the state courts. With some reluctance, decisions were made on both sides. For example, in *Reynolds* v. *The State Bank of Indiana,* 18 Ind. 467 (1862), after stating that the framers of our Constitution "ordained and established, by the paramount, the fundamental law of our nation, that the currency should be gold and silver. . . and not bills of credit issued simply upon the indebtedness and faith of the government," made a simple and expedient decision that the Act was constitutional. However, other courts either limited the influence of the Act or found the same unconstitutional. In *State Treasurer* v. *Wright,* 28 Ill. 509 (1862), the Illinois Supreme Court held that U.S. Treasury notes could not be used to pay state taxes.

Two years after the rendition of the *Reynolds* case,

supra, the Indiana Supreme Court had the full opportunity to address the issue of the constitutionality of the Legal Tender Act of 1862. In a well written opinion, the Indiana Supreme Court in *Thayer* v. *Hedges,* 22 Ind. 282 (1864), found the Act unconstitutional and stated in reference thereto as follows:

"In another aspect, it enables the government to make, by indirection, forced loans as actual if not as oppressive as those of Charles I, as they are made without interest, against the will of the lender, and without repayment of but a part of the principal; thus, in this case, as an example. The government desires Thayer to loan it 500 dollars. Thayer expresses his inability or unwillingness to spare the money. The government then goes to Hedges and Kleiger and says to them, you owe Thayer 500 dollars, which you are about to pay him. The government wants that money, but he will not loan it. You pay it to the government, and it will give you a piece of paper which it will compel him to take of you, instead of the money contracted for, in payment of your debt.

"That the power to coin money is one power, and the power to declare anything a legal tender is another, and different power; that both were possessed by the States severally at the adoption of the Constitution; that by that adoption, the power to coin money was delegated to the Federal Government, while the power to declare a legal tender was not, but was retained by the States with a limitation, thus: 'Congress should have the power to coin money' and 'no State shall coin money,' and 'no State shall make anything but gold and silver coin a legal tender.' States, then, though they cannot coin money, can declare that gold or silver coin, or both, whether coined by the Federal, or the Spanish or the Mexican Government, shall be legal tender. And as Congress was authorized to make money out of coin, and the States were forbidden to make anything but coin a legal tender, a specie currency was secured in both the Federal and States governments. There was thus no need of delegating to Congress the power of declaring a legal tender in transactions within the domain of Federal legislation. The money coined by it was the necessary medium.

"It was the intention, by the Federal Constitution, to withhold this power of supplanting natural money from the general government, and to strip the states of it, and thus extinguish it, and ensure to the people and nation a sound currency forever. Of this we have not the slightest doubt. Money should be to values, what weights and measures are to quantities, the exact measure, and a uniform, stable one. The States were prohibited from making anything but gold and silver a tender for debts, and the general government was authorized touching this subject, only 'to coin money, regulated the value thereof, and of foreign coin,'...It will be observed that while the States are forbidden to make anything but gold and silver a tender, Congress is empowered to coin money, without being limited to the two kinds of coin to which the States are restricted.''

It must be noted that before 1870, the U.S. Supreme Court was not required to address the issue of the constitutionality of the 1862 Legal Tender Act. Thus so undeterred, the Supreme Court made rulings which further affirmed the proposition that specie coin was the only constitutional currency. In *Bronson* v. *Rhodes*, 74 U.S. 229 (1869), the Supreme Court discussed the purposes for coinage of gold and silver. In *Butler* v. *Horwitz*, 74 U.S. 258 (1869), the Court required the payment of a judgment in specie coin. In *New York* v. *Supervisors, County of New York*, 74 U.S. 26 (1869), the Supreme Court stated that a ''dollar was a certain amount of gold or silver; it also held that ''greenbacks'' could not be taxed by any state authority.

The groundwork for the first U.S. Supreme Court decision in reference to the constitutionality of the 1862 Legal Tender Act was laid in 1865 with the decision of *Griswold* v. *Hepburn*, 63 Ky, 20 (1865). In this case, the constitutionality of the Act was in issue and the majority decision, in a lengthy and well-reasoned opinion, was that the Act of 1862 was unconstitutional. Upon an application for certiorari, the Supreme Court agreed to hear the case, and finally with the decision in *Hepburn* v. *Griswold*, 75 U.S. 603 (1870), the Supreme Court found that the Act violated the Constitution. In its opinion, the Court stated as follows

''We are obliged to conclude that an Act making mere promises to pay dollars a legal tender in payment of debts previously contracted, is not a means appropriate , plainly adopted, really calculated to carry into effect any express power

vested in Congress; that such an Act is inconsistent with the spirit of the Constitution; and that it is prohibited by the Constitution.''

This decision, which had been pending for approximately two years, should have ended the controversy, but with its rendition, the advocates of paper money already had a plan for reversing this decision which they did not like.

The number of Justices on the Supreme Court in 1870 was eight, and the Chief Justice was Salmon P. Chase, who had been Secretary of the Treasury during the War and had been the principal architect of the Legal Tender Acts. However, it was Chase who wrote the opinion in *Hepburn*, supra, and it must have taken considerable courage for a man to say his actions were unconstitutional. The decision in *Hepburn* was a five to three decision, but Justice Grier, a member of the majority, resigned from the Court in 1870 for health reasons.

In 1869, Congress had enacted legislation to increase the number of Justices on the Court from eight to nine. With Grier's resignation and on the same day as the rendition of the opinion in *Hepburn*, President Grant nominated William Strong and Joseph Bradley to be Justices on the Court. These two new Justices were obviously paper money advocates because the Court, after the appointment of the two men, decided to reconsider the issue upon motion of the U.S. Attorney General.

Coming through the Courts at the time of the rendition of *Hepburn* were several other caes involving the legal tender issue and to these cases the Supreme Court granted certiorari. Finally, in *Knox* v. *Lee*, 79 U.S. 457 (1871), the Supreme Court, with a new majority, rendered the famous decision which held that Congress had the power to make U.S. Treasury notes a legal tender. In making this decision, the Court discussed at length the powers of Congress granted in Article 1, section 8, clause 5, but the opinion was still based upon the power of Congress to borrow since Treasury notes were considered, in the context of the Legal Tender Act, to be bills of credit. Although the Court found that Congress had the power to emit bills and make the same a legal tender, it affirmatively stated that no attempt was being made to make paper a standard of value. ''What we do assert is that Congress has power to enact the government's promises to pay money shall be for the time being equivalent in value to the representative of value.'' The opinion didn't sanction the making of money out of valueless material, nor did the court envision that the Treasury notes would never be paid. Some thirteen years after the rendition of this opinion, the Supreme Court reaffirmed *Knox* in *Juilliard* v. *Greenman*, 110 U.S. 421 (1884) by stating as follows:

> ''Congress is authorized to establish a national currency, either in coin or in paper, and to make that currency lawful money for all purposes, as regards the national government or private individuals.

The above two cases of *Knox* v. *Lee* and *Juilliard* v. *Greenman* are utilized by opponents of the ''specie'' issue as the authority for the propositions that legal tender is whatever Congress so designates and that Article 1, section 10 does not prohibit the states from utilizing irredeemable Federal Reserve notes. It is important to note that at the time of the decision in *Juilliard*, Treasury notes were redeemable in specie and the Court, in *Knox* and *Juilliard*, did not expressly authorize the above interpretation. The important passage in *Juilliard* stated that such national currency was lawful ''as regards the national government or private individuals,'' and the Court carefully avoided any mention of utilization of such notes by the States. The power of Congress to issue such a national currency is based upon its constitutional authority to tax and borrow, see *Knox* v. *Lee*, supra. But, as noted by the Supreme Court in *Knox* as well as the Court in *Thayer* v. *Hedges*, the issuance of such Treasury notes is tantamount to the government forcing the citizens to loan it; such notes are nothing more than evidences of government debt which, as the Supreme Court stated in *New York* v. *Supervisors*, supra, can't be taxed by state governments. Since the issuance of Treasury notes are in fact forced loans, can the federal government compel states to loan to it when the states have as much need to survive as the national government? Can the federal government in fact force the states to operate, in collecting taxes and making expenditures, through the use of such evidences of federal government debt? These questions or issues were not addressed or resolved through the Legal Tender Cases, and the Court carefully in these cases avoided addressing these issues.

Whereas, the Supreme Court did not resolve these particular issues in the Legal Tender Cases, such questions were resolved by the same Court which rendered such cases. Prior to the decision in *Knox*, the Supreme Court held, in *Lane County* v. *Oregon*, 74 U.S. 71 (1869), that a county tax collector, who had received tax payments in ''greenbacks,'' was required to pay the State of Oregon gold coin since state law required this form of payment. In this case, the Court found it necessary to construe the word ''debt'' as used in the Legal Tenter Act. In ruling that the state taxes had to be paid in gold coin pursuant to state law, the Court stated that the term ''debts, public and private'' applied only to obligations arising from express or implied contracts and since state taxes were imposts, ''greenbacks'' could not be used to discharge a liability for state taxes. Some fifteen years later, and after the decision of *Juilliard*, the Supreme Court followed *Lane County* when rendering its decision in *Hagar* v. *Reclamation District No. 108*, 111 U.S. 701 (1884). If the Court had chosen to give *Juilliard* the expansive interpretation that states are constitutionally required to utilize whatever currency standard Congress adopts, the decision in *Hagar* would have been different.

There can be but one interpretation of the cases of *Land County*, *Knox*, *Juilliard* and *Hagar*, in relation to the issue of the power of Congress to emit Treasury bills and the corresponding constitutional prohibition upon the states to make nothing but specie a tender for debts. Obviously the state codes involved in *Lane County* and *Hagar* required specie payment of state taxes and also redemption of notes issued by state banks with specie; these provisions in such state codes were necessary to comply with the requirements of Article 1, section 10. The Court in *Knox* and *Juilliard* upheld the challenged Congressional power upon the express condition that such notes did promise to pay money and would ultimately be redeemed. But the Court found that even these notes could not be used to discharge state taxes, hence the Court did not allude to any power in Congress to override the dictates of Article 1, section 10. Therefore, there exists a fine line and distinction between the reach and power of Congress to issue legal tender Treasury notes and this constitutional prohibition. Suffice it to say that this fine line or boundary upon this Constitutional power is surpassed whenever Congress removes the promise to redeem. In such situation, the States can't utilize nor compel its citizens to accept such notes for the identical reasons that states can't allow issuance of notes by state banks otherwise than upon a specie basis.

The powers of Congress granted in Article 1, section 8, clause 5 of the Constitution and the prohibitions upon the states as set forth in Article 1, section 10, are obviously related to the subject of currency and are therefore "of the same family." But the power of Congress to establish a national currency is based upon its power to borrow and this power is not a member of the above noted "family." The Constitution, and no construction thereof, does not grant the power to Congress to force the states to utilize notes representing anticipated federal tax receipts, although Congress itself can accept such notes in discharge of federal tax liabilities. It is for this reason that no interpretation of the *Juilliard* powers of Congress will support the proposition that States must accept such notes in discharge of state tax liabilities. In truth and fact, states are required to operate by use of a currency redeemable in gold or silver coin as required by Article 1, section 10, clause 1.

On December 23, 1913, in the haste of Congress to leave Washington for the Christmas holidays, the Federal Reserve Act was enacted, thus establishing the Federal Reserve System composed at twelve privately owned Federal Reserve Banks (see 12 U.S.C. section 221, et seq., particularly sections 282 and 321). In effect, what was created by this act was a central bank owned and controlled by the banking industry and this banking system was empowered to create credit and expand the money supply on the basis of fractional reserve banking principles. The federal legislation which created this system ostensibly granted to the system the *Juilliard* powers of Congress.

By the date of the United States' entry into World War I, this system was in place and functionally operative. The system flexed its muscle and authority during this war by purchasing securities of the U.S. Treasury by the mere creation of such credit by the Federal Open Market Committee to pay for such securities. This credit expansion was the direct cause of the inflation our country experienced during WWI. This activity of credit expansion generally continued until the Fall of 1929, when a decision to abruptly halt the money supply expansion of the previous decade was made.

In 1933, President F. D. Roosevelt, as one of his first acts as President, declared a banking holiday and ordered all U.S. citizens to turn in all gold in their possession to the Treasury. Congress ratified the President's actions in 1934, most notably by passage of the resolution found at 31 U.S.C. section 463 which stated that it was against "public policy" to discharge obligations in gold coin. Great significance must be placed upon the fact that section 463 (b) defined the term "obligation" as exclusive of currency. Also in 1934, the statutes at 31 U.S.C. section 315 (b) and 31 U.S.C. section 408 (a) were passed to prevent the redemption of currency with gold coin. Much emphasis is placed by the proponents of paper money upon the cases of *Norman* v. *Baltimore and O.R. Co.*, 294 U.S. 240 79 L. Ed. 885, 55 S. Ct. 407 (1935), *Nortz* v. *United States*, 294 U.S. 317, 79 L Ed. 907, 55 S. Ct. 428 (1935), and *Perry* v. *United States*, 294 U.S. 330, 79 L. Ed. 912, 55 S. Ct. 432 (1935); however, these cases dealt only with very limited issues, none of which concerned the interrelationship between the currency powers of Congress and the prohibitions of Article 1, section 10. For an excellent analysis of these cases, reference is made to the law review article at 39 Brooklyn Law Review 517, entitled "How Americans lost their right to own gold and became criminals in the process."

Whereas, gold coins were withdrawn from circulation in 1934 pursuant to 31 U.S.C. section 315 (b), Treasury notes and Federal Reserve notes after such time were still redeemable for silver coin. For the reason of the redeemability of such notes for silver coin between 1934 and 1968, the states were not in violation of Article 1, section 10 by enforcing payment of debts in such medium. However, in 1968, pursuant to 31 U.S.C. section 405 (a) (3), redemption of the circulating currency in silver likewise followed the path of gold and was withdrawn from circulation. Since 1968, the national currency, consisting entirely of Federal Reserve notes and dollar denominated credit units issued by private banks, has not been redeemable for any specie coin. For this reason, since 1968, the States of our nation have been wantonly negligent in protecting the economic and property rights secured to their state citizens through Article 1, section 10, all of which is a gross violation of our Constitution.

The Federal Reserve System as it operates today is probably the most profitable business concern in existence in the United States. The Federal Open Market Committee, which is a part of the System, has power to create credit (money) out of nothing whenever a decision is made to purchase federal notes or bonds. If the Committee desires to make such a purchase, it merely gives the U.S. Treasury a check for the bonds, which are then transferred to F.O.M.C. The credit created by F.O.M.C. and given to the Treasury is ultimately spent and this credit ends up as a deposit in the banking system as a whole. This net new deposit into the banking system will support an expansion of the money supply to an amount approximating the sum of the deposit multiplied by the inverse of the reserve requirement ratio (referred to as the "multiplier"). This expanded money supply is then loaned out at prime interest or better and the banking industry reaps large sums in the form of interest income. To "put the icing on the cake" of this bonanza arising from fractional reserve banking principles, the U.S. Treasury must pay interest on the bonds held by the System.

It must be remembered that the above noted banking system is almost identical with the banking system of England during our colonial history. The Bank of England, at that time as well as today, was owned by the Rothschild family and it functioned in much the same manner as our own privately owned Federal Reserve System. While Benjamin Franklin was in London in 1763 as our Ambassador to England, a Rothschild banker became infuriated when Franklin told him the colonies did not use the interest bearing currency issued by the Bank of England. In 1764, the Rothschilds pressured the King of England to force the colonies to use such currency and this was a primary factor in the reason for the American Revolution. Our forefathers did not like this type of banking system and neither do their descendants, the modern day Americans.

In addition to the above hatred of a banking system such as the Bank of England, our forefathers experimented with irredeemable fiat currency and found the same to be fraught with danger and extremely hazardous. The issuance of such fiat currency caused severe inflation and greatly depressed trade and commerce. Our forefathers, having firsthand knowledge of interest bearing currency, fractional reserve banking and fiat money sought to dispense with and forever prohibit these things from our land by inserting Article 1, section 10 in our Constitution.

The intent of our founding fathers was to establish a form of popular republican government which could exist in perpetuity and could survive all possible and foreseeable crises, including, without limitation, civil disorders, insurrections, war and natural disasters. It is incumbent upon the three branches of our national government to determine if this intent concerning perpetuity and survivability is fulfilled. If a foreseeable or possible crisis could in any way adversely affect our nation or society, then our government has the responsibility to remedy the situation and at least prepare for such crisis.

Our present banking system is extremely labor and capital intensive. It is dependent upon the vast consumption of human resources and is dependent upon fancy electronic banking machinery, such as computers and electronic communications systems, to function. Should any natural or man made disaster arise, this system would be severely impaired in its functioning and this would adversely affect the citizens of our country.

An example of natural disasters which could affect the States of our nation are earthquakes, tornadoes, and volcanic eruption. Earthquakes could disturb dams constructed on or near fault lines in the earth and the breach of such dams would cause the curtailment of hydroelectric power. The same could also have an effect upon nuclear power plants, and thus earthquakes and even tornadoes and volcanoes could cause the electrical generation capacity of our nation to drop. With either reduced electrical power or no production of electrical power, the aggregate credit we as a nation have stored in memory banks of computer terminals in our nation's financial institutions would be unavailable to us. Our society would not function very long on the Federal Reserve Notes we carry on our person. Whereas the above may be natural phenomena it must be remembered that the technology developed on the principles of Nicholas Tesla allows man to also create these natural occurrences.

It is clear that our current banking system is not designed to withstand even certain foreseeable natural or man-made crises. Since the U.S. Congress enacted legislation establishing this system, and since our society is totally dependent upon this system, it is apparent that Congress has failed in its duty to provide for the perpetuity of our Constitution and society and has not created a completely survivable system.

However, by the re-establishment of a valuable metallic currency available in a sufficient quantity, or a paper currency redeemable in specie, we can overcome the deficiencies apparent in our banking system, insure the perpetuity of our Constitution and society, and can enable our important banking industry to survive. With either a metallic or redeemable currency having an actual existence, we can withdraw the same from our banks in sufficient quantities in times of crises to insure that our trade and commerce remain viable. A metallic currency will not be dependent upon the labor and capital intensive nature of our banking system, will have an actual existence, and will not be destroyed by the lack of power to run electronic banking devices. By having an actual and valuable currency circulating in every community of our nation, crises resulting from natural or man-made disasters would not destroy our currency and our society could still maintain trade and commerce and this would lessen the adverse effects of any such disaster.

Not only are there certain practical drawbacks to our present banking system and currency, there are also serious constitutional problems as well. The *Juilliard* powers of Congress in relation to the "national currency" are strictly legislative in nature. But the Federal Reserve Act delegated to the privately owned Federal Reserve System a legislative function without retaining any control over the corporation created. This Act is unconstitutional for the reason that Congress cannot delegate to any other entity a legislative function without at least prescribing a policy, a definite standard for administrative action to implement that policy, and administrative procedures and actions which comply with due process of law. *Field* v. *Clark*, 143 U.S. 649, 12 S. Ct. 495 (1892); *Panama Refining Company* v. *Ryan*, 293 U.S. 388, 55 S. Ct. 241 (1935); *Schechter Poultry Corp.* v. *United States*, 295 U.S. 495, 55 S. Ct. 837 (1935); *Hampton and Co.* v. *United States*, 276 U.S. 394, 48 S. Ct. 348 (1928); *Butterfield* v. *Stranahan*, 192 U.S. 470, 24 S. Ct. 349 (1904); *Union Bridge Co.* v. *United States*, 204 U.S. 364, 27 S. Ct. 367 (1907); *United States* v.

Shreveport Grain and Elevator Co., 287 U.S. 77, 53 S. Ct. 42 (1932); and *United States* v. *Grimaud*, 220 U.S. 506, 31 S. Ct. 480 (1911); see also "Is the Amended Federal Reserve Act Constitutional? A study in the Delegation of Power," at 23 Va. L. Rev. 629.

The important United States Code sections which relate to this issue and which are in Title 12 of the Code are sections 152 and 411. Section 152 defines "lawful money of the United States" as "gold or silver coin of the United States." Section 411 states that Federal Reserve notes are obligations of the United States and must be redeemable "in lawful money on demand." Since such notes are obligations of our federal government, the Secretary of the Treasury directs the "form and tenor" in which such notes must be designed and issued; 12 U.S.C. section 418.

Other important U.S. Code sections relating to the money issue also appear in Title 31 thereof. 31 U.S.C. section 311 establishes a policy of bimetallism and requires the federal government to establish a stable currency based upon gold and silver coin. 31 U.S.C. section 314 defines a "dollar" as 25.8 grains of gold 90% fine, which is the standard unit of value. 31 U.S.C. section 371 establishes the various units of a "dollar," such as dimes and cents.

Notwithstanding the above unrepealed U.S. Code sections, certain other sections of Title 31 dispense with the redemption of currency with specie coin. In sections 315 (b) and 408 (a) of this title, the redemption of "currency of the United States" with gold coin was prohibited. In section 405 a (3), redemption of silver certificates with silver was prohibited. Thus, there exist major conflicting provisions in the United States Code with reference to this issue, some requiring redemption of currency with specie and others dispensing with the necessity of such redemption.

SUMMARY OF MEMORANDUM

Outside the scope of this memorandum is an in-depth analysis of the subject of common law legal tender; for more history concerning the same, reference is made to the law review articles at 20 Corn. L.Q. 52, "Legal Theories of Money," 23 Georgetown L.J. 359, "The Gold Clause Cases in the Light of History, Part I," 24 Georgetown L.J. 722, "The Gold Clause Cases in the Light of History, Part II," 14

Boston U.L. Rev. 485, "Monetary and Legal Tender Acts," 8 Minn L. Rev. 561, "Evolution in Paper Money in the United States," and 20 Va. L. Rev. 856, "Stare Decisis and the Legal Tender Cases."

The history and development of the monetary powers and disabilities contained in the U.S. Constitution can be divided into four separate and distinct periods. The first such period began in 1792, with the enactment of the Coinage Act if 1792, and extended to 1862 with the passage of the Legal Tender Acts. The Coinage Act of 1792 was adopted pursuant to the Congressional powers enumerated in Article 1, section 8, clause 5 of the U.S. Constitution. Both the history of the adoption of the U.S. Constitution and the subsequent court decisions construing this part of the Constitution reveal that the coining powers of Congress involve only the minting of precious metals into coins. Since the states are prohibited from coining money and making any thing but specie coin a legal tender, it is apparent that Congress must coin the money which the states must utilize as a legal tender. Irrevocably intertwined in the U.S. Constitution are the monetary powers and disabilities contained in Article 1, section 8, clause 5 and Article 1, section 10, clause 1. During this period in the constitutional history of United States currency, the courts of our nation construed, and rightly so, these two clauses together, thus establishing a specie currency for our nation.

The second period in the history of United States currency began with the 1862 Legal Tender Act and ended in 1934 with the abolition of the gold standard. During this period, it was established that through the Congressional power to borrow Congress could establish a national currency of paper, provided that such paper could be redeemed for specie coin. During this period, Congress created the Federal Reserve System which over time began supplying the nation with its own paper currency. However, during this time, Federal Reserve and Treasury notes were at all times redeemable for specie coin.

The third period in this history is the period from 1934 to 1968, during which redemption of circulating paper money for any specie coin was abrogated. Notes could not be redeemed for gold after 1934; silver likewise followed the path of gold in 1968 when U.S. citizens were prohibited from redeeming notes in silver.

The fourth period starts in 1968 and continues through the present date. During this fourth period, circulating notes have not been redeemable by U.S. citizens for any specie coin. During this period, Congress totally abrogated its responsibility to supply the nation with specie coin and allowed the Federal Reserve System and private banks to fulfill the need for a medium of exchange. All of the presently existing medium of exchange has been borrowed into circulation and is totally subject to private control. For the "privilege" of using this privately created medium of exchange, our nation must annually pay interest and other tribute (foreclosed lands and personal property) just to have a medium of exchange.

Within the U.S. Constitution, the most readily apparent power to establish a national currency is found in the power "to coin money and regulate the value thereof." Ample authority exists to show that the proper exercise of this power consists in minting the precious metals into coin. However, within the body of that great instrument exist other powers to establish the national currency. In the first great effort, see *Hepburn*, supra, to find such a power, the U.S. Supreme Court, upon sufficient and lengthy analysis of the Constitution, failed to see and discern such a power. However, the subsequent examination of the Constitution in *Knox* did find such a living, but apparently well hidden, power in the Congressional power to borrow. However, a limitation upon this power to establish a national currency via the borrowing power is the command to repay that which is borrowed. This limitation on such power was explicitly demonstrated in both *Knox* and *Juilliard*. Therefore, if any national currency is established by Congress pursuant to the power to borrow, Congress must make provision for ultimately repaying the money so borrowed and that money must be gold or silver coin. Congress cannot, pursuant to this power, establish a purely fiat paper currency.

Whereas the power to establish a national currency via the power to borrow was apparently well concealed within the body of the Constitution, there may exist other powers microscopically hidden therein upon which Congress can establish a national currency. In *Norman*, supra, the Court alluded to the Congressional power over the national currency derived from tax, interstate commerce, coining and weights and measures powers plainly granted to Congress.

However, assuming such broad currency powers not apparent on the face of the Constitution, it is still a contested issue that such currency powers as Congress may have can be utilized to relegate Article 1, section 10, clause 1 to a relic of antiquity. Today, the only effort Congress makes to provide the citizens of this nation with any national currency is to coin cupranickel, "clad" coins. The federal government coins precious little money and what it does so provide is truly "small change." The remainder of our "national" currency is provided by both the Federal Reserve System and privately owned banking institutions. The Fed monetizes the federal government's debt securities and issues upon such collateral nominal amounts of Federal Reserve Notes. The Fed further provides credit to the federal government and the federal government spends such credit into circulation. Over this entire operation, Congress exercises no control; the Fed is completely without Congressional supervision with the exception of occasionally asking Congress for legislative authority for actions it would take in any event, with or without Congressional approval. The Federal Reserve Board is currently controlled by the Chairman, the master of our economy. The extent of Congressional control amounts to occasionally summoning of this person before various Congressional committees wherein he exhibits his limitless authority and effectively "bullies" Congress with the threat of depriving it of funds.

Whereas the Fed provides some of our national currency, the vast portion of our national currency is demand deposits, the creation of privately owned banks. Over the creation of bank demand deposits, Congress has virtually no control, having abrogated whatever power of control it has over private banks to the Fed.

All of our national currency has been borrowed into circulation from private financial institutions. The cost for the privilege of using this privately owned and controlled currency is the interest which the national economy must pay every year to the money creators. If any attempt were ever made to pay all of the debts owed by our society to such institutions, there would not be enough money to pay the interest owed, since currency to pay the interest was never originally created.

There exists today in our country a vast money creation monopoly which directly affects the production of wealth by our society and directly controls the price for which such wealth will command. This money monopoly is so powerful that not even the strongest Congress can obtain an audit of this federally chartered, private banking monopoly, which has obtained certain privileges and favors as the result of international treaties and agreements, such as immunity from process. If this system wherein money is created by these private interests is not changed, it is a mathematical certainty that this system will ultimately collapse, resulting in chaos and destruction in our country.

There are definite limits to the Congressional power to impose upon our country this type of currency system which is privately created, controlled and manipulated in favor of the private financial interests involved. Undeterred this system will ultimately cause our nation to experience ruinous inflation and the consequent destruction of our national economy. The states are not without the power to challenge this destructive system as such power resides within the Ninth and Tenth Amendments to the U.S. Constitution; see *National League of Cities* v. *Usery*, 426 U.S. 833, 49 L. Ed. 2d 245, 96 S. Ct. 2465 (1976). However resort need not be made to possibly living but hidden powers in these Amendments as more specific and definite authority therefore exists within the body of our national charter: "No state shall..."

Amendments to the U.S. Constitution

AMENDMENT I

Congress shall make no law respecting an establishment of religion, or prohibiting the free exercise thereof; or abridging the freedom of speech or of the press; or the right of the people peaceably to assemble, and to petition the Government for a redress of grievances.

AMENDMENT II

A well-regulated Militia, being necessary to the security of a free State, the right of the people to keep and bear arms, shall not be infringed.

AMENDMENT III

No Soldier shall, in time of peace be quartered in any house, without the consent of the owner, nor in time of war, but in a manner to be prescribed by law.

AMENDMENT IV

The right of the people to be secure in their persons, houses, papers, and effects, against unreasonable searches and seizures, shall not be violated, and no warrants shall issue, but upon probable cause, supported by oath or affirmation, and particularly describing the place to be searched, and the persons or things to be seized.

AMENDMENT V

No person shall be held to answer for a capital, or otherwise infamous crime, unless on a presentment or indictment of a grand jury, except in cases arising in the land or naval forces, or in the militia, when in actual service in time or war or public danger; nor shall any person be subject for the same offense to be twice put in jeopardy of life or limb, nor shall be compelled in any criminal case to be a witness against himself; nor be deprived of life, liberty, or property, without due process of law; nor small private property be taken for public use, without just compensation.

AMENDMENT VI

In all criminal prosecutions, the accused shall enjoy the right to a speedy and public trial, by an impartial jury of the State and district wherein the crime shall have been committed, which district shall have been previously ascertained by law, and to be informed of the nature and cause of the accusation; to be confronted with the witnesses against him; to have compulsory process for obtaining witnesses in his favor, and to have the assistance of counsel for his defense.

AMENDMENT VII

In suits at common law, where the value in controversy shall exceed twenty dollars, the right of trial by jury shall be preserved, and no fact tried by a jury, shall be otherwise reexamined in any court of the United States, than according to the rules of the common law.

AMENDMENT VIII

Excessive bail shall not be required, nor excessive fines imposed, nor cruel and unusual punishments inflicted.

AMENDMENT IX

The enumeration in the Constitution, of certain rights, shall not be construed to deny or disparage others retained by the people.

AMENDMENT X

The powers not delegated to the United States by the Constitution, nor prohibited by it to the States, are reserved to the States respectively, or to the people.

QUIT CLAIM DEED, INDIVIDUAL TO INDIVIDUAL   FORM NO. 27-M

This Indenture, *Made this 18th day of January, 1984, between David G. White, married, of the County of Stearns and State of Minnesota, party of the first part, and Ron L. Kalmoe, of the County of Stearns and State of Minnesota, party of the second part.*

Witnesseth, *That the said party of the first part, in consideration of the sum of Eleven Dollars, to him in hand paid by the said party of the second part, the receipt whereof is hereby acknowledged, does hereby Grant, Bargain, Quitclaim and Convey unto the said party of the second part, his heirs and assigns, Forever, all the tract or parcel of land lying and being in the County of Stearns and State of Minnesota, described as follows, to-wit:*

a one-half undivided interest to the tract of land described as follows:

S½NE¼, the E. 6 acres of SW¼NW¼ and SE¼NW¼, except: commencing at the N¼ corner of said Sec. 1; thence S. along the North–South ¼ line of said Sec. 1, a distance of 2017.57 ft. for point of beginning; thence S. along said line 145.20 ft.; thence W. at right angles 300 ft.; thence N. at right angles 145.20 ft.; thence E. at right angles 300 ft. to the point of beginning and there terminating, all in Sec. 1; AND EXCEPT that part of the S½NE¼ of Sec. 1, described as follows: Beginning at a point on the west line of said S½NE¼ of Sec. 1, distant 33.00 feet southerly of the northwest corner of said S½NE¼ of Sec. 1, distant 33.00 feet southerly of the northwest corner of said S½NE¼; thence easterly, parallel with the north line of said S½NE¼ a distance of 470.16 feet; thence southerly, parallel with the west line of said S½NE¼ a distance of 276.19 feet; thence northwesterly a distance of 486.74 feet to a point on the west line of said S½NE¼, distant 150.00 feet southerly of the point of beginning, thence northerly along said west line a distance of 150.00 feet to the point of beginning, containing 2.30 acres; all in Sec. 1, T125N., R32W.

The NE¼SW¼, except tract desc. as follows: Beginning at the NE corner thereof; thence W 53 rods to the center of the road; thence S. along said road 3 rods; thence E. to the E. line thereof; thence N. 3 rods to the place of beginning, Also Govt. Lots 1 & 2, except parcels:

Parcel A: That part of Govt. Lot 1 and Govt. Lot 2 desc. as follows: Commencing at the S¼ corner of said Sec. 35; thence N 89°57′W (assumed bearing) along the S. line of said Govt. Lot 2 for 1497.22 ft. to the centerline of a public road; thence along said centerline N 3°21′27″W for 1160 ft. to the point of beginning of the land to be described; thence continuing along said centerline N 3°21′27″ W for 260 ft.; thence S 86°38′33″ W for 152 ft. more or less to the shore of Freeport Lake; thence SW'ly along said lake shore to its intersection with a line draw S 86° ′38″E for 462 ft. more or less to the point of beginning.

Parcel B: That part of Govt. Lot 2 desc. as follows: Beginning at a point in the S. line thereof 53 rods 3.05 ft. W of the SE corner thereof, said point being the center of the road; thence W 41 rods; thence N 9 rods; thence E 41 rods to the center of said road; thence S 9 rods to the place of beginning and also except that part of said Lot 2 lying W. of County Highway #11, as now constructed and travelled.

S½SE¼, also a part of the NW¼SE¼ desc. as follows: Beginning at the SE corner thereof; thence N 1 rod; thence W parallel to the S line thereof 67⅓ rods; thence NW'ly to a point on the W line thereof which is 66⅓ rods S of the NW corner; thence S along said W line to the SW corner; thence E to place of beginning, all in Sec. 35, T126N., R32W.

To Have and to Hold the Same, *Together with all the hereditaments and appurtenances thereunto belonging or in anywise appertaining, to the said party of the second part, his heirs and assigns, Forever.*

In Testimony Whereof, *The said party of the first part has hereunto set his hand the day and year first above written.*

Tax statements to: [signed] David G. White
Ron L. Kalmoe
41 NE 3rd
St. Cloud, MN 56301

State of Minnesota,   )
                                    ss.
County of Stearns   )
    The foregoing instrument was acknowledged before me   *by* David G. White
this 18th day of January, 1985,   [signed] Jean A. Trunk

THIS INSTRUMENT WAS DRAFTED BY
            David G. White
            Rt. 2, Box 286
            Avon, MN 56310

STATE DEED TAX: $2.20

The total consideration for this transfer of property is $1,000 or less.

BRIEF IN SUPPORT OF MOTION FOR COURT DETERMINATION
OF JURY TRIAL DEMAND.

CASE No. _____

This brief summarizes without becoming too lengthy the case law which supports my / our right to a trial by jury in this case. All case law cited is pursuant to the intent of the U.S. Constitution as written by our founding fathers.

1. "To ascertain scope and meaning of Seventh amendment, preserving trial by jury in suits at common law where the value in controversy exceeds $20, resort must be had to the appropriate rules of the common law established at the time of the adoption of the constitutional amendments in 1791. U.S.C.A. Const. Amend. 7. *Dimick* v. *Scheidt*, 55 S. Ct. 296, 293 U.S. 474, 79 L. Ed. 603." 9A S. Ct. Digest 250

2. "The distinction between law and equity jurisdiction is constitutional to the extent to which the seventh amendment forbids any infringement of the rights of trial by jury, as fixed by the common law. *Root* v. *Lake Shore & S.R. Co.*, 105 U.S. 189, 26 L. Ed.975." 9A S.Ct. Digest 250.

3. "Seventh Amendment to Constitution preserves right of jury trial existing under English Common Law when amendment was adopted and protects it from indirect impairment through possible enlargement of courts' power of re-examination under such law. *Baltimore & Carolina Line* v. *Redman*, 55 S. Ct. 890, 295 U.S. 654, 79 L.Ed. 1636." 9A S. Ct Digest 251.

4. "A constitutional power cannot be used by way of condition to attain an unconstitutional result. *Gomillion* v. *Lightfoot*, 364 U.S. 339, 81 S. Ct. 125." S. Ct. Digest, L. Ed.

5. "A litigant may only assert his own constitutional rights and immunities. *McGowan* v. *Maryland*, 366 U.S. 420, 81 S. Ct. 1101." S. Ct Digest, L. Ed.

6. "The Constitution is intended to preserve practical and substantial rights, not to maintain theories. *El Pase* v. *Simmons*, 379 U.S. 497, 85 S. Ct. 577." S. Ct. Digest, L. Ed.

7. "Where rights secured by the Federal Constitution are involved, there can be no rule-making or legislation which would abrogate them. *Miranda* v. *Arizona*, 384 U.S.436, 86 S. Ct. 1602, 10 ALR 3rd 974." S. Ct. Digest, L.Ed.

8. "Constitutional deprivations may not be justified by some remote administrative benefit to the state. *Harman* v. *Forssenius*, 380 U.S.24, 85 S. Ct. 1177." S. Ct. Digest, L. Ed.

9. "Where the intention of a constitutional provision is clear, there is no room for construction, and no excuse for interpolation or additions. *United States* v. *Sprague*, 282 U.S.716, 51 S. Ct. 220, 71 ALR 1381." S. Ct. Digest, L. Ed.

10. "A clause in the Constitution must be given full force and effect throughout the Union. *King* v. *Mullins*, 171 U.S.404, 18 S. Ct. 925." S. Ct. Digest, L. Ed.

11. "The Constitution was intended to prohibit things, not names, and its provisions cannot be evaded by giving a new name to an old thing. *Craig* v. *Missouri*, 4 Pet 410." S. Ct. Digest, L. Ed.

12. "As used in constitutional or statutory provision, the term "jury" is ordinarily understood to mean a common-law jury if no other jury was known in law at the time of the adoption of the constitution." 47 Am Jur 2d, 627.

13. "The right to trial by jury is a fundamental right in our democratic system, and is recognized as such in the Magna Charta, the Declaration of Independence, the Federal Constitution, and the constitutions of the various states." 47 Am Jur 2d, 631.

14. "The constitutions of the several states generally contain express guarantees of the right to a jury trial. The typical provision is that the right shall be and remain inviolate, or that the right, as heretofore enjoyed, shall remain inviolate. Such rights apply to both civil and criminal cases. The right is secured, and not granted, by such a provision." 47 Am jur 2d, 633.

15. "It has also been stated that the words "law of the land" and "due process of law," when used

in considering the property rights of individuals, mean not only summons or notice, such as is ordinarily given upon institution of a suit, due appearance of the parties in interest, and pleading of the facts in issue, but also means a determination thereof by a jury." 47 Am Jur 2d, 634.

16. "The right of a trial by jury, where it is granted by constitutional or statutory provision, cannot be taken away or impaired by the courts, nor has the legislature any power to authorize the courts to take away or impair the right when it is secured in or guaranteed by a constitutional provision. The general rule is that a trial without a jury cannot be had where there is a right to a jury trial...The view has been taken that a court sitting without a jury, where there is a right to a jury trial which has not been waived, has no jurisdiction of the case, and its decree is void, the jury being a necessary constituent part of the court itself." 47 Am Jur 2d, 643.

17. "The citizens of each State shall be entitled to all Privileges and Immunities of Citizens in the several States." U.S. Constitution, Article 4, Sec. 2. The right to trial by jury having been secured in the Constitutions of several states further secures this right in this state. The right to trial by jury cannot be denied for reasons of expediency or efficiency without doing a great injustice to this party as the debtors have the same rights, privileges and immunities as the wealthy and powerful. There are no provisions in the Constitution that exempt the wealthy from jury trials at their discretion. If the courts were to exempt them from having to defend themselves before juries, then it would have created an umbrella of sovereign immunity to protect the wealthy from answering and defending themselves against allegations of wrongdoing. This clearly would not be in the interest of justice. It is hoped that the court, having examined this information will declare that this case is triable to a jury on all the facts in dispute in this case pursuant to the U.S. Constitution, our State Constitution and the statutes and case law made in pursuance thereof.

Being duly sworn on oath, I affirm that this brief in support of the Motion for Court Determination of Jury Trial Demand is true and correct, to the best of my knowledge and belief.

Date _____   X _____

       State of _____

       County of _____

       _____

       Subscribed and sworn to before me,

       this _____ day of _____, 19____

       Notary Public, State of _____

       My Commission expires _____

Caption   Case No. _____

MOTION FOR COURT DETERMINATION
OF JURY TRIAL DEMAND.

Now comes the [plaintiff or defendant], [your names], and present to the court the following facts to support this motion for a court ruling on our jury trial demand:

1. The [plaintiff or defendant] in this action is not an attorney, but is a layman who is aware of the fact that we live in a Republic based on the Constitution of the United States and that this Constitution is the Supreme Law of the Land and that all courts and their officers, and the presiding judges are sworn to uphold the same.

2. That all statutory law or Case law contrary to the intent of the Constitution is a usurpation of power and can only be enforced under color of law.

3. That misrepresentation of a material fact, otherwise known as fraud, is contrary to all principles of law and equity and is an integral part of this case. That fraud knows no statute of limitations and is a just basis for the voidance of contractual obligations.

4. That the writing of bad checks to circulate as money and the laundering of these checks otherwise known as "check kiting," is a material misrepresentation of facts and contrary to both Federal and State law and is an integral part of this case.

5. That verbal representations and actions, that suggest a particular course of commitment, constitute representation, and a failure of the other party to fulfill such is a violation of a contract between the parties and is an integral part of this case.

6. That the interest rate charged for the amount of coins and currency risked by the lender in this transaction is at least 20 times greater than the amount agreed to in the note / mortgage note / deed of trust that this party signed and constitutes a second violation of a contractual obligation.

7. That the other party in this action has violated Federal Racketeering laws by creating an unlawful debt and using the U.S. Mails more than twice to collect on this debt.

8. That the plaintiff / defendant in this action has admissible evidence to support these allegations and is competent to testify to the above.

9. That the plaintiffs / defendants complaint / counterclaim / third party complaint is a "suit at common law" within the meaning of the 7th amendment to the Bill of Rights and that the case is estimated at a value of ? . The 7th amendment says: "In suits at common law, where the value in controversy shall exceed twenty dollars, the right of a trial by jury shall be preserved." The right to a trial by jury is further preserved in the state constitution which says:...

10. That the plaintiff / defendant in this action has filed a written demand for a trial by jury in his Answer / Counterclaim / Complaint and has filed a brief in support of this demand and an affidavit in support of both and asks the court to rule and to make a determination on this demand as soon as possible and before the hearing of any motions or demurrers that would constitute a final disposition of this case. The plaintiff / defendant asks the court to set the date of the trial by jury as at least 60 days after making its determination so as to allow the parties to complete Discovery and no later that 90 days after making this determination, if it is possible and within the court's calendar. If the other party to this action would like the trial by jury to begin sooner, we are agreeable to any other date the court chooses.

Date _____   X _____

FORM NO. 1

VOLUNTARY PETITION

United States Bankruptcy Court

For The _____ District of _____

In re

_____

Debtor [set forth here all names including trade names used by Debtor within last 6 years].

} Case

No. _____

Social Security No. _____

and Debtor's Employer's Tax Identification No. _____

VOLUNTARY PETITION

1. Petitioner's mailing address, including county, is

2. Petitioner has resided [*or* has had his domicile *or* has had his principal place of business *or* has had his principal assets] within this district for the preceding 180 days [*or* for a longer portion of the preceding 180 days than in any other district].

3. Petitioner is qualified to file this petition and is entitled to the benefits of title 11, United States Code as a voluntary debtor.

[*If appropriate*]
4. A copy of petitioner's proposed plan, dated _____ , is attached [*or* Petitioner intends to file a plan pursuant to chapter 11 *or* chapter 13 of title 11, United States Code].

[*If petitioner is a corporation*]
5. Exhibit "A" is attached to and made a part of this petition.*

[*If petitioner is an individual whose debts are primarily consumer debts and is proceeding under chapter 7*]
6. Petitioner is aware that [he or she] may proceed under chapter 7 or 13 of title 11, United States Code, understands the relief available under each such chapter, and chooses to proceed under chapter 7 of such title.

[*If petitioner is an individual whose debts are primarily consumer debts and such petitioner is represented by an attorney*]
7. A declaration or an affidavit in the form of Exhibit "B" is attached to and made a part of this petition.

WHEREFORE, petitioner prays for relief in accordance with chapter 7 [*or* chapter 11 *or* chapter 13] of title 11, United States Code.

Signed: _____
Attorney for Petitioner

Address: _____

_____

[*Petitioner signs if not represented by attorney*]

_____
Petitioner

I, _____ , the petitioner named in the foregoing petition, declare under penalty of pejury that the foregoing is true and correct.

Executed on _____

Signature: _____
Petitioner

*[For unsworn Declaration on Behalf of a Corporation or Partnership, see Form 4 on next page.]

EXHIBIT "B"

[If petitioner is an individual whose debts are primarily consumer debts, this Exhibit "B" shall be completed and attached to the petition pursuant to paragraph 7 of the Form No. 1 Petition and paragraph 6 of the Joint Petition.]

United States Bankruptcy Court

For The _____ District of _____

In re

FOR COURT USE ONLY

_____
Date Petition Filed

_____

Debtor [set forth here all names including trade names used by Debtor within last 6 years].

_____
Case Number

Social Security No. _____

_____
Bankruptcy Judge

and Debtor's Employer's Tax Identification No. _____

   I, _____ , the attorney for the petitioner named in the foregoing petition, declare that I have informed the petitioner that [he or she] may proceed under chapter 7 or 13 of title 11, United States Code, and have explained the relief available under each such chapter.

Executed on _____

Signature: _____
Attorney for Petitioner

FORM NO. 4

UNSWORN DECLARATION UNDER PENALTY OF PERJURY
ON BEHALF OF A CORPORATION OR PARTNERSHIP

I,   , [the president *or other officer or* an authorized agent of the corporation] [*or* a member *or* an authorized agent of the partnership] named as petitioner in the foregoing petition, declare under penalty of perjury that the foregoing is true and correct, and that the filing of this petition on behalf of the [corporation] [*or* partnership] has been authorized.

Executed on _____

                                     Signature: _____

FORM NO. 6

SCHEDULES OF ASSETS AND LIABILITIES

United States Bankruptcy Court

For The _____ District of _____

In re

_____

Debtor [set forth here all names including trade names used by Debtor within last 6 years].

Case

No. _____

SCHEDULE A.—STATEMENT OF ALL LIABILITIES OF DEBTOR*

Schedule A-1, A-2 and A-3 must include all the claims against the debtor or his property as of the date of the filing of the petition by or against him.

SCHEDULE A-1.—CREDITORS HAVING PRIORITY**

(1) Nature of claim	(2) Name of creditor and complete mailing address including zip code (if unknown, so state)	(3) Specify when claim was incurred and the consideration therefor; when claim is subject to setoff, evidenced by a judgment, negotiable instrument, or other writing, or incurred as partner or joint contractor, so indicate; specify name of any partner or joint contractor on any debt	(4) Indicate if claim is contingent, unliquidated, or disputed, [use appropriate abbreviation(s)]	(5) Amount of claim	
a. Wages, salary and commissions, including vacation, severance and sick leave pay owing to employees not exceeding $2,000 to each, earned within 90 days before filing of petition or cessation of business (If earlier specify date).					
b. Contributions to employee benefit plans for services rendered within 180 days before filing of petition or cessation of business (If earlier specify date).					
			Total	$	

*[In chapter 11 cases counsel's attention is directed to the additional requirement mandated by Rule 1007(b) which requires a list of creditors by class in addition to the information already called for by this Schedule as well as a list of equity security holders.]

**[List all creditors in alphabetical order within each of the sections above. Where spaces are inadequate, use additional sheets.]

Sheet 1

SCHEDULE A-1.-CREDITORS HAVING PRIORITY (CONT.)*

(1) Nature of claim	(2) Name of creditor and complete mailing address including zip code (if unknown, so state)	(3) Specify when claim was incurred and the consideration therefor; when claim is subject to setoff, evidenced by a judgment, negotiable instrument, or other writing, or incurred as partner or joint contractor, so indicate; specify name of any partner or joint contractor on any debt	(4) Indicate if claim is contingent, unliquidated, or disputed, [use appropriate abbreviation(s)]	(5) Amount of claim
c. Deposits by individuals, not exceeding $900 for each for purchase, lease, or rental of property or services for personal, family, or house hold use that were not delivered or provided.				
d. Taxes owing [itemize by type of tax and taxing authority] (1) To the United States (2) To any state (3) To any other taxing authority				
			Total	$

SCHEDULE A-2.-CREDITORS HOLDING SECURITY *

(1) Name of creditor and complete mailing address including zip code (if unknown, so state)	(2) Description of security and date when obtained by creditor	(3) Specify when claim was incurred and the consideration therefor; when claim is subject to setoff, evidenced by a judgment, negotiable instrument, or other writing, or incurred as partner or joint contractor, so indicate; specify name of any partner or joint contractor on any debt	(4) Indicate if claim is contingent, unliquidated, or disputed, [use appropriate abbreviation(s)]	(5) Market value		(6) Amount of claim without deduction of value of security
		Total			$	

SCHEDULE A-3.—CREDITORS HAVING UNSECURED CLAIMS WITHOUT PRIORITY*

(1) Name of creditor (including last known holder of any negotiable instrument) and complete mailing address including zip code (if unknown, so state)	(2) Specify when claim was incurred and the consideration therefor; when claim is contingent, unliquidated, disputed, subject to setoff, evidenced by a judgment, negotiable instrument, or other writing, or incurred as partner or joint contractor, so indicate; specify name of any partner or joint contractor on any debt	(3) Indicate if claim is contingent, unliquidated, or disputed	(4) Amount of claim
		Total	$

*[List all creditors in alphabetical order and leave adequate space between listings.]

SCHEDULE A-3.—CREDITORS HAVING UNSECURED CLAIMS WITHOUT PRIORITY (CONT.)*

(1) Name of creditor (including last known holder of any negotiable instrument) and complete mailing address including zip code (if unknown, so state)	(2) Specify when claim was incurred and the consideration therefor; when claim is contingent, unliquidated, disputed, subject to setoff, evidenced by a judgment, negotiable instrument, or other writing, or incurred as partner or joint contractor, so indicate; specify name of any partner or joint contractor on any debt	(3) Indicate if claim is contingent, unliquidated, or disputed	(4) Amount of claim
		Total $	

*[List all creditors in alphabetical order and leave adequate space between listings.]

SCHEDULE B.—STATEMENT OF ALL PROPERTY OF DEBTOR

Schedules B-1, B-2, B-3, and B-4 must include all property of the debtor as of the date of the filing of the petition by or against him.

SCHEDULE B-1.—REAL PROPERTY*

Description and location of all real property in which debtor has an interest [including equitable and future interests, interests in estates by the entirety, community property, life estates, leaseholds, and rights and powers exercisable for his own benefit]	Nature of interest [specify all deeds and written instruments relating thereto]	Market value of debtor's interest without deduction for secured claims listed in Schedule A-2 or exemptions claimed in Schedule B-4	
	Total	$	

*[Where spaces above are inadequate for detailed listing of assets, please use additional sheets.]

Sheet 6

SCHEDULE B-2.—PERSONAL PROPERTY *

Type of property	Description and location	Market value of debtor's interest without deduction for secured claims listed on Schedule A-2 or exemptions claimed in Schedule B-4	
a. Cash on hand			
b. Deposits of money with banking institutions, savings and loan associations, brokerage houses, credit unions, public utility companies, landlords and others			
c. Household goods, supplies and furnishings			
d. Books, pictures, and other art objects; stamp, coin and other collections			
e. Wearing apparel, jewelry, firearms, sports equipment and other personal possessions			
f. Automobiles, trucks, trailers and other vehicles			
g. Boats, motors and their accessories			
h. Livestock, poultry and other animals			
Total		$	

*[Where spaces above are inadequate for detailed listing of assets, please use additional sheets.]

Sheet 7

SCHEDULE B-2.—PERSONAL PROPERTY (CONT.)*

Type of property	Description and location	Market value of debtor's interest without deduction for secured claims listed on Schedule A-2 or exemptions claimed in Schedule B-4	
i. Farming equipment, supplies and implements			
j. Office equipment, furnishings and supplies			
k. Machinery, fixtures, equipment and supplies [other than those listed in items j and l] used in business			
l. Inventory			
m. Tangible personal property of any other description			
n. Patents, copyrights, licenses, franchises and other general intangibles [specify all documents and writings relating thereto]			
o. Government and corporate bonds and other negotiable and non-negotiable instruments			
p. Other liquidated debts owing debtor			
	Total	$	

*[Where spaces above are inadequate for detailed listing of assets, please use additional sheets.]

Sheet

SCHEDULE B-3.—PROPERTY NOT OTHERWISE SCHEDULED

Type of property	Description and location	Market value of debtor's interest without deduction for secured claims listed in Schedule A-2 or exemptions claimed in Schedule B-4	
a. Property transferred under assignment for benefit of creditors, within 120 days prior to filing of petition [specify date of assignment, name and address of assignee, amount realized therefrom by the assignee, and disposition of proceeds so far as known to debtor]			
b. Property of any kind not otherwise scheduled			
	Total	$	

SCHEDULE B-4—PROPERTY CLAIMED AS EXEMPT *

Debtor selects the following property as exempt pursuant to 11 U.S.C. §522 (d) [*or* the laws of the State of _____ .]

Type of property	Location, description, and, so far as relevant to the claim of exemption, present use of property	Specify statute creating the exemption	Value claimed exempt
		Total	$

* [All property claimed as exempt must be itemized in detail.]

SCHEDULE B-4.—PROPERTY CLAIMED AS EXEMPT (CONT.)*

Debtor selects the following property as exempt pursuant to 11 U.S.C. §522 (d) [*or the laws of the State of* _____ .]

Type of property	Location, description, and, so far as relevant to the claim of exemption, present use of property	Specify statute creating the exemption	Value claimed exempt
		Total $	

*[All property claimed as exempt must be itemized in detail.]

SUMMARY OF DEBTS AND PROPERTY

[From the statements of the debtor in Schedules A and B]

Schedule		Total	
DEBTS			
A—1/a, b	Wages, etc. having priority		
A—1/c	Deposits of Money		
A—1/d(1)	Taxes owing United States		
A—1/d(2)	Taxes owing states		
A—1/d(3)	Taxes owing other taxing authorities		
A—2	Secured claims		
A—3	Unsecured claims without priority		
	Schedule A Total	$	
PROPERTY			
B—1	Real property [total value]		
B—2/a	Cash on hand		
B—2/b	Deposits		
B—2/c	Household goods		
B—2/d	Books, pictures, and collections		
B—2/e	Wearing apparel and personal possessions		
B—2/f	Automobiles and other vehicles		
B—2/g	Boats, motors and accessories		
B—2/h	Livestock and other animals		
B—2/i	Farming supplies and implements		
B—2/j	Office equipment and supplies		
B—2/k	Machinery, equipment, and supplies used in business		
B—2/l	Inventory		
B—2/m	Other tangible personal property		
B—2/n	Patents and other general intangibles		
B—2/o	Bonds and other instruments		
B—2/p	Other liquidated debts		
B—2/q	Contingent and unliquidated claims		
B—2/r	Interests in insurance policies		
B—2/s	Annuities		
B—2/t	Interests in corporations and unincorporated companies		
B—2/u	Interests in partnerships		
B—2/v	Equitable and future interests, rights, and powers in personality		
B—3/a	Property assigned for benefit of creditors		
B—3/b	Property otherwise scheduled		
	Schedule B Total	$	

SCHEDULE C.—SCHEDULE OF CURRENT INCOME AND CURRENT EXPENDITURES

This schedule is required by Bankruptcy Code (Revised), 11 U.S.C. §521(1), effective October 8, 1984

a. Give current monthly income, if unmarried, otherwise for each spouse whether single or joint petition is filed, unless spouses are separated and a single petition is filed. *

    (1) Husband's [or debtor's] monthly take-home pay . . . .   _____

    (2) Wife's monthly take-home pay . . . .   _____

    (3) Other monthly income (specify) . . . .   _____

                                                           Total $ _____

b. Give current monthly expenditures which are used to support debtor or dependent(s) of debtor. *

    (1) Rent or home mortgage payment (include lot rental for trailer) . . . .   _____

    (2) Utilities (Electricity _____ , Heat _____ , Water _____ ,

         Telephone _____) . . . .   _____

    (3) Food . . . .   _____

    (4) Clothing . . . .   _____

    (5) Laundry and cleaning . . . .   _____

    (6) Newspapers, periodicals, and books (including school books) . . . .   _____

    (7) Medical and drug . . . .   _____

    (8) Insurance (not deducted from wages):
         (a) Auto . . . .   _____

         (b) Other . . . .   _____

    (9) Transportation (not including auto payments to be paid under plan) . . . .   _____

    (10) Recreation . . . .   _____

    (11) Dues, union, professional, social, or otherwise (not deducted from wages) . . . .   _____

    (12) Taxes (not deducted from wages) . . . .   _____

    (13) Alimony, maintenance, or support payments . . . .   _____

    (14) Other payments for support of dependents not living at home . . . .   _____

    (15) Religious and other charitable contributions . . . .   _____

    (16) Other (specify): _____ , _____ . . . .   _____

                                                           Total $ _____

c. Excess of monthly income over monthly expenditures . . . . $ _____

* If income received or expenditures made covers more than a monthly period, pro rate and enter monthly amount.

UNSWORN DECLARATION UNDER PENALTY OF PERJURY
OF INDIVIDUAL TO SCHEDULES A, B AND C

I, _____ , declare under penalty of perjury that I have read the foregoing schedules, consisting of _____ sheets, and that they are true and correct to the best of my knowledge, information and belief.

Executed on _____

                                    Signature:_____

UNSWORN DECLARATION UNDER PENALTY OF PERJURY
OF JOINT PETITIONERS TO SCHEDULES A, B AND C

We, _____ , and _____ , declare under penalty of perjury that we have read the foregoing schedules, consisting of _____ sheets, and that they are true and correct to the best of our knowledge, information and belief.

Executed on _____

                                    Signature: _____

                                    Signature: _____

UNSWORN DECLARATION UNDER PENALTY OF PERJURY
ON BEHALF OF CORPORATION OR PARTNERSHIP TO SCHEDULES A AND B

I, _____ , [the president *or other officer or* an authorized agent of the corporation] [*or* a member *or* an authorized agent of the partnership] named as debtor in this case, declare under penalty of perjury that I have read the foregoing schedules, consisting of _____ sheets, and that they are true and correct to the best of my knowledge, information and belief.

Executed on _____

                                    Signature: _____

FORM NO. 7

STATEMENT OF FINANCIAL AFFAIRS FOR DEBTOR NOT ENGAGED IN BUSINESS

United States Bankruptcy Court

For The _____ District of _____

In re

⎫ Case

⎬ No. _____

_____

Debtor [set forth here all names including trade names used by Debtor within last 6 years].

STATEMENT OF FINANCIAL AFFAIRS FOR DEBTOR NOT ENGAGED IN BUSINESS

[Each question should be answered or the failure to answer explained. If the answer is "none" or "not applicable" so state. If additional space is needed for the answer to any question, a separate sheet, properly identified and made a part hereof, should be used and attached.
The term, "original petition," used in the following questions, shall mean the petition filed under Rule 1002, 1003, or 1004.]

1. Name and residence.

   a. What is your full name?

   b. Have you used, or been known by, any other names within the six years immediately preceding the filing of the original petition herein? (If so, give particulars.)

   c. Where do you now reside?

   d. Where else have you resided during the six years immediately preceding the filing of the original petition herein?

2. Occupation and income.

   a. What is your occupation?

   b. Where are you now employed? (Give the name and address of your employer, or the address at which you carry on your trade or profession, and the length of time you have been so employed or engaged.)

   c. Have you been in a partnership with anyone, or engaged in any business during the six years immediately preceding the filing of the original petition here? (If so, give particulars, including names, dates and places.)

   d. What amount of income have you received from your trade or profession during each of the two calendar years immediately preceding the filing of the original petition herein?

e. What amount of income have you received from other sources during each of these two years? (Give particulars, including each source, and the amount received therefrom.)

3. Tax returns and refunds.

a. Where did you file your federal, state and municipal income tax returns for the two years immediately preceding the filing of the original petition herein?

b. What tax refunds (income and other) have you received during the year immediately preceding the filing of the original petition herein?

c. To what tax refunds (income or other), if any, are you, or may you be, entitled? (Give particulars, including information as to any refund payable jointly to you and your spouse or any other person.)

4. Financial accounts, certificates of deposit and safe deposit boxes.

a. What accounts or certificates of deposit or shares in banks, savings and loan, thrift, building and loan and homestead associations, credit unions, brokerage houses, pension funds and the like have you maintained, alone or together with any other person, and in your own or any other name within the two years immediately preceding the filing of the original petition herein? (Give the name and address of each institution, the name and number under which the account or certificate is maintained, and the name and address of every other person authorized to make withdrawals from such account.)

b. What safe deposit box or boxes or other depository or depositories have you kept or used for your securities, cash, or other valuables within the two years immediately preceding the filing of the original petition herein? (Give the name and address of the bank or other depository, the name in which each box or other depository was kept, the name and address of every other person who had the right of access thereto, a brief description of the contents thereof, and, if the box has been surrendered, state when surrendered, or, if transferred, when transferred, and the name and address of the transferee.)

5. Books and records.

a. Have you kept books of account or records relating to your affairs within the two years immediately preceding the filing of the original petition herein?

9. Receiverships, general assignments, and other modes of liquidation.

a. Was any of your property, at the time of the filing of the original petition herein, in the hands of a receiver, trustee, or other liquidating agent? (If so, give a brief description of the property, the name and address of the receiver, trustee, or other agent, and, if the agent was appointed in a court proceeding, the name and location of the court, the title and number of the case, and the nature thereof.)

b. Have you made any assignment of your property for the benefit of your creditors, or any general settlement with your creditors, within one year immediately preceding the filing of the original petition herein? (If so, give dates, the name and address of the assignee, and a brief statement of the terms of assignment or settlement.)

10. Suits, executions, and attachments.

a. Were you a party to any suit pending at the time of the filing of the original petition herein? (If so, give the name and location of the court and the title and nature of the proceeding.)

b. Were you a party to any suit terminated within the year immediately preceding the filing of the original petition herein? (If so, give the name and the location of the court, the title and nature of the proceeding, and the result.)

c. Has any of your property been attached, garnished, or seized under any legal or equitable process within the year immediately preceding the filing of the original petition herein? (If so, describe the property seized or person garnished, and at whose suit.)

11. a. Payment of loans, installment purchases and other debts.

What payments in whole or in part have you made during the year immediately preceding the filing of the original petition herein on any of the following: (1) loans; (2) installment purchases of goods and services; and (3) other debts? (Give the names and addresses of the persons receiving payment, the amounts of the loans or other debts and of the purchase price of the goods and services, the dates of the original transactions, the amounts and dates of payments and, if any of the payees are your relatives or insiders, the relationship; if the debtor is a partnership and any of the payees is or was a partner or a relative of a partner, state the relationship; if the debtor is a corporation and any of the payees is or was an officer, director, or stockholder, or a relative of an officer, director, or stockholder, state the relationship.)

b. Setoffs.

What debts have you owed to any creditor, including any bank, which were setoff by that creditor against a debt or deposit owing by the creditor to you during the year immediately preceding the filing of the original petition herein? (Give the names and addresses of the persons setting off such debts, the dates of the setoffs, the amounts of the debts owing by you and to you and, if any of the creditors are your relatives or insiders, the relationship.)

12. Transfer of property.

a. Have you made any gifts, other than ordinary and usual presents to family members and charitable donations, during the year immediately preceding the filing of the original petition herein? (If so, give names and addresses of donees and dates, description, and value of gifts.)

b. Have you made any other transfer, absolute or for the purpose of security, or any other disposition, of real or personal property during the year immediately preceding the filing of the original petition herein? (Give a description of the property, the date of the transfer or disposition, to whom transferred or how disposed of, and, if the transferee is a relative or insider, the relationship, the consideration, if any, received therefor, and the disposition of such consideration.)

13. Repossessions and returns.

Has any property been returned to, or repossessed by, the seller or by a secured party during the year immediately preceding the filing of the original petition herein? (If so, give particulars, including the name and address of the party getting the property and its description and value.)

14. Losses.

a. Have you suffered any losses from fire, theft, or gambling during the year immediately preceding or since the filing of the original petition herein? (If so, give particulars, including dates, names, and places, and the amounts of money or value and general description of property lost.)

b. Was the loss covered in whole or part by insurance? (If so, give particulars.)

15. Payments or transfers to attorneys.

    a. Have you consulted an attorney during the year immediately preceding or since the filing of the original petition herein? (Give dates, name and address.)

    b. Have you during the year immediately preceding or since the filing of the original petition herein paid any money or transferred any property to the attorney or to any other person on his behalf? (If so, give particulars, including amount paid or value of property transferred and date of payment or transfer.)

    c. Have you, either during the year immediately preceding or since the filing of the original petition herein, agreed to pay any money or transfer any property to an attorney at law, or to any other person on his behalf? (If so, give particulars, including amount and terms of obligation.)

    I, _____ , declare under penalty of perjury that I have read the answers contained in the foregoing statement of financial affairs and that they are true and correct to the best of my knowledge, information, and belief.

Executed on _____

                Signature: _____

                            Debtor

STATEMENT OF EXECUTORY CONTRACTS

United States Bankruptcy Court

For The _____ District of _____

In re   Case

_____   No. _____
Debtor(s) [set forth here all names including trade names used by Debtor(s) within last 6 years].

Debtor(s) is (are) a party to the following executory contracts:

[Give names and addresses of the parties to and the terms and conditions of, each contract.]

I (we), _____ , debtor(s) in this case, (or, the president or other officer or an authorized agent of the debtor corporation) (or, a member or an authorized agent of the debtor partnership) declare under penalty of perjury that the foregoing is true and correct to the best of my knowledge, information, and belief.

Executed on _____ .

Signature : _____

Signature : _____
Debtor(s)

STATEMENT OF INTENT WITH RESPECT TO THE RETENTION
OR SURRENDER OF PROPERTY WHICH SECURES CONSUMER DEBTS

[If an individual debtor's schedule of assets and liabilities includes consumer debts which are secured by property of the estate, this statement of intent shall be completed and filed with the Clerk of the Bankruptcy Court.]

[The Bankruptcy Code (Revised), 11 U.S.C. 521(2)(A), effective October 8, 1984, states that:

 "(2) if an individual debtor's schedule of assets and liabilities includes consumer debts which are secured by property of the estate —

  (A) within thirty days after the date of the filing of a petition under chapter 7 of this title or on or before the date of the meeting of creditors, whichever is earlier, or within such additional time as the court, for cause, within such period fixes, the debtor shall file with the clerk a statement of his intention with respect to the retention or surrender of such property and, if applicable, specifying that such property is claimed as exempt, that the debtor intends to redeem such property, or that the debtor intends to reaffirm debts secured by such property;"]

United States Bankruptcy Court

For The _____ District of _____

In re

               FOR COURT USE ONLY

               _____

               Date Petition Filed

_____

Debtor [set forth here all names including trade names used by Debtor within last 6 years].

               _____

               Case Number

Social Security No. _____

               _____

               Bankruptcy Judge

and Debtor's Employer's Tax Identification No. _____

List each item of property which secures a consumer debt together with the name and address of the creditor. State whether the property is claimed as exempt, and whether you intend to surrender it to the creditor, redeem it, or reaffirm the debt.

Executed on _____

        Signature : _____

                 Debtor

UNITED STATES BANKRUPTCY COURT

For the _____ District of _____

NOTICE TO INDIVIDUAL CONSUMER DEBTOR(S)

If you intend to file a petition for relief under the bankruptcy laws of the United States, and your debts are primarily consumer debts, the Clerk of Court is required to notify you of each chapter of the Bankruptcy Code under which you may seek relief. You may proceed under:

Chapter 7—Liquidation, or
Chapter 11—Reorganization, or
Chapter 13—Adjustment of Debts of an Individual
with Regular Income

If you have any questions regarding the information contained in this notice, you should consult with your attorney.

CLERK OF COURT

ACKNOWLEDGEMENT

I hereby certify that I have read this notice.

Dated: _____

_____
Debtor

_____
Joint Debtor, if any

Bibliography

Allen, William Richard. *Midnight Economics. Choices, prices, public policy.* Introduction by Milton Friedman. 1980, Norton, N.Y.

Brown, Lester. *Building a Sustainable Society.* 1981, Norton, N.Y.

Herschman, Albert O. *Shifting Involvements: Private and Self Interests and Public Action.* 1984. Macmillan

Geroge, Henry. *Economics. Increase of Want. Increase of Wealth.* Norton, N.Y.

Jacobs, Jane. *Cities and Wealth of Nations: Principles of Economic Life.* Random House. (1984)

Greenwald, Douglas. *Dictionary of Modern Economics.* 1985. McGraw Hill

McClelland, David. *Achieving Independence.* Van Nostrand. (1981)

Schumacher, E. *Small Is Beautiful. Economics as if people mattered.* Harper Row (1973)

Ackerman, David. *A Smart Woman's Guide to Successful Money Management.* Harper (1980)

Brownstone, David M. *Dictionary of Business and Finance.* (1981) Van Nostrand.

German, Don R. *Consumer's Guide to Personal Finance.* Facts on File (1984) N.Y.

Graver, Fred. *How to Gain Control of Your Financial Affairs.* Little, Brown (1982)

Morris, Hal. *Real Estate Investing.* (1984) Beaufort, N.Y.

Grass, Robin. *Basics of Borrowing Money.* N.Y. Times Books (1980)

Hallman, Victor. *Personal Finances, Planning (1985) McGraw Hill*

Peterson, Jean Ross. *Organize Your Personal Finances. Turn Chaos into Cash.* (1984) Betterway Publications, White Hall, Va.

Schram, Joseph F. *Fixing and Financing the Older Home.* Beaufort, N.Y.

Williams, Gordon. *Financial Survival in the Age of New Money.* 1984, Simon, Schuster.

Barnes, James A. *A Guide to Learning Systems, Proposals, Business Letters* (1983) Arco.

Other Suggested Reading:

Superior Court Law Library: Open to anyone. Librarian will assist.

    Case Research: Foreclosures
                         Bankruptcy
                         Motions
                         Court Rules and Procedures.

The Federal Reserve, Bankers Research Institute

Wealth for All, R. E. McMaster, Jr.

Truth in Money, Theodore R. Thoren, R. F. Warner.

Billpayer's Rights, P. J. Honigsber and R. Waner

Bailing out a Bankrupt World, Malone

How the Federal Reserve Works, and What It Is, Report by the Federal Reserve Bank of Chicago.

Money, E.W. Kemmerer, MacMillan

Econometrics, Buckminster Fuller

Can America Survive, Cornelius Maloney

Let's Stop Foreclosures, Le Beau

Constitutional Issue, Becraft

Book of Facts, U.S. News and World Report

How to Proceed to Stop Foreclosures, Federal Rules, 1982 Ed.

Index